Education and Society in Hong Kong and Macau

CERC Studies in Comparative Education 7

Education and Society in Hong Kong and Macau: Comparative Perspectives on Continuity and Change

Edited by
Mark Bray & Ramsey Koo

Comparative Education Research Centre
The University of Hong Kong

Comparative Education Research Centre
Faculty of Education
The University of Hong Kong
Pokfulam Road, Hong Kong, China

© Comparative Education Research Centre 1999
First published 1999

ISBN 962 8093 82 7

Layout and index by Emily Mang.

The editors and publisher acknowledge financial support from the Sik Sik Yuen Education Research Fund in the preparation and publication of this book.

CERC Studies in Comparative Education

1. W.O. Lee & Mark Bray (eds.) (1997): *Education and Political Transition: Perspectives and Dimensions in East Asia.*
    ISBN 962-8093-93-2. 115pp. HK$100 / US$20.

2. Mark Bray & W.O. Lee (eds.) (1997): *Education and Political Transition: Implications of Hong Kong's Change of Sovereignty.*
    ISBN 962-8093-90-8. 169pp. HK$100 / US$20.

3. Philip G. Altbach (1998): *Comparative Higher Education: Knowledge, the University, and Development.*
    ISBN 962-8093-88-6. 312pp. HK$180 / US$30.

4. Zhang Weiyuan (1998): *Young People and Careers: A Comparative Study of Careers Guidance in Hong Kong, Shanghai and Edinburgh.*
    ISBN 962-8093-89-4. 160pp. HK$180 / US$30.

5. Harold Noah & Max A. Eckstein (1998): *Doing Comparative Education: Three Decades of Collaboration.*
    ISBN 962-8093-87-8. 356pp. HK$250 / US$38.

6. T. Neville Postlethwaite (1999): *International Studies of Educational Achievement: Methodological Issues.*
    ISBN 962-8093-86-X. 86pp. HK$100 / US$20.

7. Mark Bray & Ramsey Koo (eds.) (1999): *Education and Society in Hong Kong and Macau: Comparative Perspectives on Continuity and Change.*
    ISBN 962-8093-82-7. 286pp. HK$200 / US$32.

Other Books Published by CERC

1. Mark Bray & R. Murray Thomas (eds.) (1998): *Financing of Education in Indonesia.*
    ISBN 971-561-172-9. 133pp. HK$100 / US$20.

2. David A. Watkins & John B. Biggs (eds.) (1999): *The Chinese Learner: Cultural, Psychological and Contextual Influences.*
    ISBN 0-86431-182-6. 285pp. HK$200 / US$32.

3. Ruth Hayhoe (1999): *China's Universities 1895-1995: A Century of Cultural Conflict.*
    ISBN 962-8093-81-9. 299pp. HK$200 / US$32.

Order through bookstores or from:

Comparative Education Research Centre
The University of Hong Kong
Pokfulam Road
Hong Kong, China

Fax: (852) 2517 4737
E-mail: cerc@hkusub.hku.hk
Website: www.hku.hk/cerc

The list prices include sea mail postage; add US$5 per copy for air mail.

Hong Kong and Macau in the Asia Pacific Region

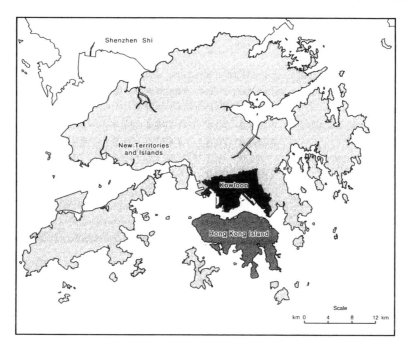

Map of Hong Kong

Map of Macau

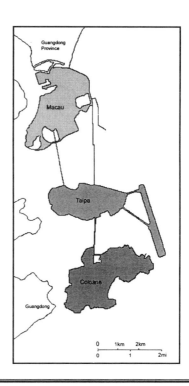

Contents

List of Abbreviations

AIOU	Asia International Open University
APA	Academy for Performing Arts
BA	Bachelor of Arts
BEd	Bachelor of Education
CBE	Catholic Board of Education
CCP	Chinese Communist Party
CDC	Curriculum Development Committee
CDC	Curriculum Development Council
CDI	Curriculum Development Institute
City U	The City University of Hong Kong
CMI	Chinese Medium of Instruction
CUHK	The Chinese University of Hong Kong
ED	Education Department
EMI	English Medium of Instruction
EPA	Economic & Public Affairs
ESF	English Schools Foundation
GDP	Gross Domestic Product
GPA	Government & Public Affairs
HKALE	Hong Kong Advanced Level Examination
HKBC	The Hong Kong Baptist College
HKBU	The Hong Kong Baptist University
HKCEE	Hong Kong Certificate of Education Examination
HKEA	Hong Kong Examinations Authority
HKEWA	Hong Kong Educational Workers' Association
HKIEd	The Hong Kong Institute of Education
HKPTU	Hong Kong Professional Teachers' Union
HKPU	The Hong Kong Polytechnic University
HKU	The University of Hong Kong
HKUST	The Hong Kong University of Science & Technology
HUCOM	Heads of Universities Committee
IEA	International Association for the Evaluation of Educational Achievement
IT	Information Technology
KMT	Kuomintang
LC	Lingnan College
MA	Master of Arts
MCEA	Macau Chinese Education Association
MEd	Master of Education

MFA	Multi-Fibre Arrangement
OECD	Organisation for Economic Co-operation & Development
OLI	The Open Learning Institute
OUHK	The Open University of Hong Kong
PCEd	Postgraduate Certificate of Education
PGCE	Post-Graduate Certificate of Education
PPP	Pre-primary Project
PRC	People's Republic of China
QAKT	Qualified Assistant Kindergarten Teacher
QKT	Qualified Kindergarten Teacher
SAR	Special Administrative Region
SCMP	South China Morning Post
SCNU	South China Normal University
SMP	School Mathematics Project
SPUC	St. Paul's University College
TC	Technical College
TESL	Teaching of English as a Second Language
TLQPR	Teaching & Learning Quality Process Review
TOC	Target Oriented Curriculum
TTRA	Targets and Target Related Assessment
UEA	The University of East Asia
UGC	University Grants Committee
UK	United Kingdom
UM	University of Macau
UPGC	University & Polytechnic Grants Committee
VTC	Vocational Training Council

List of Tables

List of Figures

Introduction

Introduction

Koo Ding Yee, Ramsey

The fundamental basis of comparative studies of all kinds is identification of similarities and differences. From this identification, analysis usually proceeds to the reasons for the similarities and differences, and to the conceptual implications of the forces which shape the objects being compared.

The field of comparative education resembles all other comparative fields in this respect. Major questions for analysts in the field of comparative education concern the reasons why education systems in different parts of the world are similar to and/or different from each other. Additional questions concern the links between education systems and the broader societies which those education systems serve. Education systems on the one hand reflect the societies in which they are situated, and on the other hand shape those societies.

Meaningful analysis is facilitated when the units for comparison have sufficient similarity as well as significant difference. In this light, Hong Kong and Macau make an ideal pair for comparison. The book shows that the conceptual lessons from comparison of Hong Kong and Macau go far beyond the small corner of East Asia in which the two territories are located.

To expand on this point, this Introduction begins by outlining the major similarities and differences in Hong Kong and Macau. It then turns to comments on the nature of continuity and change in education and society, and to specific aspects of education and colonial transition. The next sections explain the way in which the book was assembled and structured, and outline the contents of each chapter.

Hong Kong and Macau: Similarities and Differences

For comparative studies of the type presented here, analysis of the features of education systems must be couched within the framework of contextual features. For this reason, it is useful to commence with an outline of political, social and economic similarities and differences.

The most obvious similarities between Hong Kong and Macau are in location and colonial history. Both territories are located on the south coast of China; and both have been colonies of European powers. The chapter in this book by Adamson & Li describes the two territories as siblings. Macau, the chapter points out, is "the introspective elder outshone, overshadowed and greatly influenced by the more gifted and extrovert junior"; but the two territories exist in a situation of mutual support. They form a pair of Special Administrative Regions (SARs) within the People's Republic of China (PRC), operating economic, political and social systems which resemble each other but are significantly different from those in the rest of the PRC. Pursuing the metaphor of the family, China is commonly referred to as the motherland. Adamson & Li point out that the motherland was until recently politically, economically and socially estranged, and that the reunification has resulted "in a familial accommodation of differences rather than a whole-hearted embrace". Commonalties in attitudes towards the motherland are further elements of similarity between Hong Kong and Macau.

As distinguishable entities, Hong Kong and Macau are products of colonialism. Macau emerged as part of the Portuguese empire in the 16th century (C.M.B. Cheng 1999). It was chiefly needed as a port in which ships could anchor and be repaired, and as a base for trade with China and other parts of Asia. Geographically, the territory of Macau comprises the Macau peninsula and the offshore islands of Taipa and Coloane. The Portuguese arrived in southern China in 1513. Macau was ceded to the Portuguese in 1557 by the Chinese government in exchange for banishment of pirates in the Pearl River Delta. In 1974, Macau was redefined as a "Chinese territory under Portuguese administration". The 1987 Sino-Portuguese Agreement set a timetable for full reversion of sovereignty to the PRC on 20 December 1999 (Shipp 1997).

Hong Kong was established as a separate entity three centuries later than Macau, but again was chiefly valued by the British as a port and as a base for trade within the region (Endacott 1964). Geographically, the territory of Hong Kong comprises Hong Kong Island which was ceded to the British in 1841, the Kowloon Peninsula which was added in 1860, and the New Territories which were leased for a 99-year period in 1898. The scheduled expiry of the lease in 1997 was the chief factor setting the timetable for the reversion of sovereignty over Hong Kong to the PRC on 1 July of that year. Although strictly speaking the lease applied only to the New Territories and not to Hong Kong Island or the Kowloon Peninsula, it was clear to negotiators on both sides that the component parts could no longer be separated. Because of this, the whole of the territory of Hong Kong was returned to Chinese sovereignty, including the parts that had been ceded "in perpetuity". The initial arrangements for the change of sovereignty were set out in a Sino-British Agreement in 1984.

These comments show that similarities in the political histories of the two territories are not confined to colonial origins, for both have had a common destiny in the contemporary era. Although Macau had been colonised earlier than Hong Kong, its reversion of sovereignty occurred slightly later. The political negotiations allowed Hong Kong to retain many of its existing characteristics, including its legal, financial and educational systems. While China remained officially socialist, Hong Kong remained officially capitalist. This formula was known as 'One Country, Two Systems', and set the model for Macau's subsequent reversion of sovereignty (Lo 1993). The Basic Law for Macau was modelled on that already prepared for Hong Kong.

The similarities do not end there. Among other common features, some of which are identified in Table 0.1, are that:

- both are small in area;
- both are small in population, especially compared with their immediate neighbours;
- both are urban societies, with insignificant agricultural sectors;
- in both territories, the great majority of inhabitants are Cantonese-speaking Chinese;

- both have efficient financial infrastructures and free market economies with simple taxation systems;
- both have highly productive and competitive workforces, with relatively low unemployment rates; and
- both have efficient telecommunications and transport systems, providing easy access to mainland China and other parts of the world.

Table 0.1: Characteristics of Hong Kong and Macau, 1998

	Hong Kong	Macau
Land area (sq. km.)	1,097	24
Population	6,806,000	430,000
Population density (people per sq. km.)	6,200	17,900
Ethnicity	97% Chinese; 2% other	95% Chinese; 3% Portuguese; 2% other
GDP per capita (US$)	24,700	15,900
Official Languages	Chinese & English	Chinese & Portuguese
Currency	Hong Kong Dollar (HK$)	Pataca (MOP)
Exchange rate	US$1 = HK$7.8	US$1 = MOP8.0

Sources: Hong Kong, Information Services Department (1999); Macau, Department of Statistics & Census (1999).

Despite these similarities, major differences are also apparent. Among them are the following:

- Although in global terms both territories are small in area, Hong Kong is considerably larger than Macau. Hong Kong's land area is 1,097 square kilometres, compared with just 24 square kilometres in Macau.
- Hong Kong's population is much larger: 6,806,000 in 1998 compared with 430,000 in Macau.
- Although Macau's population is smaller, because the land area is smaller still, Macau has a much greater population density: 17,900 persons per square kilometre, compared with 6,200 persons in Hong Kong.
- Although Chinese form the vast majority in both territories, Macau has a slightly larger proportion of non-Chinese people than Hong Kong.
- Both territories have high per capita incomes compared with most parts of the region; but Hong Kong's per capita incomes are higher than those of Macau.
- In both territories, Chinese is an official language. However, one legacy of Macau's period under Portuguese administration is that Portuguese is the other official language. By contrast, one legacy of British administration in Hong Kong is that English is the other official language in that territory.

Turning specifically to education, again similarities and differences are evident. The main similarities are in the formal nature of schooling, some parts of the curriculum, some sponsoring bodies, and high enrolment rates. However, the structure and important aspects of the content of education differ significantly in the two territories. The reasons for this, and the implications, are among the major themes of this book. Different chapters highlight the ways that education has evolved in each territory, and make some comments about the future.

One final observation under the heading of similarities and differences is that because Hong Kong and Macau have much in common they can also be taken as a pair to contrast with other parts of the world. One particular theme in this book concerns colonial transition. The transitions in Hong Kong and Macau differed from most other colonial transitions because they occurred at the end of the 20th century rather than earlier. Also, the transitions were to reintegration with the country from which the colonies had previously been detached rather than to sovereign independence. As in other domains, politics and education have shaped each other: political forces have shaped the scale and content of education, and the nature of education has to some extent shaped the landscape of politics. In this and other respects, although the book primarily focuses on only two territories it can contribute to much wider understanding. Indeed most chapters make specific comparisons and contrasts not only between Hong Kong and Macau as separate entities but also between Hong Kong and Macau as a pair and other parts of the world.

Education and Society in the Context of Continuity and Change

One major theme running through all chapters, as indicated in the subtitle of the book, is continuity and change. The closing decades of the 20th century brought tremendous social, political, economic, and technological changes in Southeast Asia. In a review of educational policies in Asia and the Pacific, Makagiansar et al. (1989, p.1) noted that "heterogeneity of the Asian-Pacific region nations in terms of geographic location, population size, socio-political systems, stage and pattern of economic development, technological advancement and level of educational development means that there can be no singular scenario for the area's wide-ranging and complex problems, issues and approaches". It is not difficult to see how educational systems and practices could be seriously affected by these driving forces.

Furthermore, analysts sometimes note that education systems in Asia and the Pacific are primarily oriented towards coping with the 'here and now' issues and solving current problems. As observed by UNESCO (1990, p.21):

> Education helps by providing knowledge and understanding through the development of skills and the promotion of attitudes which future citizens will need in order to cope with the diverse issues they face. However, education systems often are not 'forward looking' because, in periods of rapid growth, most education systems have been oriented towards immediate problems: building and enlarging schools, providing better and sufficient equipment and books, and training teachers. Little time has remained to lift the gaze from the immediate issues to look ahead and engage in forward planning to better cope with what is likely to occur.

Hong Kong and Macau do not completely fit this pattern; but different phases of history have certainly brought different pressures.

Since education processes do not occur in a vacuum but are products of other forces, analysis of those other forces is essential for complete understanding. Oliver (1996, p.3) pointed out that "as education exists primarily in a changing social context, it is almost certain that it will be accompanied by continual transition". However, changes in a system may have different meanings, effects, and implications to different groups of people. As Oliver added (p.3):

> If change is viewed as a series of isolated events, which upset the pleasant stability of things, then it will be perceived as something to fear, and something to avoid wherever possible. On the other hand, change can be viewed as simply a continuous process of evolution, whereby transition is part of the normal sequence of events. There may well be times of greater change and lesser change, but generally an organisation or educational system is perceived as being in a state of natural flux.

Within this framework, Oliver argued, individuals will develop new approaches to change. Thus one cannot necessarily assume that continuity is comfortable and that change is threatening.

The social and political aspects of change have always been considered the important driving forces in the development of education. A.V. Kelly (1987) pointed out that education can be a powerful political tool because it is used to change attitudes and values. He wrote that, in effect (p.54):

> At every level and from every perspective, education and politics are closely interlinked. Whatever forms it takes, education must be some kind of preparation of the young for the social and political context in which their adult lives will be conducted. Nor can that social and political context be ignored in their upbringing. Whether the concern is merely to initiate them into the values and customs of their society, as is often the case in primitive societies, or to encourage them to challenge, question and possibly change those values and customs, the political dimension must be there. And even those who argue that the prime concern of education must be the development of the individual rather than the needs of society must recognise that their stance is itself a political stance.

Bearing this in mind, it is appropriate to note some further features of the political contexts of Hong Kong and Macau.

Educational Reform during Colonial Transition

The role of education in political transition has been a great concern in Hong Kong and Macau. One major reason has been that the educational systems may have been fairly well suited to their previous colonial settings and to earlier objectives, but were not necessarily well suited to the new framework. Bray (1998a, p.200) has pointed out that:

> Among the common features of all colonial transitions has been a need for reorientation of education systems. In particular, curricula need to be changed to reflect the new political circumstances. This usually requires change in syllabuses, textbooks, and perhaps also media of instruction.

At the same time, both the Hong Kong and the Macau governments had to heed changing global patterns which had little to do with local transitions. Changing global patterns required investment in information technology, for example, and efforts to make the products of the education systems competitive on an international stage. The ways in which the authorities responded may be explained by considering each territory in turn.

Problems and Issues in Education: Hong Kong
In the period leading up to the change of sovereignty, major issues ranged from questions about the structure of the government's Education Department to concerns about the low government subsidies for private kindergartens. Other questions focused on school-based management and training teachers in information technology for education in the new millennium. These particular issues were not especially linked to the political transition, and indeed would have arisen even if the colonial era was not about to end.

Other changes, however, had direct political links. Many are examined in the chapters that follow. For example, with the return of sovereignty to the motherland the government revised syllabuses for subjects at all levels to reflect constitutional, political and social developments in Hong Kong and China. Civic education received a new push, and many secondary schools were forced to teach in Chinese rather than English. For most schools, this meant the Cantonese dialect, but in 1998 Putonghua was introduced as one of the subjects in the core curriculum for Primary 1, Secondary 1 and Secondary 4. In an effort to maintain standards of English, the government provided four additional English-language teachers for each Chinese-medium school, of whom a maximum of two could be native-speaking English teachers.

Other domains given major attention included:

- reconstruction of the official aims of education;
- maintenance of balance and relevance in the school curriculum;
- setting new academic standards and competence benchmarks;
- improvement of teacher education;
- the special needs of recent immigrants from mainland China;
- greater flexibility and student choice in education; and
- strengthened educational leadership and school-based management.

However, it was not always easy to identify the role of the change of sovereignty. Thus the government insisted that the shift to Cantonese at secondary level was for pedagogic rather than political reasons. Lo's chapter in this book shows why this view should not necessarily be accepted at face value; but the fact remains that multiple justifications could be presented for particular actions.

Problems and Issues in Education: Macau
Similar comments may be made about dominant issues in Macau. However, Macau had a rather different colonial legacy. In particular, during most of the colonial period the Macau government was mainly concerned with the education of Portuguese-speaking children, even though this group comprised less than 5 per cent of the total. Large proportions of the government's educational resources were allocated to enable them to attend official schools in which Portuguese was used as medium of instruction.

This policy altered dramatically as the change of sovereignty approached, and the government found a way to reduce responsibility for its major Portuguese-medium secondary school by handing it over to a private foundation.

In general, this book shows that educational provision in Macau lagged behind that in Hong Kong. For example, whereas the Hong Kong government introduced fee-free education during the 1970s, the Macau government only did so in the 1990s – and even then Macau's provision was only for seven years of education compared with nine years in Hong Kong. One result of this was that general levels of education in the Macau population were relatively low. In 1998, for example, primary education was the highest formal qualification gained by over half of the territory's labour force. For one third of the labour force, high school certificates were the highest qualifications; and only one tenth of the labour force were post-secondary graduates (*Macau Daily* 20 August 1998, p.A4).

Due to its uncoordinated education systems explained in subsequent chapters of this book, the way in which Macau education is structured and implemented differs from its Hong Kong neighbour. Reforms at the time of the transition included the following:

- increased allocation of resources to private schools;
- plans for nine years of compulsory education;
- review of official curricula;
- development of school-based programmes with support from the government;
- strengthened teacher professionalism;
- reduced drop-out rates;
- reinforcing the training of teachers in moral and civic education at both primary and secondary levels; and
- improved educational opportunities for new immigrants from the mainland.

Most of these themes, and the rationales for them, are explored in the subsequent chapters of this book.

Construction, Organisation and Contents of the Book

The process of preparing this book went through a series of key stages. Following conception in 1996, the editors contacted appropriate potential contributors. In December 1997, the Comparative Education Research Centre at the University of Hong Kong hosted a workshop at which initial drafts of chapters were presented. Sovereignty over Hong Kong had already reverted to the PRC, which meant on the one hand that observers were keenly following the impact of the change and on the other hand that attention was turning to Macau. The workshop permitted authors to comment on each others' drafts, in order to identify domains in need of co-ordination and elaboration. The event also permitted the editors to identify gaps, following which they approached some further individuals to fill those gaps.

One particular feature of the book is that each chapter is comparative, focusing on both Hong Kong and Macau. This distinguishes it from most other works of its type. Indeed, as Bray points out in Chapter 12, many works in the field of comparative education are in practice only implicitly comparative. Instead they focus on single areas, and leave it to readers to make the comparisons. The fact that each chapter in the present book addresses both Hong Kong and Macau permits the comparisons to be much more direct and informative. As observed above, most contributors also go beyond this, taking Hong Kong and Macau as a pair and making comparisons with other parts of the world.

In structure, the 13 chapters of the book are divided into four parts. As might be expected, the parts to some extent overlap; but they also form discreet and coherent units within the book. The first part focuses on levels and sub-sectors, namely pre-school education, primary and secondary education, teacher education, and higher education. The second part focuses on political, economic and social issues. The three chapters in this part address church and state in education, higher education and colonialism, and education and the labour market. The third part then turns to curriculum policies and processes. It begins with a general chapter on curriculum reform before turning to specific chapters on civic and political education, on the history curriculum, and on mathematics education. Finally, the volume concludes with chapters on methodology and focus in comparative education as illustrated by this book, and on the overall lessons for continuity and change.

To elaborate on this outline, several comments may be made on individual chapters. The first chapter, by Wong, explores the development of pre-school education in Hong Kong and Macau. It particularly notes changes before and after the signature of the 1984 (for Hong Kong) and 1987 (for Macau) Joint Declarations with China in terms of curricula, school operations, educational resources, teacher training, and government policies. Wong points out that in Hong Kong the colonial authorities never considered pre-school education to be part of basic education, arguing that it was desirable but not essential and thus not demanding substantial investment of government resources. The Macau government, by contrast, adopted a more favourable policy and considered the final year of kindergarten to be part of basic education for the fee-free education scheme. Although other sectors of education have arguably been more advanced in Hong Kong than in Macau, this has not been the case at the pre-school level. However, Wong identifies many complexities in the nature of instruction, the quality of the curriculum, and other dimensions.

The chapter by Adamson & Li examines primary and secondary schooling in Hong Kong and Macau, and identifies the main forces that have shaped the similarities and differences that emerge from the comparison. The chapter argues that the fact that Hong Kong and Macau share a similar history, geography, ethnicity and post-colonial fate has created significant similarities in the nature of schooling. In turn, colonial history has provided both territories with education systems that are very different from the system in the motherland.

Teacher education is another area of concern which continually faces the challenges of socio-political and other changes. The chapter by Li & Kwo focuses on patterns of teacher education development in a historical perspective. It notes the limited proportions of trained local teachers in both Hong Kong and Macau, and the strategies adopted in the 1980s and 1990s to tackle the situation. Hong Kong has already achieved quantitative transition but is concerned about quality, while Macau is moving towards both quantitative and qualitative changes in its teacher education development.

Developments and changes in higher education, along with the labour market and the associated transitions in the needs of both local and global industry, have led to new challenges for university graduates. Yung examines the structure and develop-

ment of higher education in Hong Kong and Macau in terms of two spheres of knowledge in higher education, namely quantitative-structural, and organisation and governance. In both territories, the expansion of higher education in the 1990s offered
increasing access to academic qualifications. However, the increasing cost of higher
education, coupled with keen competition in the labour market, made investment in
higher education less worthwhile from the perspectives of stakeholders. Partly to avoid
the high costs of local university education, increasing numbers of students chose to
further their education in mainland universities. At the same time, Hong Kong and
Macau both hosted increasing numbers of mainland students in search of specialisms
and external connections not so readily available on the mainland. These forces
brought dimensions of national integration in the new political framework. Hong Kong
and Macau have also played important roles in meeting the needs and challenges of
the global economy and information-based world.

Leung's chapter begins the second part of the book with analysis of relationships
between church, state and education during the colonial periods. As in many other
colonies, in both Hong Kong and Macau the churches and governments worked in
partnership to provide education and other social services. With the approach of reunification with the motherland, church leaders and their congregations were concerned about the implications of operation under a communist government. However,
Leung points out that the long period of political transition provided opportunities for
churches to prepare; and in the event the government in Beijing proved much more
flexible than had been feared.

Hui & Poon also have strong historical perspectives. They analyse the ways in
which the colonial states intervened in the development of higher education in Hong
Kong and Macau, using it as a means for imperial expansion. Through four case studies – St. Paul's University College, the University of Hong Kong, the University of
East Asia, and the Hong Kong Baptist College – the chapter shows similarities, variations and trends in the ways that higher education was controlled by the two colonial
states. Hui & Poon argue that in the past, state control of higher education was a
means of regulating social mobility. The 1990s brought considerable expansion, and
this much reduced the previously elitist nature of the system.

Ma's chapter explores the links between education and the labour force, particularly in relation to economic development and supply of highly educated personnel.
Changes in the benefits and costs of education raise policy questions about the ways in
which local and overseas graduates can be made more employable. One way to do this
is through courses which combine academic education with specialised training in
broad basic skills.

The third part of the book, which focuses on curriculum policies and processes,
commences with a chapter by Lo. This chapter analyses and contrasts various areas of
curriculum reform with respect to curriculum development in the two former colonies.
The territories adopted different approaches to curriculum reform during their transitional periods. The Hong Kong authorities tended to adopt the stimulus-response
model before the change of sovereignty and the rational model afterwards. The Macau
authorities were in favour of the rational model in their educational reform, along with
the use of stimulus response in the face of ad hoc events.

With reintegration with China, the study of civic education has gained particular
attention in both Hong Kong and Macau. Tse provides an insightful account of continuity and change in political education in the two territories, and discusses the impli-

cations for future civic education programmes. Tse notes that in both places the reforms in civic education produced changes which, as in many other post-colonial societies, were likely to be more apparent than real. The major institutional constraint, he suggests, lay in the conservative constitutional framework adopted in Hong Kong and Macau.

The following chapter, by Tan, focuses on the history curriculum. Using literature review, interviews, and analysis of the history curricula of selected secondary schools in Hong Kong and Macau, Tan examines the development of the history curriculum during colonial transition. Because of the centralised nature of the curriculum, wide variations in the political content were not found in the implemented history curriculum in Hong Kong secondary schools. However, the uncoordinated nature of Macau's educational systems allowed pro-PRC, pro-Taiwan, and Lusocentric curricula in history to coexist and evolve.

The final chapter in this part, by Tang, focuses on mathematics curriculum. Using Margaret Archer's morphogenetic systems theory as an explicit basis for part of his study, Tang examines the nature and causes of stability and change in Hong Kong and Macau. Macau's idiosyncratic socio-historical background and the more visible effects of links with the mainland were the major influences responsible for its different curriculum development track in mathematics. Thus, local socio-historical background and efforts of local mathematics educators must be identified for the understanding of stability and change in these places.

The fourth part of the book contains two concluding chapters by Bray. The first comments on the previous chapters within the framework of methodological literature in the field of comparative education. Illuminating the approaches used by the various authors, the chapter adds useful discussion to the broader literature on methodology in the field. The second chapter discusses the principles of continuity and change in education. It revisits the model used by Thomas & Postlethwaite in 1983, and also incorporates insights from other theorists. The chapter shows ways in which the book adds to understanding not only of Hong Kong and Macau but also of other parts of the world.

Conclusions

This Introduction has provided some background and an overview of broad areas of education and society. Hong Kong and Macau are similar in their colonial histories, ethnic composition, geographic location, and status as SARs of China. However, significant differences exist within their social, political and economic systems. This pattern has an impact on education as well as on other sectors, and helps explain many aspects of continuity and change.

Underlying each chapter in the book are several common premises. They include the following:

- the phenomena of continuity and change relate to all aspects and levels of education and society;
- some aspects of the relationship between education and social processes of continuity and change are universal, but patterns are complex and different in individual societies;

• education in general, and schooling and curriculum processes in particular, can be understood more deeply if contextualised within wider frameworks;
• comprehension of the complex phenomena associated with educational processes is enhanced by comparative and multidisciplinary analysis and interpretation.

Finally, although this book takes its subject much further than previous studies, a great deal remains to be done. Individual components of education systems could be examined in greater detail; and the processes of change will require continuing monitoring and analysis. It is hoped that scholars will take the book as the basis for further work which will deepen exploration and understanding.

Levels and Sub-sectors

1

Pre-school Education

Wong Ngai Chun, Margaret

Almost all researchers and practitioners in early childhood education believe, in the words of Bronfenbrenner (1992, p.191), that "the developmental outcomes of today shape the developmental outcomes of tomorrow". The experiences of children during the formative years have a major impact on their subsequent social, emotional and cognitive growth (Sigel 1991). This perspective has antecedents in an old Chinese saying "A child at three determines what the adult is like at eighty", and in the Jesuit maxim "Give me a child until he is seven, and he will be mine forever". Research on early childhood has demonstrated that early experiences also have a strong impact on children's readiness for primary school (Barnett et al. 1987; Sylva & Wiltshire 1993).

The quality of pre-school education is therefore an important determinant of the quality of child development. In the USA, the National Day Care Study (Ruopp et al. 1979) emphasised the significance of adult-child ratios, group sizes and staff qualifications as components of quality. These indicators are mediators of a major qualitative construct, teacher-child interaction, which as Phillips & Howes (1986) maintained, is strongly influenced by the number of children to be cared for and by teachers' professional competence. Other factors of pre-school quality may include a curriculum of active learning, parental involvement, and buildings and equipment (Ball 1994).

In Hong Kong, pre-school institutions are in the private sector and are in two categories: kindergartens regulated by the government's Education Department, and child-care centres regulated by the Social Welfare Department. Most kindergartens offer bisessional classes of around three hours each, while most child care centres offer whole-day programmes. In Macau, kindergartens operate on whole-day basis. The government operates a small number of kindergartens through the Department of Education & Youth, but the majority are private institutions which operate under the regulations of the same Department. In both territories, almost all children aged three to five are enrolled in some form of pre-school education. This reflects the value that Chinese parents traditionally attach to early childhood education. It also reflects the practical value of getting children prepared for formal schooling, success in which is perceived to lead to social and economic mobility (Opper 1989).

This common belief in pre-school education is one of the many similarities between Hong Kong and Macau. However, differences arise from contrasting colonial legacies and divergent economic strength and population size. This chapter reviews pre-school education in the two societies, paying attention to both quantitative and qualitative dimensions and to the role of government. Discussion begins with historical perspectives, to highlight the nature of continuity and change.

Pre-school Education in Macau before 1987

The signature in 1987 of the Sino-Portuguese Joint Declaration was a watershed for education in Macau. To understand the far-reaching reforms stimulated by the Declaration, knowledge of prior patterns is needed.

Operation and Control of Educational Institutions
During most of the colonial period, the Macau government, in so far as it was concerned about education at all, was chiefly concerned with the education of Portuguese-speaking children. Education for the Chinese-speaking population was mainly left to churches and other voluntary agencies. In the pre-school sector, the first government kindergarten was established in 1923 and operated in Portuguese. In the 1950s, a second government kindergarten, operating in Portuguese and Chinese and known as a Luso-Chinese institution, was opened and affiliated to an official primary school. The number of government kindergartens remained at two until after the signature of the 1987 Sino-Portuguese Declaration.

Private kindergartens were much more numerous. The first, operating in Chinese, was set up by the Catholic church in 1919. In 1987, the territory had 55 private kindergartens. Of these, 53 were Chinese-medium, one was Portuguese-medium, and one was English-medium (Macau, Department of Statistics & Census 1990). Thus in Macau the education of three to five year olds was mainly undertaken by the private sector.

The differences in government attitude towards the education of the Chinese-speaking and Portuguese-speaking communities created different patterns of control. The government exercised full control over the two official pre-schools, through the Official School Inspectorate of the Department of Education. The Inspectorate's main duties were construction and maintenance, recruitment of teaching staff, allocation of educational resources, overseeing the curriculum, and occasional assessment of the performance of the teachers. Private pre-schools, in contrast, were managed with considerable autonomy. The Department of Education did have a Private Schools Auxiliary Unit, but it was staffed by education officers rather than inspectors. It mainly played a liaison and advisory role in registration of new schools and distribution of grants. Quality issues were generally beyond the authority of the unit, and its officers were not empowered to supervise the pre-schools. Institutions were left to be self-regulating, and the government did not even set standards of minimum quality. Licensing criteria referred mainly to the legal requirements of safety and hygiene.

Disparities in Resources
The Macau government became slightly more active in the sector after the 1974 overthrow of the socialist government in Portugal. A 1977 law permitted private schools to receive direct subsidies and exemption from taxation, and families of students in financial difficulty could apply for assistance. A 1985 policy took intervention further by facilitating subsidy of private school teachers at all levels. In financial terms, however, these changes were minimal when compared with total expenditures. Less than one-third of government education expenditure was distributed to the private schools, while the rest was for administration of the Department of Education and the official schools (Wu 1994).

As a result, great disparities in resources existed between official and private pre-schools. Even after 1987, two-thirds of private kindergartens' total incomes came from school fees, and government subsidies only accounted for 19 per cent (Macau, Department of Statistics & Census 1994). About 56 per cent of the expenditures of private kindergartens were on staff salaries. Few resources were available for the maintenance or enhancement of quality. However, variations existed between the private kindergartens according to the financial conditions and philosophies of individual governing bodies.

The resource bases of official and private schools also diverged in other respects. In the mid-1980s, class sizes ranged from 20 in the official schools to over 70 in the private schools (Macau, Department of Statistics & Census 1989). All teachers in the official schools were required to possess professional qualifications, but almost half of the private kindergarten teachers were untrained. The learning environments of the official kindergartens were designed and equipped according to Portuguese standards which catered for a child-centred, activity-based type of learning; and a guideline on space and furniture issued by the Portuguese Ministry of National Education in 1973 was used by the Macau official schools as a reference point. In contrast, children in most private kindergartens were crowded in rows and had few resources for learning activities. This disparity raised major questions about the fairness in distribution of educational resources.

Adult-Child Ratio
An appropriate adult-child ratio has been identified in many studies as one of the most important prerequisites for programme effectiveness (Howes 1986; Kontos & Fiene 1987). It is considered an important quality indicator on the assumption that adults mediate children's contact with the physical and social world. An adult's responsiveness to individual children is dependent on the number of children under the adult's charge (Phillips & Howes 1987).

After 1979, Macau's pre-school population increased dramatically because of immigration from mainland China. Between 1979 and 1983, the pre-school population increased at an average annual rate of 10 per cent (Table 1.1); and from 1983 to 1988 the average annual increase was 13 per cent. However, growth in the number of teachers did not match that in the number of children. Between 1979 and 1988 the number of kindergarten teachers only increased by half while the number of students doubled. By 1987, the adult-child ratio had reached 1:40. This figure included Portuguese-language teachers in the Luso-Chinese kindergartens, and subject teachers in some private kindergartens. Thus average class size was even higher.

Teacher Training
The link between the pre-school teacher and child development can be expressed by Doyle's (1978) mediating process paradigm: teachers mediate children's experiences in pre-school, which in turn, affect their development. Teacher training affects programme effectiveness by influencing the educational goals, values and classroom behaviour of the teachers. Teacher training is thus considered an important indicator of pre-school quality (Ruopp et al. 1979; National Association for the Education of Young Children [NAEYC] 1991).

Table 1.1: Kindergarten Population and Teacher Numbers, Macau, 1979/80 - 1988/89

	1979/80	1982/83	1987/88	1988/89
Number of children	8,041	11,192	18,250	19,054
% increase		39	63	4
Numbers of teachers	307	314	451	481
% increase		2	44	10
Teacher-child ratio	1:26	1:36	1:40	1:38

Source: Macau, Department of Education.

Traditionally, teacher training in Macau also fell on the shoulders of the private sector. A teacher training unit was established in 1951 in St. Joseph's College, a Catholic secondary school. The college operated a two-year full-time programme of kindergarten teacher training for junior secondary graduates from 1953 to 1980. From 1980 to 1987, secondary graduates who wished to be kindergarten teachers could join its one-year full-time course, which also entitled them to teach in primary schools. Between 1945 and 1966, Tak Ming Middle School also operated a one-year full-time programme of kindergarten teacher training for senior secondary school graduates; and Choi Kou Middle School had two cohorts of one-year trained kindergarten graduates from 1967 to 1969. Because of these inputs, the supply of trained teachers for kindergartens was superior to that of primary and secondary schools. In 1988, 56 per cent of Macau kindergarten teachers had received professional training compared with only 27 per cent of primary teachers (Macau, Department of Statistics & Census 1989). Nonetheless, the fact that nearly half of the kindergarten teachers remained untrained was far from satisfactory.

The first attempt by the Macau government to contribute to teacher training was a joint effort with the pro-China Macau Chinese Education Association and the South China Normal University in Guangzhou, which launched a three-year distance-learning diploma course in 1985. This course mainly focused on primary education, but some kindergarten teachers also enrolled.

Pre-school Education in Macau after 1987

Government Policy
Economic growth combined with the accelerated development stimulated by the anticipated political handover in 1999 created considerable demand for quality human resources. A competent workforce was considered crucial for promoting social and economic development and for effective management in the government following the conclusion of Portuguese administration. In 1991, the Macau government released a new policy on basic education (Government of Macau 1991). The document envisaged a unified education system from pre-school to high school, indicated the government's intention to provide fee-free basic education, and specified the degree of autonomy to which private schools were entitled in relation to government subsidy. In short, it was a blueprint of educational development for transition into the era of the Macau Special Administrative Region (SAR). The document was followed by a set of regulations for private education (Government of Macau 1993), a policy on curriculum for pre-primary education, primary schools and secondary schools (Government of Macau 1994), a law on fee-free basic education (Government of Macau 1995), a set of regulations for

teaching staff (Government of Macau 1996), and a law for teacher training (Government of Macau 1997).

Complementary to the proposed educational reform was the Macau government's intention to increase control over the private schools. In 1993, the Department of Education underwent a series of reorganisations as part of the exercise to localise the civil service, especially in senior positions, and to facilitate implementation of the proposed education laws. The Department of Education was renamed the Department of Education & Youth. A Pre-primary and Primary Department replaced the Official School Inspectorate and the Private School Auxiliary Unit, and was made responsible for both official and private schools. However, implementation of the new policies was hampered by the shortage of human resources and absence of the necessary legislative procedures empowering the Department to execute control of the private schools.

The tide finally turned in 1995, when the Macau government declared in Law 29/95/M that seven years of fee-free education would be provided for all five-year-olds in pre-schools and for children at all levels of primary school. Private schools were encouraged to join the scheme and become members of the subsidised school network, on condition that class sizes did not exceed 45. Schools were given two years to make adjustments. This step was arguably the first serious attempt by the government to regulate educational quality.

Impact on Macau Kindergartens
The most significant impact of the 1991 law on the pre-school sector was the demarcation of kindergarten education into two parts: pre-primary education for three and four year olds, and the preparatory class of primary education for five year olds. The latter became part of the scheme for fee-free basic education.

Table 1.2: Statistics on Pre-schools in Macau

	1993/94	1994/95	1995/96	1996/97	1997/98
No. of pre-schools					
Official	8	8	8	8	8
Private	58	59	61	58	57
Total	64	67	69	66	65
No. of pre-school pupils	20,974	20,476	19,770	18,964	18,291
No. of pre-school teachers	748	724	695	696	715

Source: Macau, Department of Statistics & Census, *Inquérito ao Ensino, 1993/94 – 1997/98.*

The reform also had a dramatic impact on the number of kindergartens. In 1989 and 1990, five Luso-Chinese kindergartens had been opened in the densely-populated northern part of the peninsula. This was a measure to meet the demand for kindergarten places due to the immigration from China over the previous decade. To ease further the shortage of kindergartens, the Macau government decided not to open new official schools but instead to encourage the private sector to open schools. In 1993, the government announced the first list of 16 new private schools to be built before the end of 1997. This list included five kindergartens. Between 1993 and 1997, the number of kindergartens remained steady, but student numbers shrank by 13 per cent (Table 1.2), reflecting a drop in the birth rate. In 1997, about 93 per cent of children aged three to five attended kindergartens (Macau, Department of Statistics & Census 1998b).

By 1998, over 70 per cent of private schools had joined the fee-free education scheme. The pre-schools within this public education network had maximum class sizes of 45. The reduction in class size may be considered important progress, though the figure remained very high compared with international standards (NAEYC, 1991).

In the domain of curriculum, up to that time the Portuguese-medium kindergartens had followed models designed in Portugal, while the Luso-Chinese kindergartens had used a mixture of Hong Kong and Portuguese models, and the majority of private kindergartens had adopted a Hong Kong model. Teaching materials published in Hong Kong were used in all private Chinese-medium kindergartens and in the Luso-Chinese kindergartens. The Curriculum Organisation Law for Kindergartens, Pre-primary and Primary Schools, which outlined a centralised framework of curriculum development for Macau schools, was issued in 1994. A Curriculum Development Committee consisting of teachers from private and official schools and lecturers from the University of Macau was subsequently formed to design provisional teaching syllabuses and teaching materials for each class level. Teaching materials organised around themes were trialled in the official kindergartens beginning in 1995 with the lowest classes. By 1997, the initiative had been extended to all three kindergarten levels. The reform was jointly monitored by the Department of Education & Youth and by specialists at the University of Macau. In 1999, the consolidated curriculum was recommended to the private kindergartens.

Various initiatives were also embarked upon in teacher training. In 1987, what was then called the University of East Asia (in 1991 renamed the University of Macau) was authorised to run day-release in-service courses for pre-primary and primary teachers. Students were awarded a Diploma in Education after two years' study. Also in 1987 St. Joseph's College stopped all full-time courses, continuing only with part-time evening ones. Two years later, the government declared that pre-school and primary courses offered by St. Joseph's College, the University of East Asia and South China Normal University were given official recognition. Graduates from those institutions were eligible for standard subsidies from the government. This treatment raised the question whether the courses should all be considered equivalent to each other despite differences in the mode of teaching, course hours, course design, student assessment, and qualifications of the teaching staff. For example, the course offered by the University of East Asia was the only one to include supervised teaching as a major component, and to make a pass in this domain a precondition for graduation. The fact that the Macau government disregarded these inequalities seemed to imply that the main target was to have as many 'trained' teachers as possible, preferably reaching 100 per cent by 1999. In this sense, quantity was the main concern.

Pre-service courses for pre-primary and primary education were launched by the University of East Asia in 1989. These were three-year full-time courses with full school attachments in the third year. In 1991, the Faculty of Education was established at the university. It offered three-year part-time BEd courses for pre-primary and primary teachers, for three cohorts up to 1994. In 1996, the Diploma in Education courses were upgraded to bacharelato (advanced diploma) level. Meanwhile, the South China Normal University offered in 1990 and 1994 two courses specifically for pre-primary teachers.

As a result of the ample opportunities available for teacher training through the three venues, the proportion of kindergarten teachers who had been trained rose from 56 per cent in 1987 to 80 per cent in 1995 (Macau, Department of Statistics & Census 1997b). In order to reach the target of an all-trained teaching profession, Law 15/96/M stated that new entrants to the teaching profession in the 1996 academic year must have relevant professional training. Those who were already teaching but without professional training were expected to enrol in in-service courses if they were under 40 years of age and had less than 10 years of teaching experience. In 1997, Law 41/97/M stipulated criteria for teacher training and a general framework for teacher education courses. It aimed to promote parity in academic rigour among courses offered by different institutions. Teacher training had therefore become a fairly well established part of the machinery of Macau education.

However, at that time the private kindergartens did not receive much increase in government subsidies. Although education expenditure had increased prominently in the previous few years, and the government policy proclaimed a goal of equity in resourcing of both private and official schools (Government of Macau 1991), discrepancies remained. A substantial amount of the government's education expenditure was still allocated to official administration and to government schools. This situation improved considerably after 1995, when the fee-free education scheme was introduced. By 1997, government subsidy contributed to about one third of the total income of the private schools (Macau, Department of Statistics & Census 1988b).

Pre-school Education in Hong Kong

General Background

In Hong Kong, a clearly-defined and unified school system which included the kindergarten sector emerged during the 1950s. One major cause of the growth of education was the rapid increase in population as a result of the influx of refugees from China. Educational development from then on swept through the second half of the 20th century. The government, however, resolved to implement what Sweeting (1995) describes as a "sequential" arrangement in the expansion of education, beginning with the primary level in the 1950s and 1960s, proceeding to the secondary level in the 1970s and 1980s, and reaching the tertiary level in the 1990s. Pre-school education remained neglected by the government, though it expanded significantly through private provision.

Pre-school Provision

In Hong Kong, most kindergartens provide bisessional programmes of around three hours a day for children aged three to five. Child-care centres serve children under six years of age. Some are whole-day centres, while others are half-day nurseries, and yet others are residential institutions. All kindergartens are in the private sector, but most are operated by non-profit-making agencies. In 1998, 439 of the 735 kindergartens were in that caegory (Hong Kong, Education Department 1998). Child-care centres are also private, except one run by the Social Welfare Department Training Section, but are mostly run by charitable bodies and aided by the government. In 1999, 232 of the 341 day nurseries were in that categories (Hong Kong, Social Welfare Department 1999).

The bulk of pre-school enrolment has always been in kindergartens, because parents have considered kindergarten education to be a pre-requisite for primary school entrance. However, the 1990s brought a slight shift in enrolment towards child-care centres. Official statistics (Table 1.3) indicate that the kindergarten enrolment rate dropped from 80.3 per cent of the age group in 1994 to 77.0 per cent in 1996 (Hong Kong, Education Department 1997a). On the other hand, provision of day nursery places increased from 36,378 in 1995 (Hong Kong, Social Welfare Department 1995) to 43,377 in 1999 (Hong Kong, Social Welfare Department 1999). The increased popularity of child-care centres reflected the fact that most centres had adopted a curriculum more in line with the kindergarten sector, which in turn had reduced parents' fears that child-care centres were inadequately oriented to the transition to primary school. The whole-day operation of child-care centres was also a great asset to families with working mothers.

Table 1.3: Kindergarten Numbers and Enrolment Rates, Hong Kong, 1994-97

	1994	1995	1996	1997
Estimated population aged 3-5 years	221,300	223,100	231,900	
Number of kindergarten pupils	177,772	177,773	178,489	174,588
Enrolment rate (%)	80.3	79.7	77.0	
Number of kindergartens	711	706	702	705

Source: Hong Kong, Education Department.

Pre-school education in Hong Kong has evolved through three phases of development since the 1950s. Phase I was a very rudimentary stage without a clear orientation. Phase II was a period of quantitative growth; and Phase III brought stronger emphasis on quality. The following paragraphs review the various phases and identify the role of government policy.

Phase I: Development up to 1981
In the period immediately following World War II, the government gave priority attention to primary and secondary schools, and demand for kindergartens was mainly met by untrained persons in the private sector. In 1953, a Kindergarten Section was set up in the Education Department to provide advice in planning and implementation. Quality issues such as adult-child ratio, class size and teacher qualifications were neglected. Kindergarten enrolment increased rapidly from 19,000 in 1957 (Government of Hong Kong 1958) to 141,000 in 1971 (Government of Hong Kong 1972). The rise in student numbers was not matched by an equivalent increase in teacher numbers, with the result that the adult-child ratio deteriorated from 1:25 in 1958 (Government of Hong Kong 1959) to 1:35 in 1971 (Government of Hong Kong 1972). The percentage of trained teachers also declined. The government had limited training resources, and trained teachers were not welcomed by profit-making kindergartens since the owners were unwilling to pay the higher salaries demanded by such teachers.

The situation in the child-care sector was more favourable. In 1948, a Social Welfare Office had been established to protect and care for children; and in 1958 a Child Welfare Section was created in the Social Welfare Department. However, a clear government policy on child care did not emerge until the mid-1970s. An advisory inspectorate for child-care centres was set up in the Social Welfare Department (Hong Kong, Social Welfare Department 1977); and in the early 1980s a new ordinance and set of regulations provided the legal framework (Government of Hong Kong 1982a, 1982b).

Systematic training for kindergarten teachers started in 1950, when a two-year part-time course was launched in the Northcote College of Education. However, the course was discontinued two years later. In 1956, the Kindergarten Section of the Education Department started a two-year part-time course with a biennial intake of 50 students. The intake was too small to meet demand, and during that period a significant number of junior high school students went to Macau to join the full-time kindergarten course at the St. Joseph's College. In addition, trained teachers from Taiwan and mainland China and especially Macau came to teach in Hong Kong kindergartens.

Government contribution to the training of child-care staff began in 1958 when the Child Welfare Section and the Young Women's Christian Association jointly ran a five-week part-time course for nursery staff. In 1962, the newly-established training section of the Social Welfare Department took over responsibility for training 50 nursery workers every year (Hong Kong, Social Welfare Department 1963). The 1976 ordinance and regulations accelerated the trend by requiring child-care workers to have received training within a year of their initial employment. The Social Welfare Department ran a five-week course with an extended one-year full-time or two-year part-time course offered by the Hong Kong Polytechnic starting in 1977 and 1979 respectively.

Phase II: Developments from 1981 to 1994
By 1980, concern by stakeholders and the general public about the state of pre-school education had reached a critical point. In that year, over 85 per cent of children aged four and five were enrolled in kindergartens, but 84 per cent of the teaching staff were untrained. Responding to public concern, the government prepared a White Paper (Government of Hong Kong 1981) which set out Hong Kong's first official policy on the subject.

The White Paper highlighted the need to accelerate training for kindergarten teachers, and advocated in-service training as the way to upgrade existing staff. Training at that time was in two categories: a two-year part-time Qualified Kindergarten Teacher (QKT) course run by the Grantham College of Education, and a 12-week Qualified Assistant Kindergarten Teacher (QAKT) course run by the Inspectorate of the Education Department. The government set the target of 45 per cent of kindergarten teachers being trained by 1986, rising to 90 per cent by 1992. An allied target was for all principals to attain QKT status by 1986. However, since the figures on trained teachers referred to both QKT and QAKT, it appeared that the government was only willing to commit limited resources. In the child-care sector, the government was satisfied with having 70 per cent of staff trained. The authorities decided to continue with existing training provision for that sector, but envisaged creation by 1984 of a joint programme for training kindergarten and child-care staff. In addition, the government raised issues about class sizes, adult-child ratios, minimum space, materials, and equipment. Curriculum development for the kindergarten sector was also highlighted as an important need.

In 1981, an international panel of educators was invited by the government to review Hong Kong's education system (Llewellyn 1982). The panel urged vigorous implementation of the 1981 White Paper's recommendations on pre-school education, and even suggested that early childhood education should be given priority over other levels. The report argued that eventually kindergartens should become part of the aided sector.

However, the recommendations of the visiting panel did not gain full support. In 1986, Education Commission Report No.2 addressed the question whether kindergarten education was essential, and therefore deserving aided-sector status. It argued that kindergarten education only had a short-term effect on later academic achievement. Although an American study by scholars at Cornell University claimed that children with pre-school experience had more positive attitudes towards learning, the Education Commission doubted if the same results could be achieved in Hong Kong. The Commission concluded that kindergarten education was not essential, and therefore recommended that it should not become part of the aided sector. However, the Commission did raise questions about equality of access, and advised the government to introduce a scheme to assist applicants from poor families to pay fees and other costs. The government accepted this advice, thus making some improvement but in effect confirming that it was not prepared at that time to embark on a fundamental overhaul.

The Education Commission also raised questions about the fragmentation of the sector. The Commission advised the government to work towards uniting all pre-school services in order to promote uniformity in provision. The Commission recommended that the process should begin with improvement of teacher-child ratio, teacher qualifications, and space per child. In the long term, the Commission suggested, all kindergarten teachers should be trained and the maximum adult-child ratio should be 1:15, which is close to 1:14 for child care centres. A committee was set up to compile plans for unification of the sector. However, in 1986, only 23 per cent of kindergarten teachers had received training, far below the 45 per cent target set out in the 1981 White Paper. Realising the importance of training, the Commission recommended immediate expansion of QAKT courses and, from 1990, expansion of QKT training in the Grantham College of Education.

Despite the lukewarm views expressed in Education Commission Report No.2, the public continued to remind the government of the importance of pre-school education. In 1993, a motion on the matter was passed by the Legislative Council (Ieong 1993, p.112); and a report was issued on the training needs of pre-primary teachers (Hong Kong Council of Early Childhood Education & Services 1993). The Board of Education decided to form an ad hoc sub-committee to devise measures to improve kindergarten education. The report, released in 1994, affirmed the value of pre-schools in the local context by drawing on a wide spectrum of overseas studies, and concluded that the government should be more directly involved in the sector. The proportion of trained teachers had increased to 46 per cent in 1992, but this was far below the 79 per cent target set by the Education Commission in 1986. The sub-committee proposed a new target of 60 per cent trained teachers in 1999, and advocated a long-term target teacher-child ratio of 1:15. On the question of unification of pre-primary services, the sub-committee recommended development of a common curriculum for all pre-schools, and common teacher training courses which would be recognised by both the Education Department and the Social Welfare Department.

Phase III: Developments after 1994
The 1994 government policy address stressed an official commitment to education, including the pre-school sector. One component was a pledge to spend HK$163 million in the subsequent four years for training kindergarten teachers. This was expected to provide courses for 1,130 serving teachers in 1995/96. In addition to the certificate course for serving teachers scheduled to start in 1995 was a full-time pre-service course

scheduled to start in 1997. All these initiatives were subsequently implemented in the Hong Kong Institute of Education, which opened in 1994 and took over the responsibility for teacher training from the four Colleges of Education and the Institute of Language in Education. Other initiatives included specification that new entrants to the profession after 1995 should have at least two passes in the Hong Kong Certificate of Education Examination; and the government declared that by 1997 at least 40 per cent of the teachers in each kindergarten should have attained QKT status. In order to enable kindergartens to employ teachers according to the government's recommended salary scales, policy makers promised to explore the possibility of subsidising kindergartens. These moves indicated government intention to implement several of the recommendations of the ad hoc sub-committee of the Board of Education on pre-primary education. It was the first time that substantial government investment was promised for the sector.

A working party on kindergartens had been formed in 1989 to consider the issue of unification of pre-primary services recommended by the Education Commission. This working party was initially limited in its effectiveness, but in 1994 it was reconstituted to study the practicalities of unifying all pre-primary services. In 1995, the working party recommended that unification or harmonisation of the various aspects of pre-primary service should be pursued within the context of available resources and practical administration. It proposed amalgamation of the 'Guide to the Kindergarten Curriculum' (Hong Kong, Curriculum Development Council 1984) and the 'Activity Guidelines for Day Nurseries' (Government of Hong Kong 1986) into a single Curriculum Guide. This was done, and the resulting document was subsequently endorsed by the Curriculum Development Council (Hong Kong, Curriculum Development Institute 1996). In addition, a harmonised pay scale was introduced. Coordinated training for kindergarten teachers and child-care workers was also endorsed by the Working Party, and a framework on a basic training programme was formulated. All graduates of basic training courses developed according to this framework could seek recognition from either the Education Department or the Social Welfare Department.

In 1997, the Education Commission released its seventh report, on quality school education. The document was timed to enlighten the SAR government on the quality of education as Hong Kong advanced into a new era. The report focused mainly on primary and secondary schools, but did not exclude other levels of education. Recommendations on management and performance, for example, were considered to be generic for all levels. The report advocated creation of a Quality Education Fund open to bids. Although the place of kindergartens in this HK$5 billion project appeared to have been overlooked in the SAR government's 1997 policy address, which mentioned only primary and secondary schools, the public felt that kindergartens should also be permitted to participate in the venture. Eventually, when details of the Quality Education Fund were announced in 1998, kindergartens and child care centres were invited to apply alongside other sectors. Following the first call for applications, 67 pre-primary projects, totalling $9 million were approved (Hong Kong, Quality Education Fund 1998). This could be taken as a practical move by the government to promote quality in pre-school education, and the beginning of a quality culture in the early childhood field.

The goals set in the 1994 policy address were reiterated in the SAR government's 1997 policy address. By 1996, about one-third of the serving kindergarten teachers were without training and only slightly less than one-third had attained qualified teacher status (Table 1.4). Teacher qualifications and the kindergarten subsidy scheme were therefore two items of major concern. By 2000, the government declared, at least 60 per cent of teachers in each kindergarten should be qualified, and by 2004 all newly-recruited kindergarten principals would have to be graduates of the Certificate in Kindergarten Education or an equivalent course. Parallel to these measures was the plan to expand the training by providing 660 extra places between 1998 and 2002. The kindergarten subsidy scheme which had been implemented in 1995 to encourage kindergartens to employ more trained staff was reviewed in 1996. Amendments were made both to include more kindergartens and to adjust the subsidy every year.

Table 1.4: Statistics on Kindergarten Teachers in Hong Kong, 1994-97

	1994	1995	1996	1997
Number of Kindergarten Teachers	8,107	8,232	8,436	8,619
Number of Qualified Kindergarten Teachers	1,917	2,034	2,680	3,168
Number of Assistant Kindergarten Teachers	2,342	2,709	2,644	2,568
Number of Other Trained Teachers	89	93	97	144
Number of Untrained Kindergarten Teachers	3,759	3,396	3,015	2,739

Source: Hong Kong, Education Department, *1997 Teacher Survey*

Implications of Similarities and Differences

From this review of pre-school education in Macau and Hong Kong, several major similarities and differences will be evident. The most striking similarity is that in both places the sector was long neglected by successive governments, but that this situation changed in the 1980s and 1990s. Differences include the factors which caused the change of government attitude, and the pace of change. The following paragraphs enlarge on these and related matters.

The Driving Forces of Change

The projected return of the two colonies to their motherland had different effects in Macau and Hong Kong. In the former, the 1987 Sino-Portuguese Declaration marked the beginning of a new era for education. Never before had the government been so involved in devising and executing educational innovations. During the subsequent dozen years, much legislation concerning education was processed because the 1999 handover date seemed to be the deadline for completion of the proposed changes. One notable achievement in the pre-school sector was the upgrading of the teaching force from half trained to nearly fully trained. Another achievement was inclusion of part of the pre-school sector in the fee-free basic education scheme.

In Hong Kong, the change of sovereignty had less effect on pre-school education. The education sector as a whole was well developed prior to the 1984 Sino-British Agreement. Within the education sector, pre-schools were neglected by the government; but that did not greatly change in the period immediately following 1984. In 1997, pre-school education remained largely in the private sector, and about one third of kindergarten teachers were still untrained. However, the government did inject more resources after 1994. This was not so much because of the impending political transition as a response to the public view that the sector was in need of qualitative attention.

Underlying this comment is an observation about the role of government. The delayed development of pre-school education in both Macau and Hong Kong can be attributed to the way that the sector was viewed by the respective governments. The Hong Kong government preferred to heed the views of the 1986 Education Commission Report No.2 rather than the 1982 Llewellyn Report, and stated that pre-school education was desirable but not essential. The official perception created a 'Cinderella' syndrome (Opper 1993) in which pre-school education was deemed inferior to her three sisters namely the primary, secondary and tertiary sectors. Reported government expenditure in 1997 was just HK$1,088 per kindergarten pupil compared with HK$15,305 per primary pupil, and $23,519 per secondary pupil (Hong Kong, Education Department 1997a).

The Macau government has in one sense been less discriminatory against the pre-school sector since all levels of education were neglected. Once this general neglect changed, some aspects of pre-school education gained almost as much attention as primary education. When the top grade of kindergarten became part of the fee-free education scheme, it was in effect being viewed as the preparatory class for primary education. The other two kindergarten grades were given less attention, but were still considered to be an integral part of the emerging Macau education system. Kindergartens joining the fee-free education scheme were restricted to a maximum class size of 45 in the top grade, and were expected in the long run to adhere to this maximum in other grades. Even more significantly, teachers of all kindergarten grades received the same government subsidy as their counterparts in primary schools. The pilot scheme for the kindergarten curriculum also applied to all three levels.

For Hong Kong, one lesson from Macau is that fee-free education can be separated from the question whether kindergarten education is essential. In Macau, the sector attracted more attention when the government affirmed the importance of pre-school education, with increased private as well as public investment. The Macau framework had parallels elsewhere in Asia. In Japan, for example, pre-school education is a shared venture between the government and parents. The Japanese government does not offer fee-free pre-school education, but substantial financial support is given to pre-schools and stringent requirements on quality are enforced. Governments in other parts of Asia, such as mainland China and Taiwan, do not offer fee-free pre-school education but have acknowledged its place in the education system and monitor the quality of provision. These observations strengthen the argument that the Hong Kong government should declare pre-school education to be desirable and perhaps even essential, and should legitimise it as part of the education system. Considerably more resources should be allocated to enhance quality, particularly of teachers. The Hong Kong government could follow its neighbour in Macau by making the top grade of kindergarten fee-free as a possible step towards fee-free education in the entire pre-school sector.

Teacher Training
The NAEYC (1991) in the USA rightly identifies staff quality as the most important determinant of pre-school quality. The rationale is that the teacher's ability to facilitate children's learning and development depends on the teacher's knowledge and training. Results of the National Day Care Study (Ruopp et al. 1979) indicated that child-care related training was associated with higher levels of positive adult-child interaction, higher levels of language stimulation, more co-operative behaviour, greater task persistence of children, and gains in children's general knowledge. Similarly, the National Child Care Staffing Study (Whitebook et al. 1990) showed that specialised training at the post-secondary school level is more likely to provide a good preparation for child

care provision than is child care-related training at the secondary school or vocational school level. However, a bachelor's degree has now become the targeted benchmark in many countries. For example, in 1995 the Taiwanese government declared a vision of having most kindergarten teachers at degree level by 2000 (Taiwan 1995). Research has also shown that well-trained staff can offset poor material environments (Crahay 1990) and high adult-child ratios (Howes & Marx 1992).

These observations suggests that the governments of both Macau and Hong Kong should give priority to teacher training in resource allocation. As noted above, in 1994 the Hong Kong government did make a major step by allocating HK$163 million exclusively to pre-school teacher training; and the Macau government has offered fee-free teacher education courses up to the degree level for in-service pre-school teachers since 1987. These steps are to be applauded, though further improvements are needed.

The role of the private sector, particularly in Macau, also deserves full recognition. Before 1987, output from the private sector considerably reduced what would otherwise have been a wide gap. Although the quality of these courses may have had shortcomings, the courses did demand minimum entry levels initially of Secondary 3 and later Secondary 5. At no time was pre-school teacher training ever offered at lower than the certificate level, and at no time was it inferior to primary teacher training. This framework greatly helped to build a positive image for the pre-school profession, and in turn attracted people to join.

In these respects, practices in Macau were ahead of practices in Hong Kong. Pre-service training started in Macau during the 1960s, while in Hong Kong it started only in 1998. Benchmarks for teacher training in Macau were the Certificate course in the 1960s, the Diploma in Education since 1987, and the Advanced Diploma since 1996. Even BEd courses for pre-school teachers were offered in Macau from 1991 to 1997, and plans were subsequently prepared to offer a BEd as an add-on to the Advanced Diploma course. By contrast, the benchmark for teacher training in Hong Kong is the Qualified Kindergarten Teacher course, which is below the Certificate level. The Certificate in Kindergarten Education Course launched in 1995 is a benchmark only for kindergarten principals. However, Hong Kong provision did begin to catch up in the late 1990s. As noted above, in 1997 a BEd course in early childhood education was jointly offered by the Baptist University and an overseas institution, and another local BEd course was offered solely by the Baptist University in early 1999. The Hong Kong Institute of Education launched its own BEd course for pre-school teachers in 1999 in collaboration with two overseas universities.

In Hong Kong, pre-school teacher training was under government operation almost from the start. Although this implied a guarantee of minimum quality, resources were so limited that the capacity was too small to meet the needs. Since pre-school education itself was in the hands of the private sector, and there was no legislation on professional requirements, the kindergartens mainly employed untrained teachers with low academic levels. Most assistant teachers had only received 12-week crash courses, which created an image that pre-school professionals were of low calibre. Low salaries further increased turn-over rates, and created obstacles for those who wished to attract applicants with higher qualifications. This longstanding legacy will make it difficult for Hong Kong to reach the standards evident in Macau. In 1997, 31.8 per cent of 8,619 serving kindergarten teachers had no training, while 29.8 per cent had only QAKT training (Table 1.3). The most pressing need was to help this large number of teachers attain QKT status as soon as possible. Meanwhile it was equally important to upgrade qualified teachers and administrators to the next level of their career paths in order to enhance the credibility of the profession. Certificate courses should gradually replace QKT to become the benchmarks of pre-school teacher training; both for the kindergartens and child-care centres. Another challenge for the pre-school sector was turning pre-service training into the mainstream, as in the primary sector.

In Macau, there are two dimensions to pre-school teacher training: the 'vertical' upgrading of professional qualifications offered as regular courses and the 'horizontal' widening and refreshing of professional competencies offered as short courses, mainly in the summer block. Both have been substantially subsidised by the government. In Hong Kong, pre-school teacher training has always been 'vertical'. It is therefore essential for government effort to extend to the 'horizontal' arm as well.

Teacher Trainer Preparation

In Hong Kong, in the 1980s pre-school teacher trainers in general had their training experience in either primary or secondary sections, while some followed add-on courses in child development or early childhood education abroad. The need for pre-school teacher trainer preparation was highlighted in Education Commission Report No.2 (1986), and noted again in the Report of the Ad Hoc Sub-Committee for Pre-primary Education (Hong Kong, Board of Education 1994). Between 1983 and 1997, the University of Hong Kong had three intakes in its Master of Education (MEd) programme in early-childhood education. The majority of graduates from the MEd course continued in or proceeded to the field of pre-school teacher training, and some pursued further studies at doctoral level. They were supplemented by colleagues with overseas qualifications, with the result that the general quality of teacher trainers for the kindergarten sector rose significantly.

In Macau, the qualifications of teacher trainers were not scrutinised by policy makers, professional bodies, or the public. No statistics were publicly available on the qualifications and experience of the teacher trainers. Since advanced education programmes at MEd level were offered only after 1996 at the University of Macau, most teacher trainers had received their training abroad. When the programme for primary and pre-primary teachers was first offered by the University of East Asia in 1987, all teacher trainers were recruited from Hong Kong. In the late 1990s, few teacher trainers in the pre-school programme in Macau had backgrounds in early childhood education.

This phenomenon should be viewed as a serious drawback to the development of quality pre-school teacher education in Macau, particularly as teacher training had moved from the initial phase towards a more sophisticated one. Teacher trainers are crucial to the efficacy of the training programmes, for they usually assume the multiple roles of programme developer, implementer and quality controller. School attachments and/or collaborative action research with practitioners would reduce the deficiencies of trainers without the necessary qualifications or experience. The training institutions could also collaborate with nearby institutions such as the University of Hong Kong or the normal universities in China to arrange upgrading courses for their staff.

Adult-child Ratio

Adult-child ratio is one of the three major indicators of pre-school quality, which Phillips (1988) described as an iron triangle. This quality indicator is addressed quite differently in Hong Kong and in Macau. In Hong Kong, the mandated maximum of 30 pupils to one teacher has been enforced since 1986. In 1994, it was further revised to 20 pupils per teacher for full-day kindergarten classes and nursery (three year-old) classes (Hong Kong, Education Department 1994). Education Commission Report No. 2 (1986) recommended a target kindergarten teacher-child ratio of 1:15, which was close to the ratio in child-care centres. Although not yet a legal requirement, this ratio was in fact found in many kindergartens. It was common for kindergartens in Hong Kong to have one teacher in charge of one session in the bisessional system but to be present also in the other session to help children learn. In some kindergartens, a second teacher was shared among two or three classes to help in small group activities. Macau's classes were much larger, and most had only one teacher. In this respect the quality of provision may be assumed to have been inferior.

Language Policy

The clauses in the Basic Laws of Macau and Hong Kong which protect the continuing places of Portuguese and English as official languages in the post-colonial era have far-reaching implications. However, governments in the two territories have had different attitudes towards the learning of the colonial languages by pre-school children.

In Macau, Portuguese has always been a substantial part of the curriculum of the official schools, albeit mixed with Chinese in the Luso-Chinese schools. In most private kindergartens, Chinese is the medium of instruction with English taught as a second language. The Law on Curriculum Organisation for Pre-primary and Primary Schools (Macau, Government of 1994) stated that a second language could be taught in the preparatory class through games and activities, in order not to tamper with development of the mother tongue. This legitimised the teaching of Portuguese in the official schools and English in the private schools. Understanding that Portuguese is not such a strong international language as English, the Macau government could only enforce the teaching of this colonial language within the arena of the official sector. However, since most Macau kindergarten teachers were graduates from the Chinese high schools with limited English competencies, the quality of English learning in the pre-school deserved close monitoring.

In contrast, the Hong Kong government never advocated the teaching of English or any other second language at the pre-school age. The early years are perceived primarily as a time for the development of mother tongue language. Consequently, official documents such as the guidelines on pre-school curriculum (Hong Kong, Curriculum Development Council 1984; Hong Kong, Curriculum Development Institute 1993, 1996) made no mention of the teaching of English, and it was not included in teacher education programmes before 1995. In practice, every kindergarten in Hong Kong teaches some English as early as the first grade. Some kindergartens advertise the fact that English is taught by expatriates, but in most kindergartens it is taught by local practitioners with insufficient English proficiency and little understanding of second-language learning in the early years. English is valued partly by parents because of its value as a route for advancement in the education system and society. Kindergartens know that English is required in primary school, and therefore teach it at the pre-school level as a preparation.

After the political handover in 1997, the Hong Kong SAR government declared that secondary school leavers should be trilingual and biliterate (Government of Hong Kong 1997). In the primary schools, Putonghua, which is the national language of China, became a compulsory subject in 1998. Although the pre-school sector was not included in these innovations, kindergartens were influenced by the language shifts and some began to teach Putonghua. Again, no Putonghua teaching was offered in pre-school teacher education courses before 1995, and in many pre-schools immigrants from mainland China become part-time Putonghua teachers. The fact that these two languages were now taught in pre-schools without a proper quality assurance mechanism highlighted the need for the Hong Kong government to review the state of language learning in the pre-school sector, taking into consideration both professional judgements and societal needs. The Macau government was more pro-active over the issue of language teaching but, as in Hong Kong, did not address the issue of the quality of second language learning in pre-schools.

Patterns of Child Development

In Hong Kong, details on the developmental areas of three- to five-year-old children were documented as part of the Phase I study of the Pre-primary Project (PPP) of the International Association for the Evaluation of Educational Achievement (IEA) (Opper 1996). They covered motor, personal, social, cognitive, language, and pre-academic learning. Results indicated that Hong Kong children were seemingly inferior to children elsewhere in social development, but were consistently ahead in pre-academic learning. This finding suggested that in Hong Kong pre-schools, pre-academic learning was over-emphasised at the expense of social development.

In Macau, a study of the relationship between pre-school quality and child development was conducted in 1993 using some of the IEA Phase II Study instruments (N.C.M. Wong 1997). Child development measures were used to document the profiles of four-year-old children. Results indicated that the quality of the learning environment contributed most substantially to children's social development, but that it did not relate to pre-academic development. On the other hand, children had better pre-academic development in pre-schools with large classes. In Macau, as most private kindergartens were rated poor by the Pre-school Environmental Rating Scale (N.C.M. Wong 1997), which was an adapted version of the Early Childhood Environmental Rating Scale (Harms & Clifford 1980), deficiency in social development was shown also to be a common pattern among Macau children. At the same time, Macau's mandated maximum class size was 45, which, though slightly smaller than actual class sizes in 1993, was still enormous. With only one teacher in each class, the learning of academic skills inevitably precluded more interactive types of learning. Therefore, although the advocacy of an all-round development of young children was addressed in official papers of Hong Kong and Macau, the discrepancies between policy and practice remained to be resolved.

Links with Mainland China

Hong Kong and Macau are two Chinese societies which, despite having been administered by two different colonial powers, have retained similar ideologies in education. These ideologies have Confucian roots. The cultural legacies of the colonial powers are in general not conspicuous in the pre-school except in official kindergartens in Macau. The differences in the development of pre-school education in these two territories, as revealed previously, are attributed to government operation. As Hong Kong and Macau have now strengthened their bonds with China because of the return of sovereignty to their motherland, it is useful to review the various dimensions of pre-school education in the context of patterns in mainland China.

Although a communist nation by legislation, China has the same child-centred orientation in pre-school education as advocated in Hong Kong and Macau. A 1987 document issued by the State Education Commission stated that games should be the major form of activity for children, and that their choices of games should be respected (China, State Education Commission 1996b). The document declared that children should be happy in pre-schools, where they should have a comprehensive development of capabilities and character and where individual differences should be catered for. Moral education, which means the education of feeling and the development of good behaviour, was also emphasised, as in all pre-schools in Hong Kong and Macau.

In terms of policy, mainland China is arguably ahead of both Hong Kong and Macau in pre-school education. In 1987, the State Education Commission announced a policy on kindergarten class size and staffing. The mandated class sizes for three-year-olds was 20-25, while for four-year-olds it was 26-30 and for five-year-olds it was 31-35. Each class was expected to be staffed by two teachers and one child care worker. The adult-child ratio so formed is close to the international standard. In 1989, the Kinder-garten Management Regulations (China, State Education Commission 1996a) declared that all kindergarten teachers must be graduates from the early childhood training insti-tutions or equivalent. A previous document, released in 1988 (China, National Affairs Office 1996), had related the government's conception of the impact of early education on the enhancement of the quality of the whole nation.

However, while mainland China has a comprehensive set of pre-school rules and regulations, it must be recognised that they are only observed in urban areas. Eighty per cent of the population in the rural areas still staggers along because of resource scarcity. Therefore, in a country of 1.2 billion people the Chinese government has an agenda quite different from that of Hong Kong and Macau. The government's main concern is to ensure the dissemination of a general framework of pre-school education across the country, while allowing flexibilities in pace, capacity and methods of implementation at the local level. To this end, Beijing and Shanghai formulated their own pre-school education guidelines in 1996 and 1998 respectively.

Conclusions

The prospective change of sovereignty in Macau ignited a series of changes in the edu-cational scene, which partially remedied the laissez-faire policies of the Portuguese colonial regime. In Hong Kong, change in the pre-school sector in the 1980s and more prominently in the 1990s was more a response to perceived practical needs and profes-sional advocacy than to political considerations. As in Macau, the reforms partially remedied the government's indifference to the sector. Yet in neither territory were explicit changes in the orientation of the pre-school curriculum brought by the impend-ing political hand-over.

Although Hong Kong has a better-established education system than Macau, neglect of the pre-school sector has left it in private hands. For Hong Kong, the over-arching agenda in pre-school education is the quest for a well-defined status in the education system which would generate parity in government concern and resources with the primary sector. Enhanced legislative and financial support could then become the critical force for quality in the sector. For Hong Kong, pre-school teacher training is one dimension of the iron triangle that needs particularly urgent attention.

Macau appears to be more advanced than Hong Kong in the area of pre-school teacher training, but is weaker in the other two quality constructs, adult-child ratio and class size. The high adult-child ratio reflects an underlying problem confronting the Macau pre-school education scene, namely that the territory has too few trained teachers to permit an adult-child ratio that will allow strong child-centred activity-based learning. The key need is for financial input from the government. Meanwhile, one interim measure which could quickly untie the deadlock of funding would be a move to have bi-sessional operation. This is one domain in which Macau could learn from Hong Kong, and which would help to maximise use of resources.

Improvement of teacher training and adult-child ratios would demand considerable financial input from the government. Compared with mainland China, Hong Kong and Macau are very affluent and should be in a good position to cope with the financial demands of high quality education. However, whether this quest for high quality pre-school education could be actualised hinges more on the government's value judgements about pre-school education than on financial considerations. To change government attitudes, tertiary institutions need to conduct research in the local context that will inform government of the efficacy of pre-school education. Meanwhile, equally important is the building of a quality culture among the stakeholders. Hong Kong's Quality Education Fund might provide a model for the Macau government. This could be a vital step to move pre-school education from the licensing level, the 'floor of quality', towards the professional level, the 'ceiling of quality' (Morgan 1985, p.15).

Hong Kong and Macau will continue to face problems and challenges in pre-school education long after the political handovers. Although similar problems will arise in each territory since both are SARs within China, they might be tackled in different ways due to contextual differences. The political handovers will permit more contact and exchanges between the pre-school professionals in mainland China and Hong Kong and Macau, thus cross-fertilising the early childhood sectors. A framework of quality early childhood programme embracing both the international perspectives and Chinese values could then emerge and become the mainstream.

2

Primary and Secondary Schooling

Bob ADAMSON & LI Siu Pang, Titus

As this volume shows, Hong Kong and Macau are siblings: they have fundamental similarities and individual traits, and they exist to some extent in a relationship of mutual dependence. Macau is the introspective elder – outshone, overshadowed and greatly influenced by the more gifted and extrovert junior, but nonetheless a source of support to Hong Kong. Both are ports situated on the south coast of China; and there are strong parallels in their historical development, although Macau has not experienced to the same degree the tigerish leap into economic prosperity of Hong Kong. Both are in the process of decolonisation under special circumstances: it comprises re-unification with a 'motherland' that was until recent years politically, economically and socially estranged, resulting in a familial accommodation of differences rather than a whole-hearted embrace. For pragmatic politicians in the People's Republic of China (PRC), the presence of two colonial problems left over from Chinese history (together with the vexed question of Taiwan) has conveniently provided legitimacy to what might have been an anomalous and potentially untenable conception of a "special administrative region with a high degree of autonomy" had only one colony existed.

The mutuality is reflected in primary and secondary schooling. As gateways into and out of China, Hong Kong and Macau are peopled with migrants (settlers and transients) seeking access to and egress from the Chinese mainland, including merchants, missionaries, educators and colonial administrators who bring multicentric perspectives of the purposes of schooling. At the interface of East and West, schools in both places mark a key point where the twain do meet and thus represent either contested cultural territory or a melting pot. In the main, Macau has been influenced by educational practices and curriculum materials from Hong Kong rather than vice versa, but this sibling dependency has not simply been a one-way process, especially in Hong Kong's early days as a colony.

Common issues have emerged, most notably fundamental questions concerning the provision, scope and orientation of primary and secondary schooling within the colonial and post-colonial contexts. Whose responsibility is it to provide such education? Who should receive it? What should be the aims and content? Interestingly, the answers show significant similarities and differences. This chapter provides a comparative, chronological analysis of schooling in Macau (where primary and secondary schooling are closely integrated) and Hong Kong (where the two levels are now generally distinct). It describes and compares the main features of educational provision at primary and secondary levels, and identifies some of the main forces that have shaped the similarities and differences that emerge from the comparison. It suggests that geographical proximity and contemporaneous experiences produce the similarities, while the respective colonial practices of Portugal and the United Kingdom largely account for the differences. To place this discussion in context, the chapter first refers to the evolution of school systems elsewhere, particularly those places which have undergone processes of decolonisation.

Schooling, Colonialism and the Transition to Post-Colonialism

Much of the literature on schooling and colonialism is concerned with the imposition and impact of Western thought on other countries, most notably the European sea powers and industrialised nations since the 16th century and, in more recent times, the United States of America. Although this emphasis is apposite for the comparative study of Hong Kong and Macau, the transition to post-colonialism is also worthy of study, in that the two colonies have returned to Chinese sovereignty after developing divergent socio-economic and political characteristics from those of the mainland.

The emergence of nation-states in the past few centuries has reshaped the nature and structures of schooling (Green 1990; Ramirez 1997). Previously, much education was informal and took the form of personal apprenticeships and other mentoring to prepare children to contribute to the survival of the clan or other social structures. The nation-state focused on industrial development and expansion of economic power at the national level, and schooling became more formal, and characterised by the provision of mass education and the cultivation of patriotic sentiments. The presence of the Portuguese and British in Macau and Hong Kong respectively is explained by this search for an expansion of trade, facilitated by the development of military technology. However, in colonial societies, the question of mass education (with its resource implications) and the cultivation of patriotism (for which country?) were problematic for colonial authorities, and the situation in many settings was made more complex by the existence of pre-colonial forms of schooling. In Macau and Hong Kong, pre-colonial schooling was oriented towards the maintenance of the dynastic system in China. The focus of the schools was on instilling the classical Chinese virtues of filial piety, loyalty and righteousness through the study of the great literary works with a view to maintaining social harmony (Cleverley 1991).

Colonial authorities around the world, faced with at least two different modes of schooling, adopted a variety of solutions (Kelly & Altbach 1984, pp.2-4). One was classical colonialism – imposing their own imported modes on the colonies. A second approach was to promote schooling in its indigenous form. A third method was to adopt a mixed system, either by generating a synthesis of the two modes, or creating a parallel system, or some other, more complex, admixture. The most common form of schooling in colonial societies was a mixed mode, as the local administration of education (as opposed to direct control located in the colonial country) meant that the nature of schooling was often strongly influenced by the particular conditions of the colony and by those directly responsible for its provision (Kelly & Altbach 1984). This mixed mode commonly had a strong centre-periphery orientation, whereby government schooling heavily favoured colonial nationals and those proficient in the colonial language who would serve interests of the ruling power, while missionaries and local organisations mainly provided schooling of various kinds for other children. The curriculum in the elite government schools was academic and geared towards producing administrators for the government sector (Bray 1997a; Ball 1993). An example is the French system in Algeria in the 19th century. Other modes emphasised convergence, for political and/or economic reasons. For instance, the British Orientalists in India sought to graft modern Western ideas on to indigenous learning to promote industrialisation and social reforms without generating cultural resistance (Kopf 1984).

The nature of schooling during the processes of decolonisation has commonly been affected by the amount of time available for preparation; the attitude of the colonial powers towards decolonisation; the available human resources; and the end product, including self-government or transfer of sovereignty (Bray 1997a). When the process was rapid or violent (such as in India in the 1940s and many countries in South East Asia during the 1950s), or when the colonial powers were ill-disposed towards the process, the scope for schooling to be adjusted was limited – although educational initiatives might be high on the agenda of the indigenous authorities that assumed power. However, in some African countries – Ghana and Nigeria, for instance – the provision of education was expanded and reoriented to prepare for self-rule through co-operation with the colonial power (Bray et al. 1986). Macau and Hong Kong's reunification with their neighbour, as opposed to achieving independence, was not unique: the Portuguese colonies of Goa and East Timor, for example, were transferred to Indian and Indonesian sovereignty respectively. Realignment rather than independence creates an added dimension to debates concerning the nature and content of post-colonial schooling.

As far as the curriculum is concerned, school subjects deemed ripe for reorientation at a time of decolonisation (either to independence or to merger with another state) are those connected with national identity, especially history, social studies, literature and languages (Jansen 1989). Thus the content and orientation of history might be changed to reflect the perspectives of the new power, as happened in Ireland in the early 1920s; social studies programmes rooted in local experiences and environments might be introduced, as in Tanzania in the 1960s; and the colonial language might be under pressure and indigenous languages promoted in its stead, as was the case in Malaysia in the 1970s and 1980s. A countervailing trend in many post-colonial countries has been retention or even strengthening of aspects of the imported curriculum for technological progress and international trade (Jansen 1989). This may be illustrated by the renewed status that English enjoyed in the school curriculum in Singapore in the 1960s (Jason Tan 1997) and Malaysia in the 1990s (Pennycook 1994). This tension between the desire to strengthen national identity and the imperatives of economic globalisation is discernible in the school curriculum in Macau and Hong Kong.

Primary and Secondary Schooling in Macau

The development of schooling in Macau has been influenced by two principal factors: its geographic location and the style of colonisation. Both of these had political, economic and cultural implications that impacted upon education. Geographically, Macau was initially an attractive port for the Portuguese, providing access to Chinese and other Asian markets. In the event, its golden years were short. Macau's value was drastically reduced around 1640 by a concurrence of disparate blows. The fall of the Ming dynasty, with which the Portuguese had carefully cultivated connections, the rise of the Dutch in securing and monopolising trade routes, and the expulsion of the Portuguese from Japan all contributed to Macau's economic decline (Cremer 1991). The colonisation of Hong

Kong, which had a superior harbour, condemned Macau to serving much of its colonial life as a place of rest and recreation for visitors. It has provided a safe haven for political refugees from the mainland, but the proximity to China has also left it vulnerable to political, economic and social problems emanating from over the border.

The second factor influencing schooling in the territory was the style of colonisation. Portugal perceived Macau as a settlement and granted it the status of a Portuguese city in 1586 (Cremer 1991, p.35). In 1749, the Macau government decreed that only 184 Chinese were permitted to reside in the main fortified city, as opposed to the outlying islands (Choi 1991, p.64). The emergent community of Portuguese expatriates, Macau-born Portuguese and mixed race Macanese was the major concern of the government, as the Chinese population were officially classified as foreigners (Rosa 1991). This enclave mentality created a centre-periphery dichotomy that was evident in the development of schooling. Also, Portugal's strong religious tradition meant that Christian missionaries have played an important role in education in Macau (greater than in Hong Kong), although relationships between the Church and Macau authorities have not always been harmonious. Many of the religious schools were designed to educate Chinese children. As the missionaries did not attempt completely to eradicate Chinese culture from Macau, their schooling for the indigenous population maintained a local flavour, and it existed alongside traditional schooling provided by the Chinese community.

Historical Development of Schooling in Macau

Historically, a multi-track system of primary and secondary schooling emerged: religious, government and community schooling. Until the return of sovereignty loomed, the government left the education of more than 90 per cent of the student population in private hands. Although government subsidies have a long tradition – in 1574, the King of Portugal started to give some of the tax revenue from Malacca to subsidise the running of St. Paul's College in Macau (Lau 1994) – government provision of education for local Chinese children was negligible and mainly limited to those from poor families. The decline of Macau's economic value to Portugal was a disincentive for the government to invest in the education of sectors of the population that were viewed as peripheral (K.C. Tang 1999, p.76). This resulted in "enormous inertia", as one Governor admitted (Government of Macau 1984, p.4), in social sector provision, other than for Portuguese and Macanese.

Despite their travails with an occasionally unsympathetic government, foreign missionaries (principally the Jesuits) and their converts were very active, providing Chinese children with a basic education mainly in Western subjects, such as Latin, English and Portuguese. Indeed, from the 16th to 18th century, they were the sole providers of such education. Struggles between the State and the Church in Europe spilled over into Macau. The Jesuits were expelled from Macau in 1762, and schools were abandoned. The schools reopened when the missionaries returned in 1801 (Pires 1991), but further disruption occurred sporadically during the 19th century. The most active groups in the 20th century included the Diocese of Macau; Catholic missionaries, such as the Jesuits and the Canossian sisters; Protestant missionaries; and various charities with religious links. Many of the religious and charitable organisations in Macau set up schools in Hong Kong after the British established the colony in 1841. Over time, this link led to transfer between the two territories (although later it was generally from Hong Kong to Macau rather than vice versa) of curriculum, pedagogical approaches and teaching materials. Given the inertia displayed by the Macau authorities towards peripheral communities and the different affiliations and national origins of the religious groups, it is not surprising that these schools developed a plethora of curricula. Most used Chinese or Chinese and English (for its commercial value) as the medium of instruction, but parts of curricula were based on those of the home countries of the religious organisations, or Taiwan or Hong Kong (Bray & Hui 1991a, p.187).

Formal Chinese schools developed rather late in Macau. Kiang Vu Charity School was established by Liu Long Shan in 1874; and the Tong Sin Tong charity society set up tutorial classes for the poor in 1892. The latter were extended to become Tong Sin Tong Charity School in 1924 to provide free education for Chinese boys, and girls were accepted to the school starting from 1937 (Tong Sin Tong 1992; Macau, Department of Education & Youth 1997a, p.205). Away from the Macau peninsula, two schools were founded for poor Chinese boys in Taipa and Coloane in the 1880s. They were built by local residents and were subsidised by the government (Pires 1991, p.17). The Hundred Days Reform movement in the latter days of the 19th century and the overthrow of the last emperor in China in 1911 led to an increase in the number of Chinese schools in Macau. In 1898, Chan Tse Bo and other Qing Government loyalists set up the Tung Man School (H.C. Tang, 1995, p.411). As with other new institutions, this school sought to combine Chinese and Western learning, in accordance with the principle of 中學爲體 西學爲用 (Chinese learning for the essence, Western learning for utility) which had guided the reformist Self-Strengthening movement in China. The goal was to create a strong, modern nation that could resist the encroachments of Western countries by using imported technology but without losing cultural integrity. Between 1910 and the 1930s, more than 10 Chinese schools using Western teaching methods were established by individual scholars. These schools tended to develop their curriculum according to models from the mainland and, following the civil war, Taiwan. During the Republican era in China, a liaison developed between the ruling Nationalist Kuomintang (KMT) Party and the schools in Macau established by Chinese patriotic associations. Most of these schools registered with the Education Department of Guangdong and, after the founding of the PRC in 1949 and the flight of the KMT forces from the mainland, with the Taiwan Government (Cheung 1955, 1956; Macau, Department of Education & Youth 1994c, 1997a).

In the 1930s and 1940s, both the Japanese invasion of China and the civil war between the KMT and the Communists had an impact upon schooling in Macau. Over 20 schools in Guangdong province moved to Macau to escape the Japanese, and many Chinese educators – refugees from the mainland – set up their own schools in Macau. This sudden expansion of schooling in Macau was not sustained, because of the shortage of resources and teachers. After the war, many of the schools that had moved from China returned to their original locations (H.C. Tang 1995, p.413). However, some maintained sites in Macau, such as Pui Cheng School whose kindergarten, primary and secondary sections grew to accommodate over 3,000 students. Other schools were formed by associations of KMT sympathisers who fled to Macau after 1949.

Government schooling was also a late development, dating from 1894. As noted above, the main concern of the Macau authorities was traditionally for Portuguese or Macanese residents. The centre-periphery divide was reinforced until recent times by large discrepancies in the funding of schools: government schools generally have had superior resources and smaller class sizes than other schools (Bray & Hui 1991a, p.188). The handful of government secondary schools transplanted the school curriculum from Portugal and taught through the medium of Portuguese. The only Chinese-medium government schools were Luso-Chinese primary schools, offering a curriculum based on the Portuguese model. Since 1985, Luso-Chinese secondary schools have been established to serve the Chinese community, offering a similar curriculum through the medium of Chinese, with the exception of Portuguese language.

The period since the founding of the PRC in 1949 has been one of fluctuating tension between Macau and the mainland. Problems have been exacerbated by the lack of a 'buffer' class of local officials in the colonial service such as the one in Hong Kong. The link between Macau and the KMT was a source of irritation to the PRC. This culminated in 1966 in the event that is known colloquially in Cantonese as the '1-2-3 Incident' (after the Chinese styling of the date, December 3rd, when the episode began). Controversy arose when a group of trade unionists sympathetic to the radical Cultural Revolution political movement then erupting in the mainland, attempted to establish a primary school without following registration formalities. When the Macau government chose to close down the school, there was organised resistance and a political campaign that gained the support of mainland groups. At one stage, food supplies to Macau were cut, Chinese warships menaced, and militant Red Guards briefly overran the enclave. The Portuguese retreated, literally and metaphorically, and at the height of the crisis Portugal even offered to quit Macau within a month. However, this offer was declined by the PRC leadership, who were concerned about the continued prosperity of both Hong Kong and Macau as go-betweens in conducting foreign trade with capitalist co-untries (Edmonds 1989). Eventually, the Macau government permitted the school to open and undertook to ban all organisations with strong KMT links.

The signing of the Sino-Portuguese Agreement of Returning Macau to China in 1987 marked a shift in stance with regard to schooling. Changes included consultations with school principals and management bodies on improving education (Bray & Hui 1991b) and the design of a Macau-oriented curriculum for Luso-Chinese kindergartens, primary and secondary schools that was introduced on a trial basis in 1996. The Macau government also started providing formal teacher education and 10 years fee-free education to all children (comprising the final year of kindergarten, six years of primary and three years of junior secondary schooling) and undertaking curriculum reform in Chinese schools (H.K. Wong 1991). Improvements were funded by economic development, most notably in tourism, the casino trade and the textile industry. New schools were built, and many existing schools acquired new buildings. Two technical secondary schools were established in 1998 to prepare a suitable workforce for the business and industrial sectors. These improvements, together with various infrastructural and developmental projects, may be attributed to the Portuguese wanting to leave Macau with honour, like the British in Hong Kong, in order to retain good relations with China.

Administration of Schooling in Macau

In 1997/98, Macau had 73,383 primary and secondary students and 3,409 teachers (Macau, Department of Education & Youth 1997a). Schooling is provided by a variety of bodies from three broad categories. Of 127 schools, only 33 schools (26%) were run by the government, 25 (19.7%) by religious groups, and the rest by trading or cultural associations, individuals, societies and co-operatives (Table 2.1).

Table 2.1: Sponsors of Schools in Macau, 1997/98

Sponsor	Number of Schools*
Government of Macau	33
Religious groups	25
Community organisations	62
Trading associations	7
Total	*127*

* includes evening schools, and schools for adults
Source: Macau, Department of Education & Youth 1997a

The multiple providers of education in Macau created a muddled system of administration and curriculum, although the reforms in the 1990s began to improve the situation. In the past, both Portuguese and Luso-Chinese schools run by the government followed a 4+2+3+2+1 system based on the model in Portugal. However, schools catering to expatriate Portuguese children registered with authorities in the mother country and offered a curriculum based on the national system, whereas schools for Macanese children registered with local authorities and until 1996 largely designed their own curricula. In the 1990s, Luso-Chinese schools operated a 6+5+1 system similar to some of the English religious schools. Chinese-medium and English-medium sections of religious schools either followed a 6+3+3 system (borrowed from mainland China or Taiwan) or a modified Hong Kong model of 6+5+1 (Figure 2.1). Some English-medium schools such as the School of Nations and the College of Santa Rosa de Lima (English section) still maintained a 6+5 system. However, in the late 1990s, the College of Santa Rosa de Lima changed to the 6+5+1 system in order to prepare students for the University of Macau entrance examination. Religious schools were registered locally, but many tended to borrow from the Hong Kong curriculum – not least because no local public examinations were available in Macau, so some students gaining approval to do so travelled to Hong Kong to sit for examinations administered by the Hong Kong Examinations Authority. Some schools prepared their students to sit for the General Certificate of Education examination set by an examination board in England which had approved those schools to operate as examination centres in Macau.

Schools run by Chinese associations affiliated to the KMT were registered first in Guangdong and, after 1949, in Taiwan, and until recently followed their own curriculum without input from the Macau government (Cheung 1955, 1956; Macau, Department of Education & Youth 1994c, 1997a; K.C. Tang 1998). After the watershed 1-2-3 Incident, the practice of allowing schools to register with Taiwan was stopped and schools run by associations sympathetic to the PRC were set up, again determining their own curriculum and operating a 6+3+3 system as in the mainland. As the reunion with China approached, many schools adopted textbooks from the mainland and started preparing students to sit for the entrance examinations for universities in China.

Figure 2.1: Primary and Secondary School Systems in Macau

Secondary	17	3+2+1	5+1*	3+3	5+1†	
	16					5
	15					
	14					
	13					
	12					
Primary	11	4+2	6	6	6 (+1)‡	6
	10					
	9					
	8					
	7					
	6					
	Age	Portuguese-medium Schools	Luso-Chinese Schools	Chinese-medium Schools	English-Chinese Schools+	English-medium Schools

Notes
* students may leave school after Form 5 with a general secondary school certificate issued by the
  school, or a senior secondary school certificate after Form 6
† some schools do not have Form 6 classes, so students further their studies in other
  secondary schools or in the pre-university classes in University of Macau
‡ a one-year preparation class is added for students who are weak in English before they can
  study in Form 1
+ These schools have English-medium and Chinese-medium streams

Table 2.2: Number of Schools by Type and Level*, Macau, 1997/98

Type	Primary	Secondary	Preschool & Primary	Primary & Secondary	Preschool, Primary & Secondary	Special	Total
Official Portugue-se medium	0	0	0	1	0	0	1
Offical Chinese medium (Luso Chinese)	7	2	0	0	0	1	10
Private, Portu-guese-medium	0	0	0	2	0	0	2
Private English /Chinese medium	3	3	29	8	20	5	67
Total	10	4	29	11	20	6	80

* does not include evening schools or schools for adults
+ i.e. same curriculum as schools in Portugal
Source: http://www.dsej.gov.mo/statisti/edu/971126

Unlike their counterparts in Hong Kong, many schools have two or even three
sections: kindergarten, primary and secondary (Table 2.2). Such vertical integration is
also a reflection of the lack of horizontal integration of schooling in Macau. All the
primary schools use the whole-day system even though this means larger class sizes (in
some cases reaching 50 or 60) than in Hong Kong, where a bisessional system operates

in many primary schools. There is no public examination for banding Primary 6 students for entrance to secondary schools, nor, as noted above, is there a public examination system for matriculating secondary students (although since 1990 the University of East Asia, later renamed the University of Macau, has had an entrance examination). Schools are free to assess the ability of their students, and an increasing number prepare their students to sit for the Senior 6 Public Examination in the PRC for entrance to mainland universities.

The School Curriculum in Macau

Given the variety of curricula in Macau, it is difficult to generalise about the 'typical' experience of schoolchildren. However, it is clear that certain subjects receive greater attention than do others. Official statistics indicate that, in Chinese and Anglo-Chinese primary schools for instance, Chinese, English and Mathematics are allocated more lessons per week (approximately eight, six and five respectively from Primary 1 to 6) than Science, Hygiene and Social Studies (often combined, after the Hong Kong model, as General Studies), Putonghua, Physical Education, Religious Studies, Civic Education, Music, and Art & Craft (around two lessons per week each). In secondary schools, English receives the highest number of lessons per week (around nine), with Mathematics and Chinese being allocated between six and eight lessons. Science subjects, Computer Studies, Putonghua, Physical Education, History and Geography receive two to four lessons a week, while Music and Arts are allocated one lesson each. In the Luso-Chinese system, the primary schools devote around ten lessons a week to Portuguese, eight to Chinese, five to Mathematics, two each to Science, Social Studies, and Art & Craft, with Music and Physical Education receiving one to three lessons a week. In secondary schools, Portuguese (around six lessons), English (five), Chinese (five) and Mathematics (four) receive the largest allocation; Art, Physical Education, Geography and Computer Studies are given two lessons in junior secondary school, while in senior secondary schools, Physics, Chemistry, Biology, Economics, Computer Studies, Principles of Accounting and Physical Education have two to four lessons per week according to the specific year group (Macau, Department of Education & Youth 1994c).

The lack of a Macau-oriented core curriculum was addressed in the late 1990s. The Department of Education & Youth set up a curriculum development division in 1995 to prepare syllabuses for the subjects taught in kindergarten, primary and secondary schools. These were piloted in 1996-97. In preparation for the handover to China, many schools introduced Putonghua and a course on the Basic Law (Ngai 1994).

Medium of Instruction

As with Hong Kong and other places undergoing decolonisation, language is a key issue in schooling. In drawing up the Basic Law for Macau, legislators followed the Hong Kong model, which permitted the retention of the colonial language as an official language for at least 50 years following the change of sovereignty. In the case of Hong Kong, English has the advantage of being an international language of commerce and communication that Portuguese does not have. This creates an added linguistic dimension for schooling: Chinese (which is ill-defined, and could include oral Putonghua and

Cantonese, as well as Modern Standard Chinese) and Portuguese are the official languages and English is a desirable international language for economic development. This complexity is reflected in the choices of medium of instruction. In 1998, Chinese-medium schools predominated (68.5%); 12.6 per cent of schools used Chinese and Portuguese as the medium of instruction, 11 per cent used English, only 7.1 per cent used Portuguese, and 0.7 per cent used all three languages (Macau, Department of Education & Youth 1998). Thus despite being an official language, Portuguese is the medium of instruction in a small minority of schools.

Teachers in Macau

Teachers in Macau come from a variety of backgrounds. In 1996/97, only 42 per cent of the teaching force (then numbering 4,135) had been born in Macau. A large proportion (34.4%) had been born in the PRC, while 8.8 per cent and 6.4 per cent had been born in Portugal and Hong Kong respectively (Macau, Department of Statistics & Culture 1998, p.47).

Primary teachers in private schools teach specific subjects, as in Hong Kong, but in the government Luso-Chinese schools, teachers teach all subjects except Portuguese, Physical Education, Music, English, and Computer Studies. They stay with the class for nearly the whole day and are even promoted with the class at the end of the school year, until Primary 5 when the subject teacher system is used. The class size in Luso-Chinese schools is small, around 20 in the late 1990s, but increasing as a large number of new immigrants arrived from China. In private schools, class sizes vary enormously, but the Department of Education and Youth has set a maximum of 45 students per class for all schools joining the Free Education Scheme. In secondary schools, the class size is generally less than 45.

Subject teachers in primary and secondary schools usually teach four to six periods out of seven or eight periods per day. In 1996/97, teachers taught an average of around 21 periods per week (Macau, Department of Education & Youth 1998, p.49). Each period lasts 35 to 40 minutes, followed by a short break of five to ten minutes. After normal school hours, many teachers take tutorial classes to assist students with their homework. This extra work is paid separately from the normal salary. Some schools run from Monday to Friday, while the rest run from Monday to Saturday morning. The school year normally runs from September to early June, with a short break of two weeks before summer school starts in July. In the past students were commonly required to attend four weeks' summer school in preparation of the new school year, but the practice generally changed to make summer school into a remedial programme for students who performed poorly in examinations.

There are two salary scales for teachers in government schools: one for kindergarten and primary teachers, and the other for secondary teachers. The starting monthly salary for those on the first scale was around MOP$17,500 (HK$17,000 or US$2,200) in 1999, and the highest salary, normally for a teacher approaching retirement was MOP$24,000, although senior staff, such as principals may receive MOP$29,000. According to the other scale, a secondary teacher with a degree and a teacher education qualification would start on MOP$21,500, rising (over a period of about 25 years) to MOP$32,500. All teachers receive an additional month's salary half-yearly. These starting salaries are on a par with those in Hong Kong, although the top of the scale is much lower: a school principal in Hong Kong could earn around three times the salary of a Macau counterpart. Conditions in private schools in Macau are much less favourable: in 1999, kindergarten and primary teachers started at around MOP$7,000 and secondary school teachers received a starting salary of about MOP$10,000 per month. All teachers were granted an extra allowance according to their qualifications and their salaries are tax free. The retirement age is 60 in government, with a possible extension to 65. There are no fixed retirement ages for private schools, so there are a number of old teachers in such schools: in 1996/97, the oldest teacher was 83 years old (Macau, Department of Statistics & Census 1998, p.47).

Primary and Secondary Schooling in Hong Kong

The development of schooling in Hong Kong has been linked to shifts in the socio-economic and political climate, which, in turn, has been strongly influenced by the relationships with and between the colonial power, the United Kingdom, and China. As with Macau, the harbour of Hong Kong and its gateway to China provided the economic motivation for the colonial presence. Likewise, the events leading up to and following the founding of the Republic of China in 1911; the Sino-Japanese war; civil war, violent political movements and sporadic famine in China; and the return to Chinese sovereignty all affected schooling in Hong Kong. But to a greater extent than Macau, economic factors (most notably the industrialisation of Hong Kong in the second half of the 20th century and the modernisation of China after 1978) were significant in shaping educational provision at primary and secondary levels.

The form of colonialism practised in Hong Kong was different from that in Macau. Sweeting (1992, p.65) compares Hong Kong society to a wok rather than a melting pot, in that "various separate ingredients are rapidly and briefly stir-fried in a very heated and high-pressured atmosphere". But instead of an enclave approach, the colonial authorities created a buffer class of local elites well-educated in Western and Chinese learning to work in the administration and thus reduce potential racial friction between rulers and colonised. This policy was facilitated in the early days of the colony by a degree of convergence between colonial educational practices and traditional Chinese schooling. Government schooling served mainly to furnish civil servants and commercial go-betweens not only for Hong Kong, but also for China. British interest in modernising China was partly altruistic and partly motivated by the aim of establishing influence there (Ng Lun 1984, p.82). Community Chinese schools also supplied personnel for the modernisation of China, working, for example, in the customs service (Bickley 1997), and both British and Chinese schooling used an academic, examination-oriented curriculum. The inclusion of Chinese subjects in the government school curriculum and the social and economic benefits which accrued to graduates facilitated local acceptance of this liberal form of colonial schooling, a pragmatism that remains a feature of education debates in Hong Kong today. Indeed, pressure from the local community was cited in 1878 by Governor John Pope Hennessy as one reason for not introducing more Chinese components in to the curriculum (Sweeting 1990, p.233). Modern schooling in Hong Kong reflects the synthesis of the two systems in the continued use of traditional features of British education (for example, school uniforms, straight rows of desks facing a blackboard, and students standing up to speak to the teacher) and of Chinese education (such as memorisation, and an emphasis on diligence).

Historical Development of Schooling in Hong Kong

After 1841, initial moves to set up public schooling came when the Morrison Education Society and various other missionary groups transferred or extended their Macau activities. Village schooling continued to be provided on a community basis, largely undisrupted by the change of sovereignty. Government provision of schooling was initially small scale and elitist – although it catered for all races – and it was left to charities and neighbourhood organisations to educate the majority of children. From 1873, when a Grant-in-Aid scheme was set up, providing private groups with government funding for education, the number of missionary schools grew further.

Two major events were instrumental in effecting educational change in Hong Kong early in the 20th century: the establishment of the Republic in China after the fall of the Qing Dynasty in 1911, and World War I. The first event intensified nationalist sentiments among Chinese in Hong Kong, creating unease in official circles that Chinese nationalism and anti-foreign propaganda might be spread in non-government schools and threaten Hong Kong's social and political equilibrium. This perceived threat produced a bureaucratic response from the government. The Education Ordinance of 1913 sought to impose control over the proliferating non-government schools by requiring them to register with the Director of Education, who would then be responsible for ensuring that the schools adhered to government regulations. This ordinance marked a shift in government concern from just the elite schools to all schools, and although the major forces for developing mass education were the economic imperatives and the population boom after World War II, the tensions of the inter-war period placed the general provision of schooling in an increasingly important position on the government agenda.

The demands of World War I for military hardware encouraged divergence in Hong Kong's economic activities, with light industry as well as shipbuilding and repairs developing in importance (Sweeting 1992). The impact on education was greater attention to fostering vocational skills. The emergent curriculum was designed to meet perceived local needs better, while still basically anglocentric in orientation in the case of government and Grant-in-Aid schools, and sinocentric in the case of private traditional schools. The Burney Report (1935), by a visiting inspector of schools from Great Britain, suggested (p.25) that:

> educational policy in the Colony should be re-orientated so as eventually to secure for the pupils, first, a command of their own language sufficient for all needs of thought and expression, and secondly, a command of English limited to the satisfaction of vocational demands.

World War II was a serious body blow to the British Empire, which declined rapidly. The occupation of Hong Kong by the Japanese from 1941 to 1945 also represented a considerable loss of face for the British administration, rendering its legitimacy more tenuous even after its resumption of sovereignty. The Chinese civil war and sporadic turmoil of revolutionary movements in the early years of the PRC placed economic, political and population pressures on Hong Kong. Bereft of its role as an imperial outpost, Hong Kong had to reinvent itself: light industry (including plastic goods and textiles) and entrepot services provided the capital to house and educate the huge numbers of political and economic refugees who touched base, many after swimming from the mainland. But far from proving a burden, these immigrants, rich and poor, made a major contribution to Hong Kong's emergence as an economic powerhouse. Hong Kong's relative independence from the United Kingdom and desire to remain politically independent from the communist mainland accelerated the de-coupling of schooling from anglocentric and sinocentric models. At the secondary school level, Chinese-medium schools increased in number, offering a curriculum similar to that of Anglo-Chinese schools (which purported to teach through the medium of English) – although the powerful economic pull of English as an international language bestowed low status on Chinese-medium schools in the eyes of many parents. The distancing from communism and from the rival KMT was reflected in legislation such as that which established the Standing Committee on Textbooks in 1948, which primarily aimed to ensure that no propaganda from either camp be allowed to permeate teaching materials.

Gradually, the provision of schooling was improved to cater for the burgeoning population and the demands of the growing industrial sector for human resources with at least basic education. A seven-year expansion programme in primary education was introduced in 1954. One feature of this programme was the use of bisessional schooling, whereby the same premises were used for two schools, one operating in the morning and the other in the afternoon. Intended as a temporary measure, such primary schools were still common at the end of the century, despite the government's stated commitment to move towards all-day schooling, as policy priorities had shifted first to secondary schooling and then to tertiary institutions. Nevertheless, given the tripling of the population since the 1940s, the attainment of universal and compulsory primary education by 1971 was a considerable achievement and a marked shift from the former elitist orientation.

The use of the private sector for providing education led to occasional tensions. Schools sponsored by organisations sympathetic to the mainland were active in the riots of 1967 (which were countered mainly by local police acting as a buffer for the British army). In 1978, students from one subsidised secondary school, supported by several teachers, embarked upon a campaign criticising the general management of education by the government's Education Department (ED). Events escalated to street marches. The government responded by closing down the school (Cheng 1992b, p.110). The toughness of the response contrasts with the capitulation of the Macau authorities when faced by the 1-2-3 Incident, although, in fairness, the circumstances were more politically fraught in the latter case.

The final years of colonialism in Hong Kong were paralleled by far-reaching changes on the mainland, which impacted strongly upon education in the territory. The PRC's embrace of open-door economic modernisation policies in the late 1970s resulted in another adjustment to Hong Kong's own economic profile, as much of the light industry was relocated over the border in Guangdong, where special economic zones were created. The reorientation in the PRC's priorities was reassuring to many people in Hong Kong once the territory's future was decided with the signing of the Sino-British Joint Declaration in 1984, but anxieties were reawakened by the bloody suppression of the student-led democracy movement in and around Beijing's Tiananmen Square on June 4th 1989. During this period, Hong Kong's self-identity became stronger (Sweeting 1995, p.49) and eyes were fixed on the post-1997 era and the credibility of the promise of "fifty years without change" made by China's leaders.

The establishment of nine years' universal and fee-free education was achieved in 1978, providing six years of primary and three of secondary schooling. But 1978 was also significant in marking the beginning of the 'Four Modernisations' drive in the PRC. When Hong Kong developed its service and financial sectors to compensate for the loss of its manufacturing base to the mainland, schools came under pressure to groom versatile and multilingual citizens conversant with sophisticated technology and Wall Street wisdom. This pressure was reinforced by parental expectations – a prosperous, well-travelled and increasing influential middle class had emerged – and by the determination of the government's Education Department (ED) to adopt and/or adapt the latest fashions from Western countries.

The various pressures resulted in a series of reports by the Education Commission, which had been created in 1984, and of curricular initiatives. The latter included the attempts to improve Chinese and English language standards in Hong Kong, which were portrayed as declining; the establishment of the Hong Kong Institute of Education (HKIEd) in 1994 as part of a move towards an all-graduate and qualified teaching profession; and the introduction of new approaches to teaching, learning and assessment, such as the Target Oriented Curriculum (TOC), which was underpinned by a humanistic orientation, constructivist views of learning and the promotion of task-based learning as a key pedagogy. The influence of the forthcoming reunification with – or, as Law (1997) argues, recolonisation by – China was evident in the promotion of Putonghua as a core school subject from its previously very low status (Adamson & Auyeung Lai 1997), and a lively debate over civic education, which some educators argued should be associated with patriotism. Textbooks were rewritten by commercial publishers, with a degree of self-censorship that was apparently encouraged by the ED. In 1994, the Director of Education suggested that history books should avoid covering the past 20 years (which would encompass the Tiananmen Square events) on the grounds that it would be difficult to achieve historical objectivity (Lee & Bray 1995, pp.365-366). After the handover, the ED promoted ill-defined "Asian values" in the civics curriculum in an attempt to strengthen Hong Kong students' identification with the mainland, where a similar promotion was seeking to fill the vacuum in philosophical worldview that had been created by the demise of the imperial system and communism (Agelasto & Adamson 1998). Daily ceremonies raising the national flag were introduced in many primary schools.

But apart from these instances, few changes to the school curriculum could be ascribed to political motives in the immediate post-colonial period – perhaps because the PRC government was eager to be seen to adhere to its promise of a high degree of autonomy for Hong Kong. In his speech to celebrate the inauguration of the Hong Kong Special Administrative Region on July 1st 1997, the Chief Executive, Tung Chee Hwa, identified education as "the key to the future", which "should encourage diversification and combine the strengths of the east and the west" (Tung 1997a). Economic competitiveness remained a strong influence: nationalism had to be tempered with internationalism. Later in 1997, Tung visited Singapore and returned impressed with the education system there – in particular, the provision of computers and their use in teaching and learning. In his first policy address, Tung announced the development of Information Technology (IT), with each primary school to be allocated 42 computers and each secondary school 84 computers (Tung 1997b). A target of 25 per cent of the curriculum was to be taught through IT. He instituted the HK$5,000 million Quality Education Fund for school initiatives and research projects, and other measures including benchmarking of teachers' linguistic and pedagogical competence.

Quality education for the masses replaced quality education for the elite. Educational change was fuelled by economic dynamism and constrained by political forces.

But to a large extent, under a facade of modernity continued deep set conservatism. The traditional Chinese and British practices noted above still held sway in many aspects of schooling at the turn of the century. Continuing concerns among the business sector, parents and other influential stakeholders prompted the Education Commission to undertake a comprehensive review of education in Hong Kong.

Administration of Schooling in Hong Kong

In 1997/98, Hong Kong had 846 primary schools and 468 secondary schools with enrolments of around 450,000 in each sector. Over half of the primary schools were still bisessional at that time, with morning and afternoon schools sharing the same premises, although the government planned to phase in whole-day schooling. Primary schooling in government and aided schools was free but approximately 10 per cent of the enrolment attended fee-paying private schools. The secondary schools comprised 422 grammar schools, 19 technical schools and 27 prevocational schools, with the latter two categories focusing on commercial, technical and practical subjects (Government of Hong Kong, 1998, pp.141-143).

Government schools only accounted for some 10 per cent of the total (Table 2.3). The remainder were sponsored by various bodies with financial assistance from the government. The great majority of more than 400 school sponsoring bodies are religious groups (mainly various Christian denominations) or charitable organisations, such as the Po Leung Kuk. Other bodies include specific trading groups (e.g. the Cotton Spinners Association), families commemorating a deceased member, associations of people from the same hometowns in China (e.g. Toi Shan Association), and alumni of educational institutions (e.g. Queen's College Old Boys' Association). In Hong Kong, subsidised schooling has existed since 1873, as noted above. However, the total number of places offered by government and aided schools does not meet demand, which has meant that the government had to buy places from private schools under the Bought Place Scheme since the 1960s. This scheme has been gradually replaced since 1991 by the Direct Subsidy Scheme, whereby private schools meeting government standards in terms of class size and teacher quality can receive a subsidy and thus offer a private education in parallel to the mainstream schools in the public sector. This also enabled previously excluded schools with strong political links to the mainland to receive government funding. Aided schools could also opt out of the mainstream by joining the scheme (Bray 1995b).

International schools, which serve the non-Chinese (and increasingly the Chinese) population, are aided or private. The largest group, the English Schools Foundation (ESF), was set up in 1967, and at that time had two schools. In 1979, the government's schools offering education for expatriates were transferred to the ESF, thus permitting the government to concentrate on education for the Chinese majority. ESF schools receive the same financial assistance as other aided schools, but are permitted to charge fees in order to pay for superior facilities and higher salaries. In 1998/99, the ESF had 15 primary and secondary schools, plus one kindergarten. The ESF's autonomy has allowed it to respond to shifts in the social make-up of Hong Kong, so that its student base has become increasingly multi-ethnic (Bray & Ieong 1996). Some so-called international schools would be better described as foreign schools operating in Hong Kong. Examples are the Japanese, Korean, Indonesian and Singaporean schools. Others serve more multinational clienteles, e.g. the Canadian International School and the Hong Kong International School. Demand for private education among local parents (or those returning from emigration) has led to such schools broadening their student bases.

Table 2.3: Providers of Primary and Secondary Schooling in Hong Kong, 1998

Level	Sector	Day	Evening & Part-time	Both Day & Evening
Primary*	Government	45		45
	Aided	696		696
	Private	89	2	91
	All sectors	830	2	832
Secondary+	Government	37		37
	Aided	352		352
	Private	82	36	118
	All sectors	471	36	507
Special Schools	Aided	63		63
Practical Schools	Aided	4		4
Skills Opportunity Schools	Aided	7		7

Notes

*Including nine English Schools Foundation schools in the aided sector and 24 international primary schools in the private sector

+Including five English Schools Foundation schools in the aided sector, 18 international secondary schools, nine caput schools (where places are bought on a per head basis), and 18 private schools with bought places in the private sector

Source: Hong Kong, Education Department 1998, p.9

The School Curriculum in Hong Kong

In 1997, public schooling in Hong Kong had the following official aim, as displayed on the cover of Education Commission Report No.7 (1997):

> School education should develop the potential of every individual child, so that our students become independent-minded and socially-aware adults, equipped with the knowledge, skills and attitudes which help them to lead a full life as individuals and play a positive role in the life of the community.

However, the emphasis on individualism and well-roundedness, drawn from the Western humanist school of thought and adopted by the business community in Hong Kong, is not reflected in the implemented curriculum, where attempts to promote problem-solving and other active forms of learning have been passively resisted by teachers (Morris et al. 1996). Indeed, schooling is mainly perceived by parents as a means to gain access to tertiary education. As a result, it is academic in orientation with strong subject boundaries and with great value ascribed to examination performance, report cards and homework. Therefore, as observed by Bond (1991, p.18):

> ... parents exert massive pressure on their children to do well in school. Homework is supervised and extends for long periods, extracurricular activities are kept to a

minimum, effort is rewarded, tutors are hired, and socialising is largely confined to family outings.

In this respect, little has changed since the heyday of traditional Chinese schools.

Mainstream schooling (international and foreign schools might have variants) is organised on a 6+3+2+2 system. The common system allows for more horizontal integration across schools, which creates competition for entrance to what are perceived as more successful schools at each stage. This competition reinforces the high status attached to examinations noted above. Children enter primary school at age six, after the large majority have already attended kindergarten for three years. The primary curriculum is subject-based, with a common-core of seven constituent subjects: Chinese Language, English Language, Mathematics, General Studies, Music, Art & Craft, and Physical Education. Table 2.4 shows the curriculum arrangement adopted by one primary school sponsored by a religious association in Hong Kong. The subjects allocated the most periods per week – Chinese Language, English Language and Mathematics – form the basis of the Secondary School Placement Allocation exercise, by which, at the end of six years' primary schooling, the children are streamed into five bands for placement in secondary schools.

Table 2.4: A Curriculum Map for a Primary School (Periods per Week), Hong Kong, 1997

Subject \ Level	Primary One	Primary Two	Primary Three	Primary Four	Primary Five	Primary Six
Chinese Language	10 (11)+	10 (10)	10 (9)	10 (8)#	9 (8)#	9 (8)#
English Language	10 (5)	10 (6)	10 (7)	10 (8)	10 (8)	10 (8)
Mathematics	7 (5)	7 (5)	7 (5)	7 (5)	7 (5)	7 (5)
General Studies*	5 (5)	5 (5)	5 (5)	5 (5)	5 (5)	5 (5)
Art and Craft	2 (3)	2 (3)	2 (3)	2 (3)	3 (3)	3 (3)
Music	2 (2)	2 (2)	2 (2)	2 (2)	2 (2)	2 (2)
Physical Education	2 (2)	2 (2)	2 (2)	2 (2)	2 (2)	2 (2)
Library	1	1	1	1	1	1
Biblical Knowledge	1	1	1	1	1	1

Notes:
+ figures in brackets are the minimum allocation of periods as suggested by the Curriculum Development Council
# Unlike many other schools, this school does not offer Putonghua in Primary 4 to Primary 6.
* Social Studies, Science and Health Education
Source: Adapted from Adamson & Morris 1998, p.189.

There are seven forms in secondary schooling, with exit points at Form 3, Form 5 and Form 7. This system reflects the one that was prevalent in England and Wales in the 1950s. A typical curriculum map is shown in Figure 2.2. Once again, the dominance of Chinese Language, English Language and Mathematics is evident. Noteworthy too is the common practice of replacing a five-day Monday to Friday timetable of 40 periods with a six-day cycle incorporating 48 periods. This arrangement allows greater curricular breadth. However, the number of cycles per year is obviously fewer than the number of weeks, and in the long run, the marginal subjects such as Physical Education lose out because they are allocated the same number of periods per cycle as they would have received in a five-day timetable, while the dominant subjects receive larger allowances.

Figure 2.2: A Typical Curriculum Map for a Secondary School (Periods per Cycle) in 1997

Year	Subjects & Allocated Periods						
7 6	3 Arts subjects & Use of English OR 3 Science subjects & Use of English						
5 4	English Language (10)	Chinese Language (9)	Maths (9)	3 Arts subjects OR 3 Science subjects (15)	1 elective Science subj. OR 1 elective Arts subj. (3)		PE (2)
3 2 1				Integrated Science (5)	Geog, EPA, Hist., Chin. History/Social Studies (9)	Music, Art, P.E., Home Eoon, ctc. (5)	Computer Lit. (1)

Source: Adapted from Morris 1998, p.74

Public examinations take place at Form 5 (Hong Kong Certificate of Education Examinations) and at Form 7 (Hong Kong Advanced Level Examinations). The system is essentially elitist. Although these examinations are based on syllabuses that are largely standardised, success is limited to the top 20 to 30 per cent of students, most notably those who are literate in English – a throwback to the time when schooling was a feeder for the colonial civil service (Biggs 1996, pp.4-6).

The school curriculum at the time of the political handover was undergoing a major revision. Official documents, as noted above, stressed whole-person development, which was reflected in curriculum terms as a multi-dimensional approach to schooling (Figure 2.3).

Figure 2.3: Diagrammatic Representation of the School Curriculum in Hong Kong

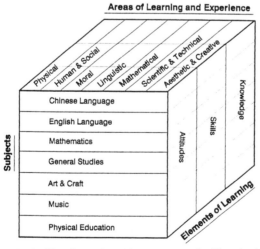

Note: The emphasis of learning and experience may vary in different subjects.
Source: Curriculum Development Council 1993, p.56

At the centre of the curricular reform was the incremental introduction of TOC starting in Primary 1 in 1996. TOC addresses concerns that prevailing approaches to schooling emphasised factual knowledge were taught through teacher-centred and textbook-driven pedagogy, and relied on norm-referenced procedures for assessing children's learning. TOC promotes cross-curricular, whole-person competencies through task-based learning with criterion-referenced assessment. Students' learning is mapped against a hierarchy of learning targets for each subject and five cross-curricular principles of learning: communicating, inquiring, conceptualising, reasoning, and problem-solving. Progression is divided into three Key Stages (Primary 1 to 3; Primary 4 to 6, and Secondary 1 to 3). Although it claims to encourage an integrated, cross-curricular approach, TOC was initially introduced only in the three core subjects, English, Chinese and Mathematics.

The reform proved problematic when implemented in primary schools. Teachers complained of its complexity and inherent contradictions. Schools interpreted TOC in a wide variety of ways amidst concerns over the tension between criterion-referenced assessment and the high stakes norm-referenced assessment at Primary 6 for placing students in secondary schools. The government, after demonstrating initial commitment to the initiative, gradually appeared to lose interest in pushing through the reform whole-heartedly (Morris et al. 1999).

Medium of Instruction

An enduring debate in Hong Kong concerns the medium of instruction for schooling. A twin-track system emerged historically, with secondary schools which used English as the medium of instruction (EMI) enjoying a higher status than their Chinese medium (CMI) counterparts. Most primary schools are CMI, but parents favour those that achieve good results in English and therefore give access to prestigious secondary schools. In the 1990s, various policies were instituted. Firstly, schools were permitted to teach in either medium according to their resources and capabilities, with Bridge Programmes established to assist students to move from CMI to EMI education at appropriate points. In 1997, this policy was changed, with 100 secondary schools being designated by the Education Department as EMI schools. This created consternation among some of those that were omitted from the list and who feared a drop in status that was associated with CMI education. On appeal, 14 more schools were deemed to be capable of delivering EMI education. At the heart of the issue is the tension between the post-handover government's determination to promote trilingualism (in Cantonese, Putonghua and English) and biliteracy (in Chinese and English), as well as whole-person education – considered to be best fostered in most cases through the mother tongue – and parental aspirations for their offspring, which include the social, academic and economic benefits that competence in English can bring.

Teachers in Hong Kong

The teaching profession came under the spotlight in the 1990s as part of the movement towards quality mass education. The provision of teacher education was upgraded (see the chapter by Li & Kwo in this volume) and moves instigated to set benchmarks for teacher performance, most notably in language competence. Teaching in Hong Kong, while not highly prestigious, does not have the low status and poor economic rewards that the profession has in some Asian countries, such as mainland China and, to a lesser extent, in the private schools in Macau. It is seen as a haven of stability in times of economic turmoil, and as the source of a respectable salary, comparable with other careers requiring similar qualifications.

A teacher's day typically starts early in the morning (or early in the afternoon for half of the bisessional schools) and comprises an average of around five lessons, plus extra-curricular activities and other teaching duties. Class sizes (around 35 in primary schools and 40 in secondary schools) make for crowded classrooms and a hindrance to more active, student-centred pedagogy, and in some instances encourage the teacher to use a microphone for addressing the class. Marking exercise books consumes a considerable amount of non-teaching time, as many teachers set great store by the objective results that marks can provide for assessment purposes (Morris et al. 1999, pp.18-19). There is a tendency among teachers to see themselves as 'small potatoes', having little influence over the curriculum. However, while this might be the case in terms of teacher representation on policy-making committees, they are very powerful forces when it comes to implementing the curriculum or resisting change (Morris 1998, p.114). Teachers are well organised, with a strong union, the Professional Teachers' Union, and a functional constituency seat in the Legislative Council. Overall, teachers in Hong Kong are better off than their Macau counterparts in terms of salary, status and political influence. This has meant that teaching is a relatively attractive profession and has managed to maintain an almost closed shop: there is just a small number of foreign teachers, mostly confined to language teaching, and, unlike Macau, mainland teachers have yet to obtain a foothold in Hong Kong schools.

Comparison

Hong Kong and Macau are linked by geography, ethnicity, Western colonisation and post-colonial fate. The geographical convenience for missionaries and traders with designs on Chinese souls and markets brought institutionalised education with Western characteristics to large sectors of both populations, while traces of traditional modes of schooling have endured. Neither colonial government has adopted a strong hands-on approach to education, except when the reversion of sovereignty to China approached (or, in Hong Kong, in times of crisis). The common destiny of Hong Kong and Macau – their respective reversions of sovereignty took place within two and a half years of each other – meant that the political and social arrangements for Hong Kong provided a convenient blueprint for Macau. This had long been the tradition in schooling. Although the initial provision of schooling in colonial Hong Kong had been made possible by charitable bodies branching out from Macau, most educational transfer took place in the opposite direction because of Hong Kong's more rapid development of a unified system of mass education.

The disparity in the rate of educational development stemmed from the different modes of colonialism and the different impact of socio-economic changes. Portuguese colonial authorities generally limited the provision of education to their own citizens in the enclave, whereas the British system embraced the local population, albeit only the elites at first. This is reflected in the fact that mainstream schooling in Hong Kong dates back to the Education Ordinance of 1913, whereas a similar measure was only passed into law in Macau in 1991. The rapid economic growth of Hong Kong that arose from the exogenous pressure of Britain's decline (fostering Hong Kong's economic independence) and China's mixed fortunes (providing an influx of human resources or stimulating new areas of commercial activity) has been paralleled by attention to the improved provision of mass education. Macau, being a comparatively sleepy backwater belonging to a colonial power whose decline had arrived much earlier, was relatively immune to the kind of shocks felt by Hong Kong. It took the major awakening occasioned by the timetabled return of sovereignty to move the Macau authorities to pay any serious attention to mass schooling. Meanwhile, the laissez-faire approach created political problems: Macau was a fertile territory for educators with KMT or Communist Party sympathies, and schooling was also affected by political events in Portugal. In Hong Kong, laissez-faire has been less indolent in this regard. The colonial authorities were more prepared to suppress political issues in education that the authorities deemed threatening to their tenuous legitimacy.

Different attitudes towards the schooling of the local population are evident in the school sponsors. Although the proportion of government schools in Hong Kong is about 6 per cent and in Macau is about 25 per cent, Hong Kong has a large number of aided schools which are run by charitable bodies with financial support from the government. Macau has no aided schools: most schools are run by the private sector with minimal government subvention. These arrangements have facilitated a greater degree of horizontal integration across schools in Hong Kong, and have encouraged individual schools in Macau to be more vertically integrated, providing primary and secondary schooling in a single location. As a result, the school curriculum in Hong Kong shows more uniformity than its pluralistic counterpart in Macau.

The curriculum, clearly defined in Hong Kong (mainly by economic and political exigencies) but less so in Macau, has gained a facade of modernism. However, the implemented reality is academic with firm subject boundaries and oriented towards examination success. As such, the curriculum reflects a union of traditional Chinese education and the more conservative ideas of schooling as access to high culture that have held sway in Europe. The implemented curriculum has been more resistant to progressivist changes because of deeply held beliefs about the nature and purposes of schooling among parents, teachers and other stakeholders. Bureaucratic inertia has also hindered efforts to reform the curriculum. These characteristics are not unique to Hong Kong and Macau. They are typical of schooling developed in territories under colonial administration (such as India under the British), although the interplay of forces that have shaped schooling are particular to the locality. The post-colonial authorities will face similar resistance if resourcing and educational administration are not improved or if the various stakeholders do not share the goals of change.

The relatively long run-up to the restoration of Chinese sovereignty permitted preparatory changes to be initiated in schooling in Macau and Hong Kong, which, even if not implemented whole-heartedly, were generally accepted by the respective communities. There were opportunities for improvements to the quality of provision and the curriculum, as demonstrated by the building of new schools and the curricular reforms, and this may be linked to a desire on the part of the colonial administration to leave with honour. The smoothing of most contentious issues before the handover and Hong Kong's role in the global economy meant that the school curriculum has not been radically reformed in an anti-colonial backlash, and it also allowed the in-coming administration to gain kudos by promoting the non-controversial goal of quality in education. The return to Chinese sovereignty spurred reform in primary and secondary schooling in Macau. The centre-periphery model began to break down as the old centre virtually disappeared with the handover and its remnants became the new periphery. Education for the Chinese sector of the population is now the central concern, and the curriculum reflects the new political order (as manifested in the increased teaching of Putonghua) and the international economic order (as shown by the importance of English).

The lead-in time allowed alignment with the mainland, as indicated by the increased attention to Putonghua and Chinese cultural subjects in both places. Interestingly, the alignment is with an external rather than innate culture: the emphasis was placed on getting to know the mainland and its official language. (Putonghua, the dialect promoted as the standard in mainland China, is not native to either Hong Kong or Macau.) Despite a close ethnic bond with China, many inhabitants of Macau and Hong Kong shared the misgivings of Portugal and United Kingdom about features of the political and social systems operating on the mainland, especially when these have fostered turmoil and violence. In terms of schooling, neither Macau nor Hong Kong has been greatly influenced by the mainland, which has largely adapted practices at different times from the USA and the Soviet Union (Hayhoe 1984); colonial status has kept Hong Kong hermetically sealed, and Macau in a state of neutral balance. Consequently there is a large gulf between these two places and the rest of China, most notably manifested in the organisation and orientations of schooling (although the recent drive towards economic modernisation on the mainland has narrowed the gap in the case of the latter). This suggests that the changes to primary and secondary schooling around the time of reversion of sovereignty that moved practices in Macau and Hong Kong closer to those on the mainland also reflect the characteristics of changes to tertiary education that Law (1997) labels 'recolonisation' rather than 'decolonisation'. Comparisons with other places show that the experiences of Macau and Hong Kong are particular but not unique. Planned, non-violent decolonisation has been experienced, as noted above, in a number of places, and preparatory adjustments have been made to the school curriculum. The cases of Hong Kong and Macau are unusual in the length of the lead-in time.

As elsewhere, language remains an interesting aspect of the curriculum in post-colonial Hong Kong and Macau. Chinese embraces spoken Cantonese (which is the dialect spoken by the majority of people in the two territories) and Putonghua, as well as Modern Standard Chinese characters. The continued promotion of English in Hong Kong is understandable – its attraction as the international language of commerce and communications are too strong. But the retention of Portuguese on the school curriculum in Macau is more surprising, and its presence is mainly due to the Basic Law for Macau following the Hong Kong model, with Portuguese substituted for English as an official language. The debate over the medium of instruction has become redefined, but no less complex, in both places. English has largely lost its colonial associations in Hong Kong because of its stronger international attractions and thus remains highly desirable; Cantonese has been invigorated by the handover through the CMI policy but may face future pressure from the claims of Putonghua as the national unifying language of China. Macau has the added complication of Portuguese. The retention of English in post-colonial societies is familiar – in Singapore, South Africa and India, for example – and subsequent tensions with indigenous languages well documented, as in Malaysia (Pennycook 1994). Efforts to promote another non-indigenous language have occurred in cases of recolonisation, such as in Cambodia when occupied by the Vietnamese (Clayton 1999), although the case of Putonghua in Hong Kong and Macau is more low key and generates less resistance.

Conclusion

This chapter has argued that Macau and Hong Kong share a similar history, geography, ethnicity and post-colonial fate, which is reflected in the development of two very similar, cross-referenced systems of schooling. Colonialism provided both places with education systems that are very different from that of the mother country, China. The two ports have been havens from the political vagaries of educational policy across the border. Although the Four Modernisations drive in China narrowed the gulf, by reducing the political components of the curriculum, education in China had goals which were not shared by Hong Kong or Macau until reunification loomed. These included the development of Chinese patriotism and the promotion of Putonghua (based on the northern Chinese dialect) as the national language. Instead, Macau and Hong Kong created a hybrid system of schooling by combining the classical humanism of the West with the rote-learning, stuffing-the-duck methods of traditional Chinese education to produce a somewhat sterile curriculum that emphasised remote propositional knowledge and avoided awkward questions. At the same time, differences emerged between Macau and Hong Kong. Economic fortunes favoured Hong Kong, turning it into the dominant partner in its relationship with Macau. It also prompted the creation of a more unified, structured system of schooling. This difference was enhanced by the variation in colonial policy. The British approach included the local population in educational provision; the Portuguese enclave system excluded them.

Convergence has been a feature of the respective handovers. Both Hong Kong and Macau have moved towards a degree of alignment with the mainland curriculum, and in doing so Macau has used more of the Hong Kong model. Yet fundamental differences remain across the three parties. Will these differences gradually disappear under Chinese sovereignty? The avowed 'One Country, Two Systems' policy would appear to suggest otherwise. It is perhaps unwise to peer too far into the future, given the historical experiences of China, but it seems likely that Hong Kong and Macau will retain autonomy in preserving their particular brand of schooling so long as the political and economic dynamics that underpin these complex relationships remain.

If the status quo remains – bearing in mind that education policy is always in a state of flux – the only major change will be that international trends among a group of advanced countries may replace the practices of Britain and Portugal as the main point of reference for educational initiatives. Alignment with the mainland will continue to be an influence, but the main determinants of schooling in Hong Kong will probably remain local social and economic imperatives. In Macau, the relative lack of cohesion within the system makes prediction difficult, but past practices suggest that the Hong Kong model will be an important guide, mainland influences will be strong, and local conditions will endow the system with its own particular characteristics.

3

Teacher Education

Li Siu Pang, Titus & Kwo Wai Yu, Ora

This chapter examines the history and development of primary and secondary teacher education in Hong Kong and Macau. In Hong Kong, formal in-service and pre-service teacher education was initiated in the 19th century, but in Macau its history dates only from the 1930s. The Macau government has worked hard to catch up with Hong Kong; but the Hong Kong authorities feel that much needs to be done to catch up with other advanced societies.

The chapter begins with broad literature on the topic, so that Hong Kong and Macau may be taken as a pair for comparison and contrast with other parts of the world as well as with each other. This broad literature points out that teacher education has been neglected in many countries, and that even at the end of the 20th century many education authorities recruited untrained as well as trained teachers for their classrooms. Various debates have also taken place over the structure of teacher education, and on its most appropriate locus. A global trend gives universities rather than specialised training colleges increasing responsibility for the training of teachers; but in some countries training is being devolved to schools in which trainee teachers work closely with experienced mentors in the classroom.

Several parts of the chapter refer to institutions for training teachers as 'normal' schools. While this terminology has ceased to be common in both Hong Kong and Macau, it is still part of standard vocabulary in mainland China. The word also remains common in some other parts of the world, particularly French-speaking ones. The term normal education originates from French term *écoles normales* (Collins et al. 1973, p.146).

The Nature and Functions of Teacher Education: International Perspectives

In almost all parts of the world, teacher training has been a neglected activity until relatively recent times. As noted by Dove (1986, p.177):

> Modern school systems have had to make do for over a century with high proportions of untrained and unqualified teachers. The planning and development of teacher education and training has nearly always lagged behind the development of schools. Popular pressures have often filled the classrooms with pupils faster than teachers could be found.

The histories of education in Hong Kong and Macau are not exceptions to that statement.

Dove (p.177) identified several reasons why teacher training has tended to have a low priority. One reason was that teacher training was (and is) only part of larger systems, responsive and reactive to developments in the schools. Another reason is that until recently, the need for training has not been put forward convincingly. Particularly at the elementary level, where the earliest expansion of school systems began, the notion was widespread that any person who had completed a particular level of education could teach students at lower levels. A further factor concerns budgets. Not only does training itself require finance, but trained teachers generally demand higher salaries than untrained ones.

Because of these factors, almost all countries, whatever their level of development, have at some point in history permitted untrained personnel to take teaching positions. Indeed in some countries it remains the norm rather than the exception. UNESCO (1998, p.45) reported that in the mid-1990s in Uruguay, for example, 70 per cent of teachers in secondary schools had not been trained; and in Togo the corresponding figure for lower secondary education was 84 per cent. Even in the USA, which is a prosperous society with high standards, over 12 per cent of new recruits entered the classroom without any formal training, and another 14 per cent arrived without fully meeting state norms. Many teachers in Hong Kong and Macau are also untrained. As will be explained below, both governments are trying to rectify this situation; but progress requires considerable expenditure and firm commitment from the authorities. Meanwhile, UNESCO pointed out that although on a global basis teachers are better educated than 30 years ago, so are general populations who are not teachers. UNESCO added (p.46) that:

> The fact that society still is willing to accept at all that people can be employed as teachers without having received any specific preparation for the job points to the difficulty for teachers in getting their claims heard. Probably no other aspect of teacher employment policies has done as much to retard progress towards recognition of teaching as a profession.

This observation would apply to Hong Kong and Macau as well as to other parts of the world.

International survey also shows diversity in the emphases between pre-service and in-service training (Gimmestad & Hall 1995). While some education authorities insist that teachers must have received training before they can be offered jobs, others are prepared to employ untrained teachers and then encourage or require them to undertake in-service training. Pre-service training is commonly provided either in colleges of education or in universities. Where universities are involved, training may be part of an undergraduate degree or it may be a special postgraduate course. In-service courses may vary in duration from days to years. Refresher courses are typically shorter than ones which seek more fundamental training in techniques and approaches. Again, this diversity in the forms of training has been evident in Hong Kong and Macau as much as in other parts of the world.

UNESCO (1998, p.67) reports a "long-term secular trend worldwide ... towards the consolidation of pre-service teacher-education programmes at the tertiary level of education". This partly reflects the shifting balance of teacher education as secondary school systems, and therefore the demand for secondary teachers, have grown proportionately to primary school systems and therefore the demand for primary teachers. Hong Kong and Macau have followed the trend towards consolidating teacher education in tertiary institutions. Hong Kong used to have a dual system in which some teacher training was conducted by universities while other training was conducted by colleges of education operated by the government's Education Department. The colleges of education have now been merged into a Hong Kong Institute of Education (HKIEd) funded by the University Grants Committee. Likewise in Macau, the expanded work of the University of Macau has greatly shifted the balance between training provided by the tertiary and the non-tertiary sectors. However, in neither Hong Kong nor Macau has an existing college of education been absorbed into a university. Thus the HKIEd was created as a free-standing body, similar in nature to normal universities in mainland China. This contrasted with the model in Australia and the United Kingdom in which many colleges of education were merged with existing multi-faceted universities.

As one might expect, the nature of teacher education in colonies around the world was in general heavily influenced by patterns in the colonising country (Dove 1986, p.181). This observation applies to Hong Kong and Macau as well as to other colonies, though in Macau the government's laissez faire approach until the late 1980s meant that government-sponsored forms of teacher education were neglected along with other aspects of education and training. Historically, in many parts of the world churches and other voluntary agencies have been involved in teacher education. This still continues in some settings, but has declined in prominence as governments have generally become more involved in education.

International survey also reveals controversy over the contents of teacher education. Courses typically seek to balance subject knowledge, teaching skills, and general conceptual understanding. This means that biology teachers, for example, must know enough biology to be able to teach their subjects well; but that they must also be equipped with an array of tools for teaching their subjects to different types of pupils and in a range of different circumstances, and they must have general understanding of psychology, sociology, the structure of education systems, and various other domains which will affect their lives and work. One difficulty, however, is a lack of consensus on where the appropriate balance between these different elements should lie. Professionals also differ in their conceptions of the roles of the practicum, appropriate relationships with school-based mentors, and many other issues.

Finally, one specific factor which affects the nature of teacher education, as well as of education systems more generally, is the scale of the operation. Systems which are fairly large can afford much more specialised training than can systems which are smaller. This is evident in mainland China, for example, which has many normal universities entirely devoted to the task of teacher education. Hong Kong also has a fairly large education system, and is therefore able to provide considerable specialised training by subject, level, and special need (such as mentally handicapped children, or gifted children). As shown in other chapters of this book, Macau's education sector is not only small but also fragmented. Macau's Portuguese-medium schools, for example, have rather different cultures, traditions and needs from the Chinese-medium schools. Small size and fragmentation has in the past obstructed development of teacher education in Macau; and it remains the case that some forms of specialised training are better sought outside the territory than in Macau itself.

Historical Perspectives

To explain the origins of contemporary patterns, this section of the chapter charts the growth and development of teacher education in the two territories. It begins with Hong Kong before turning to Macau, and primarily focuses on the period up to the 1980s.

Hong Kong

The colonial Hong Kong government declined to play anything more than a minimal role in teacher education until the 20th century. St Paul's College, an Anglican school founded in 1849, introduced teacher education to Hong Kong in 1853 by setting up a pupil-teacher scheme which prepared teachers of English. Frederick Stewart, who held a dual appointment as the first headmaster of the government's Central School (later renamed Queen's College) and the first Inspector of Government Schools, launched another pupil-teacher scheme in the mid-1860s in the Central School. This scheme was similar to the monitorial teacher education system in England (Sweeting 1992, p.60). Also, in 1881 the authorities set up the Wanchai Normal School to train Chinese teachers to teach English. However, the school was short-lived. It only admitted 10 student-teachers, and only two managed to graduate before its closure in 1883 (Yau et al. 1993, p.75).

The next government initiative was in 1906 when an Evening Continuation Class for pupil teachers was introduced in Queen's College. The following year the class was transferred to the Technical Institute. Then, a decade later, a four-year undergraduate course was launched at the University of Hong Kong by the newly established Department for the Training of Teachers (Sweeting 1998a, p.4). The course aimed to prepare teachers for both primary and secondary sectors.

Vernacular (Chinese) teacher training started in 1914 at the Technical Institute. In 1920, the government opened two Vernacular Normal Schools: one for men and the other for women (Yau et al. 1993, p.76). A third institution, the Government Tai Po Vernacular Normal School, was founded in 1925 to supply teachers for rural schools. In 1926, the Government Vernacular Middle School was founded. It absorbed the Government Vernacular Normal School for Men under its Normal Division.

In 1938, Governor G.A.S. Northcote appointed Mr Justice Lindsell to form a special committee to study teacher education. The following year, as a result of his report, the first Teacher Training College was opened to replace the existing normal schools in temporary premises. It provided teacher training for both Anglo-Chinese and vernacular schools in a two-year full-time course. Thirty-seven of the 48 student teachers graduated in 1941, and in the same year the college was moved to its own premises. However, its activities were interrupted by World War II. At first named the Northcote Training College, in 1967 it was renamed Northcote College of Education (Sweeting 1990; H.T. Wong 1993).

The post-war period brought continued expansion. To serve the New Territories, a Rural Training College was established in 1946; and five years later the Grantham Training College was established in Kowloon to prepare Chinese primary school teachers. The Grantham Training College absorbed the Rural Training College in 1954, and was renamed Grantham College of Education in 1967. The college trained primary and secondary teachers from the outset, and kindergarten teachers after 1981.

Another teacher education institution of this type was set up in 1960 to support the expanding primary school sector. It was initially called the Sir Robert Black Training

College, but was renamed the Sir Robert Black College of Education in 1967. In 1981, the college set up a special unit for in-service training of special education teachers. The basic course structure for pre-service primary and secondary teacher education was a two-year full-time Certificate of Education course for Secondary Form 5 or 7 graduates. In the 1980s, three-year full-time courses were introduced for Secondary Form 5 graduates in order to upgrade the quality of teachers.

To strengthen the expertise for industrial development, the Hong Kong Technical Teachers' College was formed in 1974. The college trained teachers of practical subjects for secondary and prevocational schools. Technical Diploma graduates from Technical Institutes or Polytechnics with industrial working experience were allowed to take a one-year full-time Technical Teacher Certificate course, while Secondary Form 5 graduates had to study for two years. Following the other three colleges of education, the two-year Technical Teachers' course was extended to three years in the 1980s.

Hoping to advance the language ability of teachers, the fifth government teacher education institution was opened in 1982. The Institute of Language in Education was established to provide in-service Chinese and English language courses for primary and secondary teachers. Language teachers were released by schools to attend three-month or six-month courses in the institute.

In addition, much teacher education was provided by local universities. The long history of teacher education at HKU has already been mentioned (Sweeting 1998a, 1998b). In 1965, the Chinese University of Hong Kong (CUHK) also established a Faculty of Education. The university courses mainly provided training for secondary teachers, on a pre-service and in-service basis.

Macau

The history of teacher education in Macau is shorter and more modest than that in Hong Kong. In the initial decades it was mainly provided by churches rather than by the government.

The first of these formal arrangements for teacher education was initiated in the 1930s. Courses were taught in Chinese, and provision was rather limited and unstructured. According to Lau (1997), 12 independent institutions provided normal classes to prepare teachers for Macau Chinese schools between 1935 to 1985 on either an in-service or pre-service basis. For example, Hou Kong Middle School launched a one-year normal class for junior secondary school graduates in 1952; and St. Joseph's College introduced a normal class in 1953. In the same year, Tak Meng School started kindergarten teacher education for female Senior Secondary 3 graduates; and Zhongshan Normal School and the Anglican Church Teachers' College within Choi Kou Middle School also offered normal classes (Fu et al. 1994; Lai 1995).

Few of these programmes were sustained, however, and the only course still running in the 1980s was that provided by St. Joseph's College (K.I. Chan 1991). Even St. Joseph's changed the structure of training and suspended classes several times. However, it continued with in-service and pre-service courses for kindergarten and primary teachers even when other institutions launched programmes in the 1990s. The private sector gained few resources from the government because until the 1970s the authorities were mainly concerned with education for Portuguese-speaking children (Rosa 1991). Moreover, before the 1966 riots, most schools were registered with the Taiwan government. In 1954, for instance, 51 of the 70 schools in Macau were registered in Taiwan (C.F. Cheung 1956). This further distanced the schools from the Macau government. After the 1966 riots, many schools turned to mainland China for assistance (Macau Chinese Education Association [MCEA] 1967, 1968).

Teacher education for secondary schools was even more limited than for primary schools. The chief reason was that the whole sector was very small. In 1934, Macau had only eight Chinese secondary schools with 350 students, serving a total population of just 120,000 (Lau 1996). Rather than establishing local institutions for training, sponsoring bodies found it easier to recruit teachers from abroad who had already been trained. Supply of teachers was also increased by immigration. During and after World War II, many highly educated Chinese scholars migrated to Macau and took up teaching posts (Lau 1996; K.K. Tang 1997). Also, many schools were run by religious bodies in which priests and nuns were available to teach. Finally, teachers were in effect trained on the job. A common practice was to promote teachers of junior secondary classes to the senior classes after they had received a few years of experience.

Government-provided teacher education in Macau began in the mid-1960s, when the authorities set up a Division of Initial Teacher Education for Portuguese-medium primary schools in the official Pedro Nolasco da Silva Primary School (later converted to the Luso-Chinese Central Primary School, and then to the Gomes Luso-Chinese Secondary School). In 1973, the two-year full-time primary teacher education course was abandoned, because student-teachers preferred to take scholarships for study in Portugal. After a long break, teacher education for Portuguese-medium primary schools was resumed in 1995 at the University of Macau (Li 1997).

During the 1980s, under pressure from the MCEA and other bodies, the government abandoned its laissez-faire policy in teacher education for Chinese schools. A partnership was arranged with the South China Normal University (SCNU) in Guangzhou. In 1985, the SCNU's College of Adult Education launched an external part-time in-service course leading to a diploma in teacher education. The three-year course was conducted by correspondence and without a practicums, and was administered by the MCEA (Chiu & Ng 1991; C.L. Wong 1995). Among the 141 enrolled in-service primary and secondary teachers, 120 received full financial support from the Macau government. The government also paid for a two-year in-service special course for primary and kindergarten teachers at the private University of East Asia (UEA). This course was launched in 1987 (Wang 1996).

Developments in the 1990s: Pre-Service Teacher Education

The 1990s brought substantial change and maturation in teacher education in both Hong Kong and Macau. This section comments on pre-service provision while the following one comments on in-service provision.

Hong Kong

Among the most significant developments in Hong Kong teacher education during the 1990s was the establishment of the Hong Kong Institute of Education. It was formed in 1994 by amalgamating the five existing colleges of education (C.K. Leung 1995). The chief goal, following recommendations in Education Commission Report No.5 (1992), was to upgrade the quality of teacher education. The HKIEd moved into a new campus in Taipo in 1997. All the pre-service programmes were conducted in Taipo, while many in-service programmes were retained in the Institute's Town Centre, the former Grantham College of Education. Two types of pre-service primary teacher education were run by the HKIEd. One was for Form 7 students, who could be admitted to the Certificate in Primary Education (Chinese) course which lasted two years full-time. Form 5 school leavers could enrol in the Certificate in Primary Education (Chinese) course which lasted three years full-time. The students were trained to teach four primary subjects.

Education Commission Report No.5 (1992, pp.45-46), which was subsequently endorsed by the government, had set a target of achieving graduate status for 35 per cent of primary teachers in 2007. Initially, the HKIEd focused on non-graduate teacher education; but graduate teacher education for primary teachers was provided by the CUHK, HKU and the Hong Kong Baptist University (HKBU). Many primary school teachers also obtained degrees from overseas universities, either through full-time study in those universities or through a combination of residential and distance education. Most of these courses provided part-time or full-time courses for graduates from the colleges of education or the HKIEd. For instance, holders of the HKIEd Certificate of Primary Education could transfer directly to two-year full-time courses at the CUHK and HKU in order to become graduate primary teachers.

The HKIEd also provided pre-service courses for junior secondary teachers and technical teachers. The format of courses and the types of student-teachers selected for the junior secondary tracks were similar to those in primary teacher education. Secondary 7 graduates were eligible to join the two-year full-time Chinese or English Certificate in Secondary Education courses, while Secondary 5 graduates with reasonable results in the Hong Kong Certificate of Education Examination (HKCEE) could join the three-year Chinese or English courses. However, the three-year English Course was terminated in 1997/98. The one-year full-time Technical Teacher Certificate Course was for post-secondary graduates with technical Diplomas or above as well as a minimum of two years relevant post-qualification industrial experience. These fresh technical student-teachers were prepared to teach one technical subject and mathematics or technical drawing at junior secondary level in prevocational schools.

HKU, CUHK and HKBU also helped build up the team of specialist secondary teachers. HKU offered a four-year BEd in Language Education (Chinese/English); and HKIEd fresh graduates could join the BEd two-year course in Physical Education & Sports Science at the CUHK. In addition, both HKU and CUHK offered one-year full-time Postgraduate Certificate of Education (PCEd) or equivalent courses. The courses were designed for fresh graduates, though also attracted applicants who wished to move to teaching after having worked for some years in other sectors. Subjects offered included geography, physics, chemistry, history, Chinese, English, biology, economics, accounting, mathematics, and computer science.

Other courses in tertiary institutions (Sweeting 1998a, p.32) included:

- the Postgraduate Diploma in the Teaching of English as a Second Language (TESL) at the City University of Hong Kong, launched in 1989, and the Bachelor of Arts (BA) in TESL (1991) and the Master of Arts (MA) in TESL (1992); and
- the BA in Music taught at the Hong Kong Baptist College, launched in 1989 and followed by the BA in Physical Education & Recreation Studies (1992), the Postgraduate Diploma in Education (1994) and the Master of Education (MEd) (1995).

Macau

Realising the urgent need for high quality teachers for rapid educational reform, in 1989 the Macau governor appointed an eight-person committee to plan innovations in education. A School of Education was created in the UEA later that year to provide courses in early childhood and primary teacher education. In 1989, 34 pre-service primary student teachers enrolled in the School Education Diploma course at the UEA. The following year, a special one-year Advanced Diploma in-service teacher education course was initiated for practising teachers who were graduates from St. Joseph's College and similar institutions. From 1992 to 1996, the School of Education offered a three-year Bachelor of Education (BEd) course for advanced diploma and pre-service diploma graduates. Thus, at this stage three different bodies were offering courses for Macau primary school teachers in the Chinese stream: St. Joseph's College, the South China Normal University, and the UEA (F.K. Ng 1992; K.C. Cheung 1996; Lau 1997).

As before, however, teacher education for secondary teachers received less emphasis. The Macau government did not provide any local training for teachers in Portuguese-medium secondary schools, preferring instead to send personnel abroad for training and/or to recruit expatriates. For teachers in Chinese-medium secondary schools, a full-time pre-service course was introduced in 1991 at what had previously been the privately-operated UEA but which in 1988 had been purchased by the government and in 1991 had been renamed the University of Macau (UM). Initially, just under 20 students were admitted to the four-year full-time BEd with arts/Chinese and arts/English majors. One year later, the BEd with science/mathematics major was also launched by the Faculty of Education. The intention of the university was to prepare teachers of Chinese, English and mathematics for local Chinese-medium and English-medium secondary schools.

In 1995, the UM Faculty of Education launched a three-year pre-service Bacharelato degree of Educational Science (Primary) course, to replace the Diploma of School Education Course. In the Portuguese system, the Bacharelato degree normally takes three years of study while the Bachelor (Licenciatura) degree normally takes four years.

Table 3.1 summarises the nature of pre-service primary teacher education offered at the HKIEd and UM. For simplicity, it omits provision by the other bodies. It shows that the courses had similar entrance levels, but that the UM required a written examination as part of the entrance requirement. It also shows that the HKIEd gave a heavier credit weighting to academic subjects, and had a different arrangement for the practicum. At the HKIEd, students could apply for a loan to cover the fees, but they were required to repay the loan after graduation. At the UM, by contrast, more generous availability of grants meant that loans were not needed. Another interesting difference concerns the ratio of male and female student primary teachers. From 1989 to 1997, the UM course had only nine males among 149 students (6.0%). This may have reflected the low social status and salaries of primary teachers compared to secondary teachers in Macau. The situation in Hong Kong was better since the working conditions and salaries of primary teachers were more acceptable.

Table 3.1: Pre-service Primary Teacher Education, HKIEd and UM

	Hong Kong Institute of Education	University of Macau
Entrance requirement	Form 5 or Form 7 students with reasonable results in 'O' level and 'A' level examinations	Form 5 or Senior Secondary 3 graduates
Entrance examination	Oral examination & aptitude test	Written examination & oral examination
Form of course (qualification awarded)	(i) 2 year Certificate of Primary Education ('A' level student) (ii) 3 year Certificate of Primary Education ('O' level student)	3 year Bacharelato Degree of Educational Science (Primary) Course
Weight of subject knowledge and teaching methodology	Credit weighting for academic studies is heavier than that of pedagogy	Academic studies and teaching methodology of each subject given equal credits
Duration of practicum	2nd year: 2 + 4 weeks 3rd year: 4 + 4 weeks	1st year: 3 weeks 2nd year: 3 weeks 3rd year: whole year
Ratio between male and female student teachers	male < female	9 male out of 149 student teachers (1989-1997)
Grants/loans	Grants and loans available from the government. Loans repayable after graduation.	Grants available from the government.

Table 3.2 shows comparable information for pre-service secondary teacher education at the HKIEd and the UM. The HKIEd had courses of different lengths depending on the starting points of the entrants; and the HKIEd courses (unlike those of HKU and CUHK) led only to a certificate. Whereas HKIEd students were expected to have knowledge of English as well as Chinese, UM students were expected to have knowledge of Portuguese as well as Chinese.

Developments in the 1990s: In-Service Teacher Education

In both Hong Kong and Macau, in-service courses were available to give initial training to practising teachers and to upgrade the knowledge and skills of teachers who were already qualified. These are explained and commented upon here.

Hong Kong
Two different types of in-service primary teacher education courses were offered by the HKIEd to give initial training to practising teachers. The three-year part-time in-service course for teachers in primary schools was designed for teachers who had obtained reasonable HKCEE results; and the two-year part-time course was offered to untrained primary teachers with higher academic qualifications. A parallel set of in-service evening courses was offered for teachers in Chinese-medium and English-medium secondary schools. The courses lasted three years part-time or two years part-time according to students' entry qualifications, but the two-year part-time Certificate of English Secondary Education course was discontinued in 1997/98 (HKIEd 1998).

Table3.2: Pre-service Secondary Teacher Education, HKIEd and UM

	Hong Kong Institute of Education	University of Macau
Entrance requirement	Form 5 or Form 7 students with reasonable 'O' level and 'A' level results	Senior Secondary 3 graduates
Entrance examination	Oral examination & aptitude test	Written examination
Form of course (qualification awarded)	(i) 2 year Certificate of Secondary Education ('A' level student) (ii) 3 year Certificate of Secondary Education ('O' level student)	4 year Bachelor Degree of Education (Chinese, English, Mathematics)
Subjects expected to teach	Limited	One major subject for English, One major and one minor for mathematics and Chinese class
Levels of teaching	Form 1 to Form 3 (junior secondary)	Form 1 to Form 6 (both junior and senior forms)
Subjects offered	All subjects taught in secondary schools	Limited subjects. Only English, Chinese, mathematics, physics and Chinese history
Weight of subject knowledge and teaching methodology	Credit weighting for academic studies heavier than that of pedagogy.	Similar to that in HKIEd
Duration of practicum	2nd year: 2 + 4 weeks 3rd year: 4 + 4 weeks	4th year: half year (above 10 periods)
Colonial language	Expect to speak English	Learn to speak Portuguese
Grants/loans	Grants and loans available from government. Loans repayable after graduation.	Grants available from the government. No need to repay.

In 1997, the HKIEd Division of Extension Studies offered 22 professional development programmes. For secondary teachers, the HKIEd offered several in-service courses to advance the professionalism of teachers. Some of the courses aimed to advance the Chinese and English language ability of secondary teachers. Others helped panel chairpersons of Chinese or English Language, and yet others focused on curriculum development and other subjects.

Teachers with Certificate of Education (Primary) qualifications had many channels to upgrade themselves to degree status both within Hong Kong and abroad. The CUHK and HKU offered BEd part-time degrees for primary teachers; and two consortia of local tertiary institutions offered similar courses. One consortium comprised the Open University of Hong Kong (OUHK), the Hong Kong Polytechnic University, the City University of Hong Kong and the HKIEd. The second consortium comprised the School of Continuing Education of the HKBU, the HKIEd and the School of Professional & Continuing Education of HKU. Australian and UK universities offered additional BEd courses through part-time distance learning, sometimes in conjunction with blocks of full-time study.

The HKIEd also provided upgrading courses for non-graduate teachers of cultural, practical and technical subjects with the one-year full-time Advanced Course of Teacher Education. Practising teachers who were nominated by their Heads of Schools were considered to undertake specialised studies in one of the following subjects: Art &

Design, Commerce, Design & Technology, Home Economics (Dress & Design), Music and Physical Education, plus the compulsory professional and general studies.

Certificated secondary school teachers in the past normally either studied in the UK for one or two years to upgrade themselves to be graduate status or through the six-year part-time evening bachelor degree of mathematics or science in the Hong Kong Polytechnic or the City Polytechnic. Later, many Australian and UK universities set up teaching points in Hong Kong so that non-graduate teachers could take the part-time distance learning BEd course in Hong Kong. Another resource was the OUHK, which launched a BEd (Secondary) degree in 1995 and an MEd in 1996.

Macau
Three institutions offered initial in-service primary teacher education courses in Macau. First, the UM provided a three-year in-service part-time Bacharelato degree in primary education for untrained teachers who had at least one year's teaching experience. The course content and structure was similar to that of the pre-service programme. Second, St. Joseph's College offered a mixed two-year evening part-time certificate in primary education for both non-trained in-service teachers and adults with no teaching experience. And third, the SCNU offered a part-time distance three-year diploma course and a five-year BEd course in education and Chinese language teaching for in-service teachers as well as Macau citizens with no teaching experience. All these courses were recognised by the Macau government.

The UM's three-year Portuguese Bacharelato degree of Educational Science (Primary) was a mixed course for untrained teachers and other Portuguese-speaking adults who wished to become teachers (University of Macau, Faculty of Education 1997a). The course content and structure of the Portuguese programme was similar to that of the Chinese programme.

Opportunity for holders of primary teachers' certificates to upgrade to BEd was more limited in Macau than in Hong Kong. The UM did have a three-year part-time BEd in primary education, but suspended it in 1995. Although the UM introduced an MEd course in 1996, and a number of BEd graduates were enrolled in two MEd courses in management and in psychology, analysts expected Macau to suffer a shortage of graduate primary teachers. As a result, some non-graduate primary teachers took the five-year part-time BEd course provided by the SCNU. This course did not give them credit for their existing post-secondary studies, and in this respect seemed to waste government resources and teachers' energy and time.

Compared to provision for primary teachers, in-service provision for secondary teachers in Macau was neglected. When the full-time BEd secondary teacher education programme was launched, the UM did allowed a small number of in-service initial student teachers to study under a part-time structure. However, the last group of this type graduated in 1996/97.

Nevertheless, since 1991 the UM has offered a two-year part-time Post-Graduate Certificate of Education (PGCE) for practising secondary teachers with Bachelors' degrees in any subject. Fifty six in-service secondary teachers had been awarded the PGCE by the end of 1997 (University of Macau 1997b). The SCNU also provided in-service opportunities for secondary teachers. A number of secondary teachers joined the three-year Education Professional course in 1985; and in 1989 the university extended a two-year Bachelor course for these graduates. In the 1990s, a five-year distance Bachelor degree of Chinese Language was introduced to upgrade the status of language

teachers. In addition, the Macau government has established two special Bachelor Degree Courses in Physical Education and Arts & Design under the administration of the
Macau Polytechnic and the Institute of Arts.

The University of Macau also works with the government's Department of Education & Youth in offering summer courses for practising teachers in all school levels to
upgrade their professional knowledge through 15-hour or 45-hour courses yearly. Some
courses have been extended to last for a full year. For instance, the Department in conjunction with the UM has conducted several special programmes for school teachers and
administrators in Putonghua teacher education, school management & administration,
special education, and computer-based education (University of Macau 1996). Several
private organisations such as the Macau Chinese Education Association and the Macau
Catholic Schools Association have also conducted short refreshment courses or seminars in educational issues.

Tables 3.3 and 3.4 summarise these points. They map the provision of in-service
primary and secondary teacher education in Hong Kong and Macau, highlighting similarities and contrasts.

Table 3.3: In-service Primary Teacher Education, Hong Kong and Macau

	Hong Kong	Macau
Channels for in-service further studies (e.g. BEd)	Many channels. Many local and overseas institutions offered BEd and MEd courses	Limited. UM stopped the BEd course in 1995, but resumed in 1999. SCNU offered only 5-year degree programmes
Institutions offering in-service initial course	HKIEd	UM; St. Joseph's College; SCNU
Form of initial evening teacher education courses (qualification awarded)	(i) 2-year Certificate of Primary Education (post-secondary stan-dard) (ii) 3 year Certificate of Pri-mary Education ('O' level student)	3-year Bacharelato Degree of Educational Science (Primary) Course
Subjects expected to teach	3 core subjects: Chinese, mathe-matics and general studies, plus optional subjects including English, physical education and arts	All subjects: Chinese, mathematics, English, general studies, history, geography, arts [in Chinese], music [in Chinese], and physical educa-tion [in Chinese]
Weighting for subject knowledge and teaching methodology	Weighting for academic studies heavier than that for pedagogy	Academic studies and pedagogy of each subject weighted equally
Practicum arrangement	4 times each year	twice each for 1st and 2nd year; 4 times for 3rd year

The Future: Development and Innovation

In Hong Kong, major thrusts in the mid- and late 1990s focused on quality school education and excellence in education. Education Commission Report No.7 (1997) stressed
that it was time to raise the professional standards of principals and teachers. In 1997,
the Chief Executive, Tung Chee Hwa, announced that the government would enhance
the professional status of primary teachers by advancing the date for 35 per cent of posts

being graduate positions from 2007 to 2001, and would require all new primary and secondary teachers to be trained graduates (Tung 1997b). Thus, Hong Kong was following the steps of other advanced societies to raise the quality of teachers.

Table 3.4: In-service Secondary Teacher Education, Hong Kong and Macau

	Hong Kong	Macau
Channels for in-service further studies (e.g. PGCE, BEd, MEd)	Many channels through HKIEd and local and overseas universities.	Limited. UM offers PGCE and MEd courses while the SCNU offered 5-year degree programmes
Institutions offering in-service initial course	HKIEd, HKU, CUHK	SCNU
Form of initial evening teacher education courses (qualification awarded)	(i) 2-year Certificate of Secondary Education (Post-secondary standard); (ii) 3-year Certificate of Secondary Education ('O' level student)	5-year BEd or Bachelor Degree in Chinese

However, K.M. Cheng (1997a) asserted that these innovations came 20 years late. Furthermore, Pong (1997) asserted that the quality and quantity of teachers of physical education, music and arts trained by the HKIEd could not meet the demand of the primary schools. One problem was that these subjects were treated as minor subjects, and thus given less time and attention. Secondly, many full-time primary student-teachers who learned arts subjects in their secondary schooling were weak in science. Hence, the quality of primary science teachers was not up to standard. Further, the reform of subject curriculum to integrate Social Studies, Science and Health Education into General Studies made the situation even more complex.

Secondary teacher education was not seriously discussed by the Chief Executive or by Education Commission Report No.7. The most challenging tasks in secondary schools were to raise the language ability of both Chinese and English teachers, promote mother-tongue language teaching in secondary schools, and increase the use of information technology in teaching. All these challenges reflected the weakness of secondary teacher education in Hong Kong. The institutions endeavoured to meet the challenges, but themselves found it a major task.

In Macau, the authorities commenced with a lower starting point but during the 1990s achieved great strides in upgrading the large team of non-trained teachers. In 1995/96, 60 per cent of primary teachers had completed both secondary schooling and teacher education, while 20 per cent of secondary teachers had received training and 71 per cent of secondary teachers had received tertiary education (Macau, Department of Statistics & Census 1997b). This situation may be compared with that in 1983/84, when only 512 (23.7%) out of 2,163 teachers of all levels had teaching qualifications. In 1996, the Macau government issued the 'Regulation on Teachers for Private School Organisations' to raise the status and academic qualification of teachers. The Department of Education & Youth also restricted the freedom of schools which had joined the Free Education Scheme to employ new untrained teachers. Only private schools outside the scheme were permitted to employ untrained teachers.

Foreseeing the shortage of students for initial in-service primary teacher education, the UM planned to offer an in-service evening Bachelor degree of Primary Education to upgrade the Bacharelato degree primary teachers. Even though the UM would not provide a pre-service BEd in primary education in immediate future, a plan to upgrade the qualifications of non-graduate primary teachers was widely considered essential. In fact, a number of practising teachers and others with no teaching experience were enrolled in the five-year part-time distance learning BEd course offered by the SCNU and the MCEA. Furthermore, the SCNU had built an annex in Zhuhai, across the border from Macau, in order to change the model from distance teaching to face-to-face teaching. This was expected to grow, and was an interesting way through which Macau could benefit from the growing city just beyond its gate. However, Macau suffered from a dispute about the standard of teacher education, particularly comparing the quality of graduates from SCNU, UM and St. Joseph's College. This matter needed resolution for harmonious future development

Conclusions

This chapter has highlighted several similarities in teacher education in Hong Kong and Macau. Beginning with historical features, in Macau, and to some extent in Hong Kong, teacher education was mainly developed by the private sector before the governments started to offer formal programmes. When governments did commence activities, they were more interested in the colonial languages than in Chinese.

Allied to this point, the nature of provision in each territory was strongly influenced by traditions in the colonising country. Hong Kong's colleges of education were initially run by the Education Department, which commonly invited experts from the UK to evaluate and supervise programmes. The UM's Bacharelato degree has a similar duration, curriculum and length of practicum to its counterparts in Portugal.

Another similarity has been that innovation in teacher education has been strongly linked with political events. Most obviously, investment and reform during the 1990s was strongly related in both territories to the prospect of reunification with China.

On the other hand, several important differences have been observed in this chapter. One concerns the stage of development of teacher education and pace of change. Although the Macau government started proper teacher education much later than its counterpart in Hong Kong, it made major strides during the 1990s. Hong Kong was taken as a specific reference point, and the authorities were anxious to catch up. Indeed, in some respects they endeavoured to overtake Hong Kong, setting the goal that all Macau student teachers should have graduated from the four-year BEd course. In Hong Kong, by contrast, the target for secondary teachers was for all of them to be graduates before aiming for them all to have received training.

However, several features of Macau teacher education needed special attention. For instance, in 1995 over 40 per cent of practising teachers had been trained by SCNU through the part-time distance learning. In addition, over half of Macau's teachers were migrants from the mainland who had qualifications from their places of origin. At the same time, many Portuguese teachers had been recruited from Portugal, and very few Portuguese teachers had been trained in Macau. As a result, the number of local trained teachers was rather small. Such a phenomenon does raise the question how far the Macau government can build an education system which is separate from and independent of that in mainland China. According to the Basic Law (China 1993, Article 121), the government is allowed to operate its own education system independently from the rest of China. However, the large proportion of teachers who have received teacher education in mainland China might create obstacles in this respect. To some extent, this reflects Macau's small size and limited domestic capacity to provide specialised training for teachers.

Another distinctive feature of Macau was the large proportion of teachers who had received in-service teacher education. This was chiefly because full-time pre-service teacher education was only offered by the UM, and had only been launched relatively recently. In 1997/98, just 54 secondary and 25 primary Year One student-teachers were enrolled at the UM. Such numbers were very small compared to Hong Kong. It seemed to show an imbalance between in-service and pre-service initial teacher education.

In summary, this chapter has highlighted the development and innovation of teacher education between the two regions under different stages. The Hong Kong government has achieved the quantitative targets, and is making a qualitative transition while the Macau government is trying its best to make both quantitative and qualitative achievements in teacher education. It is time to restructure and innovate the curriculum and content of teacher education courses in both territories so that all trained primary and secondary teachers may be both competent and effective teachers equipped with enough professional knowledge, information technology and professional ethics to face the challenges of changes in education.

4

Higher Education

Yung Man Sing, Andrew

This chapter focuses on the structure and development of higher education in Hong Kong and Macau, paying particular attention to the nature and impact of quantitative and qualitative growth during the 1980s and 1990s. It also notes the ways in which the two higher education systems were influenced by forces of globalisation in higher education. The chapter begins by analysing higher education in the two territories in the context of broader literatures on comparative higher education and the economics of education. Teichler (1996) pointed out that comparison is a basic methodological approach in the social sciences, and argued that international comparison is indispensable for analysis of macro-societal phenomena in higher education. He identified four "spheres of knowledge" in higher education. This chapter focuses mainly on two of these spheres, namely aspects of organisation and governance of higher education, and quantitative-structural aspects of higher education.

Comparative analysis of the policies and development of higher education in Hong Kong and Macau during the 1980s and 1990s exposes major issues concerning size, shape, planning, and financing. These matters can be classified under Teichler's first sphere, namely organisation and governance. Concerns about shortfalls or surpluses of qualified applicants for higher education and the output of graduates for the labour market belong to the second sphere, namely quantitative-structural aspects. These matters are frequently discussed by policy-makers, administrators, researchers and students in both Hong Kong and Macau. Identification of patterns and trends helps to chart possible courses for future development in the two territories.

Higher Education Institutions and Enrolments

To set the context, Table 4.1 shows key economic and educational indicators in the mid-1990s. It highlights major differences between the two societies in terms of population, area, and economy, resulting in different paces and outcomes of higher education development.

In Hong Kong, higher education institutions offer both degree and non-degree programmes to post-secondary students. Most of the degree courses use English as the medium of instruction except for the courses related to Chinese languages and history. The Chinese University of Hong Kong is distinctive in offering a considerable number of courses in Chinese. In 1998, Hong Kong had 21 higher education institutions. Eight,

Table 4.1: Key Economic and Educational Indicators, Hong Kong and Macau

Territory	Population 1997 (millions)	Per capita GDP 1996	GNP real growth rate 1980-97 (%)	No. of degree granting insti- tutions 1997	Public expenditure on education as a % of GDP 1996
Hong Kong	6.5	US$24,500	6.0	8	3.0
Macau	0.454	US$14,100	5.2	4	0.8

Sources: Hong Kong, Census & Statistics Department (1997); Macau, Department of Statistics & Census (1997a).

shown in Table 4.2, were funded by the University Grants Committee (UGC). The others were the Academy for Performing Arts, the Open University of Hong Kong (until 1997 called the Open Learning Institute), two technical colleges, seven Technical Institutes operated by the Vocational Training Council, Shue Yan College, and Chu Hai College. In 1996/97, the higher education sector enrolled over 139,450 students, forming approximately 24 per cent of the relevant age group (UGC 1996, pp.4-5). About 2 per cent of students came from mainland China and overseas countries. The UGC indicated in 1996 that it planned to increase the participation rate of non-local students to 4 per cent in the next two years, and to increase the proportion of non-local research postgraduates from 20 per cent to one third. This policy aimed to strengthen academic and cultural exchange.

Table 4.2: UGC-Funded Institutions, Hong Kong, 1998

Name of Institution	Founded
1. The University of Hong Kong (HKU)	1911
2. The Chinese University of Hong Kong (CUHK)	1963
3. The Hong Kong Polytechnic University (HKPU, formerly Hong Kong Polytechnic)	1972
4. The City University of Hong Kong (City U, formerly City Polytechnic of Hong Kong)	1984
5. The Hong Kong Baptist University (HKBU, formerly Hong Kong Baptist College)	1956
6. The Hong Kong University of Science & Technology (HKUST)	1988
7. Lingnan College (LC)	1967
8. The Hong Kong Institute of Education (HKIEd, created by amalgamating four Colleges of Education and the Institute of Language in Education)	1994

Macau has a much smaller population and more limited public resources. In 1998, it had one university offering degree programmes, a Polytechnic Institute offering diploma and bacharelato (professional degree) programmes, an Institute for Tourism Training which offered a degree programme, and the Asia International Open University offering diplomas, and bachelors and masters degrees by distance learning. Other bodies included the School of Judiciary & Police, and a branch of the United Nations University. The total enrolment in Macau's higher education institutions in 1996/97 was approximately 6,400 (Table 4.3). About 25 per cent of students were from mainland China and from Portuguese-speaking countries, such as Angola, Mozambique, Cape Verde, Guinea-Bissau and São Tomé & Príncipe. This proportion of non-local students was thus much greater than in Hong Kong.

In addition to the institutions mentioned above were various partnerships with external institutions. For example, in Macau an Inter-University Institute was established in 1996 as a partnership between the Diocese of Macau and the Catholic University of Portugal. Similarly, in Hong Kong the Australian Catholic University operated programmes in conjunction with Caritas, an education and social service organisation operated by the Catholic church. Many other external universities offered degrees in conjunction with the schools of continuing education of the UGC-funded institutions.

Table 4.3: Enrolments in Hong Kong and Macau Higher Education Institutions (Full-Time Equivalents), 1996

Hong Kong	Enrolments	Macau	Enrolments
UGC Institutions	87,000	University of Macau	3,100
Academy for Performing Arts (APA)	700	Macau Polytechnic Institute	1,000
Open Learning Institute (OLI)	8,000	Institute for Tourism Training	90
Vocational Training Council's Technical Colleges (VTC – TCs)	4,700	Asia International Open University (distance learning)	n.a.
Shue Yan College (Privately funded)	2,500	Others	n.a.
Others	26,000		
Total	128,900		6,400

Sources: UGC (1996), p.6; Chow (1997); Macau, Department of Education & Youth (1997b), p.9.

Planning of Higher Education Expansion

Education systems and policies develop under the influence of economic development, political considerations and social values (Psacharopoulos & Woodhall 1985, pp.14-15). Higher education systems and policies in Hong Kong and Macau are no exception to this general statement.

Trow (1974) defined higher education systems which enrolled up to 15 per cent of the age group as elite systems. He defined ones which enrolled between 15 and 40 per cent as mass systems; and defined ones with enrolment rates above 40 per cent as universal systems. On this definition, Hong Kong entered the era of mass higher education in 1993/94.

The Hong Kong government's decision to enter a system of mass higher education was based on a number of factors. First was the postulate of human capital theory that investment in higher education would increase the productivity of the population for further economic growth (UGC 1996). According to economists such as Schultz (1961), Becker (1964), Blaug (1970), Psacharopoulos (1985), McMahon (1991), and Weale (1992), education contributes directly to the growth of national income by improving the skills and productive capacities of the labour force. Based on this notion, from the mid-1970s the Hong Kong government used manpower forecasting as a planning tool for education policy (Bray 1997b; K.M. Cheng 1997b). In the first half of the 1990s, three manpower projections – in 1990, 1991 and 1994 – forecasted higher education manpower requirements up to 2001. The first two forecasts served as basic indicators for manpower requirements in Hong Kong in the 1990s, and higher education expanded correspondingly. The 1994 forecast projected a surplus of graduate labour. This projection, taken in conjunction with the report of a study on Preparation of Students for Tertiary Education (POSTE Team 1996), led to a policy change which slowed the pace of expansion and shifted attention to efficiency and quality.

The expansion in the late 1980s and early 1990s was also embarked upon for other reasons. First, it was to meet the government's long term goal of providing equal access to higher education. Second, it was a response to the strong social demand for higher education by the public. Third, many educators in Hong Kong believe that the decision made in October 1989 to accelerate expansion of higher education was a short-term reaction to a perceived crisis of confidence and credibility in the context of brain drain relating to the 1997 issue and the aftermath of Beijing's Tienanmen Square incident in June 1989 (Morris et al. 1994).

In 1993/94, Hong Kong's two polytechnics were upgraded to university status. In 1997, the Open Learning Institute and Lingnan College were also upgraded, and given the status of self-validation. These moves transformed university education from a binary to a unified system, and facilitated the administration of funding for degree pro-grammes. Since then, higher education in Hong Kong has operated in a segmented market where degree programmes are offered mainly by the UGC-funded institutions and the Open University of Hong Kong, and diploma and other sub-degree programmes are offered by the Hong Kong Institute of Education, technical institutes, and the Academy for Performing Arts.

Macau's system of education has been less developed, but made great strides during the 1990s. Portugal did not give Macau as much attention as the United Kingdom gave Hong Kong, and education services were not generally regarded as a public good throughout the bulk of Macau's 400 years of colonialism (Tang & Morrison 1998, p.246). Education was almost wholly dependent on private rather than public providers. The main reasons for this were twofold. First, at some points in history Portugal itself had a lower per capita GNP than its colony, and lacked public resources for development. Second, the Portuguese colonial regime was little interested in emancipating the peoples of its colonies (Cross 1987; Errante 1998).

In Macau, by the late-1980s it was clear that government neglect of education could no longer satisfy the social and economic needs of the global knowledge-based society of which the territory was increasingly becoming a part. The task at hand was considerable, and in the 1990s higher education in Macau was at an early stage of development. This reflected demand as well as supply. Because Macau's economy greatly relied on tourism and small labour-intensive industries, and because per capita incomes were lower, social demand for higher education was more limited than in Hong Kong. On the supply side, before 1988 public investment in higher education was almost non-existent. To some extent the gap was bridged by the private sector, but only in 1981 did a group of entrepreneurs establish Macau's first modern university, the University of East Asia (Mellor 1988). In 1988, the university was purchased by the Macau government and became a public institution. In 1991 it was renamed the University of Macau, and in 1997 it had 3,140 students.

Following the establishment of the Macau Polytechnic Institute in 1990, Macau's higher education system began to resemble the binary higher education system in Portugal (and also Hong Kong and the United Kingdom). The Macau Polytechnic Institute was created from the Polytechnic College which had been part of the University of East Asia. The Macau Polytechnic Institute offers diploma and bacharelato programmes, mainly in vocational subjects. The private Asia International Open University (AIOU) had a similar origin, having been formed in 1992 from the East Asia Open Institute which had previously been part of the University of East Asia. The AIOU operates in partnership with the Open University of Portugal, and offers distance courses particularly in business administration.

Shortfalls in Supply of Qualified Applicants and Concern about Quality

During the mid-1990s, Hong Kong educators became increasingly concerned that the supply of adequately qualified secondary school students was insufficient to fill all the places in the fast-expanding tertiary sector (J. Cheng 1995). In systems of mass higher education, not only the outstanding but also the average students are admitted to colleges and universities. During the mid-1990s, many educators in Hong Kong queried whether the latter could fulfil the expectations and requirements of this level (J. Cheng 1995; Postiglione 1996b; French 1997). To maintain quality, most higher education institutions introduced extra-academic programmes to enrich their students' competence. For instance, the HKUST, HKU, the two Polytechnic Universities and the HKIEd set up centres to upgrade their students' language competence. The allocation for extra language training for undergraduates in the UGC-funded institutions in the 1995-98 triennial funding period was HK$214 million. This included grants to assist the institutions to enhance students' oral and written English, oral Putonghua, and written Chinese. In 1996, HKU introduced a general education programme on the recommendation of its Careers Advisory Board to strengthen the core competencies of its students; and the CUHK proposed to extend the basic curriculum by one year to implement general education programmes and upgrade language and communication skills.

To ensure that graduates meet international standards, the UGC has undertaken periodic Teaching & Learning Quality Process Reviews (TLQPRs) of all UGC-funded institutions (Massy 1997; Imrie 1998). TLQPR panels have examined the internal and external validation processes, peer evaluation and assistance, students' evaluations of teaching, and facilities for teaching and learning. The panels have also examined informal communication channels between staff and students to see how well they supplement the formal processes. In response to the demand for quality assurance, between 1993 and 1998 seven UGC-funded institutions set up centres or units to improve the quality of teaching and learning.

In 1996, the University of Macau received official recognition to enjoy status similar to universities in Portugal, and the university has established links with over 70 foreign universities around the world (Zhou 1997). Regarding quality assurance measures, the University of Macau developed a self-validation process in 1997. The fact that the university is staffed by a team of international scholars helps to maintain a high standard (Koo 1999).

University Structure

The nature of university structures has major implications for the allocation of finance, design of curriculum, and strategies for teaching and learning. Structures also reflect societies' educational aims, and affect local academic relationships with global academic communities. For instance, structures may affect international recognition and facilitate or obstruct further study by local students who wish to go abroad.

When the quality of university students in Hong Kong became a major concern of higher education educators during the early 1990s, some Hong Kong participants suggested that the basic length of degree programmes should be extended from three to four years. For the CUHK this would have been a reversion to the basic structure which the institution had between its establishment in 1963 and the 1991 change forced upon it by the government. The change or reversion to a basic four-year degree, it was argued, would facilitate curriculum reform and strengthen general education as a supplement to students' major fields of study.

The argument about university structure was restarted by a report entitled 'Re-proposing the University Structure' published in 1996 by the Consultative Committee of the CUHK. The report stated that if the government refused to increase funding, the CUHK would rather accept fewer high-quality students than many low-quality students. The report also stated that a three-year degree structure could not satisfy the need to implement general education programmes which the CUHK had been pursuing in its curriculum. The proposal for a four-year university structure was echoed in a subsequent meeting of the heads of the eight UGC-funded institutions. Their request was stimulated by the growing concern about the quality of university education and the demand for a more liberal university education.

The debate about university structure has always been vigorous. Many educators in tertiary institutions are among those who favour a four-year structure and who argue that the extra year would permit improvement in the quality of products. Many educators in schools, by contrast, point out that the university sector already consumes a huge amount of resources and that an extended university structure would probably be at the expense of lower levels. In 1996 the government did not respond to the request for a four-year university structure, probably because of funding difficulties and the approach of the transfer of sovereignty. Education Commission Report No. 7 (1997, p.47) proposed a review of the entire education system, since the education structures of basic and higher education were interconnected. In 1998, two working groups were set up by the Education Commission to focus on (a) primary and junior-secondary education, and (b) post-junior-secondary education. The first stage of the review focused on the educational aims of different levels of education.

An ad hoc Working Group convened under the Heads of Universities Committee (HUCOM) was also set up in 1998 to examine the issues associated with the proposal to extend the basic duration of undergraduate education from three to four years. The committee's consultation document proposed a 5+1+4 post-primary education system, i.e. five years of basic secondary, one year of senior secondary, and four years of tertiary. The document proposed to use Hong Kong Certificate of Education Examination (HKCEE) results as the basic criteria for admission to Secondary 6 and universities. Two-thirds of university places were to be reserved for HKCEE candidates, this ratio being subject to revision as the internal secondary schools appraisal system developed. The new admission requirements, it was argued, could minimise examination pressure on students because in one-year matriculation programmes they would not sit for any public examination and therefore could develop talents in other aspects (HUCOM 1998, pp.7-8).

By the end of the consultation period, only 20 responses had been received. They did not include responses from either the Hong Kong Subsidised School Council or the

Hong Kong School Principals' Association. Secondary school personnel remained sceptical about the 5+1+4 structure, and were particularly concerned about the interface between post-secondary and tertiary education. School principals feared that the proposed 5+1+4 structure would threaten the survival of the sixth-form colleges; and they pointed out that shortening of the matriculated curriculum would change resource distribution in secondary schools. It was obvious that there were divided opinions on the 3+3+4 structure, the proposed 5+1+4 structure, and the 5+2+4 structure. The government decided to stall by preparing another consultation document in 1999.

Macau has also experienced a change of university structure. In 1981, the University of East Asia adopted a three-year basic structure. This was partly because the founders and administrators were mostly educators from Hong Kong, the United Kingdom and other Commonwealth universities, but was more strongly because the private university aimed to recruit not only local high school graduates but also applicants from Hong Kong, Malaysia, Singapore and other countries in the region which had education systems fitting a three-year university structure.

The change to a four-year structure began after the University of East Asia was purchased by the Macau government in 1988. The university became a public institution under the Higher Education Act of Macau (Hui 1994). Thereafter, the basic degree structure of the University of Macau matched that of the 13 state and eight private universities in Portugal with which it had close relationships. This provided more convenience to study or work in some of the European Community countries. By chance, it also matched the structure in mainland China, Taiwan, Canada and the USA, but this did not have strong implications for the work of the University of Macau.

Funding for Higher Education

Hong Kong's higher education system absorbs about 6 per cent of total recurrent public expenditure, and about one third of the government's education budget (UGC 1996, p.23). Direct public expenditure on tertiary education also accounts for about 0.7 per cent of Gross Domestic Product (GDP). This figure may be compared with that for member countries of the Organisation for Economic Co-operation & Development (OECD), whose allocation to tertiary education averaged 1.0 per cent of GDP in 1994 (OECD 1997, p.64). Among the OECD countries, the lowest in 1994 were South Korea (0.3 per cent) and Japan (0.5 per cent). However, these countries have large private sectors in tertiary education. At the other end of the scale, Canada devoted 1.6 per cent of GDP to direct public expenditures on tertiary education, and Finland devoted 1.5 per cent.

Given the range of these figures, it is difficult to reach firm judgements about what the 'right' level of public expenditure might be. Hong Kong's higher education has traditionally been dominated by the public sector – to the extent, as indicated in the chapter by Hui & Poon in this book, that the government actively prevented some private entrepreneurs from establishing institutions. This is very different not only from such OECD countries as South Korea and Japan, but also from such countries as Philippines, Indonesia, Colombia and India (World Bank 1994, p.35). The Hong Kong government did allow the Open Learning Institute (later called the Open University of Hong Kong) to operate on a self-funded basis following its establishment in 1989, but during the 1980s and 1990s the government seemed to move towards greater rather than less public funding for higher education by providing subsidies to the Baptist College and Lingnan College. Similar moves were evident in Macau, where, as noted, the private University of East Asia was purchased by the government in 1988, and then supplemented by other public institutions.

Within both territories, however, have been major shifts of policy on student fees in public tertiary institutions. Internationally, policy makers are split into two major groups on this topic. Some argue that higher education benefits the whole society and so should be financed out of general taxation. Others argue that since individuals gain both financial and non-economic benefits from their education, they should contribute to its cost by paying fees. The latter group points out that governments can still provide subsidies in the form of grants or loans to help students who could not afford to pay the fees without financial assistance (Woodhall 1995a, pp.427-428).

In order to cope with the growing cost, in 1991 the Hong Kong government decided on substantial increase of fees on the principle that the beneficiaries should pay more. International survey highlights three main ways through which students can contribute (Williams 1996). First, they can pay fees while studying. Second, their studies can be free of charge but their subsequent taxes can be higher to help pay for their successors' education. And third, students can borrow while they study and repay when they are earning. The Hong Kong government decided on a combination of the first and third options. In 1992/93, students' fees represented an average of 8.2 per cent of the recurrent cost of their education. This proportion was increased to 18.0 per cent in 1997/98 (Table 4.4). The argument behind the policy was that tuition fees combined with student aid were more efficient than fee-free education, and more equitable because fee-free education often favoured the children of rich parents more than the poor (Bray 1993, p.38; Woodhall 1995b, p.419).

Table 4.4: Tuition Fees for Degree Courses, Hong Kong, 1992/93–1997/98 (HK$)

	1992/93	1993/94	1994/95	1995/96	1996/97	1997/98
Degree courses	$11,598	$16,996	$24,000	$30,568	$37,346	$42,096
Sub-degree courses	$8,993	$12,745	$18,002	$23,267	$28,002	$31,574
Rate of increase (%)	16.0	46.6	41.2	29.3	12.7	12.7
Cost-recovery rate (%)	8.2	10.5	13.5	16.0	17.0	18.0

Source: Hong Kong, Education & Manpower Bureau (1997)

In 1996 the government commissioned a management consultancy firm, Ernst & Young, to review the situation. The firm proposed two basic areas of change. First, was that on equity grounds the government should make financial assistance available to all students requesting it. The consultants proposed that any student should be able to borrow up to a ceiling based on the student's tuition fees, academic expenses and living costs. Any grant assistance received would be subtracted from the maximum allowable loan. Second, the consultants recommended an increase in the annual interest charged on loans from 2.5 to 4.0 per cent. Other recommended changes included extending the loan repayment period from the first five years following graduation to 15 years, and reducing repayment amounts during periods of low or no income (Ernst & Young 1996).

The announcement of increased fees and the proposed changes in interest rates incited opposition from the students and the public. The government extended the public consultation period, during which it negotiated with student representatives. Finally, the

Chief Executive of the Hong Kong Special Administrative Region (Tung 1997b, p.97) announced that a non-means-tested student loan scheme would be made available for all students. The new scheme would charge annual interest of 1.5 per cent plus the current civil service housing loan scheme interest rate. This formula was expected to allow the government to cover the cost of borrowing and defaults. The interest rate was lower than the expected rate of inflation, which meant that the value of the loan principal was expected to depreciate in real terms during the period of the loan. The non-means-tested loan interest rate would be subject to review every six months, and the maximum loan would be capped at the tuition fee level, which in 1998/99 was HK$44,500 for degrees and HK$33,375 for diplomas. Students were expected to repay the loan in 40 quarterly instalments within 10 years of graduation. A student who borrowed up to the loan ceiling would have to pay about HK$1,700 each month. The new non-means-tested student loan complemented the existing means-tested student loan. It became available to all 70,000 full-time equivalent students of UGC funded programmes, 23,633 part-time tertiary students on courses of the Open University of Hong Kong, and about 3,000 full-time students of the Hong Kong Shue Yan College.

However, doubt remained on whether these provisions could meet all needs. Critics asserted that the vetting method for means-tested loans was unable to estimate accurately the assets and incomes of the applicants' families. Also, students considered the 8.2 per cent interest rate charged on the non-means-tested student loan – a rate which was based on the housing loan scheme for civil servants – to be rather high. Most students were reluctant to apply for non-means-tested loans unless they had no alternative. Students were worried about the burden of accumulated debt in circumstances of rising unemployment and economic downturn. Partly because of this, in 1998 the government announced that fees would be frozen at the level of the 1997/98 academic year.

The individual private costs of higher education were also high in Macau. The annual fee for a full-time degree was MOP$64,000 in 1997. However, all permanent residents of Macau were eligible for a 40 per cent fee reduction at the University of Macau (University of Macau 1997). In 1997, about 85 per cent of students at the University were local residents. Also, needy students could apply for loans from the Macau government's Department of Education & Youth if they were prepared to work in Macau after graduation (Koo 1994b); and a few scholarships were provided by local charitable organisations.

Worries about Graduate Unemployment

Higher education expansion in Hong Kong between 1990 and 1997 greatly increased the supply of graduates. Worries about unemployment emerged as a new issue, especially during the economic downturns in 1995/96 and 1997/98. Table 4.5 shows the student enrolments in six UGC-funded institutions from 1989/90 to 1995/96, and Table 4.6 shows the graduate numbers from six UGC-funded institutions from 1989/90 to 1995/96. Competition in the labour market intensified when the first and second groups of graduates after the higher education expansion in the early 1990s began to enter the labour market in 1995. These new graduates needed a longer lead time to find jobs. Many of them, including those with higher degrees, were unemployed at first (Y.T. Wong 1995). Graduate unemployment intensified in the second half of 1995, when overall unemployment hit 3.4 per cent. As explained in more detail by Ma's chapter in this book, this scenario had not been anticipated by planners earlier in the decade.

Table 4.5: Student Enrolments in Six UGC-funded Institutions, Hong Kong, 1989/90 to 1995/96

	1989/90	1990/91	1991/92	1992/93	1993/94	1994/95	1995/96
Sub-degree	12,198	12,446	13,407	12,090	10,214	9,370	9,414
Under-graduate	24,027	26,265	29,793	33,593	38,150	41,782	44,659
Taught Post-graduate	2,250	2,608	2,931	3,565	3,904	4,236	4,691
Research Post-graduate	729	783	1,348	1,943	2,276	2,547	3,012
Total student enrolment	39,205	42,102	47,480	51,190	54,544	57,935	62,045
Student enrol-ment (headcount)	54,833	57,824	64,942	68,109	70,181	72,154	75,520
Total head-count of stu-dents per 1000 population	9.6	10.1	11.3	11.7	11.9	11.9	12.2
Fte first-year first-degree places	7,426	8,575	10,665	12,090	12,726	14,253	15,073
% of relevant age group (age 17-20)	8.6%	10.2%	12.6%	14.5%	15.3%	17.4%	18.8%

Source: UGC Statistics, 1996

Table 4.6: Graduate Numbers from Six UGC-funded Institutions, Hong Kong, 1989/90 to 1995/96

Graduate Number	1989/90	1990/91	1991/92	1992/93	1993/94	1994/95*	1995/96*
Sub-degree	7,513	8,387	8,609	8,324	7,465	6,337	4,997
First degree	5,973	6,740	7,792	8,169	10,690	12,529	13,609
Taught post-graduate	1,719	1,867	2,117	2,274	2,668	3,227	3,810
Research Postgraduate	215	225	263	325	515	1,055	835
Total graduate number	15,420	17,219	18,781	19,092	21,338	23,148	23,231

* projected
Source: UGC Statistics, 1996

Competition in the graduate job market was intensified by an increasing number of returning emigrants (UGC 1996) and a new group of elite graduates migrating from mainland China. In 1998, the issue became more acute because of the Asian economic crisis. The annual economic growth rate dropped from 5.0 per cent to -5.6 per cent in the first three quarters of 1998, with prices sliding both in the stock market and real estate market, and overall unemployment surging to 6.2 per cent – the worst figure recorded in 23 years (*South China Morning Post*, 20 April 1999, p.1). Fresh university graduates anticipated more difficulties in seeking employment which matched their fields of study and with satisfactory remuneration. In November 1998, the graduate unemployment rate in Hong Kong reached 4.3 per cent (Hong Kong Census Household Survey 1998).

Since graduate unemployment was previously practically unheard of in Hong Kong, the situation greatly worried many university students and especially those in non-vocational programmes. Many students and parents who viewed the main function of higher education as preparing students directly for employment considered that higher education should generate a higher return than employment immediately after secondary education. When the graduate unemployment rate hit 3.3 per cent in 1995, and when graduate unemployment among medical graduates, teachers and social workers was reported again in 1997, this inevitably deepened worries about the possible occurrence of large scale graduate unemployment should the Hong Kong economy deteriorate seriously.

Similar patterns were evident in Macau. The establishment of the new higher education institutions in the 1990s increased the supply of graduates. In addition, many graduates came to Macau from abroad. As shown by Ma's chapter in this book, these included graduates from mainland China, Taiwan, Hong Kong and Portugal. During the 1990s, increasing numbers of Macau students chose to study in mainland China. In 1997, 600 undergraduates and 108 postgraduates were enrolled in higher education institutions in the mainland (*Macau Daily* 1997). Some students enrolled in professional subjects that were not available at the University of Macau, but others chose to study in mainland China because they considered qualifications from key Chinese universities to have a higher status than local qualifications. Lower tuition fees and living costs were also an important attraction. However, as Macau's economic performance slowed due to structural transformation during the mid- and late 1990s, low-cost labour-intensive manufacturing and real estate were badly affected. From 1993 to 1995, annual growth was maintained at a level between 3.6 and 5 per cent while unemployment surged from 2.1 to 3.6 per cent (Liu & Lee 1997). In 1998, unemployment reached 5.4 per cent (Bruning 1999, p.6), when the economy deteriorated further due to the Asian economic crisis and escalating violent crime. This situation badly affected the export industry and tourism, and created more difficulties for fresh graduates entering the labour market.

Implications for the Future

Higher education developments in Hong Kong and Macau before the 1990s were slow relative to other industrialised societies due to the lack of priority in government allocation of resources. During the 1990s, the sector achieved significant quantitative and qualitative progress in both territories. For policy makers, this undoubtedly was a great achievement. However, while students who would otherwise have been excluded benefited from increased access, the increasing private cost of higher education together with competition in the labour market diminished the benefits. As noted in other contexts (e.g. Ashworth 1997), private rates of return declined in the short term and the investment in higher education appeared more risky from the perspectives of students and their families. However, the long term social and individual benefits of higher education in relation to national economic growth should not be underestimated (McMahon 1998, p.449).

The reversion to China of sovereignty over Hong Kong and Macau will certainly increase linkages between the territories' higher education systems and that of the Chinese mainland. The participation rate in the mainland at the end of the 1990s was only about 2 per cent, and thus much lower. Economic and social reforms in the mainland had already increased demand for highly educated personnel, and both Hong Kong and Macau appeared to be obvious locations for providing the necessary training.

In terms of governance, Hong Kong's system of higher education system remained modelled on the dominant system in the United Kingdom, even after the 1997 change of sovereignty. English remained the medium of instruction in most institutions, and most courses had the type of three-year structure followed in English (but not Scottish) universities. Requests were renewed by universities to move to a four-year structure, but the matter was not immediately settled by the government. In parallel, Macau's institutions of higher education maintained close links with counterparts in Portugal as well as mainland China and Hong Kong. The concept of 'One Country, Two Systems' allowed policies in both Hong Kong and Macau to be decided by local educators, but academic cooperation with universities in mainland China education increased. At the same time, links with Europe did not imply continued ties to a fixed model. Thus, higher education was set to change markedly in the United Kingdom and Portugal, in line with the needs of the global economy and learning society (Scott 1995; Dearing 1997). Continued investment in human capital was clearly essential for maintenance of competitive edges in the global society.

From the perspective of continuity and development, higher education in both Hong Kong and Macau was incorporated into the global higher education system. This was greatly promoted by information technology, which speeded up the dissemination of knowledge extensively and effectively (Carnoy 1996; K.M. Cheng 1998; Spring 1998). Information technology in learning and teaching in higher education around the world has reduced the significance of national boundaries. Higher education has also become an institution of society and not simply an institution in society (Barnett 1994). Both in Hong Kong and Macau, higher education is seen as essential for economic survival, not simply for welfare. Being members of the global society, higher education in these two territories will continue to converge with what Kerr (1982) called the huge global multiversity.

Political, Economic and Social Issues

5

Church, State and Education during the Colonial Period

LEUNG Kit Fun, Beatrice

In different parts of the world, the relationship between church and state has historically ranged on a scale extending from relatively mild tensions in western democracies to fundamental conflict of authority in authoritarian and especially communist states (Weigel 1987; 1992). In many colonies, church and state worked in partnership, sharing the workload in education and other services, with the government granting land and financial aid for recurrent expenditure to church schools (Holmes 1967; Igwe 1987). However, colonial education was usually designed for facilitating colonial rule rather than for national development (Tsurumi 1977; Altbach & Kelly 1991). To make the programme of education for the maintenance of imperialism more acceptable, colonisers commonly sought the cooperation of missionaries (Boutilier 1978; Blakemore & Cooksey 1980; Brock & Tulasiewicz 1988; Carmody 1992). Since church-run education played an important role in colonial education systems, the decolonisation process has also involved church-run education. However, some scholars argue that education can be a vehicle for resisting as well as promoting decolonisation of attitudes and structures (Lee & Bray 1995; Bray 1997a).

This chapter particularly focuses on the Roman Catholic church, since it has been the largest single provider of education in both Hong Kong and Macau. As the chapter will show, the Roman Catholic church cooperated in education with both the British authorities in Hong Kong and the Portuguese authorities in Macau. Education provided by the Roman Catholic church calls for attention not only because its missionaries were among the first educators to establish Western-type schools in the two colonies, but also because its schools remain prestigious and continue to attract many applicants.

The chapter begins by discussing the partnership between the church and state during the main colonial period. It then turns to Catholic education and its interaction with the societies of Hong Kong and Macau in the processes of decolonisation. This includes consideration of the degree to which the return of sovereignty over the two territories to the People's Republic of China (PRC) has affected Catholic educational policies. Discussion is in the context of Catholic-China relationships, which have been an underlying problem for Catholic education policy in the decolonisation processes (Leung 1992; Tan 1997).

All religions, including Catholicism, hold a world view which is irreconcilable with the atheist ideology of Marxism-Leninism, and the Chinese Communist Party (CCP) has indicated that it has no intention of endorsing any religious beliefs. CCP leaders from the beginning held negative feelings towards all religions because religions were considered to be part of cultural imperialism. Being nationalists, CCP leaders who treasured national pride and dignity particularly disapproved of Christianity, which they considered to be a foreign religion. The Catholic problem was aggravated by the claim of the Vatican to exercise authority over its clergy in organisational and theological terms, and by the Vatican's sovereign status in international law (Hanson 1978; Lazzarotto 1982). Article 26 the Chinese constitution (PRC 1982) prohibited any education run by Christian churches.

Catholic Education during the Main Colonial Period

Hong Kong

The British rulers did not show strong favour to the French and Italian Catholic missionaries who headed the Catholic church in Hong Kong at different periods, as the British had a closer affinity to the Anglican Church. However, soon after the British occupied Hong Kong in 1841, both Protestant and Catholic missionaries started to provide care for abandoned and other children (Sweeting 1990, pp.143-153). Italian missionaries began to provide education for both British and Chinese boys in 1843. Later, both Catholic and Protestant missionaries became allies with the government in education and other services. In 1848, with the arrival of the Catholic French Sisters of St. Paul de Chartres, an orphanage and an old people's home were established (Ticozzi 1983). Many church schools received financial support from the Hong Kong government (Hong Kong Public Record Office [HKPRO], series 147 2/1). These church schools included many prestigious institutions, including the Diocesan Boys' School, the Diocesan Girls' School, the French (St. Paul's) Convent School, De La Salle College, Maryknoll Convent School, Wah Yan Branch Senior School, and St. Mary's School. In the government's Board of Education during the initial period after World War II, three church leaders (two Catholic and one Protestant) were among the 17 appointed members who advised the government on education policy (HKPRO, series 147 2/2 (2)).

The civil war between the Kuomintang and the Chinese Communist Party broke out in China after World War II with the withdrawal of the Japanese from Chinese soil. The defeat of the Kuomintang and the establishment of the People's Republic of China caused hundreds of thousands of mainlanders who refused to live under a communist regime to migrate to Hong Kong. Most of them needed relief services, including medical assistance and education for their children.

During the early stages of the influx, the Hong Kong government viewed the immigrants as temporary asylum seekers, and made no long term plans to provide education or housing for them. Because resources were limited, government officials and local newspapers felt that priority provision should be given to people who had been born in Hong Kong (Editorials, *South China Morning Post [SCMP]* 15 and 19 December 1949, 10 April 1950). However, the refugees from the mainland were accompanied by missionaries who had been expelled by the atheist CCP for political reasons. The influx of personnel and relief goods enabled the Christian churches in Hong Kong to initiate some social services for refugees including education and housing. The American Foreign Missionary Society (Maryknoll Fathers) was an example. From 1945 it was affiliated to the American Catholic Relief Service, which was headquartered in New York and which had provided social services including education to backward areas of China (Maryknoll Archive no. MPBA Hong Kong 9/8). After the arrival of the Maryknoll Fathers in Hong Kong in the 1950s, the China projects funded by the Catholic Relief Service were diverted to Hong Kong for Chinese refugees. Thus, large scale relief and education services were launched by churches in Hong Kong even before the government was stimulated to begin refugee services by such disasters as the Shek Kip Mei squatter fire of 25 December 1953.

The initiative taken by churches in Hong Kong in the areas of education and relief work not only reduced the burden on the government but also presented the church as an ideal partner when the government later sought contractors in a channelling mechanism for education services. During the 1950s, this channelling in the education field was only through Christian churches and not through Chinese traditional civil organisations such as the Tung Wah Group of Hospitals or the various workers' unions.

Political considerations were the principal determinant of this policy. In the international political arena, Soviet-American rivalry dominated international relations during the Cold War period (1945-91). The United Kingdom was a traditional ally of the USA, and was anxious to minimise the spread of communism in Hong Kong. The CCP's policy during this period was to spread its ideology in Hong Kong, and to encourage Hong Kong workers to support activities in Southern China (Deng & Lu 1997, p.228). The CCP also exported its ideology and provided financial aid to political groups in Vietnam, Cambodia, Burma, Thailand, the Philippines, Indonesia and Malaysia.

The Hong Kong government's stand may be illustrated by the remarks of its governor, Sir Alexander Grantham, when opening a school in 1948. He highlighted what he called the communist practice of "deforming and twisting ... youthful mind[s]", and stated that the government would not tolerate political propaganda in schools (*SCMP* 16 December 1948, p.7). For political reasons, the government deported the principal of Heung Tao Middle school in 1950, deregistered several teachers at the Portland Street Motor Car Workers' Children's School in 1950 and 1951, and closed Nanfang College in 1951.

In each of these cases, the Hong Kong Teachers' Welfare Association and the leftist press printed sharp criticism against the government action (Sweeting 1993, p.53). However, support for such a stance was provided by the views of Malcolm Macdonald, British Commissioner-General for South East Asia. Macdonald had experience with the CCP's subversion of British rule in Malaya and Singapore, and after a visit to Hong Kong stressed the dangers of infiltration there. One safeguard, he suggested, lay in prohibition of political parties. Macdonald argued that it would be better to prevent the birth of the CCP than to try to control it later. He also recommended the government to work with Christian churches rather than with the traditional Chinese associations when it sought partners or contractors in education and other social services (HKPRO 1949, April 30).

The challenges facing the government were greatly exacerbated by rapid population growth. After the Japanese occupation of Hong Kong, Chinese civilians, many of whom had moved into China during the war, returned to Hong Kong at the rate of almost 100,000 a month. The population, which by August 1945 had been reduced to about 600,000, rose to 1.8 million by the end of 1947. In 1948-49, Hong Kong received an influx unparalleled in its history, and by mid-1950 the population reached 2.2 million (Hong Kong 1998, p.393).

To assist in the education sector, in 1950 a British expert, Norman Fisher, was invited to advise on policies. However, his report gave little attention to the immediate needs of the Chinese refugees (HKPRO, series 147 2/2 (1), 127). The Board of Education met from time to time to discuss strategies to cope with the rapid increase of children and the great demand for primary education. One member was Bishop R.O. Hall, the Anglican bishop of Hong Kong. He suggested that only Christian church schools, not non-religious secular schools, should be used to provide the urgently needed primary education. One of his memoranda included the statement that:

> In view of what was said by two members of the Board who do not share my Christian faith, I could not say publicly that my main concern is with the use of Christian churches by subsidy in primary education. The government both in UK and in its colonial policy recognises that by and large only religion can resist Communism and that non religious secular primary education on a large scale will produce atheistic proletariat as prepared ground for Communist sowing. I very much hope that the Roman Catholic Church will with encouragement from the Department strengthen and enlarge their primary school work. I think the Director understands my view on this matter, but it's not easy to say it publicly (HKPRO, series 147 2/2 (1), 119).

The reply from the Secretary of Board of Education on 21 September 1950 reveals support for Bishop Hall's perspective:

> I agree entirely with your view.... I consider myself that religion should play a more and more important part in school since it is the very essence of cultured civilisation.... I read the report of your address with interest and can well sympathise with your feelings (HKPRO, series 147 2/2 (1), 120).

The Anglican bishop's stance may be interpreted as one of Christian compassion for school-aged children who would otherwise have been denied access to schooling; but it was clearly also influenced by political considerations and by anxiety to resist the possible spread of communism.

As a result of such forces, the cooperation between the government and church leaders led to tremendous growth of church schooling. In 1953, 22 new Catholic schools were opened (14 in the New Territories, and eight in Hong Kong and Kowloon); and by 1963 a further 33 Catholic schools had been added (16 in the New Territories, and 17 in Hong Kong and Kowloon). During this period, the number of students going to Catholic schools increased from 3,909 to 28,029 (Hong Kong Catholic Diocesan Archive no. HK-DA S.6-01, F/03). In most cases the government constructed the school buildings and then invited the church to run the schools with government subsidy covering the recurrent expenditure. The government at first allowed school halls and playgrounds to be used for Sunday worship, and later provided land adjacent to schools for two thirds of the lease prices, together with land for the priests' living quarters at full lease prices.

These measures gave a political dimension to the partnership or contractorship between the Hong Kong government and Christian churches. The two parties cooperated closely for their own interests with the common foundation of anti-communism. Subsequently, however, the partnership created a serious problem for the Catholic and other Christian churches. The churches were instruments for the government to achieve its political ends in the 1950s and 1960s, but after the 1967 pro-leftist riot in Hong Kong had been crushed and the CCP's underground network had been cracked (Xu 1995 p.75), communist influence in Hong Kong was greatly reduced. The government then redistributed some of its subsidies to schools sponsored by religious bodies to those sponsored by traditional Chinese associations such as the Po Leung Kuk and the Tung Wah Group of Hospitals. The move signified that the value of Christian education to the government had considerably decreased in the 1970s. However, the anti-communist label remained attached to the Catholic church and its education, and the ideological incompatibility created a heavy psychological burden for local Catholics vis-à-vis the handover of Hong Kong to Chinese rule (Chan & Leung 1996). The anti-communism within the Catholic education circle nurtured by the British in Hong Kong gave extra anxiety to Hong Kong Catholic leaders responsible for running Catholic education in the post-colonial framework. In Macau, the Catholic church did not have a similar direct link with the government in anti-communist activities, and the Catholic leadership there found it easier to adapt to the prospect of the post-colonial era in both education and other domains.

Macau
The Macau Catholic church, with its first Portuguese bishop, Melchior Carneiro, became part of the governing group before Lisbon sent its first governor to Macau in the 16th century (Teixeira 1969, 1991). This laid the foundation for the harmonious church-state relationship in Macau. Like the church-state cooperation in Hong Kong, this relationship was strengthened by the partnership between the Macau Catholic church and the government in education and other social services.

Shortly after their arrival, the Jesuits in Macau opened a school for reading and writing (Gomes dos Santos 1968, p.8) in 1572; and, as recounted by Hui & Poon in this book, in 1594 the General of the Jesuits in Rome authorised the creation of a college offering university-level level instruction in Macau by upgrading the Madre de Deus school. The resulting St. Paul's University College offered degree courses from 1597 to 1762. Also worth noting is that educational provision was initiated for Portuguese orphans in 1718 (Teixeira 1982, p.280). This was the origin of what today is the prestigious Catholic school, Colégio Santa Rosa de Lima, with Portuguese, Chinese and English sections. In Hong Kong, the government 30 years after the arrival of the British took up leadership in education even at the risk of a row with the Catholic church in the period 1873-78 on the issue of religious education in schools (HKPRO series HK-DA S6.2, F/01). In Macau, by contrast, the government avoided responsibility for education even of Portuguese children until nearly 300 years after commencement of the colonial era. Even then, the government paid no attention to education for Chinese children. Nevertheless, in 1819 the first Macau Chinese private school, run by a Chinese association, came into being. Then in 1903, both the Canossian Sisters and the Salesian Fathers opened girls' and boys' schools for Chinese orphans, which in the course of time developed into Chinese primary schools for the public (Cheong 1991). This was the beginning of Church education for the Chinese who constitute 95 per cent of Macau's population.

In terms of education policy and administration, for many decades even in the 20th century the Macau authorities held a non-interventionist attitude. This led to a great diversity of models of educational provision; and the environment depended heavily on Catholic education. Although the Macau government formed a Department of Education in the 1960s, its initial role for the non-government sector was limited to registration of schools. In the 1970s the government began to subsidise not-for-profit private schools, but Catholic education in poor areas like Green Island received only a small subsidy.

Even with the great flow of refugees to Macau from mainland China in the 1950s, the Catholic church rather than the government took up the responsibility to provide education, building 12 primary and secondary schools for the refugees. As in Hong Kong, many of the personnel operating these schools were missionaries and others who had either been expelled or had fled from the mainland. The Macau branch of the American Catholic Relief Service was established, and provided food and medical care for refugee children in the schools.

The December 1966 riot in Macau, which was a spill-over of the Cultural Revolution in the mainland, was a turning-point in economic, social and political spheres. While the Hong Kong government was able to stand firm in the face of similar pressures, the Macau government crumbled. This led to Lisbon's humiliation, and the Portuguese government sent the Macau governor to make a public apology to the local Chinese. The Portuguese lost much of their popular support in Macau, and for some years social order and security were chiefly maintained by the pro-China neighbourhood associations and other influential social, religious and economic organisations rather than by the government.

During the 1966 riot, the Macau Catholic church, being a traditional ally of the Portuguese government, was also a target. The largest diocesan secondary school, St. Joseph's, was surrendered to pro-leftist demonstrators. Slogans were chanted, and big character posters were put on the exterior wall of the school. The posters demanded the removal of the pro-Taiwan principal, a Macau diocesan priest, who had to make an immediate departure to Hong Kong and spent the rest of his life there. After this incident, the rise of pro-China influence was mirrored in reduced support for the Catholic church. The victory of the pro-leftists in Macau frightened the Catholic personnel, including many of those working in education.

For political and ideological reasons, even before the riot the Catholic church had become introverted and had begun to give up its leadership in education. The history of the Macau Chinese Education Association reflects this change. The Association was a trade union for teachers, which had been founded in 1920 under the leadership of a Chinese Catholic priest, Fr. James Liu. When the Association became pro-China in the 1950s, Catholic priests and nuns who were members left the Association in disagreement with the new political stance (Lai 1996). The leadership vacuum in the Association was filled by pro-leftist educationists, and has remained with them. After the riot, religious congregations in Macau transferred some of their personnel to Hong Kong and elsewhere, which further weakened Catholic services including education and encouraged further growth of the pro-China sector.

The departure of some religious orders from Macau led to the restructuring of Catholic schools under the Catholic Macau diocese. A network of six diocesan secondary schools under the name of Colégio Diocesano de São José was established, with six schooling locations scattered around the territory. In 1993, the six campuses had 6,024 students and 132 classrooms, and formed the largest school in Macau (Macau, Department of Education & Youth 1994c). The restructuring of diocesan schools improved the management and quality of education, and helped Catholic sector to regain some of its strength and bargaining power.

Catholic Education during the Decolonisation Period

Immediately before and at the time of the 1984 Sino-British declaration on the future of Hong Kong, dominant attitudes within the Catholic church in Hong Kong were apprehensive about the post-colonial future of the territory. In September 1983, for example, the diocesan spokesman stated that it was "very likely" that priests, particularly foreign priests, would not be allowed to maintain ministries to nurture their believers after 1997 (Tan 1997, pp.74-75). One month after the signature of the 1984 declaration, *Kung Kao Po*, the Chinese diocesan weekly newspaper, interviewed nine principals of diocesan schools. Five of them expressed doubts that the promises in the declaration would be honoured by the Chinese government, and none of the other four expressed confidence (Tan 1997, p.76).

As time progressed, however, attitudes became more positive. The Hong Kong prelate's 1989 pastoral exhortation was entitled *March Towards a Bright Decade*, and included education as a focus of attention (Wu 1989, section 6). One result of the focus on education was a reform of the Catholic Board of Education, which had been founded in 1977 to increase unity among Catholics schools. In 1995 the Board was restructured to include superiors of religious congregations which sponsored large numbers of schools. With their leaders in the restructured body, there was a stronger chance that religious congregations and the diocese could work together and even adopt a common stand on important issues. The Board was convened by the Cardinal, the highest Catholic leader in Hong Kong, and chaired by the Episcopal Delegate for Education. A Catholic Development Committee was added, with representatives from Catholic schools as members, to implement policies made by the Board. The Catholic Education Office was created to serve the Board and the Committee and meet secretarial needs.

The restructuring promoted unity and communication among Catholic schools, and was considered particularly important in view of the impending political transition. Although no one could predict the exact changes in the first few years of post-colonial rule, preparation was considered prudent and a way to strengthen the bargaining power of Catholic education. One project of particular importance, examined in detail by Tse's chapter in this book, focused on textbooks and teaching materials for civic education. The project covered both primary and secondary levels, and was a joint effort of the Catholic Education Office and the Catholic Centre for Religion & Society. The Catholic Board of Education also addressed the question whether secondary schools should teach in English or Chinese. While this topic had a pedagogical element, it was also widely considered politically significant in the prevailing climate (Tan 1997, pp.77-78).

Parallel developments were evident in Macau. During the 1980s, the Macau Catholic Schools' Association had been formed to bring Catholic school principals together to discuss common problems. When Catholic education did not have specific problems calling for action, the Association still gave members a framework for mutual collegial support. Perhaps the most obvious policy domain in which the Association played a role was in opposition to the government proposal to make Portuguese a compulsory second language starting from primary school. The Macau Catholic Schools' Association acted as a focal point for opposition not only by Catholic schools but also by other schools, arguing that the proposal aimed in an inappropriate way to perpetuate Portuguese culture in the post-colonial period. In this particular instance, rather in contrast both to previous patterns in Macau and to patterns in Hong Kong, church and colonial state were in conflict. Moreover, for the first time in history the Macau Catholic Schools' Association discussed the problem of teaching Portuguese with the pro-leftist Macau Chinese Education Association. The Catholic schools and pro-leftist schools did not agree to publish a joint communiqué, but on this particular issue they operated in harmony. Catholic leaders learned that strength lay in collaboration, and that such collaboration sometimes needed concession and compromise.

Like its counterpart in Hong Kong, the Catholic church in Macau also embarked on significant initiatives in civic education. The bulk of the materials were prepared by a priest who was also principal of the Instituto Salesiano da Imaculada Conceição. The initiatives were less comprehensive, and were undertaken later than in Hong Kong. As explained in Tse's chapter in this book, however, they were another important dimension of the education sector in Macau's transitional period.

Preparation of civic education materials was not a simple task because it demanded delicate balances. Since in both Hong Kong and Macau the materials were intended for use in the post-colonial period as well as during the transition, the writers had to heed the perspectives of the PRC government as well as of the church. It seems that they achieved the necessary balances, for the Hong Kong books were endorsed by the Catholic Education Office and then accepted for republication and sale throughout the PRC by the Lanzhou People's Press. Finance for the Macau project was provided by the Salesian congregation.

The preparations for Chinese rule by Hong Kong and Macau Catholic leaders in the education sector were influenced by political considerations. The fear of revenge in the post-colonial period because of the church's explicit anti-communist partnership with the government in Hong Kong, and the fear in both territories of being undermined by patriotic schools, prompted Catholic leaders to take two steps for protection. First was an effort to promote unity within the Catholic education circle for mutual support in case of adversity; and second was the decision to prepare civic education materials before pro-China materials were launched. Concerning the latter, the leadership hoped that early action would permit their materials to be accepted by both the Catholic church and the governments of the respective Special Administrative Regions (SARs).

In general, however, the Catholic churches in Hong Kong and Macau lacked comprehensive policies on education. As had been the case before the decolonisation period, they mainly reacted to government policies and social pressures. The civic education issue was a response to the criticism that mission schools were insufficiently patriotic. The compromise in the civic education materials was a point of departure which showed that the Catholic authorities in both Hong Kong and Macau were willing to be flexible in cooperating with the post-colonial regime.

Conclusions

Issues in church-state relations in Hong Kong and Macau have had both similarities and differences. Historically, the chief commonality was in the ways that churches and governments worked together to provide education. During the 19th century the Hong Kong government gave more active support to the churches, but the Macau government was ideologically well-disposed towards the mission schools. In more recent times, the chief commonality has been the China factor. The nature of the church-state partnership in Hong Kong education during the 1950s was strongly influenced by the British goal of curbing the spread of communism from China. On the other side of the Pearl River estuary, there was a power struggle between the leftists and the Macau authority in the 1966 riot, and the Macau government, which had been the traditional partner of the

Catholic church, was humiliated. Subsequently, the education sector had to be shared more evenly with pro-China groups. Left-wing so-called patriotic schools grew substantially in number, and by the early 1990s embraced almost one third of the student population in the private sector (Chen 1994). By that time the share of Catholic education had declined from above 80 per cent in the 1950s to just 52 per cent.

Due to ideological incompatibility between Marxism-Leninism and church teaching, in the international arena the Catholic church in general has had a cool or even negative relationship with socialist states. However, both the PRC and the SAR governments have considered it appropriate to cooperate with civil organisations including the Catholic church to maintain prosperity and stability in the two territories after the handover. On their side, the Hong Kong and Macau Catholic churches wish to survive and to continue their service to their peoples. MacKenzie's international portrait (1993, p.47) pointed out that in general:

> The decline of missionary school provision in the latter part of the twentieth century, and the diminution in the status of colonialism as an acceptable relationship between nations, has evolved new interactions between Church and state, which despite their many variations, can rarely be characterised any longer as 'religion supporting imperialism'.

Some of the changes in Hong Kong and Macau occurred later than in other colonies, chiefly because the colonial transition itself occurred later. However, MacKenzie's observation is applicable to both Hong Kong and Macau in the late colonial era. In both Hong Kong and Macau, the long period of political transition allowed the churches to find new roles for themselves and to anticipate relationships with their new government counterparts. This was facilitated by the termination of Cold War political tensions, and circumstances in the 1990s were very different from the clashes between churches and communists in post World War II Czechoslovakia, Hungary, Yugoslavia and Romania (Tan 1997, p.71). Thus, broader forces softened the hard stances previously evident both in the Roman Catholic church and in the PRC. It remains to be seen how much further the two sides will go in their adjustment and mutual compromise. Meanwhile, the new political frameworks have permitted considerable continuity as well as requiring various changes.

6

Higher Education, Imperialism and Colonial Transition

Hui Kwok Fai, Philip & Poon Lai Man, Helen

This chapter poses a historical question: how did colonial states intervene in the development of higher education and use it as a means of colonisation and imperialism as evidenced by Macau and Hong Kong? The history of higher education in the two colonies illustrates how higher education was controlled by the two colonial states and served the interests of their suzerains, Portugal and the United Kingdom (UK).

A case-based comparative strategy is employed in the chapter. Four institutions are selected to illustrate the practices and rationales underlying higher education development and its relationship to state intervention. Table 6.1 lists the institutions at different periods of colonial rule. The two oldest institutions selected are St. Paul's University College (SPUC) which was founded in Macau in 1594, and the University of Hong Kong (HKU) which was founded in 1911. These were the only universities in the two territories during the main colonial period. The other two institutions selected are the University of East Asia (UEA) which was founded in Macau in 1981, and the Hong Kong Baptist College (HKBC) which was founded in 1956. These institutions were established as private bodies and then transformed into public ones during the late colonial period. We posit that colonial governments commonly try to maintain their influences in colonies in post-colonial periods, and that education is one of the major social institutions for actualising such influence. This is what Law (1997, p.42) defines as neocolonialism, which is "the adjustment of colonial mechanism, practice or traditions or creation of new ones by the departing sovereign power or its allies to support the preservation of their interests". In Hong Kong and Macau, the colonial governments initiated higher education expansion during the period of political negotiation over sovereignty, and the change of status of HKBC and UEA occurred within the same period.

Table 6.1: Four Higher Education Institutions in Macau and Hong Kong, Compared in Different Periods

	Macau	Hong Kong
Main colonial period (before 1970s)	Establishment of St. Paul's University College	Establishment of the University of Hong Kong
Late colonial period	Establishment and transformation of the University of East Asia	Expansion and transformation of the Hong Kong Baptist College

Using the four cases, the chapter compares the development of higher education in the two colonies across a time span of four centuries, and explores how the colonial governments intervened and determined the pace and course of higher education development. Despite decades of neglect of higher education, both Macau and Hong Kong witnessed abrupt expansion and reform during the period of state power transition. The authors argue that higher education systems in the two colonies were used as an instrument for Portuguese and British imperialism. Hong Kong was treated as a British pawn in relationships with China and in international political manoeuvres, and Macau was the base for disseminating Portuguese culture to China. Colonial policies, including higher education policies, were influenced by Sino-British and Sino-Portuguese relationships. This socio-economic dynamic has not been previously studied within the historical contexts of Macau and Hong Kong, and is a neglected topic in other parts of the world. The chapter builds on existing literatures on comparative higher education and on education and colonialism.

Theories of Imperialism, Colonialism and Education

Theories of Imperialism
'Imperialism' is a catchword that has brought people together in both self-assertion and self-defence. Reynolds (1981) proposed four modes of imperialism: the power-security theory of imperialism, economic imperialism, ideological imperialism, and socio-biological imperialism. The first two are the most relevant here. The power-security hypothesis argues that by seeking and gaining power in the world, the state can create its own security and achieve a position of hegemony in international politics. Such imperialism extends power through the subjugation of weaker states by force or diplomacy.

Most economic theories of imperialism revolve around Marxism, in which Karl Marx's ideas of contradiction and conflict emerging from the capitalist mode of production and the notion of capital accumulation are the essence. According to this perspective, the main reasons for imperialist expansion were the need to guarantee sources of raw materials, to provide outlets for surplus capital, to create profits from investment, and to ensure markets. When the advanced capitalist states entered into that mode of production and were forced to compete for economic territory, it is argued, wars and the partition of colonies were inevitable (Reynolds 1981, pp.70-75).

Colonialism and Education
Colonialism has been defined as "the oppression, humiliation, or exploitation of indigenous peoples" (Nadel & Curtis 1964, p.3). Hong Kong and Macau were colonised in the classical manner. Altbach & Kelly (1984) collected case studies of colonial schooling to illustrate colonial educational practices and their underlying rationales. For example, France gained control of Indochina between 1858 and 1900, and provided some schooling from elementary to university level for the colonised (Kelly 1984). However, by 1937 only 631 indigenous students had enrolled at the university level. The United States adopted an inequality policy in the Philippines, expanding the school system in agricultural villages but encouraging private schools from elementary through college to serve the urban and provincial elites (Foley 1984). Treating Taiwanese as second-class citizens, the Japanese colonial government implemented ethnic discrimination in education in Taiwan during the colonial period (Tsurumi 1984).

Carnoy (1974) has conceived of colonial education as an instrument through which the imperial powers attempted to train the natives to do the empire's bidding. This may be exemplified by the impact of colonialism on African education. Nkabinde (1997, p.184), with particular reference to South Africa, has noted that:

> Colonial education for Africans did not lead to true knowledge and understanding. Such education prepared Africans to be servants to their colonial masters.

Nkabinde added (p.185) that "educational expansion, far from rendering social uplift-ment and/or economic development, served to render education little more than a sophisticated mechanism for the recruitment of elites". Throughout the continent, Afri-cans were not generally allowed to plan or structure their own education systems. The colonial languages (mainly English, French and Portuguese) were used as the principal languages of instruction in formal schooling. This has left a legacy in which colonial languages remain dominant in many independent African states, and African languages are devalued. Similar phenomena may be observed in Hong Kong and Macau, though with some distinct features arising from the complex socio-economic structures of the two societies.

Macau and Hong Kong under Colonial Rule

Review of the history of Macau and Hong Kong helps clarify understanding of the development of higher education in these two small but unique colonies. Despite de-velopment along different paths, the histories of the two colonies were directly influ-enced by the relative political strengths of, and relationships between, their original and colonial mother states, namely China, the United Kingdom and Portugal.

Hong Kong under British Rule

Table 6.2 classifies the 155-year colonial history of Hong Kong into five periods ac-cording to political changes in Hong Kong and China. In 1842, China was for the first time opened up to international mercantile interests when the Qing Dynasty was de-feated by the British in the First Opium War. Using Hong Kong as the stepping stone, Britain became the dominant Western imperial power compelling China to open its treaty ports to trade, and set up the extra-territoriality system to enjoy foreigners' pri-vileges (Tang 1992). From this point onward, China, which was militarily weak, became a semi-colony of the Western imperial powers. As Hong Kong was chiefly a base for penetration of China, the welfare of the people living there was not a strong concern of the British colonisers. Accordingly, the colonial regime held an indifferent attitude in social welfare, including education.

After the establishment of the Republic of China in 1911, the British changed their colonial policy in Hong Kong. While keeping a harmonious relationship with the Re-publican government, the British took a more aggressive approach towards education in Hong Kong, especially higher education. They felt that educating the youths in Hong Kong helped actualise Britain's imperial education policy. The development of the University of Hong Kong following its establishment in 1911 is a good case in point. The higher education policy resonated with British diplomatic policy of appeasement.

Table 6.2: Relationships between Hong Kong, Britain and China, Mid-19th to Late 20th Centuries

Period	Polity		Colonial status of Hong Kong	State power		Diplomatic policy		Higher education policy in Hong Kong
	China	Britain		China	Britain	China	Britain	
1842-1911	feudal empire	monarchy/ parliament	British colony	weak	strong	ignorance, tolerance	expansion by gunboat	indiffer-ence
1911-1949	Republic	monarchy/ parliament	British colony	weak	strong	tolerance	balance of power appeasement	State inter-vention
1949-1971	com-munist republic	monarchy/ parliament	British colony	strong	strong	self-reliance, anti-imperialism	conciliatory	State inter-vention
1971-1984	com-munist republic	monarchy/ parliament	British territory	strong	strong	full diplomatic relations	full diplomatic relations	State inter-vention
1984-1997	com-munist republic	monarchy/ parliament	British territory	strong	strong	cooperation, conflict	cooperation, conflict	State inter-vention

In 1949, the Communist Party seized power in China and became a strong regional force. The British government employed a policy of 'keeping a foot in the door' in China, and attempted to accord formal diplomatic recognition to revolutionary China in order to preserve British interests there. Britain and China exchanged chargés d'affaires in 1954, and maintained bilateral relations until the two countries established full diplomatic relations in 1971. In the same year China established formal diplomatic relations with the United States, and subsequently resumed its seat in the United Nations. In 1972, China successfully demanded that Hong Kong and Macau be removed from the United Nations' ordinary category of colonial territories, setting a necessary precondition for future resumption back to Chinese sovereignty.

From 1911 to 1984, the colonial government in Hong Kong controlled the development of higher education by restricting financial support for private tertiary institutions and denying recognition of their qualifications. Even at the end of the period, only 2 per cent of the age-appropriate population was admitted to local universities. However, in 1984 when the British government realised that their reign over Hong Kong would definitely end in 1997, the Hong Kong authorities started to plan for major expansion of tertiary education. Official recognition of the Hong Kong Baptist College and granting it university status was a step in the expansion plan. It was a clear example of linkage between higher education policy and wider diplomatic policy.

Macau: From Portuguese Settlement to Portuguese Colony
Table 6.3 shows interrelationships between Macau, Portugal and China, with the corresponding higher education policies at different colonial periods. Macau has a distinctive history in that the strategies of settlement employed by the Portuguese were neither superior military strength nor diplomatic efforts, unlike those in most parts of Africa and Asia, but by through bribery and deception. In 1557, the Portuguese were able to break through China's enclosure policy and lease Macau for trading by bribing the Chinese officials (Shipp 1997). Since then, as an entrepôt in China, Macau has played an im-

portant role in reaping profits for the Portuguese in sea trade. The situation did not change even when the Qing dynasty was established in China in 1664.

Table 6.3: Interrelationships between Macau, Portugal and China, 16ᵗʰ to 20ᵗʰ Centuries

Period	Polity		Colonial status of Macau	State power		Diplomatic policy		Higher education policy in Macau
	China	Portugal		China	Portugal	China	Portugal	
1557-1643	feudal empire	feudal empire	Portuguese self-governing city	strong	strong	Rejection, monitor	Bribery for Settlement	missionary participation
1664-1841	feudal empire	feudal empire	Portuguese self-governing city	strong	strong	Rejection, enclosure	Maintenance of Privilege	missionary participation
1842-1910	feudal empire	feudal empire	Portuguese colony	weak	strong	Ignorance, Tolerance	Trickery, Expansion	indifference
1911-1948	republic	republic	Portuguese colony	weak	weak	Tolerance	Expansion	indifference
1949-1971	communist republic	authoritarian state	Portuguese overseas Province	strong	weak	no mutual recognition	No mutual Recognition	laissez-faire
1972-1986	communist republic	Democratic state	Chinese territory under Portuguese administration	strong	weak	Hidden, secret Negotiation	Cooperation, Secret negotiation	state intervention
1987-1999	communist republic	Democratic state	Chinese territory under Portuguese administration	strong	weak	Negotiation, firmness	Cooperation, subservience	state intervention

In 1887, the Qing government was forced to sign the 'Treaty of Peking', affirming the "perpetual occupation and government of Macau and its dependencies by Portugal as any other Portuguese possession" (Chang 1988, p.28). Within Portugal itself, the First Republic was established in 1910, the year before establishment of the Republic of China. Yet the changes in polity in Macau's mother state and suzerain did not affect its colonial status. The Portuguese Republican government inherited the colonial system, and in most parts of the world continued existing policy. Although the Communist Party took over China in 1949, it deferred making a claim of sovereignty over Macau. Yet China assumed a stern attitude towards colonial antagonism. For instance, in 1955 the Beijing authorities prevented official celebrations of 400 year of 'Portuguese' Macau, which was seen by the Chinese as an event planned to boast Portuguese sovereignty (Marques 1972; H.C. Wong 1987).

Case 1: Establishment of St. Paul's University College

The History of SPUC
In the 16ᵗʰ century, Macau was called, at least by some observers, the "City of Schools" because many Catholic and Protestant missionaries came to the colony and provided schooling for upper-class European and Chinese residents (Chapple 1993; Thomas 1983a). In 1594, Claudio Aquaviva, the General of the Society of Jesus in Rome,

authorised the creation of a college offering university-level instruction in Macau by upgrading the Madre de Deus School. The new institution was called Colégio de São Paulo (St Paul's University College), and also called the College of the Mother of God. The college consisted of two seminaries for lay brothers, a university with faculties of arts, philosophy and theology, a primary school, and a school of music and arts. In 1597, the first degree courses were organised in theology and arts. The Portuguese declared that the college was the first Western university in the Far East. Indeed, the establishment of this college was 25 years earlier than the founding in Manila of St. Joseph's College and Seminary and the College of St. Thomas (Gomes dos Santos 1968), and 285 years earlier than the foundation of Shanghai's St. John's University (Lau 1994).

From 1597 to 1645, the period known as Macau's 'golden age', SPUC was at the height of its splendour. The college library had 4,000 books, a precious collection of paintings, atlases and maps, and a printing press. Many famous scholars taught at this college. However, due to complex theological and political disputes, Portugal seized all the Society's properties within its domain in 1759, and the Jesuits were expelled from Macau in 1762. The closure of St. Paul's University College soon followed. In 1835 a fire destroyed three quarters of the college, leading to the symbolic truncation of the history of Macau as a base of spreading Christianity in China.

The Aims, Finance and Impact of SPUC
SPUC owed much of its origin to the work of Alessandro Valignano, the head of the Eastern mission and Jesuit Visitor. Valignano recognised that Macau was not only a Portuguese trade centre in the Far East, but also the frontier for disseminating Christianity in China. He initiated an evangelical policy of cultural accommodation (Lau 1994), and believed that the goal could be achieved by establishing a higher education institute to train prospective missionaries. SPUC's task was to train missionaries in the Chinese language as well as in Chinese rituals and culture, so that they could travel inland "garbed in the dress and manners of Confucian literati to cultivate the friendship of Chinese scholars and members of the ruling class" (Thomas 1983a, p.299). SPUC was a bilingual training centre for missionaries so that they were able to proselytise effectively. Cultural exchange was a by-product: Chinese culture was spread to the Europeans, while Western knowledge was spread to the Chinese (Correia 1994; Lau 1994; Gomes dos Santos 1968).

Valignano organised the educational and institutional life of SPUC according to the Regulations of the College of Arts of Coimbra in Portugal, with adaptation to the needs for missionary assignment in China. The curriculum consisted of 1) Humanities – Chinese Language, Latin, Greek, Portuguese, Rhetoric and Music; 2) Philosophy – Metaphysics and Theology; and 3) Science – Mathematics, Physics, Astronomy and Medicine. Lau (1994) pointed out three features of the curriculum: first, it was an advanced programme for nurturing missionaries for the Roman Catholic Society of Jesus; second, it was a Middle Ages European university, with a comprehensive programme aiming to foster generalists; and third, the Chinese language was a compulsory subject and an essential tool for preaching purposes.

Money for setting up the college came primarily from donations by local people and the city Chambers, as well as taxes levied by the local government. At the outset, the Portuguese government drew 1,000 cruzados from Malacca tax every year to subsidise the college. On this basis, Lau (1994, p.2) argues that "St. Paul's University College was a government-subsidised Catholic school from its beginning". Even the money needed to rebuild the college after destruction by fire in 1603 was obtained from donations. In essence, Portugal shared little responsibility in terms of resources for the college.

SPUC had an examination system similar to that of its counterparts in Europe. Students passing the examinations were awarded university degrees, which were re-cognised by the Chinese government and which made the graduates eligible for official appointments in China. About 200 students attended the college, of whom 109 gradu-ated and became missionaries in various Chinese provinces. SPUC played a major part in the persistent efforts of the Jesuits over a period of two centuries, which led to conversion of 300,000 Chinese to Christianity.

SPUC was a centre of learning for over 150 years. The historical value of this college was to achieve Macau's role as "the bridgehead of Christianity in the Far East as missionaries came from the west to China from 1583 to 1841" (Teixeira 1991, p.43). Guillen-Nuñez (1984) believed that the primary purpose behind the Portuguese voyages of discovery and trading was the search for Christians and spices. Therefore, it was under the religious zeal of the Portuguese that higher education flourished for a period in Macau.

Case 2: The Establishment of the University of Hong Kong

The History of HKU
In the 1900s, the conditions for establishing a university in Hong Kong seemed mature for several reasons. First, the demand for university education in China and in the colony was growing, and there was a steady supply of qualified secondary school graduates. In 1910 an estimated 5,174 Chinese students were attending universities in Japan, and 400 were in Britain and the United States. Second, the early 20th century was a period of rapid expansion of university education in Britain, and the expansion policy there influ-enced colonial education policies. Third and perhaps most important, with national interests moving into the university field in China, various Western powers were begin-ning to set up colleges. For example, the Americans helped establish Tsinghua College in Peking, and the Germans were planning a university in Kiao-chow. Because of this, the British were anxious to set up a university to secure imperial relations with China (Endacott 1962).

Sir Frederick Lugard, Governor of Hong Kong from 1907 to 1912, was a central advocate of Hong Kong's first university. The institution was formed by merging the Hong Kong College of Medicine and the Technical Institute. The Hong Kong University ordinance was passed by the Legislative Council in 1911, and the university, which was regarded by the British as the first imperial university in the Far East, was opened in 1912 by Lugard (Endacott 1962; Ride 1962).

The Aims and Finance of HKU
Although the University was situated in Hong Kong, the major educational target was China. As noted by Harrison (1962, p.xv), "the higher educational needs of the Colony alone were for long regarded as insufficient to justify a full scale university-type insti-tution, and the University's main raison d'être was therefore thought to lie in service to the Chinese people as a whole". The prime goal of the institution, as Lugard (1912, p.3) stated in the preamble to the ordinance of incorporation, was "the maintenance of good understanding with the neighbouring Empire of China". Other purposes were to serve

the higher education needs of an awakening China, to be a symbol of Western cultural tradition in the Far East, to be a meeting-place for Chinese and Western cultures, to help to maintain British prestige in Eastern Asia, and indirectly to benefit British business through dissemination of modern knowledge and the English language (Harrison 1962). HKU was clearly part of Britain's broad imperial education policy. The educational needs and welfare of the local people were not the priority on the political agenda.

The take-over of China by the Communist Party in 1949 changed the relationship between Hong Kong and its motherland, and rendered questionable the purpose of HKU to serve the whole of China. To accommodate the political change, the Secretary of State for the Colonies announced in 1948 (quoted by Priestley 1962, p.96) that:

> the University should reflect in the realms of science and intelligence the success of the Colony in the realms of trade and industry...[and] at the same time be a University for Hong Kong.

This was the first time that the colonial government formally regarded HKU as a university for the people of Hong Kong. Yet such an acknowledgement did not mean that Britain had given up its imperial education policy: it was only a change in emphasis. As stated in the 1952 Keswick Report on higher education in Hong Kong (quoted by Priestley 1962, pp.96-97):

> Hong Kong should certainly be a centre for the diffusion of English ideas and for interpreting the West to China. It should also be a centre for interpreting Chinese concepts to England and the West, a centre where Chinese and English thought can meet at all levels.

In this new context, local youths were to be trained to develop Hong Kong into a modern British colony.

From the outset, HKU was required to be financially self-sufficient even though, in Lugard's words (1910, p.1), it carried the role of "upholding the British name and fame in the Far East". Lugard added (1910, p.1) that it was:

> neither just nor practicable to expect the taxpayers of Hong Kong to bear the entire burden of discharging these Imperial obligations, and of promoting single-handed interests which are common to both the British and the Chinese Governments. It is for this reason that we desire that the new step forward shall be met by a University which is largely self-supporting.

For the first few decades, the university suffered from under-financing which hindered the institution's long-term balanced development as a teaching and research centre (Mouat Jones & Adams 1950). In addition to finance from the Hong Kong government, the foundation of the university was based on support solicited from local merchants, Chinese residents and the government of the neighbouring province of Guangdong. Only after World War II did financial commitment from the government increase gradually. In the 1960s onward, the Hong Kong Jockey Club became another source of financial support. From the very beginning, the British government made little contribution. Every time commissions were set up to investigate the financial position of HKU and to recommend alternative solutions, the question of the financial responsibility of the British government arose. The idea that the university was an imperial asset and therefore an imperial responsibility was emphasised in all commission reports, urging greater financial commitments from both the British and the colonial governments. Yet positive response from Britain was rarely heard (Jones & Adams 1950).

The Impact of HKU: Chinese Ruling Chinese for Imperial Interests
The colonial government expected that HKU students would come from all parts of mainland China, and after graduation would return to China to take up leadership positions in government (Harrison 1962). Indeed, six students who graduated in 1922 had been sent to the university by the central government in Peking (Mouat Jones & Adams 1950). The future of the graduates of the university was anticipated to be very bright, at least as conceived by Lugard. The Objects of the University stated that "the graduates from the Hong Kong University will have before them all the limitless opportunities which the Empire of China offers, both in the ranks of official life, and in the fields of commerce, and the professions of Medicine, Engineering, etc. in addition to the opportunities offered by our own and neighbouring Colonies" (Lugard 1910, p.7). Such was also true at the time when China was ruled by the Nationalist government and there were diplomatic relations between the Chinese and the British governments. As Lugard had foretold, graduates served as talented representatives of the colonial motherland. Britain benefited from the graduates' British-style heritage acquired during their training at HKU, which was translated indirectly into commercial benefits.

After 1949, the linkages described above totally disintegrated. The university turned inward to serve primarily the educational needs of the colony. Consequently, the graduates of the 1950s and 1960s became the elite of the local society, and, by serving either in official capacities or in the business fields, helped the administration of Hong Kong. These people were ethnic Chinese with British-style education and excellent working knowledge of both English and Chinese. As a result, they became the best tools for explaining and implementing government policies, permitting successful implementation of the British strategy of "the Chinese ruling the Chinese".

British rule over Hong Kong was further secured by the use of English as the medium of instruction in higher education. Lugard (1909, p.4) believed that English should be the medium of instruction at HKU because the language was "the best medium for imparting Western knowledge", and because "by acquiring a fluency in it students will best fit themselves for success in after life whether they adopt a profession or become officials in the service of their country at the Capitals or abroad". However, Lugard's underlying motive was spelled out in the preamble to the ordinance of incorporation of HKU (Lugard 1912, p.3):

> the Hongkong University will be largely instrumental in making King's English the predominant language in the Far East, as pidgin English is already in business and commerce. Such a result would no doubt bring in its train important political and commercial benefits.

This strategy helped English to secure its high position in the Far East, and remained a steadfast policy at HKU. Even at the early foundation stage in 1908 when the financial situation of the University was so stringent that the scheme was almost aborted, Lugard firmly rejected a proposal to attract donations from China by launching a secondary parallel course in Chinese. Lugard insisted on English as the sole language, even risking the fate of the university (Endacott 1962; Lugard 1910).

The English-language policy remained intact throughout the decades. Although it is only one of many university academic policies, its impact has been far-reaching because it has influenced the medium of instruction in secondary schools. Since universities in Hong Kong before the early-1980s could cater for less than 2 per cent of the age cohorts, graduation from the university guaranteed a ticket to a bright future. Use of English became the most important tool for gaining access to the university. Many parents felt that they had no choice but to force their children to learn English as early as possible in order to increase the chance of entry into this prestigious university. Chinese was relegated to second class status, both in the university and in the school system. As a result, the British were successful in transplanting not only the British university model, but also parts of the British academic system and infrastructure, which in many respects dominated the indigenous culture. This may be instructively compared with SPUC (Table 6.4).

Case 3: Transformation of the University of East Asia

The University of East Asia as a Private Institution
No university education was available in Macau between the closure of SPUC in 1762 and 1981. In the latter year, a private university, the University of East Asia, was established. It consisted of five colleges working at several educational levels. Three languages were employed: English was the medium of instruction and administration; and Chinese and Portuguese were the second and third working languages.

In 1978, Peter Wong King-keung, a Hong Kong soils engineer serving as a consultant to the Macau government on industrial development, together with his friends Edward Woo Pak-hay and Ng Yuk-lun, had made a proposal to the Macau government to develop a university (Mellor 1988). The following year, the Macau government signed a land lease agreement for 100,000 square metres to be the site for this new university. At almost the same time, Portugal and China signed an agreement stating that Macau was a Chinese territory. Ng Yuk-lun, one of the founders of the university (quoted by Mellor 1988, p.117), noted that because:

> Macau [is] small, a university there must be capable of attracting students and faculty from the rest of East Asia and other parts of the world in order to grow, and indeed to survive, and such an institution would reflect the character of Macau itself as a multilingual and multicultural society. The development of an international character was key to its strength.

That was why the university was titled the University of East Asia rather than the University of Macau. The policy of serving the wider East Asian region was reflected in the student and academic staff recruitment strategies. The university obtained economic support through operation of joint programmes with other institutions and through the use of distance teaching materials originally prepared by other universities.

Table 6.4: St. Paul's University College and the University of Hong Kong: Similarities and Differences in Origins and Functions

	St. Paul's University College	University of Hong Kong
Founder	• established by a religious body, the Roman Catholic Society of Jesus, in 1594	• established by the government of Hong Kong in 1911
Functions and Roles	• training missionaries for Japan and China • graduates preached and taught in China and translated Chinese Classics • tool for cultural (religious) dissemination; base for Christianity in China	• training of intellectuals to serve China and Hong Kong • graduates worked as high ranking officials or experts in China before 1949, and as members of the social elite and bureaucrats in Hong Kong after 1949 • tool for cultural dissemination and economic exploitation
Funding	• funding from colonial government and merchants • little support from the suzerain (Portugal)	• funding from colonial government and merchants • little support from the suzerain (UK)
Colonial higher education policy	• no central higher education policy in Portuguese colonies • College closed down because of struggles between religious orders	• Imperial higher education policy • formation of Inter-University Council for Higher Education in the Colonies for coordination of universities in the British Empire
Use of language and its impact	• Chinese a compulsory subject, a tool for cultural accommodation in order to propagate Christianity • promote European understanding of China and Chinese culture	• English the medium of instruction, enhancing spread of British culture • suppress Chinese language, promote British academic model, facilitate cultural domination

In 1987, a new group of officials recruited from Portugal joined the government's Department of Education as senior administrators. They began to conduct educational research, and tried to reduce Macau's educational problems by initiating various reforms. At the same time, the Portuguese government realised that in the transitional period of Macau lay the last real chance to spread the Portuguese language and culture in East Asia. In order to achieve this, the government provided grants of 5,000 patacas per class per year to schools in which Portuguese was included in the curriculum. One Portuguese educational planner, Rosa (1990, p.19), pointed out that the grants were part of a:

> review of the current Portuguese language diffusion sub-system, with the overall redefinition of educational goals, methods and programs, so as to bring them in line with the Territory of Macau's specific needs and expectations, and to serve fully a global policy of widespread bilingualism.

In addition to providing grants to promote Portuguese language in primary and secondary schools, the Macau government decided to purchase the University of East Asia. After some negotiations, the Governor and the Directors of the company which owned the university signed a protocol in 1988, and the Macau government paid 130 million patacas to the company. Most of the institution's physical assets were transferred to the Macau Foundation, which was a public body set up by the Macau government in 1987 for cultural and educational purposes. The money for purchasing the university came from government revenue (78 million patacas), from the Sociedade de Turismo e Diversoes de Macau (Macau Travel and Amusement Company) which donated 26 million patacas, and from several commercial, industrial and financial bodies which together contributed 26 million patacas. The university was thereby transformed from a private to a public institution. In 1987, Carlos Montez Melancia, then Governor of Macau and Chancellor of the University (quoted by Mellor 1988, pp.110, 116), explained that the intention of the change was:

> to guarantee conditions which will enable [the university] to serve the interests of Macau with stability and continuity in the fields of education and scientific research, especially in the field of law studies and other types of study relevant to the training of cadres, both during the period of transition and beyond.... The University of East Asia is a reality. History will not forgive us if we do not plan wisely and ensure its future.

The University of East Asia in the Publicly-funded Stage

After becoming publicly-funded, the university was managed by the Macau Foundation, which was structured by the Macau government specifically to assume the trusteeship of UEA with safeguards for its academic autonomy. The Governor appointed an administrative board from the private sector. The change also brought adjustment to the aims of the university. Instead of serving the wider East Asian region, the focus was shifted to Macau. The original 1979 land-lease agreement had contained a clause requiring the university to develop a centre for Portuguese studies, in which were to be offered courses in philosophy, linguistics, language, literature, culture and history. However, local Portuguese students did not choose to enter UEA because few courses in Portuguese were available until an Institute of Portuguese Studies was set up in 1987. In 1986, for example, only 37 students enrolled in classes on Portuguese language and culture (Mellor 1988, p.107). Financial constraints had delayed progress in extensive provision for Portuguese Studies.

The change in institutional philosophy following the change of ownership was reflected in remarks by the President of the Portuguese Republic, Dr. Mario Soares, during an official visit to the University of East Asia in 1989. "To some of the Portuguese who are living in Macau," he declared (Soares 1989, p.1), "the attempts to spread and defend the Portuguese language have been a failure". However, he continued, "there is sufficient reason to support that from now on we need to double our effort". This speech indicated that the Portuguese government intended to use the university as a base to spread Portuguese culture and language in Macau, and in line with this goal, moves were made to strengthen the Portuguese presence at the university. One of the objectives added in the revised university charter was "to provide programmes which will educate Macau persons for positions of responsibility in the Macau community" (Mellor 1988, p.196). The university was expected to provide training of more direct relevance to the immediate needs of the territory, and to make significant contributions to Macau's stability, prosperity and further development including through localisation of the civil service. Such programmes included teacher training and courses in law, public administration, and Portuguese and Chinese translation and interpretation.

Another consequence of change in ownership was alteration in the university's composition and power structure. The governing authority was reorganised so that the university could achieve the functions required by its new role. In 1988, in a speech delivered at the Centre of Portuguese Studies, Rangel (1989, p.202) declared that:

The greatest heirloom Portugal can leave in Macau should be a university built according to the modern mode. This university will be the focus point of knowledge transmission and the bridge for eastern and western communication. For this I have for years been advocating the establishment of the Portuguese Oriental Academy and East Asia University (for short why not name it Macau University). This will be an invaluable tool. But they need the technological and academic support of the organisations of our country. Its special function will be to spread the cultural value of Portuguese; promote the dialogue between the Portuguese culture and those countries with whom Portugal has cultural or commercial relationships; study the cultural, political and economical problem of the residents of Macau and Portugal.

The Macau government gave very little financial support to the University between 1981 and 1987. After 1988, however, the university enjoyed a publicly-acknowledged mandate which, in the words of Governor Melancia (quoted by Mellor 1988, pp.116-117), was "backed by the wealth of the Territory". The university's income included fees, donations, and subventions from the Macau Foundation. Many programmes were subsidised by the government, including the in-service teacher training programme which was fully sponsored by the Department of Education & Youth. Taxation revenue from lottery tickets and other gambling businesses was another major source of income.

Another change following the government's purchase of the university was a shift from a three-year to a four-year basic curriculum. The shift was not purely for academic reasons, but was also for reasons of academic recognition since basic degree courses in Portugal followed a four-year model. The new arrangement permitted recognition by both the Portuguese and the Macau governments. In addition, programmes were set up to cater for Portuguese applicants. The Institute of Portuguese Studies offered courses in education, research, journalism and secretarial skills. Koo (1998b, p.6) revealed that the Institute:

> preferred to employ teaching staff with academic backgrounds from Portuguese institutions to teach Portuguese language and culture. Only one staff did not receive his academic qualification from Portugal... The FL [Faculty of Law] was dominated by professors from the Portuguese empire.

The governing structure, staff recruitment and curriculum of the university were also greatly influenced by Portuguese traditions.

Case 4: Transformation of the Hong Kong Baptist College

The Baptist College as a Private Institution
The Hong Kong Baptist University, originally known as the Hong Kong Baptist College, was founded in 1956. The institution, registered with the Hong Kong government's Education Department as a private non-profit making Christian college, was established by the Hong Kong Baptist Convention. The reasons for setting up such a college, as recorded by Y.L. Wong (1996, p.8), were:

- to educate young people to become competent individuals who would serve the Baptist church and the society;
- to provide further education opportunities for graduates of Chinese middle schools, who lacked such opportunities because the sole university in Hong Kong admitted students only from schools with English as the medium of instruction; and
- to offer a channel for international cultural exchange and connection with universities overseas for students who intended to pursue further study.

In 1957, 132 students enrolled in the college, which offered a four-year programme with biblical knowledge as a compulsory subject for all Year 1 to Year 3 students (Y.L. Wong 1996). The student number rose to 623 in 1959/60, becoming the greatest enrolment among all full-time post-secondary institutions at that time. In the same year, three other post secondary colleges, Chung Chi College, New Asia College and United College, joined together to form the Association of Chinese Post-secondary Colleges and began to receive government subsidy. The three colleges then amalgamated to form the Chinese University of Hong Kong (CUHK) in 1963. This brought new pressure to the Baptist College because the CUHK was explicitly set up to meet the further education needs of students from Chinese-medium schools.

In order to compete with the publicly-funded universities, the Baptist College raised its requirements on student academic performance, restructured its departments to form Arts and Science Faculties, promoted research, and refined its constitution. The chief goal was to achieve registration as an approved post-secondary college eligible for government subsidy. Initially, however, the college was denied registration on the grounds that its standards were still too low. Only in 1970, 14 years after its establishment, did the college finally achieve approved post-secondary college status. Graduates were then recognised to have qualifications equivalent to diploma level, and were permitted to teach in primary and secondary schools. However, government finance remained denied until 1979, when the college accepted a government proposal to restructure its five-year academic programme to the one outlined in the 1978 White Paper on Senior Secondary and Tertiary Education.

The new structure was a '2+2+1' system, and was introduced in exchange for being accepted into the government funding scheme. In the words of an official publication (Hong Kong Baptist College 1988, p.9):

> The first two-year programme was an integrated course designed to provide all rounded education for secondary school graduates. The third and fourth years provided students with the opportunities to enter the fifth (or final) year which allowed students to pursue in-depth studies in their chosen fields.

Under the new scheme, the government agreed to subsidise the first four years of the programme. Table 6.5 compares the 2+2+1 system with the mainstream education systems in England and the United States. In the view of Tse Chi-wai, President of the College, six factors lay behind the government's insistence on a 2+2+1 structure (Y.L. Wong 1996, pp.214-215). Three of them were related to the colonial state's higher education policies, namely:

- subsidising only the first four years of study helped to declare the government's stand of financially supporting only post-secondary education but not university education;
- allowing the government to recognise the qualification of the four-year programme in these colleges as diploma level but not degree level; and
- permitting the existence of the fifth year so as to satisfy the need of the colleges to maintain their academic standards.

The reason why the Baptist College was willing to change its programme to a 2+2+1 structure was, as revealed by a senior administrator of the college (see Hui 1999, p.243) that:

> We came to a conclusion that unless we became a publicly-funded and publicly supervised institution, it would be very unlikely that the government would ever accept our programme for degree recognition. We got approval for some funding in the late 70's and early 80's. But that was on the condition that we restructure from 4-year to 3-year, admitting students one year later. There was also an agreement that if we did this, the government would bring in a review panel to look at further development, and that occurred in January 1981.

This account clearly shows that the government was intervening in the development of higher education, even in the private sector.

Table 6.5: Comparison of the 2+2+1 Structure of the Hong Kong Baptist College with the Mainstream Higher Education Systems of England and the United States

Hong Kong Baptist College	England	United States
First year (Junior division of Basic Studies - Year 1)	Sixth Form	12th Grade
Second year (Junior division of Basic Studies - Year 2)	Seventh Form	University - Year 1
Third year (Diploma programme - Year 1)	University - Year 1	University - Year 2
Fourth year (Diploma programme - Year 2)	University - Year 2	University - Year 3
Fifth year (Honours Diploma programme)	University - Year 3 (Bachelor degree)	University - Year 4 (Bachelor degree)

Source: Adapted from Y.L. Wong (1996), p.223.

The Baptist University in the Publicly-funded Stage
In 1983 the college became a publicly-funded higher education institution, formally taken into the ambit of the University & Polytechnic Grants Committee (UPGC). The college modified its programme structure to a 2+3 structure, aspiring to degree-granting status and meanwhile providing two years of basic studies plus three years of diploma studies. The intake of students for the first two years was expected to diminish until it was completely phased out in 1985. In addition, under the advice of the UPGC, the college had to give up the Department of Civil Engineering, and to develop departments of humanities and natural science. The college was unwilling to close its Department of Civil Engineering, but was forced to do so as another compromise. The college authorities were aware that refusal to follow government's advice would mean withdrawal of

government subsidy, which in turn would seriously hamper the development of the institution.

In 1984, the Hong Kong Baptist College was permitted to launch degree programmes, one year after becoming publicly-funded. The aim of the new programme was education of the 'whole person' through a liberal education with some emphasis of vocational training. The college admitted its first batch of degree students in 1986. By 1987, all courses had a duration of three years, conferring either degree or diploma qualifications, and in 1991 the college became a fully-degree-granting institution. In 1995, it was renamed the Hong Kong Baptist University. It took 30 years for this institution to become a university; but it would certainly have taken much less time in the absence of state controls and intervention.

For the first 23 years, the Hong Kong Baptist College was running totally on its own funding and other resources. Some of its running expenses in the early years were met by the American Southern Baptist Foreign Mission Board, by churches and institutions connected with the Hong Kong Baptist Association, and by other donors (Hong Kong Baptist College 1957). Up to 1979, the college always faced financial stringency. The government had denied many times the college's requests for financial support with such reasons as:

- the government had been satisfied with the role that the college had been performing in providing sub-degree education for the community;
- the government had to support the newly-established CUHK, and to make sure that its development would not be affected by support channelled to other post-secondary institutions including the Baptist College;
- there would not be enough job vacancies to absorb so many four-year tertiary education graduates, and one-year or two-year diploma courses would be more economical, practical and beneficial to society's needs; and
- there was still considerable capacity for growth in HKU and the newly established university.

The College President, Tse Chi-wai, remarked that it was the government's policy to run universities itself, and that the idea of promoting private universities was received coldly (Y.L. Wong 1996, p.167). He felt that the government was afraid that once the Baptist College was granted a government subsidy, it would appear that the government was approving the establishment of the third university.

The college was able to get a small amount of funding from the government in 1979 on the condition that it restructured its programme from four to three years, which was compatible with the English model. A senior administrator at the institution (see Hui 1999, p.246) admitted that:

> The primary reason to become a public institution in the early 1980s was to obtain recognition for academic work so that degrees could be awarded and the graduates would have a proper credential. It also required more funding to do that, which was the secondary reason to go public. The government would never accept degrees without the institution becoming public.

The college did not insist on its four-year programme. The same administrator revealed further that:

The only condition [for funding] about four-year to three-year was laid down directly by the Education and Manpower Branch in the late 1970s... We did not propose a four-year degree programme in the early 1980s because we knew that the government and UPGC were towards three-year degrees.

The college obtained full government subsidy in 1983, and its academic qualifications were then recognised. To achieve this, the administrators sacrificed their control over programme structures. The government also restructured the institution's governing bodies through legislation, and monitored its development through official representatives on these bodies. The Council, which is the highest governing body, was chaired by a person, usually a member of the Legislative Council, appointed by the Governor. After restructuring, the college's religious emphasis and connections with the Baptist community diminished.

Conclusion

Macau and Hong Kong have been geographically significant bases for the West to enter China. The territories werse on the one hand a bridge for the Portuguese and British to penetrate China for economic exploitation and cultural dissemination, and on the other hand a base for power struggles with other imperial powers. Higher education development in Macau and Hong Kong was inevitably influenced by Portuguese and British colonial heritages.

Hui (1990) argued that the lack of formal higher education in Macau between 1762 and 1981 was due to the Macau government's generally laissez-faire social policies, the lack of demand for manpower in the small commercial sector, and, most importantly, the fact that Macau was administered by a colonial regime which did not make education a high priority. In Hong Kong, the establishment of a university in 1911 was mainly motivated by the British colonial interests to serve China rather than Hong Kong (Sweeting 1990). Tables 6.2 and 6.3 in this chapter contrasted the two developments.

It is argued that in general, colonisers control and resist the development of higher education of the colonised. However, higher education systems expanded rapidly in both colonies after China had made the agreements with the United Kingdom and Portugal that Hong Kong and Macau would revert to China in 1997 and 1999 respectively. In 1989 the Hong Kong Governor announced that the number of first-year, first-degree places would increase from 7,000 to 15,000 between 1990 and 1995, implying that university capacity would cater for an increase from 2 per cent to over 18 per cent of the relevant age group within only five years (Morris et al. 1994). Though no target figures have been made public in Macau, the number of local students studying at the university increased from 62 non-government-subsidised places in 1981 to 2,836 government-subsidised placements in 1995/96 (Rangel 1991; Macau, Department of Statistics & Census 1997b).

Different observers provide different interpretations. Regarding the development of higher education in Hong Kong, Mak & Postiglione (1996, p.57) attributed such development to three factors: "its status as a colony, its reliance on international trade, and social demand for higher education". Bray (1992a, p.332) argued that:

The timing and the scale of these higher education expansion policies appear to be directly linked to the '1997 factor'.... The government aimed through bold initiative to demonstrate that it had confidence in itself.

And Joseph Cheng (1995, p.257) pointed out:

Shortage of educated manpower has created a bottleneck hampering economic growth. Substantial emigration flows relating to 1997 is also a problem. Development of higher education and infrastructure are means to ensure sustainable economic growth.

Some scholars use the concept of decolonisation to explain the function of higher education institutions. Concerning Hong Kong, Postiglione (1992, p.3) stated that "educational reforms have the potential to act as vehicles for negotiating social transition processes, as well as instruments for resisting decolonisation"; and concerning Macau, Bray (1994) contended that education may not only be an instrument of the preparation for decolonisation but also a vehicle for extending Portuguese culture in the twilight of the colonial period. Noting examples in Central and East Africa, in the Caribbean, and in southeast Asia, Bray (1997a) concluded that the establishment or expansion of higher education was typical in colonies during the period of decolonisation.

Yet an interpretation using only the concept of decolonisation seems incomplete. This chapter proposes that the ultimate aims of establishing Western universities in the two colonies were to achieve imperial initiatives in cultural and economic expansion in China. The Portuguese exhibited a kind of cultural imperialism through higher education that was different from that of the British, as illustrated by the four cases. This difference continues to be evident in the late 20th century as more historical data is revealed, especially when it pertains to the period of state power transition.

In sum, the chapter argues that state control of higher education institutions, which in turn permitted control of social mobility, was one of the most effective tools of colonialism and imperialism. Hong Kong and Macau were used by their suzerains for economic exploitation, political influence and cultural dissemination in China, and higher education policies in these two colonies served political more than educational needs. Bray (1997a) has noted that the immediate post-colonial periods of most former colonies brought more dramatic changes in the scale of education systems than in the nature of education systems. The change and/or continuity in the higher education systems of Hong Kong and Macau in the post-colonial period will be an instructive topic for continuing research.

7

Education and the Labour Force

MA Hing Tong, William

During the 1980s and 1990s, Macau and Hong Kong greatly benefited from economic links between China and other countries, acting as entrepots and service bases for foreign investments. During the restructuring of their economies from dominance of manufacturing to dominance of services, a large supply of highly educated personnel was needed.

In Macau, educational enrolments expanded rapidly after the late 1980s. However, the need for overseas graduates remained strong because of the historical neglect of local higher education, and because of constraints on the number of specialist forms of training which could be offered in a small society. The main destinations for Macau's external students were mainland China and Taiwan. Hong Kong had greater training capacity than Macau, but even in Hong Kong local universities met less than 60 per cent of the territory's needs for highly educated personnel. Hong Kong was dependent on North America, the United Kingdom (UK), Taiwan and Australia for much higher education and training.

This chapter begins with a broad conceptual framework which shows why Macau and Hong Kong are instructive places for study and comparison. Discussion then turns to the development of Macau's economy, the effects of that development on the labour market, and the supply of skilled personnel. The chapter then provides similar commentary on Hong Kong, which sets the stage for identification of similarities and differences. The final section draws out the conceptual implications of the analysis.

Education, Development and Technological Change

Concerning the general relationship between the economy and education, a widespread perspective is that the investment of public money in 'human capital' is the one of best ways to promote economic development. Many human capital theorists (e.g. Becker 1975; Psacharopoulos 1995) have investigated the contribution of education to economic growth, and have endeavoured to measure rates of return to schooling. These theorists have focused on inputs and outputs, not what actually happens in the processes of education. Such analysts have also emphasised the value of systematic predictions of demand for skills. Manpower planning has been linked to educational provision with the goal of maximising rates of return from investment in human capital. In many situations, manpower planning has led to expansion of investment in tertiary and technical education (Maglen 1991; 1993). However, an alternative set of explanations for economic progress emphasises cultural forces. In East Asia, analysts have focused on the Confucian ethic, which is believed to have fuelled and motivated both labour and management (Tai 1989).

Most advanced industrial countries have moved from economies largely based on manufacturing to economies largely based on services. This change has affected demands on education and training systems. In general, skill requirements are higher in the service sector than in the manufacturing sector (Burke & Rumberger 1987). Harris (1995) pointed out that more highly educated labour produces more output, and that the larger the stock of human capital, the more likely labour will find ways to improve production processes and to develop new and profitable products.

In both Hong Kong and Macau, the existence of a literate and numerate workforce has contributed to economic development (Bray 1995a; Sweeting 1995). However, as the second half of the 20th century progressed, mere literacy and numeracy rapidly ceased to be an adequate underpinning for continued growth. One new element became the important link between technology and education. Carnoy's (1995) review of the effects of information technology highlighted the increased demand for highly skilled labour because of the more complex requirements of information systems and flexible production. Carnoy further pointed out that intensified global competition and the development of new information technologies have altered the international division of labour. Competition in the production of the most advanced technologies has sharply increased among the highly industrialised economies, shifting manufacturing jobs from these economies to a group of newly developing countries in Asia and elsewhere. Training of highly skilled labour has become an important public policy issue in both industrialised and less developed economies.

Although Macau and Hong Kong both had fast-growing economies during the 1980s and 1990s, their governments' higher education and skill-training policies were rather different. Comparison brings into focus questions about the quantity of higher education, the type of higher education, and its planning. The labour market in each place has differed significantly. Hong Kong moved from an economy largely based on manufacturing in the 1970s to an economy largely based on tourism and other services in the 1980s. It then moved again in the 1990s to an economy strongly based on financial services. Macau's economy has also depended on tourism, but it has had a large gambling sector not found in Hong Kong. Since skill requirements are generally higher in the service sector than in the manufacturing sector, the growth of service employment has tended to increase the average skill demands of work. These and other patterns are best discerned by considering each territory in turn.

Macau

The Economy and Labour Force

According to government statistics, the real average annual growth rate of Gross Domestic Product (GDP) in Macau rose from 5.7 per cent in 1986, reached a peak of 13.4 per cent in 1992, and dropped to negative figures in 1996 (Table 7.1). The main factor in growth was a construction boom in 1992 and 1993. A surge in public investment helped to sustain GDP growth early in the decade, but after completion of Macau's airport, fixed investment dropped by 12.4 per cent in 1995 after having risen steadily during the previous five years. In 1996, tourism and gambling together accounted for 43 per cent of

Macau's GDP and nearly half of the government's current revenue. Manufacturing output, largely textiles and clothing, accounted for about a third of GDP. The trade deficit shrank in 1995 because imports fell faster than exports.

Table 7.1: Major Economic Indicators of Macau, 1981-97

	1981	1986	1990	1992	1994	1996	1997
Real GDP growth %	n.a.	5.7	5.0	13.3	4.6	-0.5	-0.1
Population (thousand)	262	426	340	381	410	416	422
Consumer price inflation %	n.a.	1.9	9.6	7.7	6.3	6.5	3.5
Exports MOP$ (million)	3,972	8,630	13,638	14,080	14,854	13,375	15,048
Imports MOP$ (million)	4,085	7,318	12,343	15,684	16,925	15,930	16,603
Trade balance MOP$ (million)	-112	1,312	1,295	-1,604	-2,071	-32	525

Sources: Macau, Department of Statistics & Census, *Yearbook of Statistics*, various years.

In the 1980s, diversification of exports had short-lived success. Toys, artificial flowers, textiles and garments were major export products to the United States and the European Union in 1995. Textiles and apparel were still locked in by Multi-Fibre Arrangement (MFA) origin requirements. With the phasing out of the MFA, the textile industry faced difficulties. Toy exports resumed their long-term decline in 1995, but footwear exports showed a steady increase. Electronics showed the best performance, but demand then fell, especially for computer components in the United States and the European Union.

Table 7.2: Macau Labour Force Characteristics

	1981	1989	1993	1994	1995	1996
Labour force participation rate (%)	n.a.	50.8	65.2	63.9	65.3	66.7
Unemployment rate (%)	n.a.	1.5	2.1	2.5	3.6	4.3
Median monthly earnings (MOP$)	1,741	2,382	4,067	4,476	4,830	4,925
Share of employment (%)						
Manufacturing	45.0	35.9	25.0	22.9	21.7	20.6
Construction	8.0	9.6	10.0	7.5	9.5	7.5
Restaurants and hotels	18.5	19.0	26.0	26.1	25.6	27.5
Financial & business services	1.7	4.0	5.4	6.3	6.2	6.6
Public, social and private services	15.4	24.8	26.5	30.4	30.1	30.5
Others	11.4	6.6	7.1	6.8	6.9	7.3

Sources: Macau, Department of Statistics & Census, *Yearbook of Statistics*, various years.

In 1996, 206,000 people, representing 66.7 per cent of the population, were said to be economically active. This was a proportionate as well as an absolute increase on the situation in the 1980s (Table 7.2). However, this figure was only an approximation which included an estimate of the many outside workers on short-term contracts. The unemployment rate was moderate at 4.3 per cent in 1996. Manufacturing, hotels, restaurants and personal services were the largest employers. As the structure changed among the various sectors, between 1989 and 1996 the proportion of workers in manufacturing declined from 35.9 to 20.6 per cent, but the share of workers in service sectors (restaurants & hotels, financial & business services, and public, social & private services) experienced growth from 48 to 66 per cent. Less than 0.1 per cent of the labour force was employed in primary industries. The median monthly earnings of workers in 1996 were MOP$4,925, below the figure for Hong Kong.

Lack of data obstructs analysis of the demand for higher education in Macau. One source of information, however, is the 1992 government survey of skill needs in the garment, knitting and toy industries. The study showed that only 0.4 per cent of workers and 14.2 per cent of the top management had attained higher education qualifications (Table 7.3). Another survey, in 1994, showed that 44.9 per cent of Macau's employed persons had attained only primary education, and that 44.7 per cent had attained only secondary education. Just 4.9 per cent possessed university degrees, and another 1.7 per cent had non-degree tertiary qualifications (Macau, Department of Statistics & Census 1994, p.98). The figures showed that the stock of higher education qualifications was still very low, and that more resources were needed for training of vocational, technical and professional workers. Moreover, Feitor & Cremer (1991) and Sit et al. (1991) pointed out that some holders of tertiary qualifications were not working in sectors which made use of those qualifications. Many immigrants had gained their qualifications in mainland China and elsewhere from institutions which were not recognised by the Macau authorities, and therefore had to adjust to labour-market niches which did not use their formal qualifications.

Table 7.3: Educational Attainment of Workforce in Garment, Knitting and Toy Industries, Macau, 1992 (%)

	Higher Education	Secondary Education	Technician Level	Junior Secondary	N
Administrative & professional staff	14.2	64.0	0.6	21.2	655
General workers	0.4	7.7	0.2	91.7	38,452

Source: H.K. Wong (1996), p.113.

The civil service also needed more local personnel with appropriate skills, especially to replace the Portuguese expatriates in the top echelons and to reduce the over-representation of Macanese (mixed-race Portuguese-Chinese) in middle-level positions. During the period of political transition between 1987 and 1999, the Macau government greatly increased local recruitment and promotion in the civil service. The goal was to meet the requirements of the Sino-Portuguese Joint Declaration and Basic Law, which indicated that the government of the Macau Special Administrative Region would be composed of local inhabitants, and that the principal officials would be Chinese citizens who had been permanent residents of Macau for at least 15 years. Hence the supply of qualified local top-ranking administrators was an emergency issue for the Macau government. As shown in Table 7.4, the pace of localisation had been slow between 1987 and 1992. However, the proportion of locally-born people in top ranking positions increased from 43.7 per cent in 1992 to 76.6 per cent in 1996, and the proportion of people born in Portugal declined from 45.4 to 23.4 per cent in 1996 (Macau, Department of Administrative Services & Public Works 1994, p.63; Ho 1997). The Secretary level was the highest in the civil servant hierarchy. At the end of 1998, five out of seven Secretaries were expatriates from Portugal, and the other two were born in Macau but were Portuguese in race. This may still be considered a low pace of localisation, and underlined the need for continued urgent attention to higher education and training.

Table 7.4: Percentage of Top-ranking Position of Civil Servants by Place of Birth (%)

Year	Place of birth			
	Macau	Portugal	Others	Total
1987	48.6	42.4	9.0	100.0
1989	44.6	44.9	10.5	100.0
1992	43.7	45.4	10.9	100.0
1994	55.5	33.1	11.4	100.0
1996	76.6	23.4		100.0

Sources: Macau, Government of, *Human Resources in the Macau Public Administration* 1987, 1989, 1993; Macau, Department of Administrative Services & Public Works 1994, p.63; Ho 1997, p.40.

Stock of Highly-Educated Personnel
The foundation of the University of East Asia (UEA) in 1981 gave Macau a university for the first time in the modern period. In 1988, the university was purchased by the Macau Foundation with funds provided by the government. In 1991 the UEA was re-named the University of Macau, and it has since operated as an autonomous, not-for-profit public institution. In the early 1990s, the university was joined by two other institutions of higher education: the Asia International Open University (AIOU) and the Macau Polytechnic. The AIOU offered distance-learning diploma, bachelors and masters degrees mainly to Macau and Hong Kong residents. The Macau Polytechnic offered technical and vocational training through schools of administration & applied sciences, commerce & tourism, languages & translation, physical education & sport, and visual arts. All courses were employment-oriented, and included both two-year, full-time diploma programmes and three-year bacharelato (professional degree) programmes. By 1999, as noted by Yung's chapter in this book, five more higher education institutions had been formed: the Institute of Tourism Education, the Institute of Arts & Performance, the Inter-University Institute of Macau, the School of Judiciary & Police, and the United Nations University.

Before 1981, all personnel with higher education had obtained their qualifications abroad. Even in the late 1990s, external sources provided the greatest supply of skilled personnel in Macau; and it is likely that this will continue to be the case. No official statistics were compiled on the number of Macau citizens studying abroad, but information was available on the number of official scholarships for external study. The government commenced provision of such scholarships in 1981. At first the main intention was to support Macau students for study in Portugal; but in 1983 the scheme was extended to include studies in Macau, and in 1991 the scheme was further extended to provide loans and grants for overseas study (Rangel 1991; Bray 1993). In 1998/99, 1,617 students were receiving government assistance for external study. Table 7.5 shows that the number of Macau students receiving assistance had increased markedly since 1981/82. The number of students who went to Portugal was always modest and peaked in 1991/92. However, larger numbers went to mainland China and Taiwan, and those numbers continued to rise as the 1990s progressed. Particularly dramatic was the increase in the numbers going to mainland China, which rose from 17 in 1981/82 to 1,019 in 1998/99. As noted in the chapter by Adamson & Li in this book, a large proportion of Macau secondary schools used Chinese as the medium of instruction, and mainland China became a politically more acceptable destination for study. Also, universities in mainland China and Taiwan were generally less expensive than universities in English-speaking countries. Numbers of Macau students in Hong Kong were always modest, chiefly because Hong Kong institutions were unwilling to allocate places. As the 1990s progressed Hong Kong's tertiary sector expanded, but numbers of Macau students fell because they had alternative destinations.

Table 7.5: Numbers of Macau Students Receiving Macau Government Assistance, by Place of Study, 1981/82 to 1998/99

Destination	1981/ 82	1983/ 84	1985/ 86	1987/ 88	1989/ 90	1991/ 92	1993/ 94	1995/ 96	1997/ 98	1998/ 99
Macau	0	2	41	178	469	897	1,092	1,014	1,060	1,075
Mainland China	17	23	57	128	202	202	313	595	888	1,019
Portugal	54	65	97	74	73	125	68	69	54	50
Hong Kong	8	18	26	32	31	23	17	2	6	8
Taiwan	25	88	165	252	322	342	432	568	562	495
USA	1	7	22	34	27	20	17	17	21	23
Canada	0	2	10	14	12	5	0	4	3	4
Australia	0	0	2	6	9	7	0	1	4	8
Others	4	5	13	13	3	2	6	17	13	10
Sub-total	109	208	392	553	679	726	853	1,273	1,551	1,617
Total	109	210	433	731	1,148	1,623	1,945	2,287	2,611	2,692

Source: http://www.dsej.gov.mo/statisti/bolsa/9899/bol-p.htm#7.

While these figures are an indicator of the numbers of students going abroad, statistics were not available on the numbers who chose not to return home, or who chose to work in fields other than those for which they had been trained. Planners thus faced major difficulties in getting the balances right when trying to match supply with demand. The task for planners in small economies is even more difficult than for their counterparts in larger societies, because the arithmetic demands such fine tuning (Bray 1992c, pp.33-34). Small size also requires a different approach to training. Even in the long run, it is not conceivable that Macau will provide local training in all specialisms that will be needed by the economy. This contrasts with mainland China, for example, which is so huge that whole universities can be devoted specifically to agriculture, medicine, aeronautics, and various other specialisms. Small states may also find it more sensible for specific tasks, particularly ones with short durations, to recruit expatriates who are already skilled rather than to try to train locals.

Characteristics of University Graduates
In the absence of detailed figures on courses of study by local and external students, it is not easy to be precise about changing patterns. Nevertheless, some data are available from a 1993 study of university graduates in Macau (Ma 1994). Also, data have been compiled by some host countries in which Macau citizens are studying.

These studies indicate that business was the most popular specialisation both in Macau and abroad, though the popularity of other courses differed according to the destination of students. Ma's (1994) survey of local graduates indicated that 57.8 per cent had studied business, 18.8 per cent science and computer science, and 15.6 per cent arts and social science (Table 7.6). On the other hand, one quarter of the external graduates had chosen business administration, 22.2 per cent had studied engineering, and 19.3 had chosen science or computer science. A 1996 survey of Macau students in Australia showed a similar pattern: 47.6 per cent of students had chosen business administration, 18.3 per cent had chosen science or computer science, and 16.7 per cent had chosen engineering.

Table 7.6: Macau Local and External University Graduates and University Students in Australia by Courses of Study (%)

Courses of study	Survey in 1993		Student enrolment in Australia in 1996
	Local	External	
Architecture/Building	0	0	6.3
Arts, Humanities & Social Science	15.6	12.5	6.3
Business Admin. & Economics	57.8	25.0	47.6
Education	0	1.9	0.8
Engineering	0	22.2	16.7
Health, Community Services	0	0	3.2
Science, Computer Science	18.8	19.3	18.3
Law	0	1.8	0
Others	7.8	17.3	0.8
Total	100.0	100.0	100.0

Note: The 1993 survey assumed that the respondents were local Macau people, because only Macau residents were included. The survey used a questionnaire to collect information about local and overseas university graduates in the local labour market. Out of 1,407 sent questionnaires for which mailing addresses were supplied by the government, 212 responded. Zero in this table means that there was no such sample in the surveys.

Sources: Ma (1994); Australia, Department of Employment, Education, Training & Youth Affairs (1997), p.40.

The survey of university graduates in Macau (Ma 1994) showed that professional, technical, administrative or managerial positions seemed to be the target for the majority (67 per cent of local graduates and 71 per cent of external graduates). Only a small proportion were attracted by clerical, agricultural, production and related jobs. Figures for the first and present jobs showed movement to the government sector by both local and external graduates (local from 12 to 27 per cent, and external from 16 to 46 per cent). Graduates generally preferred the government to the private sector. Data on salaries revealed that 27 per cent of external graduates earned more than MOP$300,000 per annum, with 23 per cent of them earning over MOP$500,000 per annum. Table 7.2 showed medium monthly earnings in 1993 of MOP$4,067 or MOP$48,800 per annum. Thus the university graduates enjoyed substantially higher salaries than the general workforce.

Hong Kong

The Hong Kong Economy and Labour Force
During the 1980s and 1990s, the Hong Kong economy shifted significantly from manufacturing to services (Table 7.7). In 1981, manufacturing industries employed over 42 per cent of the labour force; but by 1997 the proportion had declined to 14 per cent. In

contrast, the employment share of service industries, which included restaurants, hotels, financial & business services, and community, social & personal services, increased from 40 per cent in 1981 to 64 per cent in 1997.

Table 7.7: Hong Kong Labour Force Characteristics, 1981-97 (%)

	1981	1986	1991	1995	1997
Labour force participation rate	66.3	65.1	63.5	62.0	61.8
Unemployment rate	3.9	2.8	1.8	3.2	2.2
Share of employment					
Manufacturing	42.6	35.8	26.0	18.4	14.1
Construction	8.2	6.2	8.2	7.9	9.7
Restaurants and hotels	19.8	22.3	26.6	28.4	30.3
Financial & business services	4.9	6.4	8.3	11.8	12.7
Community, social & private services	15.9	18.4	19.5	21.0	21.2
Others	8.6	10.9	11.4	12.5	12.0

Source: Hong Kong, Census & Statistics Department, various editions.

At the same time, a general upgrading of the occupational structure within individual industries was anticipated, shifting the employment demand in favour of highly skilled workers. Administrative & managerial workers and professional, technical & related workers were expected to account for increasing shares of employment across industries. Upgrading of occupational structure was expected in other services industries, and even within the declining manufacturing industries.

As a result, employment in administrative and managerial occupations grew at the fastest rate. The share of this group was projected to increase from 3.6 per cent in 1986 to 13.5 per cent in 2001. Most of the employment gain was expected to be in wholesale, retail and import/export trades, in restaurants and hotels, and in financing, insurance, real estate and business services. Fewer administrative and managerial workers were expected in the manufacturing industries as the sector contracted. Professional, technical and related employment was also projected to grow, though at a slower rate.

The rapid growth of employment in highly skilled jobs was expected to increase demand for better educated workers, in particular those with university education (see Table 7.8). While only 6.2 per cent of those employed in 1991 were graduates, 10.3 per cent of the workforce was expected to need a first degree or higher qualifications by 2001. Moreover, out of the total of 320,800 graduates required by 2001, only 41 per cent would have already been in the workforce during 1991. The balance of the requirement would have to be met by new entrants to the workforce. Economic slump allied to the broader Asian financial crisis in the late 1990s changed the scenario from that which had been projected. However, the general trend of upgrading workers to more skilled and knowledgeable levels was still expected to account for increasing shares of workers across employment sectors.

Table 7.8: Employed Persons by Educational Level, Hong Kong (Thousands)

		1991		1996		2001	
		No.	%	No.	%	No.	%
1.	Lower Secondary or below	1,469.6	53.3	1,484.3	49.9	1,410.8	45.4
2.	Upper Secondary & Matriculation	949.0	34.4	1,021.9	34.4	1,080.8	34.8
3.	Craft Level	13.1	0.5	25.7	0.9	3.4	1.1
4.	Technician Level	46.0	1.7	64.3	2.1	80.1	2.6
5.	Non-degree	106.8	3.9	43.2	4.8	180.2	5.8
6.	First Degree & above	173.0	6.2	235.4	7.9	320.8	10.3
All levels		2,757.5	100.0	2,974.8	100.0	3,106.1	100.0

Source: Hong Kong, Education & Manpower Branch (1994), p.2.

Compared with Macau, the pace of localisation of the civil service has also been more effective. The Hong Kong government began a strong localisation policy in the 1980s, and would only consider non-local recruitment if no suitable local candidates were available. Even then, moreover, expatriates were only offered employment on contract terms. Of directorate officers, the most senior ranks in government, the share of local appointees was 62 per cent in 1991. At the secretariat level, nine of the 16 Secretaries were locals (A.B.L. Cheung 1991). At the end of 1995, only three branches or departments were headed by non-local officers. Localisation of the Hong Kong policy secretary team and department heads was basically completed in 1995 (K.K. Leung 1995).

The Stock of Higher Education Graduates
Although the economic restructuring increased demand for higher education graduates, growth of local university education was very restricted until the mid-1980s. The supply of higher education graduates by the local institutions could not meet demand, and Hong Kong became heavily dependent on external training.

Hong Kong has a strong tradition of overseas study. The flow of Hong Kong students for higher education across international borders increased rapidly during the 1970s and 1980s. The most popular destinations were Australia, Canada, Taiwan, the United Kingdom and the United States. In 1975, 26,206 Hong Kong students were studying in these locations – a figure which was more than twice the number of students in local tertiary education (Table 7.9). By 1994 the proportion had changed, but still these five destinations hosted 42,650 Hong Kong students, who were equivalent in number to 80 per cent of full-time tertiary students in Hong Kong.

Most Hong Kong overseas students went to English-speaking industrialised nations. The main reason was that they had competence in English from their schooling in Hong Kong, and considered it a valuable language in which to gain further competence. Industrialised countries had more prestige than less developed societies, and some courses provided skills that could not be obtained in local universities. Some industrialised countries vigorously marketed their services in Hong Kong. This is the major explanation for the large numbers of students in Australia.

Table 7.9: Enrolments of Hong Kong Tertiary Students, Various Countries, 1975-94

	1975	1984	1986	1988	1990	1992	1994
Australia	572	1,658	1,687	1,889	*3,864	*6,707	*11,932
Canada	6,644	7,723	6,730	5,840	6,372	6,600	+6,589
Taiwan	2,626	3,817	#3,854	3,850	3,633	3,450	+2,979
United Kingdom	4,434	6,500	6,935	7,300	7,700	7,600	7,400
United States	11,930	9,000	9,720	9,160	12,630	14,018	+13,750
Sub-total	26,206	28,698	28,926	28,043	34,199	38,375	42,650
Local Enrolment	11,575	21,538	25,995	29,591	34,556	42,721	52,494

* Full-fee Overseas Students; + figures for 1992/93 only; # applies to 1987

Notes: (1) Local enrolment refers to the enrolments on full-time courses in institutions funded by the University [and Polytechnic] Grants Committee. (2) Figures for mainland China are not shown because before 1994, the number of Hong Kong students in mainland China was small compared to other countries.

Sources: The British Council , *Statistics of Students from Overseas in the United Kingdom*; Hong Kong, Census & Statistics Department, *Hong Kong Annual Digest of Statistics*; Australia, Department of Employment, Education & Training, *Overseas Student Statistics*; United Kingdom, Department of Education & Science, *Statistics on Education*; Institute of International Education, *Open Doors*; Taiwan, Ministry of Education, *Educational Statistics of the Republic of China*.

Projected Supply of University Graduates

According to the government's comprehensive 1994 survey (Table 7.10), of the more than 100,000 high-level positions required by 1996, 29 per cent were expected to be filled by returning overseas graduates, 39 per cent by local graduates and 32 per cent by immigrants and returning emigrants. In 2001, the corresponding distribution was expected to be 48 per cent local, 22 per cent returned overseas graduates, and 30 per cent immigrants or returned emigrants. In other words, during the period 1997 to 2001, local new supply was projected to be as much as overseas supply of graduates (Hong Kong, Education & Manpower Branch 1994).

Table 7.10: Supply of Manpower at First Degree Level and Above, Hong Kong, 1992-2001

	1992-1996		1997-2001	
	Number	%	Number	%
Returning graduates	31,400	29	25,900	22
Local graduates	41,200	39	56,300	48
Immigrants & returned emigrants	34,000	32	34,400	30
Total	106,600	100	116,600	100

Source: Hong Kong, Education & Manpower Branch (1994), p.14.

Upward trends were also expected in the proportions of workers with postgraduate qualifications. In 1981, only 8 per cent were post-graduates; but it was projected that the proportion would rise to 17 per cent by 1996 and 22 per cent by 2001. Local tertiary institutions produced 2,500 post-graduates in 1992, and were expected to produce 5,100 in 1997. The number of Hong Kong students going abroad for postgraduate study also increased. It was estimated that about one-quarter of Hong Kong overseas students were pursuing post-graduate study.

Comparison of the Two Territories

Through comparison with other societies, policy-makers may gain insights into the functioning of their own societies. Economically advanced countries, such as Australia and the United States stand out for the fact that 50 per cent or more of their workers have higher education qualifications. During the mid-1990s, about one-fifth of employed persons in Hong Kong and Taiwan had higher education qualifications. The proportion in Macau was lower (Table 7.11).

Table 7.11: Working Population with Higher Education Qualifications

	Macau	Hong Kong	Taiwan	Australia	United States
Year	1995	1995	1995	1994	1995
%	5.5	19.0	20.6	49.1	56.1

Sources: Australia, Bureau of Statistics (1994) p.5; US Bureau of the Census (1996) Section 13, no.618, p.395; Hong Kong, Census & Statistics Department (1996), p.18; Taiwan, Director General of Budget, Accounting & Statistics (1996), p.55; Koo (1997), p.229.

In Macau, before 1997 only two major higher institutions – one university and one polytechnic – offered full-time degree courses. In Hong Kong, growth in local university education had been kept low until the mid-1980s. The number of university places in the two societies matched neither the needs of the expanding economies nor the aspirations of their peoples (Chung 1990; Feitor & Cremer 1991; Koo 1994a). Many individuals responded to this situation by going abroad for study. The most popular courses among Macau students going abroad were in the business, scientific and technical fields. This was not because local institutions did not provide opportunities in those areas at that time, but rather because some applicants could not gain places on local courses and other applicants felt that external courses were superior in quality. This situation caused the respective governments to investigate ways to expand local courses while ensuring appropriate standards.

Other courses, however, did not exist in Macau; and, in some cases were not likely to be established because of the high costs and difficulties in achieving economies of scale. Moreover, although the government does provide some scholarships, the costs to the government when individuals go abroad for study are commonly much less than when those students stay at home. This, indeed, was a factor underlying the policy of the Hong Kong government up to the late 1980s. The fact that so many Hong Kong students used their own resources to study abroad was very beneficial to the Hong Kong government and taxpayer. For political and other reasons, the Hong Kong government greatly expanded domestic provision of higher education; but one result was a considerable increase in the burden on the public purse.

In Hong Kong, the rate of change in numbers of overseas students was not uniform across different fields of study and different industries. One study of returned overseas graduates in Hong Kong (Table 7.12) found that among various fields of study, the most drastic decreases in the percentages of overseas graduates between 1986 and 1991 were in textiles & clothing (-48.0%), computer studies (-18.5%), architecture (-16.7%), mechanical engineering (-15.2%), and electrical & electronic engineering (-13.0%). These were mainly technical fields of study, and local universities expanded their enrolments in these fields during the late 1990s. Also the percentage of employees with overseas first degrees decreased from 66 per cent in 1986 to 57 per cent in 1991. This implied that, at least in terms of quantity, Hong Kong was moving from dependence to independence in the supply of higher education graduates (Chung & Ma 1997).

Table 7.12: Changes in Fields of Study and in Employment Sectors of Overseas Graduates, Hong Kong, 1986-91

Field of Study	% change	Employment Sector	% change
Textiles & clothing	-48.0	Electricity, Gas & Water	-20.5
Computer Studies	-18.5	Electrical & Electronic	-16.8
Architecture	-16.7	Construction	-14.8
Mechanical Engineering	-15.2	Agriculture, Fishing & Mining	-11.9
Electrical & Electronic	-13.0	Finance & Business	-11.2
Education	-11.6	Medical & Health	-11.1
Maths, Natural Science	-5.3	Communication	-10.8
Accountancy	-9.5	Transport & Storage	-9.8
Other Technical Studies	-9.1	Other Manufacturing	-7.9
Medical & Health	-7.4	Education	-6.7
Finance & Business	-6.5	Textiles & Wearing Apparel	-6.7
Law	+5.0	Mechanical	-2.7
		Wholesale, Retail, Hotel & Restaurants	-3.0
		Other Services	+19.5

Note: The study only considered male graduates because the participation pattern of females was more irregular than that of males. Focus only on males is a common practice when applying the Mincerian method for this type of study.

Source: Chung & Ma (1997)

The study also showed that among various industries, the most drastic decreases in employment of the overseas graduates were in electricity, gas & water (-20.5%), electricity & electronics (-16.8%), and construction (-14.8%). The choice of employment of overseas graduates was in line with the structural change in Hong Kong economy. The share of workers in these industries had already declined significantly since 1986, and was projected to continue to decline.

Another issue concerns the earnings of local and overseas university graduates. Earnings can be considered an outcome of education and a measure of the extent to which education enables the recipient to find and hold gainful employment. University education normally offers a substantial earnings advantage in comparison with upper secondary education.

Psacharopoulos (1994, 1995) and others have argued that the concept of rates of return in education may be an important guide for decision makers in allocating resources to education by different levels. Advocates of rate of return analysis suggest that both private and social rates of return should be considered. The former views the calculation from the viewpoint of the individual, whereas the latter views the calculation from the viewpoint of the whole society. When societies subsidise education, individuals get the benefit of education without having paid the full cost. In this case, the private rate of return is higher than the social rate, unless individuals have to pay very heavy taxes on their extra earnings.

However, rate of return analysis in education has been subjected to criticism (e.g. Bennell 1996; 1998). Among the criticisms are:

- The rates are calculated on past data. They are not necessarily a good guide to the future.
- It is not always clear how much differences in earnings can be attributed to differences in education, and how much is due to other factors such as natural ability, socio-economic background, and labour force status
- Some figures were not gained from a large or representative samples across all economic sectors and geographical locations.

Moreover, for Macau no detailed studies were available; and in Hong Kong the most recent data during the late 1990s were for 1986 (K.F. Wong 1992, p.32). These 1986 figures reflected a very different set of economic circumstances from those in the late 1990s, and were thus of little direct use to policy makers.

Nevertheless, it was clear that in Macau arts graduates generally enjoyed high earnings compared with graduates in other disciplines. Overseas graduates in this category tended to be at the upper end of the income range. One reason may have been that the category included some Macau Portuguese who had studied overseas and then entered high ranks in the government sector. In general, the average annual earnings of overseas graduates were 16 per cent higher than those of the local graduates. However, patterns varied in different occupations.

The situation in Hong Kong appeared somewhat different. Overall, overseas graduates had lower earnings than local graduates: 24 per cent lower in 1986, and 14 per cent lower in 1991. However, differences in earnings depended on fields of study and employment. Generally, overseas graduates had lower earnings in professional fields, such as medicine and education. They had higher earnings in computer studies, construction, civil engineering, accountancy, business, and finance. Differences were more pronounced in 1991 than in 1986 (Chung & Ma 1997). Furthermore, 1986 data showed that male overseas and local graduates working for the government had earnings about 38 per cent higher than their counterparts in private sector, while overseas graduates working in the same sector had an earnings advantage of only 17 per cent.

Neoclassical economic theory assumes that shortages or surpluses of manpower are only temporary, and that in the long run the labour market operates in equilibrium. Competition in the labour market for limited expertise will tend to increase wages. As wages rise, the quantity demanded falls since employers substitute other types of expertise or other factors of production. Then the system reaches a short-run equilibrium stage. At the same time, the high wage rate increases the supply of skilled personnel. The adjustment process continues until the system is in long-run equilibrium with a new wage rate and employment level (Ahamad & Blaug 1973; Hinchliffe 1995). In both Hong Kong and Macau, overseas graduates in construction, civil engineering and computer studies may have had short term benefits from the massive airports constructed in each territory during the 1990s. The airports demanded outside connections, international standards and high technology. In such aspects, Hong Kong and Macau needed professionals from overseas or with overseas higher education qualification in those areas. However, this was not a sustained need.

In the real world, moreover, many inflexibilities and rigidities obstruct the efficient operation of markets. The government may use monetary incentives to bring about equilibrium in the labour market. Paying higher salary to attract expatriates and overseas graduates to return to Hong Kong has been one government policy to meet the needs of labour market. Other strategies include protection of the market by local professional bodies for medical practitioners, architects, engineers, etc..

Conclusions

What conclusions can be drawn concerning the pool of skills in the two territories? Beginning with Macau, a strong case can be made for expansion of higher education to meet the perceived needs of rapid industrialisation. Ideally, graduates will be made more employable through courses which combine academic education with specialised training in broad basic skills. Questions then arising concern the scale of costs and responsibility for meeting those costs. Courses can be provided by either the government or the private sector; and within either sector, the extent of government subsidy would need to be decided. Governments commonly subsidise private operations in education; and even in the public sector, students commonly pay fees for post-compulsory education. A further question of subsidisation policy in education is how much students should pay in fees, or cost-sharing between government and other stakeholders (students, parents or employers). This itself may be linked to discussion on taxation policies, which would require a separate analysis.

As Macau began to enter the 'take off' stage, its rapid economic development preceded the expansion of technical and higher education. The skills pool could not meet the demands of the Macau economy. At the same time, efforts were being made to localise the civil service. These two forces placed considerable pressure on the limited supply of skills. To meet future needs, government may consider carrying out periodic manpower surveys. This would provide more information for decision-makers to reduce the imbalance between labour supply and demand, such as an expansion or contraction of the public sector, the adaptability of skills in one occupation to another, and the mobility of the labour force.

Turning to Hong Kong, previous analysis suggests that workers will require higher skills to cope with their jobs as the economy becomes more knowledge- and technology-intensive. Hence there will be heavy demand for higher educational qualifications. Overseas sources of supply are subject to a number of factors, including economic and political conditions both locally and overseas. Any change in these factors will affect these inflows of graduate workers. Countries experiencing political uncertainty are likely to lose particularly large numbers of students overseas (Fry 1984). Estimates showed that the proportion of overseas graduates who returned to Hong Kong was quite high, ranging from 72 per cent between 1962 and 1976 to over 90 per cent in 1994 (Huang 1988; Hong Kong, Education & Manpower Branch 1994). This does not preclude the possibility that the overseas students may be amongst the ones who later apply for resident visas overseas. It would seem likely that large numbers of those educated overseas, with their wider horizons and contacts in the potential destination countries, might wish to move permanently. However, up to now there is no supportive data to draw such a conclusion.

The motives for migration of students and highly skilled workers are complex. For the case of Hong Kong, it is clear that the higher the level of education, the higher the tendency to emigrate. The major reason is that well-educated people have a better knowledge of the consequences of emigration, and are more adaptable to life in foreign countries, partly because of their better language skills. Also, the tendency to emigrate increases with income. This may be connected with the 'insurance effect' of a 'Western passport'. If emigration is considered a kind of political insurance, then the higher income groups have a higher probability of purchasing such insurance (Lam et al. 1995).

The demand for highly skilled workers has been on the rise since the 1970s. In the future, Hong Kong will continue to expand the rail network in the north-west of the New Territories. This will require many professionals in the fields of construction and civil engineering. In the financial sector, the Hong Kong stock exchange aims to attract listings from companies operating in China and elsewhere in Asia. More accountants, business and finance professionals will be acquired to match the needs of expanding services, particularly in information technology and entertainment (Hong Kong, Financial Secretary 1999). Although Hong Kong expanded the local higher education sector in the first half of the 1990s, demand for tertiary graduates, at least up to the late 1990s, increased faster than local supply. In consequence, overseas universities remained major suppliers of high-level personnel for Hong Kong.

Prior to the changes of sovereignty, the Hong Kong and Macau governments often gave preference to individuals with qualifications from the United Kingdom (or selected Commonwealth countries) and Portugal. The change of sovereignty has brought increased attention to the possibilities for study in mainland China. Meanwhile, however, overseas studies have helped Hong Kong and Macau students to act as a bridge in the international knowledge network. They have facilitated links through familiarity with and preferences for equipment, relationships, and management styles of particular countries.

Curriculum Policies and Processes

8

Curriculum Reform

Lo Yiu Chun, Jennifer

As shown by other chapters in this book, Hong Kong and Macau are fascinating in their similarities and differences. These are evident in the domain of curriculum as much as in other spheres of education. This chapter explores the nature of the similarities and differences, identifying both causes and outcomes. It does so within the framework of broader literature on curriculum reform, and shows ways in which analysis of Hong Kong and Macau contributes to conceptual understanding. Its focus is on primary and secondary levels of education.

To provide a conceptual framework, the chapter begins with an outline of the concept of curriculum reform. It then describes and analyses the contexts of curriculum changes in Hong Kong and Macau, before turning to the processes and products of curriculum change with particular attention to the medium of instruction and to textbooks.

The Concept of Curriculum Reform

The term 'reform' refers here to changes in education initiated from above, usually by the central government or in the political system (Fullan 1991; Bourke 1994). Curriculum reform is defined as a type of educational reform which focuses on changes to the content and organisation of what is taught. Reform may take place at the system level as well as the school level (Ginsburg et al. 1990; Marsh & Morris 1991). The former commonly stresses a national curriculum which strengthens the national identity and contributes to modernisation of the education system. The latter commonly results from the initiatives of schools and teachers to develop teaching materials for their student needs.

Hargreaves (1995) noted the interrelationship between curriculum reform and the context of change. He indicated that patterns of educational reform are greatly influenced by social forces. Rulcker (1991) also pointed out that curriculum reform movements commonly arise from demand for school curriculum to meet changes in social conditions. Reform has a pragmatic task of translating social standards into the teaching and learning content for the purpose of preparing young people for integration into society. This chapter mainly analyses and compares the curriculum reforms in Hong Kong and Macau in the 1980s and 1990s, when the two territories were experiencing rapid social changes as a result of the impending transfer of sovereignty to the People's

Republic of China (PRC). The socio-political changes set an important framework for analysis.

Havelock (1973) distinguished between the stimulus-response model and the rational model of curriculum reform. In the stimulus-response model, changes occur from instinctive actions in response to challenges which have not been anticipated and perhaps even not fully understood. The model is reflexive, unplanned and trial-and-error in nature. The rational model emphasises an identification of objectives and related strategies in the face of challenges. Different steps are commonly taken, including a decision to do something, an attempt to define the problems, a search for solutions, and an application of possible solutions. The strategy is deliberate, and emphasises logical problem-solving.

Four areas of curriculum reform are especially spertinent for analysing the impact of political change on curriculum development in Hong Kong and Macau. These include:

- *Examinations.* Examinations, especially public examinations, have significant influence on school curriculum. They determine what is taught and how it is taught in schools (Mathews 1985). Many education authorities have changed examinations in order to move the school curriculum in a specific direction (e.g. to unify the education systems across the country); to shift effective control of education towards or away from central authorities; or to achieve political goals such as to repudiate the previous government's political policy (Eckstein & Noah 1992).

- *Textbooks.* Textbooks contain basic school knowledge, and convey cultural and national identity to young people. Teachers, especially those who are unqualified, rely heavily on textbooks in their teaching. In some small states, no textbooks are produced (Bray 1992c). Their textbooks are imported from overseas either from metropolitan cities or from neighbouring countries from which the small states copied their school systems. Heavy reliance on imported textbooks can result in irrelevant teaching content for local contexts (Altbach & Kelly 1988).

- *Personnel for curriculum development.* Many small systems of education suffer from constraints in personnel for curriculum development. In extreme cases, there is a complete absence of, or only one or two specialists, responsible for curriculum development. In other small states, however, curriculum development is well organised and supported. These states may have curriculum units or centres, and specialists to define curriculum policy and manage curriculum development activities at different levels and in various subjects (Bray 1992c).

- *School-based curriculum development.* School-based curriculum development was promoted as an alternative to the centre-periphery approach that appeared to achieve limited results at the school level (Hughes 1991). In the education systems of many states, priority was initially given to developing centralised curriculum which was believed to be able to strengthen national unity. In the 1980s, schools began to realise the need to supplement the centralised curriculum as well as to substitute some of its elements so as to achieve better educational outcomes.

In this chapter, curriculum reforms in Hong Kong and Macau are described and analysed with reference to criteria such as the ones listed above. The discussion focuses separately on the processes and the products. The processes of curriculum development include decision-making for the development of school curricula. The products of curriculum development include innovative curricula which can be used in schools. Before addressing these matters, however, the chapter presents more information on contexts in Hong Kong and Macau.

The Contexts: Patterns of Educational Provision

Dominant education patterns in Hong Kong are distinctly different from those of Macau. This is evident in the school and examination systems. As pointed out by Adamson & Li in this book, Hong Kong has a fairly unified school system, albeit with a considerable number of international schools operated privately to cater for children coming from abroad. Formal schooling begins at the primary level, which lasts for six years. Secondary schools provide five years of education with an additional two years of advanced courses leading to tertiary education. Most primary and secondary schools are aided, meaning that they are funded by the government's Education Department but managed by voluntary associations such as religious or charitable bodies. The other primary and secondary schools are operated by either the government or private organisations. Until 1998, only a minority of secondary schools overtly used Chinese as the medium of instruction, and the majority claimed to use English. English-medium schools are generally perceived to have a higher status and to provide better prospects for their students.

Macau, as also pointed out by Adamson & Li, has not had a unified school system. Instead, schools have followed four diverse models borrowed from Portugal, the PRC, Taiwan and Hong Kong. Up to the late 1990s, the principal schools which adopted the Portuguese model were funded and administered by the Macau government. These schools were subdivided into Portuguese and Luso-Chinese types. Lessons in the former were taught solely in Portuguese, and those in the latter were taught in both Portuguese and Chinese. Schools which adopted the other models were private institutions and formed the majority. They were mainly operated by religious bodies and social service organisations. Most lessons in these schools at the secondary level were taught in Chinese, and only 12.5 per cent (Macau Research Centre 1994) were in English. The presence of English medium schools under the Portuguese administration reflected the market demand for keeping the international status of Macau. Two bodies coordinated most of the private schools: the Macau Catholic Schools' Association and the Macau Chinese Education Association.

The existence of the diversified and uncoordinated school systems in Macau resulted from two main factors. First, Macau was a Portuguese colony in which official schools either directly followed or, in the case of the Luso-Chinese schools, were strongly influenced by the Portuguese education system. Second, because during the modern era Macau had no local tertiary education before 1981, students who wanted to have higher education had to go abroad, most commonly to Hong Kong, Taiwan, the PRC, and the UK. In order to guarantee the educational prospects of their students, the private schools followed the education systems of those societies. Thus the schools of the Macau Chinese Education Association adopted the PRC education system and curriculum, the Chinese sections of the religious schools adopted the Hong Kong or Taiwan education systems and curricula, and English sections adopted the Hong Kong or UK education systems and curricula (Macau Research Centre 1994). The fact that the school systems were diversified and uncoordinated meant that students could not easily change from one school to another.

The Hong Kong education system has long been criticised as dominated by internal and external examinations. From the earliest stages of primary school, students are besieged by regular internal examinations; and before students get a place in Secondary Form 1, they have to pass through the Secondary School Places Allocation system which scales their marks in the internal school assessments together with those of an Academic Aptitude Test administered by the Education Department. After five years of secondary education, students take the Hong Kong Certificate of Education Examination (HKCEE). On completion of a two-year sixth form course, students sit the Hong Kong Advanced Level Examination (HKALE) before they are admitted into universities. Both the HKCEE and the HKALE are organised by the Hong Kong Examinations Authority (HKEA), which was set up in 1977. It has the major functions of conducting public examinations at the secondary level and producing examination syllabuses for use in schools.

In contrast to the examination-oriented education system in Hong Kong, until 1990 Macau had no territory-wide public examinations and depended totally on external provision of school leaving examinations. In 1990, the University of East Asia (later called the University of Macau) launched an entrance examination open to all students in the territory. However, this was a university-entrance examination rather than a school-leaving examination, and Macau still has no examinations authority comparable to the HKEA. Students in the Portuguese-medium schools sit Portuguese examinations in the local examination centre and take the examinations simultaneously with their counterparts in Portugal. Many students in the other schools take examinations organised by other overseas examination boards. As those private schools under the supervision of the Macau Chinese Education Association have close connections with the PRC, their students normally take the entrance examinations organised in the local examination centres for the universities in mainland China. Students of the Catholic or Protestant schools take either the General Certificate of Education (London) examinations or entrance examinations for Taiwan universities. Some students travel to Hong Kong and sit for the school leaving examinations there; and some students take no public examinations at all. This is not necessarily problematic, for Macau is a small community. Employers can easily get references for candidates who apply for jobs, and may not have to depend on the results of public examinations for their selection purposes.

Nevertheless, the entrance examination by the University of Macau has had an increasing influence on the schools. Bray & Tang (1994a) observed an increasing number of secondary school graduates going into the University of Macau rather than to overseas tertiary institutions for further study. Hence this examination has a substantial influence on unifying Macau school curricula even though at present there is no secondary school leaving examination like that in Hong Kong.

The Processes of Curriculum Change

Different strategies for curriculum decision-making are adopted in Hong Kong and Macau. In Hong Kong, important parts of the education system are highly centralised, and educational decision-making mostly follows a top-down, centre-periphery approach. The Education Commission is the highest body responsible for advice in the formulation of education policies.

Curriculum development is undertaken by the Curriculum Development Institute (CDI), which is the executive arm of the Curriculum Development Council (CDC). The architects of the CDI expected it to be an independent professional body staffed by subject specialists committed to curriculum development (Education Commission 1990). However, the CDI was actually made a branch of the government's Education Department. Within the CDC, a number of Coordinating Committees oversee the curricula for kindergartens, primary education, secondary education, sixth forms, special education and prevocational education. Each of these Committees brings together various subject-specific committees which develop and revise the subject syllabuses for Hong Kong schools. Various mechanisms have been used by the government to control the processes of curriculum development to ensure that decision-making is compatible with central education policies. These include control of working agendas, selection of members for the relevant committees, and ignoring recommendations which are incompatible with those of the government (Morris 1996, p.100).

The highly centralised approach to curriculum decision making was initially legitimised by a set of regulations produced by the Education Department. These regulations (Hong Kong, Education Department 1971) included:

- No instruction may be given by any school except in accordance with a syllabus approved by the Director of Education (para. 92.1);
- No person shall use any document for instruction in a class in any school unless particulars of the title, author and publisher of the document and such other particulars of the document as the Director may require have been furnished to the Director not less than 14 days previously (para. 92.6); and
- No instruction, education, entertainment, recreation or propaganda or activity of any kind which, in the opinion of the Director, is in any way of a political or partly political nature and prejudicial to the public interest or the welfare of the pupils or of education generally or contrary to the approved syllabus, shall be permitted upon any school premises or upon the occasion of any school activity (para. 98.1).

Especially during the 1970s, the Education Department at various times made use of these regulations to exercise control over the school curriculum.

The 1980s brought growing dissatisfaction with the centralised curriculum, which was regarded as not meeting the needs of pupils and schools. The influential Llewellyn Report (1982, p.56) stated that:

> To encourage curriculum development efforts, especially in the post S3 [Secondary Form 3] area, we believe there is merit in drawing the teaching service, as a professional force, into curriculum development and assessment practices. Strategies should be implemented to improve the coordination and communication between the agencies responsible for curriculum development and examinations. A genuine drive towards school-based curriculum selection and adaptation, together with school-based programme and pupil evaluation, would open up new horizons for teacher participation. This involvement would be from periphery-to-centre rather than the centre-to-periphery tradition which now permeates educational planning, policy making and innovation, limiting the number of

teachers who can become involved in these activities. Every effort must be made to encourage innovation at the school level which, after all, is where the real work is being done.

Such statements were followed by a demand for more democracy in the wider society as a result of the announcement of the 1984 Sino-British Joint Declaration and the suppression of the pro-democracy movement in the PRC. Subsequently, a number of measures were introduced to reduce the degree of centralisation in curriculum decision making. These included the School-based Curriculum Project Scheme launched in 1988, the School Management Initiative launched in 1991, and the Target Oriented Curriculum launched in 1995. All of these initiatives appeared to emphasise the value of school control and teachers' participation in curriculum decision-making. However, as these innovations were launched and administered by the Education Department, at least some analysts regarded them as a means used by the government to extend its control over the curriculum and the related activities in schools (McClelland 1991; Lo 1995; Morris 1996).

Just before the transfer of Hong Kong's sovereignty to the PRC, the government, endorsing the seventh report of the Education Commission (1997), declared its determination to improve the overall quality of school education. This long term educational reform policy was supported by a reorganisation of the Education Department which included a review of the functions and structure of the CDI and its relationship with the HKEA (Hong Kong, Education & Manpower Bureau 1998).

While the Hong Kong government was bringing a more decentralised strategy into its highly centralised approach to curriculum decision-making, Macau's government was moving in an opposite direction and promoting a more centralised approach (Bray 1992b). Until the late 1980s, the Macau government adopted a laissez faire policy in education. Essentially, the government was mainly concerned with the administration of the official schools, which comprised a small proportion in the territory, while the private schools were left to their own devices including in the curriculum domain. Education provision therefore appeared to be uncoordinated (Bray & Hui 1991a). After the 1987 Sino-Portuguese Joint Declaration, the Portuguese and Macau governments began to recognise the need for education reform to place the territory on a firmer basis in the post-1999 era. The coordinator of the Education Reform Committee (Rosa 1991, p.35) stated that:

> We have realised and already emphasised that only with the resolution of education problems can we identify policy that addresses the interest of both Portugal and China, and ensure the steady transference of Macau's sovereignty. Ignoring this fact is not beneficial to the future of Macau. If the Macau government did nothing, it would be regarded as short-sighted and violating the benefits and needs of Macau people as well as those of Portugal and China.

The first public conference on educational reform in Macau was organised in 1989. The major issues identified were the need for compulsory education and the establishment of a unified educational system (H.K. Wong 1991).

To address these issues, the Macau government passed a set of laws (Government of Macau 1991) on dimensions of educational reform. An advisory Educational Council comparable to Hong Kong's Education Commission was established. New policies also considered the establishment of a local assessment system and provision of financial assistance for the private schools. This was followed in 1993 by a reorganisation of the Education Department, which included redefinition of the various Divisions within the Department (Macau, Department of Education & Youth 1993). In this aspect, the Macau government was arguably ahead of the Hong Kong government. The work of curriculum development was first undertaken by the Education Reform Committee as mentioned earlier and then assigned to the Division of Education Research & Reform within the Department. One of the functions of the Division (Macau, Department of Education & Youth 1993, Article 7, p.44) was to coordinate and organise the work of curriculum plans and programmes, as well as to pay full attention to their experimentation.

Under the Educational Council, an ad hoc Curriculum Development Committee was set up mainly for the purpose of planning the pre-primary, primary and junior secondary curricula for achieving the goal of compulsory education. Unlike Hong Kong's CDI, which is composed of various subject and curriculum development experts, this committee was made up by government personnel, principals and senior teachers from official and private schools, and a lecturer from the University of Macau. Curriculum Reform Working Groups for various subjects were also formed for the formulation of subject syllabuses. These groups comprised relevant subject teachers with university lecturers as advisors. By 1998, provisional teaching syllabuses had been produced and were being trialled in the official schools. A public seminar was arranged to collect comments from school teachers on the syllabuses.

The Products of Curriculum Change

This section focuses on two major products of curriculum change, namely the language of instruction and the textbooks used in schools. The language of instruction has been controversial in both Hong Kong and Macau. Textbooks have been less controversial, but may also be a powerful determinant of the actual learning by school children.

The Language of Instruction

With the anticipated reunification with the PRC, the Hong Kong government encouraged secondary schools to use Chinese to replace English as the medium of instruction (Adamson & Auyeung Lai 1997). Though not usually stated explicitly, Cantonese was the form of Chinese used. Proposals for the use of mother tongue as the medium of instruction have a history dating back at least to 1935 (Sweeting 1991b). The matter was raised in the 1982 Llewellyn Report, and followed up in Education Commission Report No.1 (1984). Both reports noted the value of using mother tongue in teaching, but expressed concern about pupils' standards of English. It appeared that at that time the intention of the colonial government was to maintain the status of English in the territory. However, during the political transition, a number of measures were taken seriously by the Hong Kong Education Department to encourage schools to adopt Chinese (Cantonese) as the instruction medium.

Education Commission Report No.4 (1990) proposed that schools should use the language of instruction suitable for their pupils. At primary level, the language issue is less controversial because language learning needs to be supported by the child's daily experience. Cantonese is certainly the instructional medium in the majority of primary schools. At secondary level, schools were encouraged to stream their pupils in either

English or Cantonese as the medium of instruction. Further steps were taken by the Education Department to encourage secondary schools to use the mother tongue in teaching. These included permission for schools to appoint additional Chinese-language teachers, provision of subsidy for the publication of Chinese textbooks, and revision of the examination rules to allow pupils to take subjects in Chinese without any indication of the use of language mode at the School Certificate examination level (Leung 1992, p.269).

However, this kind of encouragement did not prove successful. Many secondary schools still claimed to use English as the medium of instruction even though in practice they used mixed code (i.e. teachers using Cantonese to explain English teaching materials). The majority of school administrators were worried that if they officially changed to Chinese medium, they would receive lower band pupils and would reduce the popularity of their schools. This was actually the experience of a pioneer secondary school in the mid-1980s. The school used to attract pupils of high academic standard from primary schools. With their formal change of language instruction from English to Chinese, this group of pupils no longer chose the school as their priority. Hence the academic banding of this school dropped until its language policy was reversed (Morris 1996, p.115). This was due to the fact that parents in general preferred their children to be educated in English on the assumption that it would provide them with better career futures. In order to attract pupils, most schools claimed to use English as the language of instruction even if in classroom practice they used mixed code.

Immediately after the return of sovereignty to the PRC, the Hong Kong Education Department took steps to impose the use of mother tongue. Although the Education Department claimed that the move was undertaken for pedagogical reasons, it was widely regarded as a sort of political action (*Wen Wei Po* 1998). Initially, all Hong Kong secondary schools in the mainstream public system were requested to use the mother-tongue for classroom teaching. However, the Education Department allowed 114 schools (23.6%) to continue to use English as the medium of instruction. The criteria for selection (Hong Kong, Education Department 1997b) included:

- in the past three years, the new Secondary Form 1 entrants belonged to language group 1 (i.e. students who are able to learn in both English and Chinese) and/or group 3 (i.e. students who would probably learn better through Chinese but could also learn in English);
- from appraisal reports and evidence provided by the school principals, the teachers had levels of English which were sufficient for effective teaching;
- there was provision of resourcing support in the school, e.g. bridging courses to help students to move from Chinese-medium instruction to English-medium instruction.

This policy was criticised by the public as having the effect of stratifying the schools, and was even regarded as a barrier to mother-tongue teaching. Nevertheless, 11 of the 114 English medium schools decided to support mother-tongue teaching by applying for the use of Cantonese in subjects such as Physical Education, Art & Design, Civic Education, and Moral & Religious Education (*Sing Tao Daily* 1998).

While the Hong Kong government was attempting to minimise the extent to which schools used English as the medium of instruction, the Macau government was promoting Portuguese in schools. Previously, Portuguese had not been widely used in Macau. It was chiefly confined to a small number of Portuguese expatriates, Macanese (i.e. mixed race Portuguese-Chinese), and civil servants. As mentioned above, Portuguese was taught as the first language in the official schools, and few private schools taught Portuguese at all. During negotiation between Beijing and Lisbon about the future sovereignty of Macau, the Portuguese government felt that there was a need to promote Portuguese culture. The Portuguese felt that even after 400 years of presence Macau, few Portuguese footprints would remain and economic prospects would be diminished. Hence the promotion of Portuguese as a way to retain their influence was considered essential. This effort was strengthened by the 1987 Sino-Portuguese Joint Declaration (Annex Section VII) and the 1993 Basic Law (Article 9), which promised that Portuguese would remain an official language in Macau for at least 50 years after 1999. The Macau Education Law (1991, Article 4.2) stated that:

> in all types of education, only Portuguese or Chinese could be used as the medium of instruction. In reasonable situations, English could also be used as a medium of instruction.

The Macau government endeavoured to include Portuguese as a compulsory subject in all school curricula including the curricula of private schools. In the draft version of the pre-primary, primary and junior secondary curriculum framework submitted for approval by the Educational Council in 1994, Portuguese was envisaged as a compulsory subject. Private schools which did not teach Portuguese as a core subject, it was suggested, would not receive grants from the government (Yue 1994). This act roused the anger of the two major private umbrella educational bodies which, though divergent in their educational ideologies, worked together and had furious disputes with the government. They argued that the government could encourage private schools to teach Portuguese, but that it should not impose the language. The disputes were exacerbated by articles in the local Portuguese-language newspapers which supported the government policy, and by articles in the local Chinese language newspapers which supported the private schools (Ieong 1994). Mutual attacks went on for a number of months until the government backed down.

The final version of the curriculum framework no longer insisted that teaching of Portuguese was compulsory, and schools were given the options to use Portuguese as the second language for teaching. It stated (Macau, Department of Education & Youth 1994a, p.28) that:

> All educational institutions starting at the primary level should begin and continue to teach the second language. At P.5 and P.6 levels, the teaching of second language should be more organised and systematic. Without any restrictions, the local two official languages should be considered the top priority.

With this change in the curriculum framework, the language battle was settled, at least for the time being. Nonetheless, to support the teaching of Portuguese in schools, special programmes were organised in the Institute of Portuguese Studies at the University of Macau. These programmes trained personnel to teach Portuguese, and to use Portuguese as a medium of instruction.

Another dimension concerned Putonghua. The governments of both Hong Kong and Macau were aware of the urgent need for Putonghua in the post-colonial era, and started to encourage the teaching of Putonghua in schools. In Hong Kong, Putonghua had been included in the primary and junior secondary curricula as an elective soon after the signing of the 1984 Joint Declaration. In a few schools (e.g. Kiangsu-Chekiang College, Sun Fong Chung Primary School), Putonghua has long been used as the medium of instruction and this could cater for immigrants from northern China. In 1996, just before the hand-over, the government announced that Putonghua would become a core subject in 1998, and that by 2000 it would become an independent subject in the Hong Kong Certificate of Education Examination. This announcement was an endorsement of the recommendations of Education Commission Report No.6 (1995). However, a major problem faced by Hong Kong schools was the lack of qualified Putonghua teachers due to the fact that there was no system to accredit the teaching qualifications obtained from mainland China. For the long term, however, Putonghua has been built into the teacher education programmes of the universities and the Hong Kong Institute of Education.

As in Hong Kong, many Macau schools (about a third) had already included Putonghua in their formal curricula by the mid-1990s (Macau, Department of Education & Youth 1994b). Provisional teaching syllabuses for Putonghua were developed by the government for pupils at Primary 3 to Secondary 3 levels. However, pupils had difficulties in coping with the demands of three written languages (English, Portuguese and Chinese) and four spoken languages (English, Portuguese, Putonghua and Cantonese). In contrast to Hong Kong, teachers with qualifications from the PRC were permitted to teach in Macau, and the territory's teaching force included many well-educated personnel who were expert in Putonghua. In some schools, particularly those associated with the Macau Chinese Education Association, Putonghua became the medium of instruction. Immigrants from northern China went to these schools because of their instructional language and the adopted school curriculum.

Textbooks
Especially during the 1950s and 1960s, the Hong Kong colonial authorities endeavoured to make school curricula politically neutral (Morris & Sweeting 1991). In particular, political issues related to contemporary China were excluded from the syllabuses. The aim was to avoid the intrusion of influences by the Nationalist Party in Taiwan and the Communists in mainland China, so as to maintain social stability. To assist the tasks of de-politicising the school curriculum, a Textbook Coordinating Committee was set up to scrutinise the textbooks provided by commercial publishers. A list of approved textbooks was then sent to individual schools for reference. With regard to those perceived as not educationally and politically acceptable, the decisions and suggestions made by the Committee were conveyed directly to the publishers (Morris & Sweeting 1991, p.263). In order to avoid any financial loss, the publishers usually made changes. In contrast, the Macau government did not have to adopt the same measure to promote apoliticisation. This was partly because many textbooks used by Macau schools came from Hong Kong and were already apoliticised.

With the impending change of sovereignty and the need to help students to increase their political awareness and become PRC citizens, the Hong Kong government introduced new school subjects including Government & Public Affairs, Liberal Studies, and Civic Education at secondary level. Government & Public Affairs stressed the study of concepts related to Western democracy and political issues of China. Liberal Studies provided contextualised and politicised studies of China and Hong Kong. In Civic Education, substantial emphasis was put on developing students' identification with Chinese culture and good citizenship. The government also added topics to the existing subjects, including History, Chinese History, Economic & Public Affairs, and Social Studies. For example, in Chinese History, modern historical events between 1911 and 1976 such as the establishment of the PRC, the Great Leap Forward and the Cultural Revolution were included; in Social Studies, the development and structure of the Chinese Communist Party and the biography of Mao Zedong were also covered. Also, topics describing the relationship between Hong Kong and the PRC were added to the General Studies syllabus for primary schools. These topics were 'Hong Kong and the PRC: Geography and History', and 'Hong Kong and the PRC: Politics and Economics'. All of these teaching materials were once regarded as contrary to Education Regulation No.98 and could have resulted in the closure of the school, a dismissal of the teacher or withdrawal of financial support from the government (Morris & Sweeting 1991).

Moreover, special teaching materials introducing mainland China were produced. For example, 'Knowing Your Own Country', developed by the Hong Kong Educationists' Association and the Hong Kong Resource Centre (1996), focused on the political, social, economic and military aspects of the PRC. "Enhancing Learning, Knowing China" produced by the Education Department (1999) includes teaching resources (such as teaching packages, CD-ROM, computer software) related to Chinese culture and history as well as the political and geographical features of mainland China. In addition, terms used in the textbooks were changed, e.g. 'Hong Kong' became 'Hong Kong Special Administrative Region', 'Mainland China' became 'Inland China', and 'Taiwan' became 'Taiwan Province'. In order not to confront the Chinese authorities, the publishers also practised self-censorship. An example is found in the Chinese History textbooks. The term (聯俄容共政策) used in the old edition, meaning the policy of forming alliance with Russia and allowing the existence of the Communist Party, was replaced by a new term (聯俄聯共政策) meaning the policy of forming alliance with Russia and the Communist Party. The former term implied that the communists had a lower status than Russia whereas the latter term placed the Chinese Communist Party on an equal status with Russia *(Ming Pao* 1997).

After publication in 1985 of the Guidelines on Civic Education, teachers were encouraged to adopt cross-curricular approaches in teaching civic education and began to develop their own teaching materials for this purpose. After July 1997, some schools started to organise extra curricular activities to build up political awareness and national identity in their students. These activities included raising the national flag, singing the national song, and organising school visits to mainland China.

Macau has a shortage of locally-produced teaching materials, and schools have to depend on imported textbooks. The main source of these textbooks has been Hong Kong (especially in the religious private schools), but others have been imported from Portugal (especially in the Portuguese official schools), and the PRC (especially in the schools of the Macau Chinese Education Association). The main reasons why hardly any textbooks have been specifically produced for Macau schools are that the Macau government has neglected the majority of schools, and the market in Macau is so small and fragmented that commercial publishers have been unwilling to invest in it (Bray & Tang 1994a). The result is that some students know more about certain features of Hong Kong than parallel features of Macau, and are influenced by the thoughts and ideology prevalent in Hong Kong. From this perspective it has been argued that Macau is perhaps a de facto colony of Hong Kong rather than Portugal in aspects of its culture.

However, one textbook in Social Studies (namely Social Studies of Macau, published by the Modern Educational Research Society) and another in Chinese Language (published by Yen Chin Publications) were produced specifically for use in Macau primary schools in 1990 and 1991 respectively. These textbooks were written with close reference to the syllabuses produced by the Hong Kong Curriculum Development Council. Also, some school teachers have prepared quasi-textbooks by compiling their own teaching materials for use in schools, and the early 1990s brought initiatives for books in other subjects (Kong 1992; Bray & Tang 1994a, 1994b). For example, a geometry book has been written and published locally by a Macau teacher (Y.N. Wong 1990). In 1993, the government (Macau, Department of Education & Youth 1993, Article 7) promised to build up conditions for the production of textbooks and other educational equipment and resources. Hence it was announced that local books for History and Geography would be published in 1997/98.

Additionally, with the production of curriculum frameworks for pre-primary, primary and junior secondary schools by the Macau government, a subject called Civic & Moral Education was developed. The aims of the subject area, as noted by Tse's chapter in this book, were to foster students' positive attitudes towards their country, ethnic group and the Macau community, and to develop the traditional Chinese moral concepts and values. A symposium was held in 1991 to explore the current situation and direction for civic education in Macau (H.K. Wong 1992). One of the main goals, as in Hong Kong, was to help students adapt to the forthcoming change of sovereignty.

Conclusions

Although an extensive literature has developed on the effects of sovereignty transfer on education policies and practice in Hong Kong and Macau, examining the territories both separately and together (e.g. Bray 1992a; Bray & Lee 1997; Morris & Chan 1997; K.C. Tang 1998), little attention has been given to comparisons of the way that curriculum development in the two territories has been affected by the political change. This chapter has endeavoured to reduce part of that gap.

The preceding discussion shows that sovereignty change caused substantial innovations, with similarities and differences, in curriculum development in the two territories. With respect to curriculum process, Hong Kong had a highly centralised education system which in the domain of medium of instruction became even more centralised but which in other aspects moved towards some decentralisation. Macau, by contrast, had an uncoordinated set of education systems and was moving towards centralised curriculum decision making in order to improve coherence. Concerning the curriculum products, during the early 1990s the Macau government tried to promote the use of Portuguese in schools, while the Hong Kong government attempted to reduce the use of English as the medium of instruction. However, both governments promoted the teaching of Putonghua, and encouraged addition of Chinese political and cultural concepts through new subjects and new topics in existing subjects.

Hong Kong and Macau followed different approaches to curriculum reform. At the government level, Hong Kong adopted more the stimulus-response model before 1997 and the rational model subsequently. The Macau government mostly employed the rational model in its educational reform with the use of stimulus response in the face of ad hoc events. In the main colonial period, the principal goal of the Hong Kong government was to preserve its authority and power. When faced by challenges, the authorities took action to maintain their status. The use of the stimulus-response model in the education system by adopting a more decentralised curriculum development strategy became evident when the government faced increasing demands for democracy from the wider society and dissatisfaction with the centralised curriculum in the 1980s. One example was Targets and Target Related Assessment (TTRA), which encountered strong resistance from teachers and schools. In order to solve this problem, the Hong Kong government set up an advisory committee which recommended the implementation of the curriculum innovation with a change of the name from TTRA to Target Oriented Curriculum (TOC), a simplification of the relevant documents, and increased provision of resources. The use of the rational model was also evident in the setting up of the Education Commission in 1984, the establishment of the Curriculum Development Institute in 1992, and the reorganisation of the Education Department in 1999.

The Macau government faced pressures which were in some respects similar but in other respects different. The government continued to administer the official schools, but gave more support to the private schools. However, the private schools were not all willing to sacrifice their autonomy when invited to fit government plans. To achieve effective educational reform, the Macau government persisted with a centralised approach and use of rational model to improve coordination among schools. This was rather different from Hong Kong, where the government used dual models in organising different curriculum reform activities. A number of stages were evident in the Macau government's process, including decision on the need for educational reform; organising public conferences/seminars on the direction of the reform activities; passing educational laws and setting up of different working committees; and planning school curricula, experimenting with syllabuses, and collecting feedback from teachers. Nevertheless the government also employed a stimulus response model in coping with issues arising in educational policy making. This can be discerned in the dispute related to the inclusion of Portuguese as the compulsory subject in the school curriculum. In face of fierce opposition from the private schools, the government changed its mind and made Portuguese one of the options for second language teaching.

At the school level, changes on a stimulus-response model were evident in both territories. Out of their own professionalism, together with their response to the urgent need to help pupils to develop identity with the PRC and Chinese culture, school teachers in both Hong Kong and Macau produced teaching materials and organised extra-curricular activities in their schools.

Returning to the observation at the beginning of the chapter about the similarities and differences between Hong Kong and Macau in terms of their curriculum development, and those between the two territories as a pair and other parts of the world which have experienced curriculum reform, four major points related to the aspects mentioned earlier may be highlighted.

- *Examinations.* Hong Kong had already established its local examination system monitored by the Hong Kong Examinations Authority during the colonial era. In Macau, the first local public examination organised by the University of East Asia appeared in 1990. This was consistent with patterns elsewhere in Asia and in Africa, the Caribbean and the South Pacific, where governments established national or regional examination boards during the period of colonial transition (Kellaghan & Greaney 1992; Bray 1998b).

- *Textbooks.* Teachers in both Hong Kong and Macau depend heavily on textbooks. Hong Kong possesses various types of publishers including locally organised overseas publishers (e.g. Oxford University Press; Longman) to produce local textbooks which are based on the requirements of the Education Department. Moreover Hong Kong has subject specialists who help in writing the textbooks. In contrast, Macau textbooks have been mainly imported from such places as Hong Kong, the PRC and Portugal. Recent attempts have been made to produce local textbooks. The situation is similar to Solomon Islands, which heavily depended on imported textbooks in the past but started to produce local textbooks for schools in the early 1990s (Bray 1992c, pp.77-79).
- *Personnel for curriculum development.* Hong Kong and Macau have very different situations in personnel. Whereas Hong Kong is relatively well-endowed, Macau is short of curriculum development specialists. Curriculum development in Macau was initially taken up by the Education Reform Committee which was headed by a government official, and then by an ad hoc curriculum development committee which was made up by teachers and university lecturers who were not experienced in curriculum development. This situation resembled some small states such as Montserrat where the curriculum development unit had only one post and Grenada which had five (Bray 1992c, p.67). However, Hong Kong's Curriculum Development Institute is a well-organised body with subject specialists who have relevant experience. This has been made possible by Hong Kong's larger population and longer record of tertiary education and high-level training.
- *School-based curriculum development.* Like their counterparts elsewhere (Lewy 1991), many teachers in both Hong Kong and Macau recognise the need of school based curriculum development, and supplement non-local textbooks with materials related to local issues. Hong Kong teachers select or adapt the teaching materials from the centralised curriculum so as to meet the learning levels of their students. In Macau, as there is a lack of localised teaching materials, some teachers take initiatives to develop their own teaching materials for use in schools.

Important insights may also be gained for an understanding of the impact of political change on curriculum development in Hong Kong and Macau. Some of these insights can be generalised to other societies at different periods of time. The first important insight is related to the nature of curriculum in schools. Although the two territories are similar in their cultural backgrounds and colonial status, the characteristics of their school curricula are very different. This is due to the fact that different strategies were adopted by the two colonial governments in curriculum development. However, because of the political change with the common goal of reunification with the PRC, school curricula in these two territories have begun to show signs of convergence.

As a pair, Hong Kong and Macau may be contrasted with other colonies which have undergone political transition. As discussed above, both Hong Kong and Macau governments placed a premium on curriculum development after the hand-over of their sovereignty had been agreed in the 1980s. This approach had similarities with patterns elsewhere, but also had differences. Since most other former colonies became independent states after their political change, the major purpose of their curriculum development was to build up new national identities. This was not the case in Hong Kong and Macau. Certainly the authorities wanted their students to identify with the territories in which they lived; but they also wanted them to identify with the PRC. Language policies also differed from those in the majority of colonies which became independent. Many of these colonies maintained the use of the colonial language, because it was seen as a unifying force and as an instrument for wider communication. Singapore and Tanzania are examples of this pattern. In Macau, the departing colonial authority did try to push Portuguese, but it was largely unsuccessful; and in Hong Kong the departing colonial regime encouraged the use of Chinese rather than English as the medium of instruction. Moreover, both territories saw stronger interest in Putonghua, the official language of the PRC.

Overall, change of sovereignty certainly did not cause the end of curriculum reform in either Hong Kong or Macau. Further changes in the processes and products of curriculum development are inevitable, and may be as radical as those seen in the period prior to the change of sovereignty. Hong Kong and Macau will certainly continue to be fertile grounds for instructive comparison of curriculum development.

9

Civic and Political Education

Tse Kwan Choi, Thomas

Civic education aroused much public concern in Hong Kong and Macau during the transitional period from the mid-1980s. Informed by the theoretical discussion of the political socialisation function of schools and the role of education in political development, this chapter analyses civic and political education programmes. It first gives an account of the continuity and change of political education in these two places in the period following World War II, and then reviews the practices and implementation of political education in the schools in the light of some previous studies of civic education. Then it contrasts and compares the cases of Hong Kong and Macau, and further discusses the implications of these results for theoretical reflection and future civic education programmes in these two places.

Some Definitions of Civic and Political Education

The terms civic and political education carry denotative, descriptive and normative meanings, and they are often used interchangeably with other terms including moral education, citizenship education, civics, political literacy, political indoctrination, and nationalistic education.

Conceptually, political education refers to "institutionalized forms of political knowledge acquisition which take place within formal and informal educational frameworks" (Ichilov 1994, p.4568). The content and orientation of political education varies from country to country, and from time to time, depending on the definition of a particular political system. Political education could be about an obedient passive subject in a despotic monarchy, or an active participating citizen in a democratic polity. In nation-states, which are the dominant political communities in the world, political education is commonly tied closely with 'citizenship' education. That is why political education is also commonly called civic education or citizenship education, in particular in the US literature. Generally speaking, 'citizenship' refers to the rights, obligations, and power inherited in the legal status of a full membership of a modern nation-state (Marshall 1950, p.2). As Heater (1991, p.4) states:

> a citizen is, after all, a person who has a relationship with and within the state that is different from that of a slave, a vassal, or a subject. Citizen is both a status and a feeling. In educational terms, therefore, it requires both cognitive and skills leading to understand and use the status, and affective learning to want to behave

in citizenly manner.

As citizenship is not a fixed or static concept, the concrete content of citizenship is always changing and evolving. The same is true of the content of citizenship education, which is multi-dimensional in nature. As Heater (1990, p.314) points out, citizenship education is like a cube with three dimensions: elements (identity & loyalty, virtues, legal or civil status, and political entitlement & social rights); geographical level (local, nation-state, regional or world); and outcomes of education (knowledge, attitudes, and skills). Generally speaking, the content of citizenship education includes knowledge, values, attitudes, and group identifications necessary for a political community as well as its members. So it usually includes knowledge of the history and structure of political institutions at both the national and local levels (sometimes even at global level), loyalty to the nation, positive attitudes toward political authority, fundamental socio-political beliefs and values, obedience to laws and social norms, sense of political efficacy, and interest and skills concerning political participation.

Since 'political education' is a contested concept intertwined with different ideologies and normative expectation, it is often used interchangeably with 'civics', 'civic education', 'citizenship education' and 'political literacy'. These titles usually represent different notions and traditions concerning the goals, expectations, nature, and practices of political education. Scholars also accord and classify different modes of political education as the conservative, liberal, and radical (Giroux 1983). Civic education or civics is frequently associated with the ideas of liberal democracy. Traditionally civics tends to carry apolitical orientations, focusing upon individuals' relations with the social and civic realms, rather than on their affinity with the political arena. The curriculum mainly relates to the structural, procedural, and legal aspects of political institutions, stressing consensus, harmony, and compliance while avoiding the discussion of controversial issues. Consequently, civics has been accused in some contexts of being associated with conservative politics, aiming to preserve the status quo. On the other hand, 'political literacy' is associated with more radical traditions and particularly with the ideas of participatory democracy. The curriculum tends to be issue-based, confronting controversial issues, and often employing activity-based teaching methods (Ichilov 1994, pp.4568-9).

The above discussion of political education points to its variety, complexity and multi-dimensionality, as well as its underlying philosophical, ideological and political bearings. Schools in all societies are political as well as educational establishments; and the socialisation function of schools has been recognised by students of political socialisation and educators, both in their discussion of the role of education in political development and in their studies of curricula.

The Role of Formal Education as Political Socialisation

Formal curricula in schools receive public attention because they are major media of cultural transmission and political socialisation. Both advocates of the so-called New Sociology of Education (Young 1971; Whitty 1985; Whitty & Young 1976) and Neo-Marxism (Apple 1990; Giroux 1983) contend that cultural transmission in schools is not a neutral process but operates through deliberate organisation, selection, classification, distribution, and evaluation which reflects both the distribution of power and the principles of social control.

Likewise, as school knowledge is strongly tied with the ideology of the dominant class and under the control of the powerful, formal curriculum is not neutral but penetrated by ideologies or values in favour of the dominant groups, whether they are about sexism, racism, political doctrines, colonialism, legitimacy of capitalism and class inequality or about other dominant socio-economic values. In recent centuries, political education has increasingly been realised in formal lessons (S.Y. Wong 1991). Accordingly, social subjects like History, Social Studies, and Civics are officially designed to acquaint students with nationalistic values, an acceptance of the established social order, and the learning of particular political ideologies (Whitty 1985).

Critical studies of colonial education commonly view the school as an institution of colonialism and imperialism which exercises political control and consolidates the legitimacy and authority of the colonial rulers. Characterised by 'alienation' and 'depoliticisation', colonial education is often accused of disseminating cultural imperialism and sustaining colonial rule over indigenous people (Carnoy 1974; Altbach & Kelly 1991). According to this view, control over colonies is exercised through a number of measures including selection of the content of education.

Development of Civic Education in Hong Kong and Macau before the mid-1980s

Hong Kong and Macau have both experienced significant socio-political changes in the post-World War II era. Accordingly, there has been a change in the educational systems dealing with political education (commonly called civic education) in these two Chinese societies.

Hong Kong
For much of Hong Kong's colonial era, political power was concentrated in the hands of the governor, career civil servants and a small group of co-opted élites (Lau 1982). Between the 1950s and the late 1960s, in co-existence with a secluded and autocratic bureaucratic polity, a loosely-organised Chinese immigrant society, and substantial economic growth was a 'parochial' and 'subject' political culture characterised by an acceptance of the status quo and the colonial government, a pervasive sense of political powerlessness and political inefficacy, and a low level of political participation (King 1981a, 1981b; Lau 1982; Miners 1996; Scott 1989). The socio-political situation changed rapidly after the late 1960s. Following the serious challenges of the riots in 1966 and 1967, the colonial state opened its political structure and played a more active role in regulating economic and social affairs and in providing public services to the community (Scott 1989).

In congruence with the socio-political circumstances from the 1950s to the mid-1980s was an officially apolitical educational system in which formal political education was marginalised (Morris & Sweeting 1991; Tsang 1984, 1994; P.M. Wong 1981, 1983). The colonial government in Hong Kong exercised tight control of the educational system through legislation which prohibited political activities in schools, control of school subjects and curriculum materials via model syllabuses, officially-approved textbooks and exhortation, and provision of official circulars and guidelines (Morris 1992a). The government was particularly sensitive and suspicious towards political issues in education, and tried to keep them under control. Political education was never stated as an explicit educational objective in any official educational document, and the orientation of political education in this period was a kind of conformity-oriented civic education, alien and subject-oriented in nature (Morris 1992c; Morris & Sweeting 1991; Tsang 1994, 1998). Hence the curriculum alienated many students from their Chinese nationality and local politics, and fostered their identification as 'subjects' rather than 'citizens'.

Although nationalistic education is the core of political and citizenship education in many countries (Schleicher 1993), nationalistic education was marginalised or even eliminated in Hong Kong for a long period. Hong Kong schools generally discouraged their students from an identification with their ethnicity, indigenous culture (Chinese and local society), or any Chinese government across the Taiwan Straits. Both Chinese culture and social subjects in the secondary school curriculum were also 'a-political' and 'a-national' in nature (Tsang 1998). Although the colonial government in Hong Kong did not deliberately foster an identity with the British authority, it did not promote an identity with the Chinese government either. By contrast, an identity with the Chinese cultural heritage and tradition, instead of a political identity, was tolerated to counterbalance the influence of contemporary Chinese nationalism (Luk 1991; Fan 1995). Till the 1980s, the objectives of teaching Chinese Language were confined to cultivation of language abilities, rather than about Chinese culture (Lan 1993). The part of Chinese history between 1911 to 1949 was even deleted from the syllabus of Chinese History between 1958 and 1972 (Pong 1987). As far as other secondary school subjects were concerned, there was little discussion of Chinese society and the People's Republic of China (PRC) in the syllabuses of Economic & Public Affairs (EPA), Economics, History, or Geography (Cheung 1987; Morris 1988, 1992b; Fung & Lee 1987; Tsang 1998) till the early 1970s. Also, these syllabuses avoided sensitive political topics such as Hong Kong's colonial status, Hong Kong's relationships with mainland China, or issues concerning contemporary Chinese history. A sense of remoteness and an absence of identity was created in the curriculum as Hong Kong history was not included in the History syllabus. In addition, owing to legal constraints over political activities in schools, nationalistic education was rare outside a small number of partisan schools (K.K. Lam 1994).

Political scientists Almond & Verba (1963) have classified political culture into three models – parochial, subject and participant – in the light of its orientation toward political objects. Accordingly, political education in Hong Kong in the period between the 1950s and the mid-1980s may be characterised as 'subject-oriented' in the sense that the concept of 'citizenship' transmitted was distorted and one-sided. The curriculum in Hong Kong reflected a kind of subject political culture concerned more with administrative output and the political system than with political inputs and rights and obligations. The formal curriculum was characterised by a transmission approach to political education, carrying supporting beliefs of the pre-existing political institution and a passive image of citizenship. For example, the EPA syllabus chiefly transmitted factual political knowledge and cultivated politically-apathetic citizens, in correspondence to a subject political culture prevailing at that period. Students' exposures to political topics were mainly restricted to the description of the structure and functions of the government, and to the government's contributions to solving various social and economic problems. Citizens were implicitly defined as passive, obedient, and complacent, and cooperative recipients of governmental services. It was not until 1984 that the EPA syllabus at certificate level saw a marked increase in attention to systems of government, especially those issues relevant to representation and consultation, and the principles of law-making (Morris 1992b; Tsang 1998).

Macau

Portugal established its rule over Macau in 1557. But as a result of the decline of the Portugal on the world stage, together with the rise of a much stronger China and the state of dependency of Macau on mainland China, the Portuguese government in Macau could not maintain its governance without the cooperation and support of the Chinese government. During the 20th century, a number of events illustrated the power of the PRC government. They include the 'Barrier Gate Incident' in 1952, the cancellation of the celebration of the 400th anniversary of establishment of Macau as a Portugese trading port in 1955, the announcement banning anti-PRC activities in Macau in 1963, and the closing of the commission of the Republic of China's government in Macau in 1965 (Yuen & Yuen 1988).

The spill-over of the Cultural Revolution and a conflict around the construction of a left-wing school in Taipa island resulted in riots in December 1966. The PRC's supporters successfully demanded an apology from the Portuguese administration and a ban on all right-wing organizations (Gunn 1996). After that event, the Portuguese authorities changed their style of rule over the people and sought to cultivate friendly relations with China. With the termination of diplomatic relations between Portugal and Taiwan in 1975 and the establishment of formal diplomatic relations with China in 1979, Sino-Portuguese relations over Macau became more harmonious and stable.

Portugal's military revolution in 1974 overthrew the Salazar-Caetano dictatorship and established a multi-party democracy (Manuel 1996). The new government commenced decolonisation of all remaining Portugese territories and acknowledged Macau as Chinese territory. In addition, the new Portuguese government allowed Macau to have a higher degree of autonomy and provided limited democratic reform such as the promulgation of the 'Organic Statute for Macau' and the setting up of a Legislative Assembly in 1976 (Wu 1998).

Although politically Macau remained a Portuguese colony, economically and culturally it was heavily dependent on mainland China and Hong Kong. After the 1966 riot, the Macau government further suffered a loss of autonomy and authority. After that, there was a dual rule in Macau: while the Portuguese formally and nominally controlled the top political leadership, China's representatives in Macau (some leaders of neighbourhood (街坊) associations, labour unions and PRC officials responsible for Macau affairs) informally and substantially governed the ordinary citizens at the grass-roots level (Lo 1995). The neighbourhood associations served an auxiliary function for the government by helping to solve problems about housing, rent, pollution, hawkers and recreation, and by explaining and implementing government policies. With the dominance of pro-PRC representatives in the legislature, as well as the neighbourhood associations as intermediary organisations between the government and ordinary citizens, the PRC shared the power of the Portuguese government and established a strong leftist influence in Macau. Also, Portuguese administration in Macau was traditionally destabilised by Portuguese politics as the governor's tenure of office was often affected by Portugal's party politics. In addition, the Macau government was plagued by bureaucratic corruption and administrative incompetence (Lo 1995). The Macau civil service was notorious for its low educational levels, insufficient training, stifling bureaucracy and inefficiency, frequent reorganisation, and intense politics of parochialism.

From the end of World War II to the mid-1970s, Macau was a polity under Chinese patronage, together with an insulated bureaucracy and a parochial and subject political culture (Yee et al. 1993a; Lo 1995). After the 1970s, Macau experienced rapid industrialisation and urbanisation, as well as a sharp increase in population due to migration. The society accommodated a large number of immigrants from mainland China, and the masses of Macau exhibited a passive political culture. The majority of the Macau Chinese were uninterested in political participation, and imbued with a top-down rather than a bottom-up concept of democracy.

Unlike Hong Kong, the role of the Macau's government in education has been very limited, particularly prior to 1987 (Bray 1992a). Under the policy of classical colonialism, the Macau government was only concerned with the education of Portuguese children, and neglected the education of the Chinese inhabitants. The government spent little on education, and most of the funding went to the Portuguese-language public schools. Partly due to colonial policies, Macau's educational provision was characterised by fragmentation, and the government's non-interventionist policy. There was no compulsory free education. Macau had no aided sector; and the majority of schools were privately managed, operating with a high degree of autonomy. Like other aspects of the education system, curriculum development was 'laissez faire'. Schools adopted syllabuses and textbooks from other places, particularly Portugal, PRC, Taiwan, and Hong Kong (Bray & Hui 1991a). Even in the late 1990s, Macau did not have system-wide examinations comparable to those in Hong Kong.

Under the laissez faire education policy, a distinguishing feature of Macau education system was the phenomenon of self-reliance and diversity in terms of the co-existence of multiple systems. Macau's education is characterised by the dominance of private schools run by religious bodies, social-service organisations, and so on. Among them, the Catholic Church and the pro-PRC Macau Chinese Education Association (MCEA) play a leading role. In the absence of a compulsory unified curriculum, individual schools could operate according to their particular preferences and backgrounds.

Because of the lack of unified curriculum, as well as the small size of student population, commercial publishers have been unwilling to publish textbooks specially for Macau students (Bray & Tang 1994). Consequently, many schools adopt textbooks from Hong Kong, mainland China or Taiwan, which are also of limited relevance to Macau. As a result, Macau students tend to know more about places other than Macau, their own society.

As far as civic education was concerned, although the Macau government did not impose a formal civic education programme on the schools, civic education had a history in Macau dating back to the beginning of the era of Republican China in 1911 because many vernacular schools followed the educational system in mainland China. Until 1966, Macau was in a precarious balance between the pro-Nationalist and pro-Communist organisations. Their rivalry was manifest in the realm of education in which each camp ran its partisan schools and introduced political indoctrination (Fung 1960; Liu 1973). In 1966, the surrender of the Portuguese Government in Macau to the supporters of the pro-Communist organisations resulted in the retreat of pro-Nationalist organisations and, in turn, the decline of pro-Nationalist schools (Tam 1994). The CEA then became a dominant educational body in Macau, parallel to the Catholic Church. No formal programme of civic and political education was introduced by the Macau government during this period until the 1990s, and civic education in Macau was basically invisible. In general, the implementation of civic education in the majority of private schools was characterised by a permeated approach or solely undertaken by the form teachers (H.K. Wong 1992). Since each school varied in background and approaches to civic education, among these schools a major difference in orientation of civic education lay in the aspect of relationships between individual and community, society, and the state.

Civic Education in Hong Kong and Macau since the Mid-1980s

While education performs a function of social control in colonial states, the corollary is that in the process of decolonisation, education performs the important functions of nation-building and national integration for the new born nation-states. This was particularly evident under the wave of decolonisation after World War II (Bray 1997a; Bray et al. 1986; Fägerlind & Saha 1986; Harber 1989). For these new nation-states, building up national unity and a new political order were pressing needs. Political education was thus utilised to cultivate a sense of national identity and loyalty. Formal educational institutions like schools were expected to supplement and perhaps replace families to socialise the new generation in a new role of national citizenry rather than in the traditional local political authority.

However, unlike other former colonies heading towards independence by building new nation-states, the experience of Hong Kong and Macau is distinctive in their reintegration with an existing nation-state and, at the same time, maintaining a high degree of autonomy and thus, a different way of life. After the mid-1980s, Hong Kong and Macau underwent significant political changes in terms of decolonalisation and change of sovereignty. Accordingly, there was a change in the shaping of civic education in these two Chinese societies.

Hong Kong
Since the early 1980s, the greatest political changes have been initiated by the process of decolonisation and the accompanying steps of democratisation. With the introduction of representative government, and the political reform package brought by Governor Christopher Patten in 1993, the scope of democratisation was extended. However, the pace of democratisation progressed slowly and tortuously. Party politics has had an extremely short history in Hong Kong as direct elections were not introduced to the Legislative Council until 1991.

The socio-economic development from the 1970s onwards produced changes in the Hong Kong Chinese ethos, particularly in the moving away from a subject political culture to an immature form of participatory political culture (Lau & Kuan 1988). While there has been a growing normative orientation towards political participation and an attentive attitude towards the mass media among Hong Kong Chinese, people's aloofness and apathy remain strong, and many people stay at the spectator level regarding political participation. Further, the people's sense of political powerlessness became stronger as a result of the turbulent political environment and the rows between Britain and China. Meanwhile, the increasing intervention of the government in social and public affairs gave Hong Kong residents a benevolent, favourable and positive image of the colonial government and increased their expectations of the government (Lau & Kuan 1988). However, the authority of the Hong Kong government declined during the 1990s. The people became less trustful of and less deferential to public authorities, and showed a less favourable evaluation of governmental performance. Political cynicism and a sense of political inefficacy also prevailed, with strong feelings of political frustration and alienation.

The long separation between Hong Kong and mainland China and the different rules of governance led to Hong Kong's distinctive socio-economic development and the development of an indigenous culture, and in turn, a sense of Hong Kong-centredness and 'Hongkongese' identity (Choi 1995; Lau & Kuan 1988). With the advent of 1997 and the designated return of Hong Kong to China, change in political membership became a pressing issue as the change of sovereignty meant that Hong Kong people would acquire new national identities as PRC citizens.

Political reform in Hong Kong after the mid-1980s and the signing of the 1984 Joint Declaration triggered a demand for 'civic education' in the Hong Kong community (H.W. Wong 1988; Bray & Lee 1993; Sweeting 1992). With the introduction of political reform toward a representative government and the stipulation of China's policy of 'One Country, Two Systems', civic education was considered as a major means to provide Hong Kong's future citizens with the necessary political orientation and competence to prepare for the political change. However, a number of Hong Kong studies showed that adolescents lacked detailed knowledge and understanding of institutions, principles and processes of government, law, and politics (Wan 1990; Cheung & Leung 1994; Educational Group of Christians for Hong Kong Society 1994; Curriculum Development Committee 1995). Also, adolescents showed only moderate concern toward politics and social issues, and tended to have favourable attitudes toward the values of democracy, albeit without much understanding. They also had favourable perceptions of the Hong Kong government. Furthermore, Hong Kong students lacked an understanding of China affairs and were particularly ignorant of Chinese politics. They had a weak sense of national identity and patriotism. A significant proportion of pupils also showed negative perceptions of the Communist Party and the Chinese government, and felt resistant to the return of Hong Kong to China. Students commonly held a pessimistic view on the future of Hong Kong, and showed little confidence in the realisation of 'One Country, Two Systems'. Moreover, there was a wide discrepancy in the students' civic awareness and involvement. A majority of students identified with the importance of voting, but they lacked confidence and enthusiasm to vote. Most of them were unfamiliar with political organisations in Hong Kong and tended to keep themselves aloof from politics. The students also lacked the intellectual and communicative skills for taking political actions, and they participated little in community activities. So it was not surprising that Hong Kong students were often criticised for their lack of civic consciousness and low awareness of their nation and state. The situation invoked worries over the political future of Hong Kong, and elicited public concern for civic education in schools to promote students' civic consciousness.

Accordingly, the Hong Kong government adjusted its education policy from a stance of 'depoliticisation' to a more active role in promoting civic education, as evident in the publication of *The Guidelines on Civic Education in Schools* (henceforth *Guidelines*) in 1985. This comprehensive document covered the passage of pupils from the kindergarten to primary school and then secondary school. For each stage it outlined details about knowledge, attitudes and skills to be transmitted, and gave advice to educators and teachers on the ways to achieve them.

Civic education was also promoted in the 1980s by revision of the curriculum in some major social subjects and, the introduction of the new subjects Government & Public Affairs (GPA) and Liberal Studies at senior secondary levels (Morris 1988, 1997; Bray & Lee 1993; Morris & Chan 1997). A salient aspect of the impact of 1997 handover on the secondary school curriculum was an increase in the topics allocated to the study of China, the relationships between Hong Kong and China, Hong Kong's political transition, and a specific references to the Joint Declaration and the Basic Law.

Following the increased politicisation of the local community, the Education Regulations concerning political control were amended in 1990. The reception of the significance of civic education was further consolidated in the official booklet *School Education in Hong Kong: a statement of aims* published in 1993, which stated that one of the central aims of school education was the promotion of social, political and civic awareness. Also, in 1996 the Education Department published new guidelines on civic education which presented an enriched and more complete conception of citizenship than the earlier one. The new framework was based on the learner's perspective and needs. The new guidelines aimed to meet the challenges of political transition after 1997 and to prepare the students to become contributing citizens to society, the country and the world. The aims included development of a sense of belonging to Hong Kong and China, understanding the characteristics of Hong Kong society, and the importance of democracy, liberty, equality, human rights and rule of law. Also, an emphasis was put on the teaching of controversial issues as well as developing students' critical thinking. Meanwhile, a major revision of syllabi of social subjects, along with drafting a new curriculum of civic education, was issued by the Curriculum Development Council in 1997.

The Education Department also promoted civic education by organising seminars for school heads and civic education coordinators, and hundreds of in-service training courses, seminars or workshops for teachers. Furthermore, a Government & Public Affairs/Civic Education Section was set up in the Advisory Inspectorate to coordinate the implementation of civic education in schools. Teaching resources centres were set up, and teaching materials and manuals, bulletins and newsletters concerning civic education were published. The Education Department also undertook evaluations of the implementation of the *Guidelines*.

Despite the change in government policy toward civic education, the effectiveness of civic education on transformation of students' socio-political orientations was doubtful. Many studies called the actual practices of civic education in schools into question (S.C. Ho 1990; Wan 1990; Yu 1990; Hong Kong Catholic Education and Studies Centre 1989; Cheung & Leung 1994; Lam 1994; S.W. Leung 1997; CDC 1995). Also, official evaluation of students' performance in the public examinations of social subjects (Tsang 1984; Hong Kong Examinations Authority 1994a, 1994b) showed that the school had insignificant effect on students' civic consciousness. At most there was only modest success in transmitting knowledge, and the effects on attitudes and values were even more problematic. Because of shortcomings in school teaching, students were generally poor in cognitive and analytical abilities, and in communication and participation skills. Furthermore, political education in Hong Kong secondary schools suffered problems of 'depoliticisation' and 'moralisation' of political education, and under-implementation of political education (Tse 1997a).

The contents and objectives of the 1985 *Guidelines* were criticised for their 'all-inclusiveness', 'conservatism', and being 'a-political' and 'a-nationalistic' (Lee 1987; S.W. Leung 1997). Civic education, it was argued, should be an instrument for promoting political education, but political education itself was depoliticised and moralised in the 1985 *Guidelines*. More importantly, depoliticisation and moralisation of civic education was even more apparent at the level of implementation in schools (S.W. Leung 1995). Depoliticisation included reduction or removal of the political components of civic education, and moralisation the dominance of moral education over other components of civic education. 'Civic education', or the notion of 'citizenship', as an ambiguous, diffused, and over-encompassing concept suggested by the 1985 *Guidelines*, allowed various interpretations and resulted in different civic education programmes with different orientations and emphases. Although a small number of schools had a clear and explicit focus on political education, the majority of the schools adopted a moralised conception of civic education with little concern for political education. Indeed, most so-called 'civic education' was a hotchpotch of moral, social and political education, containing ethical and moral creeds, moral virtues, knowledge about political institutions, current issues, environmental education and even sex education. The overlap of moral, social and political education led to the subordination and even displacement of political education. Furthermore, even when political education was mentioned, emphasis was put on cognitive aspects rather than on cultivation of political attitudes and skills, an understanding of democracy, party politics, political theories, and an identification with China (Hong Kong Christian Institute & Action Group for Education 1994). As a result, civic education programmes in many schools not only failed to achieve a cultivation of political literacy, but also fell behind most of the objectives of the *Guidelines* concerning political education.

Concerning implemention of civic education, the Hong Kong government gave the schools a free hand and proposed a whole school approach which utilised both the formal and informal curricula but which did not make civic education an independent and compulsory subject. Because the promotion of civic education rested in the hands of heads of individual schools, the concrete policies, organisation and measures of implementation among different schools were diversified. The publication of the official guidelines did not bring radical, fundamental, and swift changes in implementation of civic education at school level. This lack of change occurred for three main reasons.

First, the two sets of *Guidelines* were taken not so much as guiding documents but more as a reference and at worst were neglected completely. Few schools had an explicit and systematic agreed policy addressing the issue of civic education.

Second, the leadership function of a civic education coordinating committee at the school level was questionable (H.W. Wong 1988; Tse 1997c). Without an overall co-ordinating mechanism in planning and organising civic education programmes, civic education activities were piecemeal and fragmented. The assimilation of civic education with moral education further marginalised the status of civic education, and enhanced the tendency of moralisation and depoliticisation.

Third, under the cross-curricula policy, only a minority of schools made civic education an independent subject (Hong Kong Catholic Education and Studies Centre 1989; S.W. Leung 1995; Education Department 1986, 1987). As to the subjects closely related to civic education, such as Social Studies, GPA, Liberal Studies and Sociology, the differences in curriculum among and within schools deprived many students from learning civic education, in particular for those in senior years and/or in science streams. Also, the prevocational-school curriculum was different from the common grammar-school one as it was inclined toward vocational and practical subjects. Thus, academic subjects like Chinese History were not usually provided. Moreover, the core of political education, including nationalistic and democratic education, was crowded out of the formal curriculum (Tse 1997a). For example, the syllabuses and textbooks in lower form social subjects discarded both the contents of nationalism and state identity (Tse 1997b, 1997d). Democratic education was also constrained by the incomplete conception of curricular objectives and topics in the formal curriculum, its limited exposure to students, and the distorted, biased, formalistic, and non-critical presentation in textbooks. The textbooks entailed a strong moralised notion of citizenship by teaching the students to be 'good' citizens who were willing to cooperate with the government for the welfare of the community, but discussed little about the citizen's right to participate in government, or political principles concerning democratic orientation and civic liberties. The textbooks also misrepresented the realities of the social and political systems by portraying a harmonious relationship between the government and the people and exaggerating government efforts in promoting citizens' welfare. By depicting a highly administrative and functional conception of a government and a favourable and beneficial image of the Hong Kong government, they fostered the students' faith and trust in government.

Civic education was not well received by the teachers either. Several studies (Hok Yau Shek 1987; H.W. Wong 1988; HKCI & Action Group for Education 1994; Nicholson 1988; Auyeung 1991; P.M. Wong 1992; Morris & Tang 1992; Lan 1993; S.W. Leung 1995) showed that teachers' involvement in civic education promotion was very low, although most teachers agreed with the ideal of promoting civic education in schools. Few teachers showed a good understanding of the objectives of the *Guidelines*, the purposes of civic education, or their school policies towards civic education. Few teachers were interested in politics or put much emphasis on political education. Also, few teachers accessed the civic education resource centre, or attended any civic education courses or seminars held by the Education Department, and only a small proportion of teachers received training in political education.

Besides the government, different parties such as the District Boards, agents of mass media and community organisations became increasingly involved in promoting civic education after the mid-1980s, as evident in the proliferation of programmes for civic education and propaganda activities. Different educational organisations, such as the Hong Kong Professional Teachers' Union (HKPTU) and the Hong Kong Educational Workers' Association (HKEWA), aired their views on civic education and designed their own civic education programmes. For some educational organisations, civic education was conceived of as a form of moral and even religious education. For example, to prepare for the political transition in advance and to prevent imposition of political education from outside after 1997, the Catholic Church in Hong Kong, through the Catholic Board of Education (CBE), introduced its civic education programme in Catholic schools in 1995 (Tan 1997; Ng 1997). The programme emphasised three identities of Hong Kong Catholics: Hong Kong citizen, Chinese and Christian. Also, it assimilated a pro-Chinese government attitude and a kind of patriotic education. The Hong Kong Catholic Church defined democratic education as the cultivation of students' democratic consciousness and the practice of and training for democratic participation (Hong Kong Catholic Education and Studies Centre 1989).

On the other hand, for the Chinese government's supporters, more emphasis was put on strengthening nationalistic and patriotic education in schools for inculcating the younger generation with national identity, pride and loyalty, an understanding of the Basic Law, and China's policy of 'One Country, Two Systems'. However, many educators in Hong Kong were worried that the advocacy of nationalism in civic education would result in political indoctrination. Thus, in contrast to the pro-Communist China organisations, other educational organisations put more emphasis on the role of civic education as democratic education and accorded priority to the notions of democracy and human rights. To facilitate the transformation of a participatory political culture, and thus the pacing of democratisation, some advocates introduced the model of 'political literacy' into Hong Kong (Leung & Lau 1997). Differences of ideas concerning the proper role of civic education also resulted in different ways through which the civic education programme was to be received, adopted, and implemented.

Macau
Like Hong Kong, arrangements for Macau include its existence as a Special Administrative Region of the PRC for at least 50 years after the change of sovereignty in 1999. During the 1990s, the Macau government gradually opened and reformed its political structure, and played a more active role in socio-economic affairs (Lo 1995). During the transitional period from 1987 to 1999, the major issues such as localisation of the civil service, legalisation of the Chinese language, and translation of Portuguese laws into Chinese were put on the reform agenda. However, political reforms in Macau were implemented much more slowly and narrowly than in Hong Kong. The slow progress also aroused worries of the public and criticisms from PRC officials. During the mid-1990s, the rise in crime and vice, and the deterioration of law and order, became a serious blow to public confidence.

Educational development in Macau was rather slow and stagnant under the Portuguese administration. Only in the late 1970s did the government increase its part in education by subsiding the private schools (Y.Y. Chan 1993, 1995; H.K. Wong 1991, 1992; Koo & Ma 1994). With the advent of the transfer of sovereignty after the signing of the Sino-Portuguese Declaration in 1987, the Macau government embarked on a series of major education reforms: a marked increase in government expenditure on education; a heavy involvement in higher education by purchasing the private University of East Asia and promulgating the Higher Education Law; the proposal of providing seven years of free and compulsory education; the attempt to make Portuguese a compulsory subject in all private schools and public higher institutions; the reconstruction of the Department of Education & Youth; and the promotion of civic education (Yee 1990; H.K. Wong 1991; Koo & Ma 1994). The change of curriculum in preparation for the 1999 handover was also put on the public agenda. In 1994, the laws on curriculum organisation for kindergarten, pre-primary and primary school schools were made, followed by the provisional teaching syllabuses trialled in some Luso-Chinese schools. However, the official control over education provoked resistance from the educational sector, and many reform measures were deferred without realisation.

Like their Hong Kong counterparts, Macau adolescents are often accused of lack of civic consciousness and low awareness of their nation and state. A few studies show that Macau adolescents tend to have favourable attitudes toward the values of democracy, but without too much understanding of politics and the principles and processes of government (Yee et al. 1993b; Hong Kong Federation of Youth Groups 1996). They show moderate civic awareness but are still passive in political involvement. They also show little confidence in the Macau government and feel dissatisfied with the working performance and efficiency of official polices. Furthermore, Macau adolescents have a weak sense of belonging to Macau and lack an understanding of the Basic Law.

Only recently did the Macau government initiate a programme in civic education comparable to that in Hong Kong. However, the signing of the Sino-Portuguese Joint Declaration in 1987 brought a growing concern over the issue of civic education in Macau (H.K. Wong 1991). Different sponsoring education bodies launched their own civic education programmes during and after the late 1980s (Ng 1997). As early as 1987, the Macau Catholic Schools Association started to prepare a civic education textbook for most Catholic secondary schools. The CEA also adopted a more nationalistic approach to civic education and published a textbook on the Basic Law for secondary schools in 1995.

The shortage of local textbooks and materials, together with the 1999 handover as a catalyst, prompted the Macau Catholic Schools Association to organise its own civic education programme for secondary schools in 1991. With the topics including thinking methods and basic knowledge of Macau, the programme aimed to cultivate a sense of belonging to Macau and China, strengthen civic competence, develop open-mindedness, and promote skills and knowledge in handling social conflict.

Leftist schools also implemented their own civic education programmes with an emphasis on love for country, Macau, and school, with concern about the relationships with family, community, society, and the state (Ng 1997). Education for patriotism stood out as the main objective. Also, civic education aimed to facilitate political transition and national unity. There was strong emphasis on topics about China, and, in line with Marxist ideology, dialectics and materialism.

A salient feature of Macau education is its cultural and educational dependence. Macau, in common with other small states (Bray & Packer 1993), relies on experts and resources from outside (particularly Hong Kong) in preparing civic education programmes, producing textbooks and teaching materials, and training teachers. For example, cultural and educational dependence was reflected in the primary school social studies textbooks published in 1994. Although it was the first series of textbooks tailor-made for Macau school pupils, it was published and edited in Hong Kong. Also, at Primary 4 quite a large proportion of topics were devoted to Hong Kong, including its geography, commerce and industries, tourism, transportation, postal services, social welfare, medical services, education, and the organisation of government (Modern Educational Research Society 1994). It revealed the close connection between Hong Kong and Macau, but also the cultural and educational dependence of Macau on Hong Kong.

With the promulgation of the Laws No.38/94/M and No.39/94/M in 1994 and 1997 which stated the regulations on curriculum planning and reform for both primary and secondary schools in Macau, the development of moral and civic education became an official goal of education. In 1995, the Department of Education & Youth published the Moral and Civic Education Syllabuses at both primary and junior secondary levels.

According to the 1995 Moral and Civic Education Syllabuses, civic education is taught as a specific academic subject under the scope of moral education. It aims to prepare students to become 'good' citizens with reference to certain moral and legal principles. The official programme is to ensure a solid foundation for adaptation to a more complex socio-political environment. The general aims include: to cultivate students' positive civic awareness and skills, and to explore the skills both in the acquisition of civic knowledge and in nurturing of a moral sense of mind so as to facilitate students to adapt, learn and grow up when entering the society in future. At each level, the syllabuses specify the knowledge, skills and attitudes expected of civic education, as well as the 10 major themes of the programme: personal growth, human relationships, value systems, ways of thinking and inquiry, the individual and the group, relationships among China, Portugal and Macau, United Nations, law, and mass media. Finally, assessment is recommended in the form of observing students' performance, instead of examination. However, the syllabuses issued in 1995 were in trial form, and they only targeted the official Luso-Chinese schools. They merely served as a guide for the private schools.

The underdevelopment of civic education in Macau also reflected the lack of local studies of civic education. But like the situation in Hong Kong, one study showed that there was a considerable gap between the aspirations of the reformers and the schooling practices (Ng 1997).

Hong Kong and Macau Contrasted and Compared

With the transition to integration with China rather than to independence, Hong Kong and Macau changed their formal curricula to reflect the new political circumstances: a new emphasis on relations with China rather than on an identity of a newly-emergent nation-state as in many other post-colonial states. Compared with the past, the most salient feature in Hong Kong and Macau was an emphasis on national identity and local society in the process of decolonisation. Despite the similarities in terms of ethnicity, small size, and reintegration with mainland China, the nature and progress of civic and political education in Hong Kong and Macau remained markedly different. The primary causes lay in the differences in colonial rule and the priorities of government policies, as well as the relative degree of economic and cultural dependencies in the two places.

The colonial government in Hong Kong exercised tight control of the educational system and marginalised political education. In contrast, Macau was characterised by a fragmentation of educational provision, government's non-interventionist policy, and a lack of formal civic education until the 1990s. Also, even with a relatively long transition period of 12 years (1987-99), civic education has been less developed in Macau than in Hong Kong. While the Hong Kong government published official guidelines on civic education in 1985 and 1996, the Macau government did not publish its official document concerning civic education until 1995. Indeed, while the Hong Kong government took an initiative in promoting civic education in the early 1980s, the Macau government only initiated its civic education programme after the running of civic education programmes by other educational bodies. In Macau, the state's sluggish orientation resulted in slow progress of development in education in general and civic education in particular. In contrast, with more than 10 years of preparation, in the mid-1990s Hong Kong was better equipped with support, resources, and organisations (e.g. a civic education resource centre and a civic education standing committee) than Macau. Once again, this shows differences in state capacity, autonomy and initiative in delivering civic and political education. Since the Macau government was fully preoccupied with political and social reforms, in addition to education ones, civic education was not a top priority, of much less importance than measures such as the adoption of free and compulsory education.

As revealed in the guidelines and syllabuses (see Table 9.1), the governments of both Hong Kong and Macau have defined civic education in the broadest sense, and have treated civic education as a mixture of moral, political and lifeskills education. In Hong Kong, the composition of the civic education committee in 1996 required accommodating different opinions while reserving differences to win wide recognition and acceptance from all groups in the community. In Macau, civic education was treated as a branch of moral education, based on moral and legal norms to cultivate good citizens. The recent guidelines or syllabuses in both places combined conservative and critical modes of orientation. They juxtaposed both nationalistic and democratic education, so that patriotic education went hand in hand with an affirmation of the values of human rights and democracy. Also, both pro-establishment and participatory elements were found; and civic education in both places stressed international contexts by including elements of multi-culturalism and/ or cosmopolitanism.

However, Hong Kong and Macau also differed in the orientation of civic education. First, while the Hong Kong authorities downplayed the British influence and the British colonial legacy, the Macau government took pride in Portuguese culture and still inserted the Portuguese influence into the curriculum. Hence special topics were devoted to Portugal and Portuguese culture in the syllabuses. Second, the orientation of the Macau syllabuses was more conservative, with an emphasis on preparing the students to 'adapt' to their social life and the society at large, instead of initiating change. Third, Macau's civic education had a stronger orientation to moral and lifeskills education.

Regarding the aspect of implementation, while the authorities in Macau focused only on the formal curriculum, their counterparts in Hong Kong were concerned with formal, informal and hidden curricula. Also, in contrast to Hong Kong which allowed both permeated, specific subject and integrated-subject approaches, civic education in Macau is solely taught as a specific subject with certain number of periods, specific teaching topics, and suggested learning activities.

Despite differences in these measures of implementation, in neither Hong Kong nor Macau has civic education been made a compulsory subject. Most schools could still implement their own civic education programmes; and the actual practices still rested on the initiatives of individual school administrators and teachers. This resulted in a state of diversity and fragmentation of civic education programmes at school level. The fragmented nature of implementation was particularly obvious in Macau, given the weak government administration and the high autonomy of the private schools.

Although the critics of colonial education generally highlight the relationship between colonial domination and education, in reality colonial education may not be a direct imposition of the coloniser's education system. Moreover, history has shown divergence among different colonisers in their educational policies and practices; and colonial educational practices have been shaped by indigenous societies and cultures (Altbach & Kelly 1991; Watson 1982c). This observation underscores the complex interaction between the coloniser and the socio-political organisation of the colonised. In the cases of Hong Kong and Macau, relationships between political change and edu-

Table 9.1: A Comparative Analysis of the Distinctiveness of the Formal Curriculum in Hong Kong & Macau

Distinctiveness	Hong Kong School Civic Education Guidelines 1985	Hong Kong School Civic Education Guidelines 1996	Civic Education Syllabuses (Junior Secondary) 1997	Macau Moral and Civic Education Syllabuses (Junior Secondary) (1995-97)
Major Aims & Objectives	1. To prepare students for the political reform of introduction of representative government; 2. To promote better and healthier relationships with government & other members of society 3. An avoidance of evaluation of political ideologies, instead a certain kind of 'cosmopolitan mentality', an acknowledgment of Hong Kong as an international city.	1. To prepare students to become rational, active & responsible citizens in facing challenges arising from the change of sovereignty, Hong Kong as a SAR of the PRC; 2. To develop students' sense of belonging to Hong Kong and China; 3. To develop students' competence to observe their political rights and responsibilities, to acquire critical thinking dispositions, civic awareness & basic political knowledge.	1. To cultivate positive value systems & civic attitudes, build up a sense of belonging to family, community and nation, in order to contribute to family, community, nation & the world; 2. To understand the features of Hong Kong society, apprehend the significance of rule of law, democracy, human rights & justice and put them in practice; 3. Cultivate with critical thinking & problem-solving skills, to analyze social & political problems with objective attitudes, and to make sensible judgements.	1. To prepare students to become good citizens with reference to certain moral and legal principles; 2. To ensure a solid foundation for adapting to a more complex socio-political environment; 3. The general aims include cultivating students' positive civic awareness & skills, exploring skills in the acquisition of civic knowledge and in nurturing of a moral sense of mind so as to facilitate students with sufficient abilities to adapt, to learn and to grow up when entering the society in future.
Implementation Strategies	Whole school approach; permeated (cross-curricular) approach in formal curriculum	Whole school approach and 3 models: permeated, specific subject & integrated-subject approaches	an optional subject under the scope of humanities and social subjects	a prescribed specific subject under the scope of moral education
Coverage of curriculum: topics & key competence or skills	For kindergartens, primary & secondary schools & in the domains of knowledge, attitudes, and skills. An emphasis put on critical & logical thinking, the spirit of inquiry	5 stages from kindergartens, to primary & secondary schools; at 5 levels including family, neighbourhood, regional community, national community, & international community; & in 7 domains of knowledge, reflection, action, values, attitudes, beliefs, & competence. With a special focus on controversial issues, developing critical thinking, wise decision-making, creative thinking, independ-	6 categories: family, neighbourhood, community, nation-state, global society, citizenship & civil society	At each junior secondary level, the syllabuses specify the knowledge, skills & attitudes expected of civic education; as well as the ten major themes of programme: personal growth, human relationship, value systems, ways of thinking & inquiry, individual and group, relationships among China, Portugal & Macau, United Nations, law & mass media

Table 9.1: A Comparative Analysis of the Distinctiveness of the Formal Curriculum in Hong Kong & Macau (cont.)

Distinctiveness	Hong Kong School Civic Education Guidelines 1985	Hong Kong School Civic Education Guidelines 1996	Civic Education Syllabuses (Junior Secondary) 1997	Macau Moral and Civic Education Syllabuses (Junior Secondary) (1995-97)
		(cont.) dent judgement, self-reflective abilities & upholds principles		
Pedagogy	Suggested activities for knowledge acquisition like observation, manipulation of materials, collection, interpretation & presentation of information; Suggested activities for value orientation such as story telling, case study, simulation & role playing, class or group discussion; Suggestions for extracurricular activities	A learner's perspective; recommending the use of controversial issues in order to develop critical thinking, reflection & action	Emphasis on participatory learning activities, reflection, building up an open and mutual-respect classroom climate, adopting affirmative neutral strategies in teaching controversial issues, provision of suitable extracurricular activities for students' participation in social services & affairs	No concrete suggestions except for an emphasis on internalization with regard to moral education, recommending multiple & lively methods of teaching, including visits to government departments
Assessment & evaluation	Largely informal at the school level	Regular & systematic school-based evaluations of pupil learning outcomes & of school programme	Evaluation encompasses knowledge, attitudes, values & competence in civic learning, as well as their application in situations. Apart from standard test formats, assessment is conducted through profiling students' performances in the process of reflection & action. Evaluation should be a continuing and interactive process and reflect the learning progress of students	Assessment is recommended in the form of observing students' performance, instead of examination. Conduct assessment

(partly adapted from Morris & Chan 1997; Ng 1997, with some modification and extension) cation have been complicated and dynamic. Apart from macro socio-political change as catalyst, the process of educational change is mediated by the state-society relations embedded in a particular historical context. This chapter has shown that the role of the state in constructing civic education programmes is not only influenced by the external factors of decolonisation and national reintegration, but is also conditioned and constrained by the state capacity, autonomy and initiative vis-à-vis the civil society. In the past, observers often took for granted the role of the state in shaping political education. This might have been acceptable for most strong nation states, but it is not necessarily applicable to colonial states or dependent states. Nor should analysts accept political education merely as the result of state imposition. The cases of Hong Kong (a strong state) and Macau (a weak state) demonstrate the difference in state strength in constructing civic education programmes. Also, the state's relation to society is essentially a contested one, varying from time to time, and from country to country. Advocates of both New Sociology of Education and Neo-Marxism (Young 1971; Whitty & Young 1976; Giroux 1983; Apple 1990) convincingly argue that cultural transmission in schools is an ideological product of deliberate organisation and selection which reflects both the distribution of power and the principles of social control. However, without an adequate state theory, they fail to explicate the working of structural forces on education and the mechanism of social control at work. Instead, the present study of Hong Kong and Macau helps to fill in this vacuum by reinstating an analysis of state-society relations in shaping civic education in these places.

In addition, the divergence in definitions is evident among various organisations in the educational sector. Since different schools offer their own interpretations of civic education, the debates and disputes about the orientations of civic education and the struggle for priorities in civic education concerning democratic, nationalistic, moral and religious education are worthy of attention.

Preparing Students for Citizenship? The Challenges for Civic Education in Hong Kong and Macau

So far, this chapter has reviewed the socio-political situations and the development of civic education in Hong Kong and Macau over the past several decades. The socio-political changes have significantly influenced the shape of civic education in these two places. Unlike the cases of mainland China and Taiwan in which civic education was highly politicised (Sautman 1991; Huang & Chiu 1991), civic education in Hong Kong and Macau from the 1950s to the early 1980s was generally characterised by depoliticisation and denationalisation (Tse 1998). For the sake of self-defence (British government), or due to incompetence (Portuguese government), civic education was in a state of poverty and barely visible.

Despite the changes in the socio-political milieu after the mid-1980s, the recent status of political education in Hong Kong schools showed striking continuity with the past since the dominant messages transmitted to the students were still apolitical and detached from politics in the society at large. In most schools, political education, in terms of nationalistic and democratic education was basically absent. Instead, the dominant orientation of civic education programmes in the schools was still the mode of 'citizenship transmission' mainly concerned with developing moral virtues of good citizens and promoting co-operative relationships with the government, rather than a more reflective and critical approach to political literacy. Moreover, the implementation of civic education in secondary schools was problematic, and the effects of civic education on students' values and beliefs were insignificant. Civic education programmes in schools generally did not achieve many of the objectives stated in the Guidelines. Even worse, the schools reinforced political apathy and failed to provide future citizens with the necessary political orientation and competence in democracy and national identity to prepare for the imminent political changes happening in Hong Kong (Tse 1997a).

In Macau, official civic education programme commenced later and cannot yet be judged on effects or effectiveness. Since the implementation of civic education lay in the hands of individual sponsoring bodies, the official civic education programme was not expected to bring significant changes to a vast majority of schools.

Above all, the great barriers which persist in the implementation of civic education pose challenges to Hong Kong and Macau following the change of sovereignty. Several factors lead to the failure of school civic education programmes. Among them are the problems of coordination between planning and implementation; moralisation and depoliticisation of political education at school level; the need for infrastructural support in curriculum innovation and implementation; the limitations of a cross-curricular approach to civic education; and a transmission approach fostered by the formal curricula. Difficulties in Macau were intensified by the lack of human and financial resources and the influx of many young migrants from mainland China since the early 1990s (Koo 1997). More importantly, although new curricula have been prepared to reflect changes in sovereignty, the prospect of political education has been limited by the possibility of political development in Hong Kong and Macau. The major institutional constraint lies in the conservative constitutional framework imposed on Hong Kong and Macau. Given the above factors, one may wonder whether it will produce changes which are more apparent than real, as in many other post-colonial societies (Bray 1997a).

Note: The research reported in this article was drawn from the project "A Comparative Study of Political Education in Four Chinese Societies: Mainland China, Taiwan, Hong Kong & Macau", which was partly funded by the Direct Grant for Research of the Chinese University of Hong Kong (1997-98 ID: 2020412).

10

Secondary School History Curricula

T_{AN} Kang, John

This chapter presents a study of the implemented history curriculum in eight secondary schools in Hong Kong and Macau during the period 1980 to 1993. The Sino-British and Sino-Portuguese agreements on the future of Hong Kong and Macau were signed respectively in 1984 and 1987. These political changes, along with other features of decolonisation, are related to the development of the history curriculum in schools of different political backgrounds in each colony during the period. Inter-territorial and intra-territorial comparisons show that the history curricula in these schools were quite different from those in colonies elsewhere in the world, that curricular diversity was greater in Macau than in Hong Kong, and that the curricula of schools of a similar political background located on opposing sides of the Pearl River were often very different.

The history subject was chosen for the study because the teaching of history is intrinsically political. Sweeting (1991a, p.30) observes that history, as part of the school curriculum, often demands a form of collaboration with the existing political regime. One example was the South African history curriculum which was taught to defend the ruling Afrikaner Nationalists who saw apartheid as divinely ordained and scripturally defensible (van der Berg & Buckland 1982, p.23). For the present study, 1980 was taken as the starting point for detailed study of history curriculum since it permitted inclusion of the period prior to the 1984 Sino-British Agreement and the 1987 Sino-Portuguese agreement. The year 1993 was taken as the ending point because it was the year in which fieldwork was conducted.

There are several ways to politicise the history curriculum. The content of a favoured area (for example, imperial history) can be increased to unbalanced proportions in the curriculum. Alternatively, omission of unfavoured historical events can also present a biased picture. Judgements, especially selective commentaries, on historical events can transmit political messages. Judgements can be made on nationalist, racial, moral and religious grounds. A common form of partial judgement is the externalisation of responsibility for negatively-judged events (for example, putting total blame on colonial exploitation for economic backwardness in post-colonial countries) and the internalisation for positively-judged events (for example, putting Chinese nationalist unity as the most important reason for the defeat of the Japanese in the Second World War).

The History Curriculum in Former Colonies

The history curricula in colonies of European powers tended to be Eurocentric in nature. Memmi (1965, p.105) criticised the irrelevant nature of the French colonial history curriculum which, he said, was aimed at socialising the colonised into European language, values and norms:

> The history which is taught him [the colonised] is not his own.... He knows who Colbert or Cromwell was, but he learns nothing about Khaznadar; he knows about Joan of Arc, but not about El Kahena. Everything seems to have taken place out of his country. He and his land are nonentities or exist only with reference to the Gauls, the Franks or the Marne.

Seven years before Uganda's independence, a British teacher in the colonial education service of Uganda (Musgrove 1955, p.300) noted that although Ugandan history was taught, there was:

> no evidence that the School Certificate syllabuses ... have been designed in the light of such studies of native peoples. One aspect only of the African's situation has been regarded as relevant – his membership of the British Empire.... The basic assumption underlying the selection of such a study I have found to be false: that because Uganda is part of the British Empire the people of Uganda will be interested in the Empire's growth. My pupils do not speak of it as 'their' Empire.... Membership of the Empire has not the significance for them which is often assumed.

The West African School Certificate history syllabus called 'The Development of Tropical Africa' was used in Nigeria when it was under decolonisation, until 1965, five years after Nigeria had become independent. Despite the name of the syllabus, it was criticised by Jones (1965, p.145), who referred to its use during the period of decolonisation, for "its Eurocentrism in content and approach, when even its African section was held to deal mainly with the activities of non-Africans in African situations". However, Jones also attributed part of the blame of this Eurocentrism to teachers who "concentrated on those parts of it which offered the best prospects of examination success: viz. accounts of European exploration and British constitutional history" (p.145). An examination-oriented teaching approach, which was commonly found in Hong Kong, could accentuate the Eurocentric effects (or could reduce them if such topics were unpopular in examinations) in the history curriculum.

The existence and the orientation of local history in the curriculum was an indicator of how much and in what ways the formation of national identity among the colonised people was allowed. When local history was included in the colonial curriculum, it was often described from the colonisers' perspective. Harber (1985, p.171) noted typical derogatory descriptions of indigenous Africans found in Rhodesian history textbooks: they were a savage and blood-thirsty people; bushmen were "often ugly"; black labourers were "raw and ignorant", while white employers were "energetic, skilful and ambitious". According to Okoth (1993, p.141), Ugandan students were taught that "Africa had no history of its own; that African history started with the arrival of European explorers, that Africa was discovered by Europe." These students were also made to learn of the "great" European explorers who travelled in Africa which was referred to as the "Dark Continent" (Okoth 1993, p.141). In Australia, the existence of pre-colonial Aboriginal history was dismissed by a 1923 textbook with a sweeping statement: "From the 26th January, 1788, Australian History begins" (quoted in Firth & Darlington 1993, p.87).

While local history depicted in the above British colonies and quasi-colony was Eurocentric, history learning in Portuguese colonies bore even less relevance to the local cultures and situations. The English-language literature has not contained much discussion on history teaching in Portuguese colonies. Duffy (1959, p.312) noted that Portuguese history learned by Portuguese and Africans in Angola and Mozambique, which included "the glories of the maritime discoveries", was similar to what students in Portugal learnt. The history curriculum in Portuguese East Timor was also highly Lusocentric and contained no Timorese culture. Timorese history was not studied, and the children learned about Timor from their experience and their parents (Budiardjo & Liem 1984), in a way similar to how Estonian children learnt about their country while under Soviet rule (Tulviste 1994). Similarly, in French Cambodia, metropolitan history was difficult to master since the pupils' own past was almost totally ignored. Thion (1993, p.80) noted that students of history courses had little idea about a chronology or how a country could be different from Cambodia.

The superiority and importance of the colonisers' cultures depicted in the above colonial curricula seem to support Carnoy's assertion (1974, pp.26-27) that "in true colonialism, the colonised must be transformed from individuals with belief in themselves as capable human beings to ones who believe only in the capability of others – the colonisers". According to Whitehead (1988, p.215), however, the colonial educational experience, at least in British colonies, was not generally a deliberate policy designed to perpetuate European economic and political control. He suggests that colonial rule, in particular British colonial rule, was not planned exploitation but a complex improvisation often characterised by confused goals arising out of benevolent intentions. He believes that most colonial schooling mirrored schooling in Britain, but asserts that ample evidence suggests that colonial schooling was more a reflection of local demand on the part of indigenous peoples themselves than an indication of any deliberate British policy to colonise the indigenous intellect.

Implications of Decolonisation for the Curriculum in Hong Kong and Macau

The above descriptions of the history curricula in former colonies might not apply to the history curricula in Hong Kong and Macau over the period studied in this chapter. Though some of the above observations were made about the history curriculum in the last years of colonial rule, classical decolonisation in these places was in several aspects different to what Hong Kong and Macau experienced (Bray 1994). First, the time scale of decolonisation for Hong Kong and Macau was much less hurried. In particular, Portuguese decolonisation in Macau has been very different from the hasty and chaotic colonial withdrawal from Portugal's African colonies. The longer time scale allowed the governments and schools to make planned changes in the curriculum before the change of sovereignty. However, the longer time span also allowed the colonial government more time to set up structures for post-colonial influence.

Second, Bray (1994) observed that most colonies remaining in the 1990s would not be decolonised to full sovereignty but to some form of associated statehood or to reintegration with an original mother country. Hong Kong and Macau belong to the latter category as they were scheduled from the 1980s to become autonomous Special Administrative Regions of the Peoples' Republic of China (PRC). The cultivation of national and cultural values of China, rather than that of a new sovereign country as in classical examples of decolonising and newly independent territories, was a focus of the process of curriculum change.

Two other differences between other colonies and Hong Kong and Macau might encourage or justify the incorporation of curriculum content which may promote national identity and democratic ideals. Firstly, the nationalist feelings among the British and Portuguese colonial subjects in Africa and other parts of Asia during decolonisation were stronger than those among ethnic Chinese in Hong Kong and Macau during most of the colonial period. Strong nationalism, usually accompanied by anti-European attitudes, might prompt colonial authorities to hesitate or refuse to incorporate content which might build national identity and arouse nationalist feelings in the history curriculum. Chinese in Hong Kong and Macau generally accepted their European colonial administrations and, except for a fraction of the populations during the 1966-67 riots, did not confront them to demand the return of the territories to Chinese rule. Secondly, especially for Portugal, most of the colonies gained independence amidst wars and military hostilities. But the decolonisation of Macau has taken place under a relatively cordial relationship between China and Portugal. Though Sino-British relations were strained at times, military confrontation was obviously out of the question. The peaceful decolonisation process created fewer obstacles for the colonial government to promote a sense of national identity, democracy and other aspects of civic awareness in the history curriculum than would have a process characterised by boycotts and violence.

The Subject Curricula and Schools Studied

The 'History subject' referred to different things in Hong Kong and in Macau. In public-sector Hong Kong secondary schools, History was in effect World History, learned in Chinese or English. Chinese History as a separate subject taught in schools was not included in this study. In Macau, the history discipline was not systematically divided into different subject curricula by a recognised educational authority. Different secondary schools offered different kinds of history curricula. A government document included six differently-named curricula as the history curricula found in Macau secondary schools (Macau, Governo de 1990, p.43). They were History (*História*), Chinese History (中國歷史), Chinese History (中史), World History (*História Universal*), World History (*História Mundial*), and Foreign History (*História Estrangeira*). The curriculum in each of the Macau schools studied here belonged to one of these categories.

The curriculum studied here was essentially the implemented curriculum, as opposed to the intended curriculum officially planned by any government or educational authorities. During visits to the schools, the researcher looked for the structure and the content of the history curriculum, textbooks and notes used by students (which may or may not be based on the planned syllabus), and the focus of teaching as reported by history teachers. One focus among the questions the teachers were asked was the ways in which politically sensitive topics were handled.

Four secondary schools in Hong Kong and four in Macau were selected for study. Since this study is about political forces on the curriculum, the criterion for selection was the background (especially the political background) of the school and not the proportional representation of its type among the total number of schools in each territory. One school from each of the following four loosely defined categories was selected in each colony: pro-establishment, pro-PRC, pro-Taiwan, and relatively political neutral.

The four Hong Kong schools selected were:

1. School HK1, an Anglican aided school, one of the oldest and most prominent schools in Hong Kong. Many of its graduates had become important members of the civil service and the political and business communities of Hong Kong. HK1 was not a government school, and it did not have an overt political background. However, it has been regarded by many as a pro-establishment institution.
2. School HK2, a 'pro-China' school which had traditionally been viewed as leftist. In the 1960s and early 1970s when the Cultural Revolution spilled over to Hong Kong, it was an outright leftist school which rejected the formal curriculum of the Hong Kong Education Department (Postiglione 1992, p.9). The leftist schools were closely watched by the government for anti-British activities during the 1967 riots. Later, they were more accepted by the government, as indicated by their participation in the government-initiated Direct Subsidy Scheme, a government initiative which gave subsidies to the schools while allowing considerable administrative autonomy.
3. School HK3 was an old aided school sponsored by the Methodist Church with no obvious political background. The history panel chairman interviewed was teaching in the school throughout the 1980-1993 period. School HK3 was one of the 15 schools which participated in the pilot Form 1 local history project in 1990. This project was launched by the Education Department to test the feasibility of incorporating Hong Kong history into the junior secondary curriculum.
4. School HK4 was a private school the sponsoring body of which traditionally had strong links with the Chinese Nationalist (Guomindang) government in Taipei. School HK4 also had close relations with the Education Department of the Taipei government, especially during the 1950s and 1960s. In later years, however, such links became weaker. In the 1990s, very few graduates of HK4 went to Taiwan for further studies. During the period being studied, the history curriculum catered for students taking local public examinations and no adjustment was made for students taking Taiwan universities' entrance examinations.

The four Macau schools selected were:

5. School M1, an official Portuguese school operated by the Macau government. Most of its students were Portuguese from Portugal, who would return to Portugal after graduation. The school administration was closely connected to the Direcção dos Serviços de Educação of the Macau government and to educational

institutions in Portugal. All history teachers came from Portugal.

6. School M2 was a left-wing school of over 50 years' history. Its trained history teachers were all from China, and many graduates went to China for further studies. It was regarded as a pro-China school, and it had close links with educational bodies in the mainland.

7. School M3 was founded in Guangzhou as an affiliated branch middle school of an established university in the 1930s. It moved to Macau in 1938 because of the Japanese bombing of Guangzhou. The school had no obvious political background. Most graduates went to Hong Kong, the Chinese mainland or Taiwan, or remained in Macau for further studies or work.

8. School M4 was founded in 1961 by Fr. B. Videira Pires SJ, a prominent historian in Macau and the school's principal throughout the period studied. Fr. Pires was a Jesuit, and the school was officially sponsored by the Society of Jesus. The Jesuit order was a Roman Catholic religious congregation which helped to establish Macau as the centre of Catholicism in the Far East in the 16th and 17th centuries. The Jesuits in mainland China were among the most severely purged Catholic groups during the 1950s and the Cultural Revolution. For many years, all graduates from School M4 took entrance examinations of Taiwanese universities. These examinations were conducted at the only 'Taiwan overseas' institution in Hong Kong, Chu Hai College. Since the late 1980s, the number of students entering the University of Macau had been growing, and in 1993 it recruited about 20 per cent of School M4's graduates. Among School M4's four trained history teachers in 1993, three had been trained in Taiwan.

This selection of schools not only provides a framework for cross-territory comparison between schools of similar background in Hong Kong and Macau, it also allows intra-territorial comparison between schools of different political backgrounds. The latter comparison is especially significant for Macau, which did not have a single system of education.

The History Curriculum in Hong Kong Schools

School HK1
The selection of topics and the time periods chosen in HK1's history curriculum were traditional and conservative:

1. At Certificate level, nothing beyond 1919 was taught. Students were not taught about the Second World War II and the post-War world. Teachers felt that there was not enough time for teaching the post-1919 topics since they maintained that the more contemporary the history was, the more complicated the world was.

2. Broader analysis indicated that at Advanced level, almost all schools taught the syllabus selectively, and that the histories of Japan, China and India were always chosen. Southeast Asian history had never been taught in School HK1, and was regarded as "useless" because teachers considered it irrelevant to the needs of Hong Kong students. To prepare students for the examination of a new syllabus in 1994, the traditional selections (a chronological account of Europe 1815-1939, Chinese history until 1919, and Japanese history until the 1930s) remained.

Teachers were not interested in and did not teach Hong Kong history, a new feature of the 1994 syllabus. The panel chairperson commented: "There is nothing significant or important in Hong Kong history to justify studying it for public examinations."

For textbooks on Certificate-level European history, Crisswell's *Modern Europe 1870-1960* (1974) and Stokes & Stokes' *Europe 1870-1960* (1975) were used from the 1970s to 1986, the first year of the implementation of the new syllabus (which remained in place until 1993). These books in general provided objective historical accounts, but had a slight anti-Soviet and anti-Communist bias. Concerning the 1948 Berlin Airlift, for example, Crisswell used 'Cold War language' which was commonly found in textbooks in the 1970s:

> The Western Allies agreed that they could not afford to give way in order to appease Russia. Instead they undertook the tremendous task of supplying all the needs of two million people by air. Fortunately there were airports in all three Western zones.... The airlift had proved that the Western Powers were willing to resist Russian threats.... The loss of skilled workers demonstrated the unpopularity of the governments in Eastern Europe.... (pp.196-197)

Likewise, concerning Karl Marx, Stokes & Stokes (p.11) elaborated what they saw as the weaknesses of Marx's ideas on capitalism and class conflict:

> Capitalism in the 1970s is very different from the capitalism of 1848. Marx did not foresee that the proletariat might in time acquire property, even a lot of property.... Marx did not explain how the new Communist society was to be organized. He promised that each would receive according to his needs. He forgot that there is no end to needs... [He] failed to realize the strength of man's desire for power. In fact countries that have tried to adopt Communism have more controls than most other states. (p.11)

All these lines were underlined by the teacher in the HK1 teacher's text book. The authors concluded:

> In fact his [Marx's] theory of class conflict greatly oversimplified history.

These statements probably affected HK1 students' perceptions of Communism and the Communist countries then, while the Cold War was continuing.

In Stokes & Stokes' book, which was about European history, Hong Kong was mentioned and placed historically closer to Europe than to China. For example,

1. Patrick Manson's work in tropical medicine in Hong Kong, his role in the establishment of the Hong Kong College of Medicine for Chinese in 1887, and the opening of the University of Hong Kong which had a faculty of Medicine, were listed along with many important medical breakthroughs in the West, such as Louis Pasteur's germ theory of disease, George Mendel's work in heredity and

Fleming's discovery of penicillin, under "Some Advances in Medical Knowledge" (p.56).

2. A Permanent Court of Arbitration established as a result of an 1899 conference at the Hague called by Tsar Nicholas II was linked to Hong Kong. "The judges of this court have come from many nations: among them, for instance, were two Hong Kong-educated Chinese, Wang Chung-hui and F.T. Cheng" (p.170). These two Chinese were born many years after Tsar Nicholas II had died. The authors pulled Hong Kong into their book wherever they considered appropriate, within the European context.

3. Hong Kong's "industrial revolution" since the 1950s was regarded as a repeat of the Industrial Revolution of Western Europe in the nineteenth century. (p.56)

In their account of the First Anglo-Chinese War, Stokes & Stokes did not seem to agree with dominant views on the three causes of the war – trade, culture and opium – which were generally accepted by Hong Kong history teachers then, including School HK1's history panel chairperson. The authors apparently tried to justify British actions in the war:

> In 1839-42 Britain fought and defeated China.... The war was in fact little more than a show of British force along the coast; however, it frightened the emperor into accepting certain British demands.... To the Chinese these hostilities were the Opium War, fought to protect foreign merchants who continued importing opium into China, despite an imperial prohibition. In fact the hostilities were the direct result of British determination not to agree to a demand which according to British law was both unjust and illegal. But the real cause of the conflict was the British traders' belief in *laissez-faire* principles.... The Chinese, it is said, were forced by the West to accept unequal treaties. (p.121)

Thus the power of the British forces was mentioned, and the spirit of British law upheld; but the effect of opium on the Chinese was not mentioned.

Between 1986 and 1993, textbooks used by School HK1 had less ideologically-prejudiced wording than their earlier editions. Notes on the Anglo-Chinese wars (Opium Wars) prepared by the teacher used in recent years showed no explicit political or ideological bias similar to those observed in Stokes & Stokes' book.

The history panel chairperson, who had been teaching in School HK1 since 1969, and some HK1 students, mostly of lower academic abilities, had held anti-British views. According to the teacher, these students blamed Britain for importing opium before the First Anglo-Chinese War, and some even rejected studying Chinese history in English. In teaching this topic, the teacher insisted that opium should not be regarded as the most important cause of the war. She maintained that students should not study Chinese history only from the Chinese perspective, but should also consider it from the Western angle to form a balanced view. The notes on the First Anglo-Chinese War that she had given to students since the late 1980s were essentially summaries of standard textbook accounts. No significant political bias was observed in these pages.

While the history curriculum in School HK1 cannot be described as pro-British, one can observe Eurocentric elements in its earlier textbooks. Most of the history teachers in HK1 had studied at the University of Hong Kong. Though the options taken in the curriculum seemed to be results of pedagogic concerns and educational inertia, the academic background of the teachers, largely shaped by the university history curriculum, influenced what was taught in School HK1. The school's history curriculum, even up to 1993, did little to prepare its graduates to enter the contemporary world and a decolonising Hong Kong by teaching a minimum of post-1939 world history, let alone Hong Kong history.

School HK2

Since the introduction of the new Certificate syllabus in 1986, students were always taught sections A and B (circa 1760-1919). Section C (1919-1970) was never taught. Though sensitive topics like Guomindang-Communist relations in China during 1921-1949 and the Cold War were excluded by this curricular decision, the history panel chairperson maintained that the choice was made for pedagogic reasons:

> Students cannot learn section B (1815-1919) without understanding events in section A (1760-1815). The French Revolution and Napoleon must be mentioned while teaching the Congress of Vienna (1815); British parliamentary reforms in the 19th century must be linked to the Industrial Revolution. History learning should not be compartmentalized. And there are plenty of extra-curricular opportunities for students to learn 20th century history.

The choice of European history (the alternative was Asian history) at AS level was also made for "the good of the students": the teachers did not want students, who had already been studying Chinese history as an A level subject, to learn only Asian history at sixth form. This narrow approach to learning was regarded by the panel chairperson as a poor preparation for students who would study history in university.

Three sets of Hong Kong textbooks were used in Forms 4 and 5 during 1980 to 1993. From 1980 to 1986, *World History* (Fung 1980) was used. The teachers switched to a Longman book by Kwok Shiu-tong in 1986, and again switched to Cheung Hang-kin's *The Turbulent Years* (1990) in 1991. The changes were said to be made on pedagogic grounds. Both Kwok and Cheung had been members of the history subject committees of the Curriculum Development Committee and/or the Hong Kong Examinations Authority. The panel chairperson commented that the three sets of books mentioned above were generally objectively written and definitely could not be labelled as leftist. Except for Kwok Shiu-tong's book, of which a copy was unavailable to the researcher, the books used for the Certificate examination were not leftist in outlook. *World History* may even be considered as slightly pro-Taiwan, for example, by the usage of the term 'Guo Min Zheng Fu', meaning 'the Nationalist Government', a term which is usually only used by pro-Guomindang (pro-Nationalist) authorities. The author of *World History* apparently disapproved of Zhang Xue-liang who initiated the '1936 Xian Incident' in which Guomindang's head Jiang Jieshi was kidnapped.

According to the history panel chairperson, when Higher level world history was first taught in 1984, a well known Taiwan produced book, *Chinese Modern History* (by Chang Yu-fa), was used because "it was well written". Although the author used terms like 'gong fei' (Communist thieves) to label the Communist forces during and after the civil war 1945-49, the school authorities approved the book because the teacher regarded it as a good book for teaching purposes. Mainland history books were never used as textbooks. They could only be used as reference books in the school library because, according to the history panel chairperson, they did not conform with the Hong Kong syllabuses, they were written too much from a materialistic conception of history, and they contained too many words like 'bourgeois', 'imperialist', etc. The researcher, reviewing the panel chairperson's notes on 'The Opening Up of China', observed nothing significantly biased.

The panel chairperson claimed that he taught the First Anglo-Chinese War from a world perspective. Both China and Britain were responsible for causing the war, he said, and one should not blame Britain unilaterally for aggression. The notes he gave to students began the topic with a consideration of the conflicts and differences between China and the West in culture, commerce and law. Students were reminded not to look at the issue purely from nationalistic sentiments. The teacher asked the students which term they would like to use to name the war: 'Opium War', 'First Anglo-Chinese War' or 'War of Trade'?

It is reasonable to believe that the implementation of the history curriculum at this 'pro-China school' was largely determined by requirements of the public examinations and the educational orientation of the history panel chairperson, who had studied history in English in a local secondary and a tertiary institution. The panel chairperson insisted that history teachers and students should be true to history and should look at history from different angles. He said that changes in the history curriculum had been made for the educational benefits of the students. The school gave much autonomy to the history teachers. There was no evidence that the school authorities had manipulated the history curriculum to influence the political attitudes of their students during the period under study.

School HK3

The most significant feature of the curriculum was the school's efforts to promote local history by joining the Form 1 local history project pilot scheme in 1990. In order to promote learning interest and make the curriculum relevant to the students' lives, the teachers decided not just to stay in the Form 1 pilot scheme, but also to extend the teaching of local history into Form 2 in 1991/92 and into Form 3 in 1992/93. These moves were staunchly supported by the teachers, and the school was the champion in the 1992 Hong Kong secondary school local history project competition.

School HK3 changed its Certificate level textbooks three times during the 1980-1993 period. A change was made each time because of syllabus change, the new book's simpler content, easier English presentation, the author's comprehensive approach, or the author's inclusion of cartoons and charts. In other words, changes were made because of what the teachers considered to be the good quality of the books and their suitability to the students and the curriculum. However, the contents of the books (and their political influences) might not have totally reflected the students' perceptions of history because the history panel chairperson in School HK3 normally taught without referring to passages in the books at all. He usually wrote the main points on the blackboard, and students copied. Though the students still used the books for examinations, their reliance on books was less than that of students taught by other teachers.

Though topics like the First Anglo-Chinese War and the Cold War could not be treated in detail at Certificate level, students were informed of different factors (cultural, commercial and opium) related to the First Anglo-Chinese War. At Advanced level, debates were held in class to let students air their opinions. According to the panel chairperson, teaching was based on a rational discussion of the various causes of the conflict, and he claimed that moral judgement of the war was not a feature of his teaching.

School HK3's history panel was regarded by the Education Department as enthusiastic in curriculum development and willing to try new educationally desirable endeavours. There was no evidence of a deliberate intention of the school or the teachers to influence the students politically through the curriculum. However, there was a possible relationship between the predisposing factor of Hong Kong's decolonisation process and the direct factor of the teachers' enthusiasm leading to the promotion of Hong Kong history. It was possible that the local political climate in mid and late 1989, the year in which Hong Kong was shocked by the political clamp-down in Beijing's Tiananmen Square, might have influenced the teachers to join the local history pilot scheme in 1990.

School HK4

School HK4 selected topics 4-14 (1815-1970) for teaching at Certificate level because this period included contemporary events which the history teachers regarded as "more relevant to the students' needs".

At Advanced level, the period chosen was circa 1800-1919, and areas included European, Japanese, Chinese and Indian histories. The panel chairperson said the teachers were trained in these areas and had confidence in teaching them. Hong Kong history was not taught "mainly because of the teachers' lack of training in this area".

At Certificate level, School HK4 changed textbooks in 1986 because, according to the panel chairperson at that time, the new textbooks were more simple and the English was easier. With its multiple choice exercise books and teaching guides, and later its data-based questions workbook, the new set of books was regarded by the teachers as more suitable for their students to prepare for the Certificate Examination.

The history panel chairman claimed that all politically sensitive historical issues, especially those after the Second World War, were taught "neutrally and briskly" to students. He gave an example of the treatment of the word 'liberation' which was used in the textbook to describe the change of the Chinese government in 1949 and the unification of North and South Vietnam in 1975. 'Liberation', despite its seemingly positive implication of the changes of government, was "explained" in School HK4 as '解放', which was not an explanation at all: it was just the Chinese translation of the word. The word was not actually explained, but only translated, to "avoid any political bias", according to the panel chairperson. He reported that students had been asked not to attempt questions on sensitive issues like causes of the First Anglo-Chinese War in public examinations. This claim was debatable because students in Hong Kong are usually recommended to attempt questions based on their abilities and the difficulty of the questions, and not the political content. Though the panel chairperson reported that Chinese and Western views (Opium War, War of Commerce) on the wars in China were discussed in class, such discussion on moral judgement of historical issues was only conducted in sixth form classrooms, because in Forms 4 and 5, only what was written in textbooks would be mentioned. The panel chairperson repeatedly emphasised that in his school, all politically sensitive issues were treated "neutrally and unbiasedly" in classrooms, and that history in School HK4 was not taught from a nationalistic point of view.

Despite the traditionally pro-Taiwan nature of School HK4, its history curriculum in the period studied did not seem to have a pro-Taiwan bias. The history panel was given much autonomy from the school authority. All its history teachers during the period were locally trained. Most of School HK4's graduates continued their studies at local tertiary institutions. Therefore it was not surprising to find its curriculum following the requirements of the public examinations tightly. The history panel chairperson was keen on depoliticising the history curriculum, or at least he appeared to be keen on being 'objective' in history teaching. He was very sensitive to politically controversial events, and seemed to try to present history, at least at Certificate level, with as little political judgement as possible. This way of teaching history 'apolitically' may however be intrinsically political. This attitude could be out of fear: fear that either ideological expressions of pro-Taiwan nature or pro-Communist nature would make the members of the administration or the management body unhappy.

The History Curriculum in Macau Schools

School M1

At Grades 7 and 8, students learned Portuguese history, especially about the maritime discoveries in the 15th and 16th centuries. At Grade 9, they studied 20th century world history. They concentrated on Portuguese domestic history at Grades 10 and 11. According to a teacher, Grade 10 and 11 students were not very interested in Portuguese domestic history, not because it was Portuguese, but because they were too young to fit the investigative learning approach adopted in the curriculum. This approach required students to conduct research and look up documents. At Grade 12, students learned something their counterparts in private schools would not learn: the theory of history. They studied different ways to study history and different opinions about what kind of history should be studied. The Grade 12 curriculum in a way aimed to prepare students to become historians, rather than to give them more historical facts.

Textbooks used in School M1 were all imported from Portugal. The books were generally very Eurocentric and, according to a teacher, the very little bit about Asia was written from "the eyes of the Portuguese who came to Asia". A change of the education system in Portugal in 1992 called for more flexibility and open-mindedness of the history curriculum, and the Macau government had to follow Lisbon to make similar changes in the official schools. Since teachers felt that students in School M1, who were living in Asia, should know more about Asian history, in the early 1990s they started to include more Asian history in the curriculum. To correspond with the study of 15th and 16th century Portugal at Grade 8, students now also studied 15th and 16th century Asia, from what the teachers described as a less Portuguese perspective. Grade 9 students studied world history which included the 1911 Chinese Revolution, the establishment of the PRC in 1949 and post-1949 events in China such as the Great Leap Forward and the Cultural Revolution, the last of which was usually untouched by Hong Kong teachers at Form 3, the corresponding level. These topics were included in their Portuguese textbook, even though it was written for pupils in Portugal. According to a teacher, these topics on China had already existed in the 1980 edition of the book and lasted throughout the 1980s, and the teachers had expanded their own teaching on such topics recently. In the 1990s, teachers also prepared their own notes and showed movies to supplement the inadequate coverage of Asian history in the books. Grade 9 students were asked to conduct research studies on Macau after studying socialist China. One group chose to study the influence of the Chinese Cultural Revolution on Macau in the late 1960s, a very political and controversial subject.

The textbook used at Grade 9 by Neves & Almeida (1990) contained generally neutral and objective accounts of the 20th century world. Post-war history was divided into three parts: capitalist countries (USA, Japan, Western Europe), socialist countries (USSR, China, Yugoslavia, Cuba) and the Third World. China was classified under the socialist bloc. The map of the Third World did not show China at all (p.165). This classification of post-War history suggests that the Cold War mentality was still evident in the minds of the European authors.

The 1974 revolution in Portugal overthrew dictatorship and brought independence to almost all remaining Portuguese colonies. The new Portuguese government was portrayed in the book as the saviour of the peoples in these former colonies and a friend of these new nations:

> The proclamation of independence of Guinea-Bissau on 23rd August, 1974, of Mozambique on 26th June, 1975, of Cape Verde on 5th July, of São Tomé e Príncipe on 12th of the same month, and finally of Angola on 11th November, 1975, demarcated a straight identification with the fundamental objectives of the April 25 movement [the Portuguese Revolution]. Portugal was on its way to its own liberation, which was a measure to recognise the freedom of the oppressed colonial territories. A historical destination was reached.
>
> Now, in the long run, another destination of essential importance for Portugal, was the establishment and functioning of fruitful co-operative relationships with the new African states, ... and the consolidation of the irreversible reality as a result of the great historical step of decolonisation (p.197, translated from Portuguese)

A teacher explained that the Portuguese people were proud of the revolution which brought decolonisation of the colonies. However, nothing about Macau was mentioned in the paragraphs about decolonisation. This might be because of the lack of space, but it was more likely due to an avoidance of embarrassment. The authors might have found it impossible to explain without embarrassment why Macau was still under Portuguese administration while the other territories which remained colonies at the time of the Portuguese revolution were, with the exception of East Timor, all now independent. A teacher of School M1 who was born and educated in Mozambique and later moved to Portugal ruled out the above two explanations. He explained that most Portuguese viewed Macau very differently from Portuguese colonies in Africa, probably because Macau was not annexed through warfare. Macau was generally regarded more as a Chinese territory under Portuguese administration, not as a colony, and it was not discussed much by Portuguese in Portugal or in Mozambique. He suggested this might be the reason why Macau was missing in the list of decolonising colonies. This could be contrasted with the fact that the 'colonisation' of Macau was mentioned in Grade 8 textbooks where Portuguese maritime expansion in the 15th and 16th centuries are discussed.

The history of Macau was not in the Portuguese curriculum, except for the section that Grade 8 students studied about the early Portuguese settlements in Macau in the 16th century. In 1992 the teachers added Macau history into School M1's curriculum because they believed the students should know the history of Macau, and were facilitated by the curriculum reforms in Portugal. Macau's history was made a common topic for group projects done by Grade 7 students. They looked up historical materials and considered its future. One issue under investigation was "How would Macau's population change after 1999?" This approach of studying history, using the knowledge of the past to anticipate the future, was rarely heard in history lessons in other schools in Macau or in Hong Kong.

At Grade 9, the teacher had developed a Macau history curriculum. He started with the early settlements in the 16th century, and then went on to the first half of the 17th century. The loyalty of Macau towards Portugal was emphasised when Macau was remembered as the only territory remaining Portuguese during the 60 years when Portugal and her colonies were ruled by Spain.

While Bray & Hui's (1991a) description of the history curriculum in School M1 was valid when it was written, subsequent changes made the curriculum less Eurocentric and more relevant to the students' current political environment. Some factors behind these changes might have been of Portuguese origin. While the textbooks were still imported from Portugal and the curriculum still largely followed the Portuguese one, reforms calling for flexibility and objectivity in history teaching in Portugal had influenced history teaching in School M1. The addition of Grade 9 local history was possible because of an additional hour per week allocated to history, a result of the Portuguese educational reforms. The investigatory approach, the learning of the theory of history, and projects on the future were definitely related to the current Western approach in history learning and the training the history teachers received. Local factors, however, also played a part in these changes. All the history teachers had lived in Macau for several years and this might have caused them to realise the significance of Macau's history and include it in the curriculum. The prospective return of Macau to China in 1999 initiated a small wave of interest in examining Macau's past. There had been increasing efforts from the government and scholars to promote interest in local history. History teachers living in Macau in years following the signing of the Sino-Portuguese Joint Declaration could not be unaware of this influence. Although School M1 was financed and under the supervision of the then Direcção dos Serviços de Educação, the initiative to promote Macau's history came from the history teachers themselves, based on a spirit of curriculum flexibility which originated from Lisbon.

School M2

In Junior Middle 1 and 2 where Chinese history from ancient times to late Qing was taught, Hong Kong textbooks were used. Junior Middle 3 students studied Chinese history of the recent and contemporary periods, including such events as the Opium Wars, the May Fourth Movement, Nationalist-Communist cooperation against the Japanese invasion, the civil war, the establishment of the PRC, land reforms, the Great Leap Forward and the Cultural Revolution up to the present. Events after 1949 were covered in less detail, but were still much more prominent than in the Hong Kong junior secondary and Certificate World History curricula. In the early 1990s, even the 1989 June 4th incident was touched upon.

At the Junior Middle 3 level, Hong Kong textbooks were not used because the history teachers felt that this period of Chinese history was treated too superficially by Hong Kong authors. Since the teachers regarded 20th century Chinese history as very important in the education of Chinese students and therefore deserved deeper treatment, they used textbooks from mainland China. A senior history teacher also rejected some of the interpretations made by Hong Kong authors, such as linking the causes of the Opium War to the Chinese traditional attitude of superiority over Westerners. He named British imperialism as an important cause of the war. The teachers, he said, were however aware of the pro-Communist nature of mainland textbooks, and, he claimed, made appropriate modifications when needed. For example, not only the Communists' efforts in the fighting against the Japanese invasion were acknowledged (as is done in the mainland textbooks), but also the Guomindang (Nationalist) efforts. The period 1919-49 was regarded as controversial in Chinese history, and teachers were said to be aware of historical judgements of the Communists and the Nationalists in this period from various points of view.

From Senior Middle 1 to 3, mainland textbooks were used mainly because students had to prepare for PRC examinations. These books stressed the importance of Marxist thought and the superiority of socialism, the importance of the 1917 Bolshevik Revolution, the negative image of the imperialist United States, and China's solidarity with the colonised Third World. In a discussion on the colonial expansion of the Western powers, the author of one of these textbooks wrote that "when capitalism was transformed into imperialism, Asia suffered from colonial oppression" (Anon. 1991, p.186). About the anti-colonial revolts in Egypt, Sudan and Ethiopia, the author had this account:

> During their aggression and enslavement of Africa, the colonialist and imperialist countries encountered the brave resistance of the African people ... the Ethiopians broke the chains of colonial rule against the oppressors..." (Anon. 1991, p.190)

The 1917 Bolshevik Revolution was described as the "Great Socialist October Revolution". The US Truman doctrine was criticised as "an interference into the domestic affairs of nations in the world". The American assistance received by Jiang Jieshi to fight the Chinese Communists in the civil war was described as "American invasion into Asia". The establishment of the PRC on October 1, 1949 was described as "the most important event in human history".

On the Korean War, the author wrote:

> On June 25, 1950, the Korean War broke out. The United Nations commanded the US navy and air forces to invade North Korea, also aiming to prevent the Chinese people from liberating their own sacred territory of Taiwan. China was protecting her homeland, ... while the Americans advanced north crazily..." (Anon. 1992, p.133.)

School M2's teachers did not feel that North Korea should be blamed as an invader in the war, since the US, the main aggressor, should be also blamed for what the teacher called "its imperialistic ambitions in East Asia". They justified China's participation in the Korean War on the grounds of protection of ideological interests and national security.

Certain aspects of the history of Macau were taught throughout the period 1980 to 1993. Since no systematic local history curriculum or book was available, teaching was mainly based on the teachers' own experience and their notes, with data selectively taken from the Macau government publications. The history of Macau was presented as the evolution of a small village to a significant port and now a 'window' of China to the west. The colonial aspects were never emphasised, and whenever they were mentioned, according to the senior history teacher, they were used to demonstrate the then "cruel governorship by the Portuguese and their utilitarian rule".

The pro-PRC political inclination of School M2 had basically remained unchanged for the last two decades, with the following exceptions:

- Japan had been given a totally negative image in the classroom because of its atrocities in China during the Second World War. As Sino-Japanese relations improved during the 1970s and 1980s, when the Second World War was being taught, students were taught to differentiate between the Japanese militarists, who had to bear responsibility of the suffering they inflicted upon the Chinese, and the ordinary people, who were described as innocent.
- During the Cold War, much of the teaching about US imperialism was based on nationalistic sentiments. As the Cold War thawed, this attitude was toned down.
- The teachers noted a change of Portuguese attitude towards Chinese in Macau after the signing of the Sino-Portuguese Joint Declaration. This was briefly mentioned in the teaching of local history.

School M2's history curriculum was the most politicised one of all studied. Without a centralised curricula in the enclave, Macau's schools were free to devise their own curriculum. This allowed School M2 to teach whatever topics and use whatever books it preferred. Most content of the modern period was presented with a bias towards the mainland government, though the teachers claimed that they respected history and they would correct any extreme attitudes found in mainland textbooks. The political inclination of the history curriculum closely followed the Chinese position in foreign affairs: all the three changes during the period reflected changes in China's relations with Japan, USA and Portugal. In the teachers' views, neither the school nor the students were harmed by the teaching of such a politicised curriculum. The students would not be penalised in the entrance examinations of Chinese universities if their answers in the history paper carried leftist thoughts. The history curriculum matched the school's status as a pro-PRC school in Macau where the political winds from China were influential.

School M3

History was offered at all levels, from Junior Middle one to Senior Middle three. Junior students (1-3) studied Chinese and world history. Senior students studied Chinese history (ending at 1945) at Grades 1 and 2 and world history (ending at 1919) at Grade 3. The senior history teacher cited time as a factor limiting the teaching of more world history at Senior Middle 3, the year when students had to prepare for university examinations. The teacher said he determined what should be taught, and that no consideration was given to the university requirements of the graduates' different destinations for further studies.

On the school's textbook lists of the last few years of the period studied, Hong Kong books were recommended as reference books. The 'real' textbooks however were a set of notes compiled by the senior history teacher (though they did not carry his name) and printed by the school. The senior teacher said his 'books' were based on several sources: Hong Kong textbooks, mainland textbooks and classical history texts. Hong Kong books were regarded as not good for senior students because the Hong Kong (Chinese history) syllabus "separated political history from cultural and economic history", the importance of the Chinese culture was "not emphasised enough", and the books were "written from a British perspective".

One of the senior teacher's 'books' (Macau Ling Nam Middle School n.d.) contained many descriptions based on Chinese nationalistic and anti-imperialistic sentiments. For example:

- The British shamelessly smuggled large quantities of drugs – opium – into China. (p.167)
- Patriotic hero Lin Zexu ordered opium to be banned to show the world China's determination to resist aggression.... Britain had already planned to use force to open the doors of China. When the news of banning opium was heard, Britain decided to initiate a war of aggression. (p.169)
- On 1st June, the British forces fled in panic from Humen to their vessels. (p.171)
- The Crazy Attempt of Imperialist Partition of China (p.190)
- Chang Xun [who temporarily restored the Manchu monarchy in 1917] was a stubborn remnant of feudalism. (p.215)

In his teaching and in his materials, the senior teacher, who had been trained in a mainland Chinese university, blamed the British imperialistic invasion as the prime cause of the First Anglo-Chinese War. He said that no student had ever challenged his position on this issue. Discussion with students in class was ruled out by this teacher because of the lack of time. Chinese history in the 19th and 20th century was taught from a nationalistic perspective. When the senior teacher was asked how sensitive issues concerning relations between the Communists and the Guomindang were handled in class, he replied:

"Sensitive issues are not mentioned, em, ... not very emphasised, ... Students are left to judge history themselves."

According to the opinions given by the teacher during the interview and his writings, the last statement seems very questionable. His change of tone of voice and facial expressions when he accused the West of imperialist invasion, together with his admittedly didactic teaching method, implied that he probably conveyed a lot of nationalistic thoughts to his students.

The teacher explained that local history was not taught because there was not enough time, not enough systematic textbooks, and he did not know how to teach it. When asked whether he would consider teaching Macau history if textbooks became available in future, he replied that Macau did not have a long history.

In this school, which did not have an overtly political background, the greatest form of political influence on the history curriculum did not come from centralised bureaucracies or the school management, but from the teachers.

School M4

History, taught in Chinese, was compulsory for all students at all levels throughout the period, as there was no division into science and arts classes (even at upper levels). The curriculum remained largely unchanged for the two decades before 1993. Chinese history was given greater importance than world history because of the entrance requirements of Taiwan universities.

Students from Junior Middle one to Senior Middle 5 had used Hong Kong textbooks of the same publishers for the previous two decades. In 1993, history textbooks used by School M4, published in the early 1980s, were either not commonly used or obsolete in Hong Kong. Senior Middle 3 students did not have a textbook for world history. The teacher used a book written by a Jesuit in Taiwan as a source, and students copied notes adapted from this book from the blackboard.

At junior levels, history was taught up to 1970 (in Junior Middle 3), while at Senior Middle 3, the course ended in the year 1949. Post-1949 events were not required by Taiwan universities. The content focus at the senior level was the history of the Republic of China between 1911 and 1949.

Although the school's principal was a prominent author of the history of Macau, no local history was taught in School M4 during the period. The teachers suggested that this was because of a lack of resource materials in this topic, though such an explanation held less force in the early 1990s than it would have done in earlier years.

A teacher of School M4 said that her colleagues usually consulted several sources in Hong Kong books, mainland books and Taiwan books, before deciding how to teach politically sensitive issues. They generally considered Hong Kong books as pro-British because all such books must be approved by the government's Education Department. For example, they thought the account of the First Anglo-Chinese War in the books they used did not put enough blame on Britain as an aggressor. On the other hand, they thought the mainland authors blamed Britain too much. The teachers studied both sources and "aimed to present a balanced view to the students".

History in senior forms was taught by a very senior teacher. His specialised topic was Communist-Nationalist relations in China and the Chinese civil war, since he had personally experienced such events. In class he shared his experience during that period as a Guomindang (Nationalist) military official and even showed his certificates of honour awarded by Guomindang authorities.

Since the school had to prepare most students for further studies in Taiwan, Taiwan's political stance and vocabulary had to be considered and sometimes adopted during the teaching of history. Questions for the Taiwan universities entrance examination were set by lecturers of Chu Hai College, Hong Kong, the place where Hong Kong and Macau students took the examination. The questions generally covered topics found in the Hong Kong syllabus, and Taiwan's vocabulary was used (for example, Peiping [北平] instead of Beijing [北京]).

The content, emphasis, choice of resource materials, and to some extent the political orientation of the history curriculum were largely influenced by forces from Taiwan, namely the admission examination of Taiwan universities. The current curriculum was a reflection of the traditionally strong links between Jesuit educational institutes in Macau and Taiwan tertiary institutes. The fact that pro-Taiwan teachers and opinions were tolerated was not surprising in an institution sponsored by a religious order which had suffered bitterly under the Chinese Communists. What was surprising was the total absence of a desire among history teachers to promote Macau's history in a school headed by a scholar who had written much about Macau's history.

Analysis and Comparison

The History Curriculum in the Hong Kong Schools
In the four Hong Kong schools studied, there was no evidence of obvious political indoctrination, though a slight Eurocentric inclination in School HK1 in the early 1980s was identified. Political socialisation (the encouragement of a predisposition towards a certain set of political values) and political education (promotion of a critical awareness of political phenomena) however, was unavoidable, despite the claims by the panel chairman in School HK4 that there had been no political judgement in the school's history lessons. Most of the reasons given to explain the selections made in the curriculum and choices of textbooks were related to educational needs of the students and the suitability for public examinations, though the teachers' own pedagogic beliefs and academic backgrounds were often influential. Changes in the wider political climate before the beginning of the local history pilot project might be behind the teachers' enthusiasm for Hong Kong history in School HK3. There was no evidence that curricular decisions in history had been directed by the school authorities.

The degree of implementation of the official curriculum at Certificate and Advanced levels was quite high. Though there was a freedom in the choice of sections, textbooks, interpretations, the areas of study were confined, and there was no room for political or ideological extremism. The pressure of topical and ideological conformity created by a centralised system of public examinations was powerful. Teachers and schools gave a high priority to the students' performance in public examinations, and any political bias in content and teaching approach which would affect their prospects in such examinations would not have been considered beneficial.

The History Curriculum in the Macau Schools
In Macau, as there was practically no government intervention over the use of textbooks, the schools were able to use whatever books they preferred according to their political and educational inclinations. Few textbooks on history, if any, had been published in Macau because of the small market size of Macau and the different requirements of individual schools. The books used in Macau schools studied were published in Hong Kong, Portugal and the PRC. The situation is similar to that described by Altbach (1987) in Third World countries where imported books reflected the orientations and values of the country of publication. The Portuguese book used by Grade 9 students in School M1 clearly approved of the post-1974 Portuguese government's efforts of decolonisation. The PRC books used in School M2 showed socialist and anti-American stances which were in line with the official dogma and foreign policies of the PRC government.

Students in different types of schools prepared for different examinations. They had to study history to prepare for admission examinations into PRC, Portuguese and Taiwanese universities, but not the University of Macau (except for Portuguese studies). The need to prepare students for examinations to enter universities of a particular territory justified the teacher of a particular school to choose textbooks which could meet the examination requirements of that country. The government's non-interventionist policy on public examinations had allowed the situation to persist. The establishment of the University of Macau did not bring more unity in the history curricula used by different schools because general historical studies (in English or Chinese) were not offered by the university and therefore no history paper suitable for most Macau students had been set. (History was only offered by the university's Centre of Portuguese Studies, and the course's emphasis was on Portuguese imperial history.) Had a training programme for history teachers in the university's Faculty of Education been created, the usage and availability of history textbooks would have changed, because trained teachers are usually more willing to consider the educational needs of pupils and their pedagogic interests and may be more willing to write books than untrained teachers.

Many books in the schools studied had been used for a long time. In cases where new editions were used, such as the PRC books used in School M2, in general they did not differ much from earlier editions. The inertia in changing books might be due to the lack of need to change the curriculum because of the relatively stable examination requirements of overseas institutions, the fact that the place of publication of the books was the country where teachers of a school had received their history education, and the low level of training of the teachers. Altbach (1987) related the shortage of qualified teachers to the heavy dependence on textbooks. Only 15.8 per cent of secondary school teachers in Macau in 1992 had been trained (Cheong et al. 1992). Teachers in private schools often had to face large classes, and might tend to use books that they had been used to as this might save time and effort in lesson preparation. Another factor was the cheap price of old Hong Kong books and PRC books.

Wide diversity in the history curricula was found among the four schools studied. School M1 followed a curriculum largely based on the curriculum used in Portugal. This included not only the content but also the teaching method, which was more advanced and heuristic than the curricula in the other schools. This style of teaching was related to the fact that the teachers were all from Portugal. School M2 had a politicised curriculum, taught by China-educated teachers, following political values acceptable in mainland schools. The senior secondary curriculum of School M3 seemed to be dominated by the panel chairperson, using his own materials and following his own nationalist and anti-imperialist beliefs. School M4 adopted a curriculum adapted to the admission requirements of Taiwanese universities, though increasing numbers of students sat for the University of Macau admission examination in the 1990s. Most of School M4's teachers were trained in Taiwan or by Republican institutions in the mainland before 1949, and one teacher was reported to teach with explicit Guomindang emphasis. All schools perhaps with the exception of M3 were clearly influenced by political direct forces from territories outside Macau through institutions which had obvious political affiliations. The case of School M3 was more of individual political forces operating in the absence of strong institutional political forces. This diversity was possible largely because of the non-interventionist educational policy of the Macau government. This policy resulted in a lack of coordination in curriculum development and the absence of territory wide examinations, except for the recently introduced University of Macau entrance examinations. Resources to encourage coordination of the history curriculum like financial subsidy and teacher training were scarce, though the newly established Education Commission had begun preliminary planning in curriculum matters. With the high degree of autonomy enjoyed by the schools and the need of many students to leave Macau for tertiary studies, strong external political forces influencing the curriculum in Macau were unlikely to be wiped out in the near future.

Despite the differences between the history curricula of the four schools, two similarities are observed. First, school-based curriculum innovations, though not comprehensive in nature, have been noted. School M1's teachers had given more emphasis to Asian and Macau history, without any prompting from local educational authorities. School M2 had also begun to teach Macau history, from a perspective dissimilar to that of School M1, and was mentioning contemporary historical events not covered in the 'official textbook curriculum'. School M4's teachers, though using Hong Kong books, had studied mainland and Taiwan sources to prepare some lessons which touched political contents. A second similarity was the use of informal texts in the curriculum. This text was sometimes supplementary but at other times dominating in nature. Teachers in Schools M1 and M2 prepared their own notes on Macau history. In the senior classes of School M3, the notes compiled by the teacher have been the 'real textbook' for many years. Notes from a book written by a Taiwan Jesuit had been copied by final year students of School M4. School based curriculum innovations and the use of informal texts provided the teachers with opportunities for politicisation or depoliticisation of the curriculum. The resulting curricular flexibility could be related to the laissez-faire attitude of the government, the different requirements of examinations conducted by universities of different places, and the lack of locally published classroom materials suitable for candidates sitting these examinations.

Difference from curricula under classical colonialism
The history curricula in Hong Kong and Macau schools from 1980 to 1993 in general did not conform to Carnoy's view of the function of colonial schooling, namely "to train the colonised for roles that suit the coloniser" and "to control the colonised economically and politically" (Carnoy 1974, pp.3, 72). One possible exception to this generalisation was the focus on Portuguese domestic and imperial histories in the official Portuguese curriculum in Macau. Nevertheless, this Lusocentric curriculum was mainly offered to Portuguese children who were descendants of the colonisers rather than to the colonised people. The ethnic Chinese children in Hong Kong and Macau spent a significant amount of class time (which varied among the schools) on the history of China which, unlike the cultures of many indigenous peoples colonised by the Western powers, has a history longer than many of the colonising powers. Though textbooks used by School HK1 in the early 1980s showed signs of Eurocentrism, no textbooks used in this period contained straightforward praise of Western countries or degradation of the Chinese people. However, this was not the case for textbooks used in School M2.

Most of the history curricula in Hong Kong and Macau schools are different from those in former colonies (mostly during the 1950s and 1960s) mentioned earlier. The curricula in the latter were largely Eurocentric and of little indigenous relevance. With the partial exception of the official school in Macau, schools in Hong Kong and Macau did not show or had moved away from Eurocentrism, and local history was gaining emphasis. This difference can be related to the special features of decolonisation in Hong Kong Macau. The timescale of decolonisation in Hong Kong and Macau was longer than that in other colonies, and this allowed curriculum planning by individual teachers and schools. In contrast, the abrupt decolonisation processes in many other colonies precluded a similar degree of planning and Eurocentricism stayed in the curricula (Bray 1997a). Another factor was the fact that the two territories were scheduled to reunite with China. This prospect encouraged teachers (in Macau), or teachers and the government (in Hong Kong) to promote the study of local history from a non-European perspective. Furthermore, the absence of strong anti-colonial sentiments and violence in the Hong Kong society removed an excuse which the colonial government could have used to stop the trends of moving away from Eurocentrism and cultivating a local identity through history. Finally, in this study, history curricula near the end of the 20th century were examined. Britain's, Portugal's and their colonial administrators' and subjects' conceptions of colonialism were quite different from those in earlier decades. This difference influenced expectations from the government, teachers, students and the public on the function of history teaching.

Differences between British and Portuguese Colonial Rule; Centralisation vs Decentralisation

The different styles of British and Portuguese colonial rule have resulted in significant contrasts in educational provision in the two territories. The large amount of resources devoted to education in Hong Kong led to a higher standard but also a more centralised development of the history curriculum than in Macau. The latter's framework is perhaps better described as non-centralisation rather than decentralisation since it chiefly arose by default rather than because of deliberate policy. The fundamental differences of centralisation and non-centralisation manifested in many aspects of the curricula in the two territories, which will be elaborated below.

The use of the colonial language in the history curriculum was different in both territories. English was widely used in Hong Kong, though the use of Chinese in studying World History was increasing. Among the four Macau schools studied, Portuguese was the medium of instruction only in the official school. Chinese was used in the study of history in the other three schools. The low popularity of the Portuguese language in Macau was due to the longstanding neglect of Portuguese-language education by the government and the low value of the language in tertiary studies in Macau and elsewhere. The global influence of the Portuguese culture had diminished much since its peak four centuries ago.

The difference in the extent of centralisation of the history curricula in Hong Kong and Macau was partly a result of the different extent of devotion to education by the two colonial governments. Many of the contrasting patterns of centralised and decentralised curriculum development observed by Bray (1992b) were found in this specific study of the history curriculum.

The centralised nature of Hong Kong's history curriculum, especially from Form 4 as students prepared for public examinations, limited the schools' freedom in curriculum content. The requirements of public examinations guided curricular decisions (selection of options, textbooks, ideological interpretations of history) made by individual panel chairpersons, and such decisions were usually not related to the political background (if any) of the schools. In contrast, the non-interventionist educational policy of the Macau government allowed distinctly different curricula and political forces in imported curricula to operate in Macau schools. The degree of curriculum control by the school authority and individual history teachers was much greater in Macau than in Hong Kong. The background of the school was in many cases an important factor behind curricular decisions in the history subject. The absence of a territory-wide examination of history and the high degree of autonomy enjoyed by the schools made unification of the history curricula impossible in the near future.

The effects of centralisation are evident when political aspects of the implemented curricula of schools of similar backgrounds on both sides of the Pearl River Delta are compared. The pro-Communist and anti-imperialist nature of the curriculum of School M2 was hardly evident in School HK2. The pro-Taiwan elements in history teaching and the use of Taiwan's vocabulary found in School M4 were not reported and were probably non-existent in School HK4. The curriculum of the somewhat pro-establishment School HK1, though it had a slight Eurocentric emphasis in the early 1980s, was a far cry from the Lusocentric curriculum in School M1.

The effects of centralisation and non-centralisation are also seen in the control of textbooks and curriculum innovation. The control of political content of textbooks used in Hong Kong was largely exercised through a network of authors, publishers and curriculum experts in the Textbook Committee under the Education Department. In Macau, though the ideological beliefs of authors and publishers of the imported books were also important in determining the content, the control was largely exercised by schools and teachers, who could choose whatever books they preferred, or even produced their own materials. The promotion of local history in Hong Kong was initiated by centralised educational bodies and accepted by teachers, but in Macau it largely originated from the teachers themselves. The result of this difference was a local history curriculum which acknowledged the pre-colonial civilisation in Hong Kong, and in Macau, a Lusocentric local history curriculum in the official school, and a non-colonial one in the pro-PRC School M2.

Conclusion

This chapter began with an examination of the political nature of the history subject, followed by a review of the literature about history teaching in former colonies. The differences between the decolonisation process in Hong Kong and Macau and that in former colonies were identified. The implications of such differences on the curriculum were discussed and later related to the trends (of declining Eurocentrism and increasing interest in local history) found in the study. The study shows that because of the relatively centralised nature of the Hong Kong education system, wide variations in the political content were not found in the curriculum implemented in schools. In Macau, because of its unorganised education system, the curriculum varied much in content and political inclination according to the background of the school. Therefore, pro-PRC, pro-Taiwan, and Lusocentric curricula were found in the enclave. The difference in the degree of curricular centralisation and coordination in Hong Kong and Macau was related to the difference in the allocation of resources for education from the respective colonial governments.

The information in this study supplements the works on the implemented history curriculum in Hong Kong and Macau by Morris (1990, p.109) and Bray & Hui (1991a). This study also contributes to the literature of inter-territorial and intra-territorial comparative education by comparing the history curricula in two nearby colonial territories and the curricula implemented in different types of schools in each territory. Though Hong Kong and Macau have much in common, their patterns of curriculum development have been very different. In the case of Macau, the unorganised nature of educational provision also allows striking comparison of differences within the territory itself.

11

Secondary School Mathematics Curricula

Tang Kwok Chun

Mathematics has always been considered to be an internationally accepted subject in school curricula. In most systems, between 12 and 15 per cent of student time is devoted to mathematics. Furthermore, some comparative studies suggest that school mathematics knowledge of different systems shares many similar features. For instance, focusing on the official primary curricula of mathematics and science in a large number of countries from 1800 to 1986, Kamens & Benavot (1992) showed that by the turn of the 20th century, both arithmetic and science were firmly established in most countries. They also showed that national differences in the curricular content of mathematics and science were small, and that key indicators of socioeconomic development, economic dependence, or world system position did not correlate much with instructional time. Oldham (1989), after trying to find out whether there was an international secondary mathematics curriculum, stated (p.212) that:

> it can be said that there is indeed an international mathematics curriculum. However, the commonalty is moderated by distinct (and less distinct) patterns of diversity; so a better conclusion is that there are several international curricula, sharing many features but with roots in different mathematical and contextual traditions.

In order to understand the stability and change of school mathematics curriculum, some researchers have adopted a world system perspective by emphasising the influence of the worldwide forces dominated by Western culture, whereas others have focused on the local shaping forces in the Western developed countries. Kamens & Benavot (1992) suggested that their above-mentioned findings could be explained by the growing transnational forces and worldwide institutionalised cultural rules originating from Western culture.

In a study of stability and change of the School Mathematics Project (SMP) in the 1960s in the United Kingdom, Cooper (1985) used sociological analysis to investigate the nature of school mathematics as a subject, the process of its redefinition, the nature of the redefinition, and the control of redefinition. He identified the sources of innovations and the higher institutional decision-making processes which determine which innovations would be filtered through to schools and other educational institutions.

Moon (1986) studied the New Mathematics Movement in France, England & Wales, the Netherlands, West Germany and Denmark from 1960 to 1980. The general pattern identified was that while the universities had a major impact on the reform, the 'high status' of New Mathematics was used, or later abused, by material and ideational interest groups. He also argued that commercial publishers were an influential group in the New Mathematics debate. Stanic (1987a, 1987b) studied mathematics education in the USA at the beginning of the twentieth century. He noted the decline in the influence of 19th century mental discipline theory and the rapid societal changes brought by industrialisation, urbanisation and immigration. In response, four curriculum interest groups emerged – humanists, developmentalists, social efficiency educators and social meliorists – to argue for their distinct ideas of selection and organisation of school knowledge. In the field of mathematics, the justification question was not the heart of the issue, but conflict, continuity, and compromise emerged in the struggles and controversies.

In the light of such literature, this chapter is a comparative study of the stability and change of secondary mathematics curriculum in Hong Kong and Macau. Both worldwide and local shaping forces are examined. Adoption of textbooks before World War II is studied first in order to understand the common origin of the traditional approach to mathematics teaching and learning in Hong Kong and Macau. The communist threat in the late 1940s and the different reaction of the two colonial governments marked the point of bifurcation – the advent of locally-published textbooks in Hong Kong in the early 1960s. Differences in response to the worldwide Modern Mathematics movement by the local mathematics educators brought further diversity in their mathematics curricula. Finally, differences in curriculum development organisations are discussed in relation to the 1990s challenges; including universal free education, and worldwide advancement of information technology. The influence of the People's Republic of China (PRC) due to sovereignty reversion complicated the diversity of the two curriculum patterns. In short, the two places have a common origin in secondary mathematics curriculum, but they have moved into different paths since the early 1960s and are still running on different tracks. It is unlikely that these two tracks of curriculum development will converge in the near future.

This comparative and historical study also suggests that in order to study and compare the stability and change of school knowledge in non-Western places like Hong Kong and Macau, Western influences of school mathematics are powerful forces which should be considered but local socio-historical background and efforts of local mathematics educators cannot be ignored. Finally, the author suggests that the sociology of educational systems proposed by Archer (1979, 1981, 1983, 1984, 1993, 1995) may provide a useful framework to integrate the study of Western influences and local shaping forces into a coherent and illuminating explanatory analysis.

The Common Origin of Traditional Mathematics

Before the 1960s, the mathematics curricula in Hong Kong and Macau secondary schools were mainly textbook-driven. It was a common practice to have separate textbooks and even separate teachers for arithmetic, geometry, algebra, trigonometry, coordinate geometry and calculus. The theoretical root of this approach was established over 300 years ago. The traditional organisation of mathematical content was evident in the division of the subject into four main branches: arithmetic, algebra, geometry, and analysis, with each considered as a closed and separate field of investigation (Fehr 1970, p.200).

The most popular traditional mathematics textbooks adopted by the Chinese-medium schools in both places were Chinese translations of American textbooks of the 1910s (Tang 1999). The most popular algebra textbook was *College Algebra* written by Fine (1905). The popular geometry textbooks were *Plane and Solid Geometry* written by Schultze et al. (1901). *Plane and Spherical Trigonometry* written by Granville (1909) and *New Analytical Geometry* written by Smith & Gale (1912) were also widely adopted (Hong Kong 1955a). These textbooks were also very popular in China in the 1920s (Ngai et al. 1987).

Among the English-medium schools, UK textbooks were adopted. For instance, pre-war textbooks such as *Essentials of School Arithmetic* (Mayne 1938a), *Essentials of School Algebra* (Mayne 1938b), *Modern Geometry* (Durell 1920) and *Elementary Calculus* (Bowman 1936) were included in the approved textbook list (Hong Kong 1955b), and they were widely adopted by English-medium schools in both places from the 1930s. The few Portuguese-medium schools in Macau were in effect Portuguese schools operating in Asia. Portuguese traditional mathematics textbooks were adopted in these schools.

Finding UK textbooks in the English-medium schools and Portuguese textbooks in the Portuguese-medium schools is not surprising due to the influence of colonialism. However, the adoption of Chinese translations of the American textbooks by the Chinese-medium schools in both places deserves further examination.

In China, after the overthrow of the Qing Dynasty and the establishment of the Republic of China in 1911, a new education system adapted from the Japanese and German systems was introduced. In 1922, this system was replaced by a 6+3+3 system which was adapted from the USA. English versions of the above-mentioned American textbooks were adopted by some prestigious schools in Beijing, including the secondary section of Beijing Normal University. In the 1930s and 1940s, numerous translated versions were published and were popular in secondary schools in the Republic of China (Ngai et al. 1987).

In 1928, shortly after the establishment of the Nanjing government in China, the Overseas Chinese Education Committee was established under the Ministry of Education. Regulations were issued, and overseas Chinese schools were asked to register with the Overseas Chinese Education Bureau. Details of the curriculum used were required for the registration process (Cheng 1949; Chan 1992). The main purpose was to control the structure and curriculum of overseas Chinese schools in order to exclude communist influence. The strategic consideration behind such policy might best be explicated by Cheng's (1949) examination of the Hong Kong case (quoted in Wong Leung 1969, p.53):

> Since 1928, the Chinese Government had been trying to control the overseas Chinese schools through its consuls and Kuomintang agents abroad. As there were no Chinese Consuls in Hong Kong and Kuomingtang activities were banned, the attempt of the Chinese Government to influence the Chinese colony must be by very subtle ways....
>
> One reason why most of the bigger schools had to register themselves with the Overseas Chinese Affairs Committee was that a growing number of Hong Kong students were going back to China for higher studies, and if these schools

did not register themselves with the Chinese authorities, their students or gradu-ates would not, as a rule, be recognized in China and therefore could not join any Chinese schools or universities. As registration with the Chinese authorities carried with it an obligation to observe, whether openly or secretly, certain regulations laid down, it was clear that the Chinese authorities had been having an indirect control or influences over a number of the bigger schools.

The above strategy was found to be quite successful. In 1928, some schools in Hong Kong started to borrow the American 6+3+3 system, like the Chinese-middle schools in China (Sweeting 1990, p.352). Furthermore, as observed by Luk (1991, p.661), in the early 1930s:

> an increasing number of schools were able to operate with branches on both sides of the border and registered with both governments. In Hong Kong, such schools followed the curriculum prescribed by the Nanjing government, used textbooks published in China, mostly at Shanghai, and presented their senior middle graduates for university entrance examinations in China. They engaged teachers trained either in China or in Hong Kong. The colonial government and missionary schools also generally used the Nanjing syllabi and the Shanghai textbooks for the Chinese culture subjects, although they probably followed them less closely. For other subjects, they used textbooks from England or from Shanghai. They also employed teachers educated either in Hong Kong or in China. Hong Kong never developed an autochthonous school system before World War II and remained very much a periphery to its dual centers.

In 1929, in order to counteract the Kuomintang influences, a committee was appointed in Hong Kong to draw up a syllabus for private schools to follow. But the reaction of the Hong Kong government was not successful. In the early 1930s, the vernacular schools had always tried, "as far as the Education Department allowed, to follow the curriculum of the schools in China, using the same textbooks, and having the same subjects" (Wong Leung 1969, p.53).

In 1931, the Overseas Chinese Affairs Commission was established in Nanjing. It signified the need of the Nanjing-based government for a more comprehensive and effective policy towards the overseas Chinese because their support was found to be more necessary with the rise of the Japanese militarism. A survey was conducted in 1935 by the Overseas Chinese Affairs Commission to estimate the number of overseas Chinese schools throughout the world. About 550 overseas Chinese schools, primary or secondary, were found in Hong Kong and Macau (Chan 1992, p.256). In 1938, when Guangzhou was taken by Japan, the number of schools in Hong Kong and Macau increased drastically. They were schools moved from the north or from Guangzhou for refuge. The teachers and students of these schools carried with them their curricula and textbooks which had already been adopted by some of the schools in Hong Kong and Macau in the early 1930s. In short, the above historical account explains the social origin of the common adoption of USA textbooks by the Chinese-medium schools in both places before the early 1960s.

Point of Bifurcation for Chinese-medium Schools: Development of Local Textbooks in Hong Kong

In Hong Kong, the influence of the pre-war traditional textbooks did not diminish until the early 1950s when the colonial government wanted to exercise its own and exclusive influence on local education due to the political tensions in China built shortly after World War II. The apathy of the colonial government in Macau in response to the similar political tensions created a bifurcation for the mathematics curriculum development in the Chinese-medium schools of these two places.

The Kuomintang nationalistic programme for overseas Chinese education resumed in 1945. The proposal included the publication of textbooks and educational materials (Chan 1992, p.309). In Hong Kong, the Kuomintang started to infiltrate and direct the Chinese press. Running schools was another focus of their work. In 1946, an estimated 35 private schools were under the influence of the Kuomintang in Hong Kong (Sweeting 1993, p.194). The government's concern about who was in control of education was reflected in and increased by several incidents. For instance, in 1948 the Education Department proclaimed that amendments should "be made to the ultra-nationalistic segments of Kuomintang-sponsored history, geography, and civics textbooks, and urged that a civics textbook especially prepared in and for Hong Kong should be published" (Sweeting 1993, p.196).

In the late 1940s, the government's wariness about the activities of the Kuomintang was overwhelmed by a new kind of anxiety due to the growing success of the Chinese Communist Party and the increasing intensity of the newly developed Cold War. In order to stop the spread of Communist influence, the Education Ordinance was amended in 1948. It empowered the director to refuse to register any school teacher, deregister a registered teacher, close any school, and control the curricula and textbooks of all schools (Sweeting 1993, p.199). In 1949, a Special Bureau in the Education Department was set up to fight Communism in the schools. In 1952, as suggested by the Special Bureau, the first Hong Kong Chinese School Certificate Examination was instituted. At the same time, the separate committees on textbooks and syllabuses were replaced by the Syllabuses and Textbooks Committee to perform wider and more positive functions. The new committee's terms of reference were to draw up model syllabuses for use in schools; to advise the director on textbooks and other teaching aids; and to stimulate the writing and publication of teaching notes and textbooks suitable for the model syllabuses (Sweeting 1993, pp.210-211).

By the end of 1955, the Syllabuses and Textbooks Committee had already prepared and issued some Model Syllabuses for primary and secondary schools. A few locally-written textbooks were also produced (Sweeting 1993, p.215). As the least politically-related subject, teaching syllabuses and textbooks for mathematics were not produced until the early 1960s in Hong Kong. Anti-communism not only brought the first move towards curriculum control by the Hong Kong government, it also induced a gradual change of direction for the Chinese-middle schools, from American style to the English system which was adopted by the Anglo-Chinese schools. In 1961, the pre-war 3+3 system was replaced by the 5+1 system which was in parallel with the Anglo-Chinese 5+2 system. One year later, a simple teaching syllabus was published by the Education Department (Hong Kong 1962). This was a suggested syllabus, and was officially adopted by the government Chinese-middle schools. Although non-government schools were not required to follow this suggested syllabus, their curriculum was still strongly constrained by the examination syllabus of the Hong Kong Chinese School Certificate Examination and the entrance examination of the Chinese University of Hong Kong which was established in 1963.

The situation in Macau was very different due to the government's persisting non-interventionist attitude towards education control and provision for local Chinese. The long-established relationship between the Nationalist Party and Christianity, especially the Catholic Church, enabled the Kuomintang Government quickly to resume its linkage with the Christian schools in Macau after the civil war. In 1954, the Overseas Chinese Education committee in Taiwan started to operate the entrance examination to Taiwan universities for Overseas Chinese (Chan 1992, p.391), and attracted secondary graduates from both Hong Kong and Macau. Unlike Hong Kong, Macau did not have its own school leaving or university entrance examination, and therefore the influence of this entrance examination was particularly significant. One major impact was the continuous adoption of the 3+3 system by all the Catholic Chinese-medium schools. Therefore, the influence of the Hong Kong published textbooks designed for the 5+1 system was limited, and pre-war textbooks were more popular among these Catholic schools.

The pro-communist Macau Chinese Education Association (MCEA), as a minor opposing force to the majority of Catholic schools, also started to coordinate its member schools in the early 1950s (MCEA 1951, Vol.1-5). In contrast to the Catholic schools, these pro-communist schools were more ready to turn to the 5+1 system and the Hong Kong textbooks (MCEA 1966, Vol.25).

In short, in the early 1960s, all Hong Kong Chinese-medium schools changed to the 5+1 system and local Hong Kong textbooks became popular. Such change had political roots. However, mathematics curricula in Macau were not strongly affected. Pre-war textbooks remained popular among the Chinese-medium schools in Macau, most of which were run by the Catholic Church.

Further Diversification: The Modern Mathematics Movement

The difference between the pre-war and post-war traditional textbooks was small because both had adopted the so-called pre-1800 model (Cooper 1985, p.54). This traditional approach was not severely challenged until the upheaval of the worldwide Modern Mathematics Movement in the late 1950s. The Modern Mathematics Movement suggested that the traditional separate approach did not reflect the nature of mathematics adequately. Unity of different mathematics concepts was emphasised: Plane and Solid Geometry were integrated into a single course; Trigonometry was merged with Advanced Algebra; and deductive methods, the processes of searching for patterns, and structural concepts like sets, relations and functions were introduced (Fey 1978, pp.340-341).

Although decision-makers in different countries had different motives, much of the movement originated in the USA. The news in 1957 that the Russians had been the first nation to launch an artificial satellite, the Sputnik One, was one of the most important ignition points. Many Americans believed that in order to restore the fame of their country, the education of scientists and technologists had to be modernised. Mathematics was considered to need particularly urgent attention, and large sums of federal government money became available for innovation (van der Blij et al. 1981, p.111).

The American movement inspired curriculum developers in many other countries. This influence has been documented in countries as diverse as Hungary, Indonesia, Nigeria, France, Denmark and Sweden (Moon 1986; R. Morris 1981; Morris & Arora 1992). The influence was also felt in the United Kingdom, though many reforms there in the 1960s also had local roots (Cooper 1985; Howson 1978; Gillespie 1992). Of course, some countries did not follow the trend. They included China (K.T. Leung 1980, p.45) and Italy (Castelnuovo 1989, p.52).

In the mid-1970s, the cry of 'back to basics' in the USA led to decline of the movement. Through experience, people found that the impact of the movement was disastrous. Teachers did not understand what was expected of them, and students were lost in a maze of abstractions and fancy notations. Many textbooks had reduced set theory to lists of manipulations of unions and intersections that were quite as pointless as the worst pages of Algebra in the traditional textbooks. Disillusion in the USA was paralleled by, and to some extent the cause of, disillusion in many other countries. Some educators reverted to traditional mathematics, others used traditional books to supplement the modern ones, and yet others sought an amalgamated approach.

The Modern Mathematics movement was introduced into Hong Kong in 1964, and led to a new Certificate Examination syllabus for secondary Form 5 students in 1969. The new topics included: mathematical induction, logic, matrices and determinants, bases for integers, flow charts, three-dimensional coordinate geometry, transformation, symmetry, networks, three-dimensional figures, binary operations and modulo arithmetic, and groups and linear programming (Siu Chan et al. 1997, Unit 4). In the early 1970s, about half of the schools in Hong Kong, including Anglo-Chinese and Chinese-middle, had adopted the Modern Mathematics syllabus (Brimer & Griffin 1985, p.7). In 1980, in order to overcome the problems of the failure of the movement, an amalgamated syllabus attempting to bring together the strengths of both traditional and modern approaches was introduced. Some of the Modern Mathematics topics and much of the jargon had been cut. At the same time, the use of calculators was permitted in the public examination.

Educational organisations in Macau also felt the shockwave of the Sputnik One and the Modern Mathematics Movement (MCEA 1957, 1974, 1975a, 1975b, 1979), but their response was mild. Traditional textbooks and separate approach had never been completely abandoned in Chinese-medium schools. Most of them updated their content knowledge by devising a subtopic called set and logic at senior levels. A few of them had experimented with the Hong Kong modern textbooks for a few years and turned back to the traditional textbooks. Even in the late 1990s, amalgamated textbooks remained unpopular among the Chinese-medium schools.

The situation of the English-medium schools in Macau was quite similar to that of the Chinese-medium schools. Few of the English-medium schools joined the Modern Mathematics movement by adopting the Hong Kong Modern Mathematics textbooks; and these schools also turned to the Hong Kong amalgamated textbooks after the failure of the movement. The majority did not abandon the UK traditional textbooks until the late 1980s. The reason for them to turn to the Hong Kong amalgamated textbooks was not pedagogical but pragmatic, due to the extinction of these pre-war UK textbooks in Macau. Portuguese-medium schools in Macau adopted the Portuguese Modern Curriculum in the early 1970s, and did not change to the amalgamated curriculum until the early 1990s (Ponte et al. 1994, p.348).

In sum, the rise and fall of the worldwide Modern Mathematics movement provided a chance for local mathematics educators in Hong Kong to establish their local textbooks and curriculum. Although vestiges of UK and USA influences can still be identified, local elements have been incorporated into the curriculum and textbooks. None of the Chinese-medium schools and few of the English-medium schools in Macau were changed by the movement, and they therefore were left behind by their counterparts in Hong Kong in the early 1980s.

Different Responses to Challenges in the 1990s

During the 1970s, 1980s and 1990s, both Hong Kong and Macau experienced rapid economic, social and political development. Together with the global advancement of computers and information technology, mathematics educators in both places had to reconsider their present curricula; and on the one hand, they had to identify international trends and catch up with them; and on the other hand, they had to deal with their local problems. Again, due to the differences in socio-historical background and perception of mathematics educators in both places, their responses to these challenges differed.

Nine-year universal, free and compulsory education had been implemented in Hong Kong since 1978, and by the 1990, the retention rate in secondary Form 5 exceeded 90 per cent. Furthermore, with the rapid expansion of tertiary education, most Form 5 graduates could proceed to further study. Individual differences in capability and aptitude became an increasingly important issue after the early 1990s. The examination syllabuses of the two well-established Advanced Level subjects, Pure Mathematics and Applied Mathematics, were trimmed to become less demanding. Furthermore, two less demanding Advanced Supplementary subjects, Applied Mathematics, and Mathematics & Statistics were introduced in 1994. With these changes, the mathematics curricula at the matriculation level could more easily benefit both science and arts students.

The secondary Mathematics and Additional Mathematics curricula did not change significantly from the late 1970s to the 1980s. Only in the early 1990s was a holistic review of the mathematics curriculum urged by local mathematics educators. A new secondary mathematics curriculum was proposed to have a more balanced emphasis on process and content. It was also intended to take into consideration social and technological changes; have more balanced consideration for both science and arts students; and have more balanced emphasis on the cognitive and affective development of the students (Siu Chan et al. 1997, Unit 4).

Mathematics curriculum development in Macau was uncoordinated when compared with Hong Kong. Eclectic approaches were adopted by most schools in Macau when challenged by the rapid social, economic, political and technological changes. By the late 1980s, the traditional mathematics textbooks had become more and more obsolete. The content knowledge was on the one hand too demanding for the majority, and on the other hand too remote from an information age. Some Catholic and Protestant Chinese-medium schools tried to replace the traditional textbooks by the new Hong Kong textbooks, but most of them turned back to the traditional textbooks in the early 1990s. The incompatibility between the Hong Kong 5+2 system with its own public examinations and the 3+3 Taiwan system with the Macau Taiwan university entrance examination was one of the main reasons for their failure.

Unlike the Christian schools, the pro-Communist schools had a more coordinated and successful reform. They turned away from the Hong Kong Chinese-middle 5+1 system to the PRC 3+3 system in 1987, the year of the Sino-Portuguese Joint Declaration. By the early 1990s, most of them had adopted the PRC textbooks. The compatibility between the PRC textbooks and the examination syllabus of the PRC university entrance examination for Macau students was one of the main reasons for successful reform. Although the new PRC textbooks were less problematic than the traditional Hong Kong textbooks, the curriculum was still too demanding and out of touch with modern technology (Siu Chan et al. 1997, Unit 3).

As mentioned above, the situation of the English-medium schools in Macau was quite problematic. The majority only turned to the new Hong Kong textbooks in the late 1980s because of the extinction of the pre-war UK textbooks. But many of the mathematics teachers still supplemented the new Hong Kong textbooks with the old UK Algebra textbooks. This combined use of traditional and new textbooks reflected their traditional views on mathematics teaching and learning. The Portuguese-medium schools were in a better position because they followed the mathematics curriculum reform in Portugal in the early 1990s. The new curriculum had been designed by considering the impact of universal education and technological advancement. Most of the mathematics teachers in Macau Portuguese-medium schools welcomed this reform.

Before the 1984 Sino-British Joint Declaration and the return of Hong Kong to Chinese sovereignty in 1997, the curriculum development machinery in Hong Kong had been gradually built and had gained its own momentum for further development. The Curriculum Development Committee (CDC) was formed in 1972 in response to the introduction of compulsory primary education. Teachers were appointed to the mathematics subcommittee to advise on preparation of the teaching syllabuses. Examination syllabuses were produced by a mathematics subcommittee of the Hong Kong Examinations Authority (HKEA). Both the CDC teaching syllabuses and the HKEA examination syllabuses heavily shaped the implemented mathematics curriculum in Hong Kong. Since the establishment of the Curriculum Development Institute (CDI) in 1992, many curriculum innovations have been brought into the development of mathematics curriculum. These have included the school-based curriculum development, core curriculum tailored syllabus, and the Target Oriented Curriculum.

Curriculum development organisation in Macau appears immature when compared with its Hong Kong counterpart. The Macau government only started to take an active role in curriculum development in 1994. Curriculum development committees for different subjects were formed. Committee members included teachers from both official and private schools, and experts from the University of Macau. Provisional teaching syllabuses for different subjects at different levels were drafted by referring to the PRC, Taiwan and Hong Kong models. Although the provisional junior secondary mathematics syllabus was written to face the new challenges and has been used by the Luso-Chinese Secondary School since 1995/96, the Macau government had great difficulty in persuading the private schools to adopt this syllabus (Tang 1997).

In summary, mathematics curriculum development has been more coordinated in Hong Kong than in Macau. Mathematics educators in Hong Kong have been involved quite actively within the organisational framework, and curriculum innovations have not been lacking (Siu Chan et al. 1997, Unit 4). In contrast, mathematics curriculum development in Macau has been uncoordinated. An eclectic approach has been adopted by most schools, and political influence has always been significant even for a value-neutral subject like mathematics.

Proposing a Conceptual Framework for Further Analysis

By juxtaposing and comparing the influential historical incidents, this chapter has already answered the two questions: "What is the common social origin of mathematics curricula in Hong Kong and Macau?" and "How did Hong Kong and Macau move into different paths in the early 1960s and how were they running on different tracks in the late 1990s?" Although the deep questions: "Why did Hong Kong and Macau move into different paths?" and "Why did they run on different tracks?" are worth-posing, they are too difficult to be answered in a short chapter. Therefore, only potential conceptual frameworks are proposed and briefly examined.

One possible way is to follow the work of Basil Bernstein and Pierre Bourdieu by exposing the interests and values attached to the prevailing curricular arrangements (Cooper 1985; Moon 1986; Stanic 1987a, 1987b). These researchers suggested that how school knowledge was selected, organised and assessed should be investigated in relation to the distribution of power. The sociological assumption is that the most important and overt relation between the organisation of curriculum knowledge and the dominant institutional order will be reflected in social stratification (Archer 1983, Tang 1999). If suggested change will pose threats to the power structure of that dominant institutional order, resistance will be encountered.

The author agrees with Archer (1981, 1983, 1993) that a common feature of theories about cultural transmission and reproduction is their neglect of educational systems in which the stability and change take place. Without incorporating different elements and structures of the educational systems for different countries or places, the theories cannot account for all the variances in stability and change in educational practice. Elsewhere (Tang 1999), the author has demonstrated the fruitfulness of adopting Archer's Morphogenetic Systems Theory in explaining the stability and change of secondary school mathematics knowledge in Macau from 1987 to 1995. Results showed that in addition to cultural factors, the effects of the social origin and structure of the Macau poly-centred system should not be ignored.

In sum, the author is convinced that in order to explain the different tracks of stability and change of school mathematics in Hong Kong and Macau, it should be assumed that the channels through which the similar social groups of the two places exerted control and influenced stability or change varied with the social origins and structures of the educational systems. With this basic assumption, a detailed explanatory analysis can be accomplished by adopting Archer's Morphogenetic Systems Theory. Bray's (1992b) analysis of centralisation and decentralisation in curriculum development of Hong Kong and Macau can form part of the platform for launching the investigation.

Conclusion

This historical and comparative analysis of the stability and change of secondary school mathematics curriculum in Hong Kong and Macau shows that the two curriculum patterns have a common origin starting in the 1920s. Although colonial influence was significant in English-medium and Portuguese-medium schools, influence from the Republic of China was dominant in the Chinese-medium schools. Political motives were the main force behind this external influence.

The nature of this external influence changed abruptly after the success of the Chinese Communists in 1949. For the Chinese-medium schools in Hong Kong and Macau, the difference in response of the two colonial governments to this change marked the point of bifurcation for the mathematics curriculum in the early 1960s. At the same time, the worldwide Modern Mathematics movement gained momentum and a more sweeping influence in Hong Kong. Local mathematics educators were involved in this development, and the colonial government played a less significant role. Mathematics curricula for both Chinese-medium and English-medium schools were affected. Local mathematics educators in Macau were less willing to change Major change could only be found in the Portuguese-medium school due to the reaction of local mathematics educators in Portugal, rather than in Macau. Most of the Chinese-medium and English-medium schools in Macau were only slightly affected by this worldwide movement.

The introduction of nine-year compulsory free education in Hong Kong in the late 1970s in Hong Kong reinforced this loose tie between colonial government and local mathematics educators. Curriculum development organisation was developed further in the early 1990s in order to face the challenge of different types of internal and external challenges. Macau has also started to develop its curriculum development organisations, but it is very unlikely that they can have coordinated response to the 1990s challenges. Macau's idiosyncratic socio-historical background and its vulnerability to PRC influence are the two main forces pushing it to a very different curriculum development track from that of Hong Kong. In short, external influences on these two places have always been similar, but local socio-historical background and efforts of local mathematics educators have caused differences. Finally, Archer's Morphogenetic Systems Theory is recommended for further explanatory analysis.

Conclusions

12

Methodology and Focus in Comparative Education

Mark BRAY

The preceding chapters in this book have raised many issues from a range of perspectives. This final pair of chapters summarises and elaborates on some of the lessons that may be learned from the analyses. The present chapter comments on the contents of the earlier chapters within the framework of existing comparative education literature, particularly addressing methodological features. It begins by considering the widely-accepted purposes for undertaking comparative study of education. It then turns to dominant foci in the field, and finally to the approaches and tools commonly used by comparative educationists. The next chapter, following the subtitle of the whole book, identifies conceptual lessons concerning continuity and change in education.

The Purposes of Comparative Study of Education

The purposes of comparative study of education may be wide and varied. Much depends on who is doing the comparing, and under what circumstances. For example:

- parents commonly compare schools and systems of education in search of the institutions which will serve their children's needs most effectively;
- policy makers in individual countries examine education systems in other countries in order to discern ways to achieve political, social and economic objectives;
- international agencies compare patterns in different countries in order to improve the advice that they give to national governments and others;
- practitioners, including school principals and teachers, may make comparisons in order to improve the running of their institutions; and
- academics commonly undertake comparison in order to develop theoretical models which promote understanding of the forces which shape teaching and learning in different settings.

This particular book is published by a research centre within a university. The book does not aim directly to help parents seeking to find the best schools for their children, since that would have required a very different format and set of contents. Likewise, direct assistance to international agencies, policy makers and practitioners is not a primary goal, though the editors and authors certainly hope that people in such groups will read the book and gain insights which will assist their work. Rather, the book has been conceived principally as an academic work which aims to deepen understanding of the forces that shape education in different societies. The book chiefly focuses on the education systems and institutions in two territories on the south coast of China; but the work also aims at wider conceptual understanding.

In this context, it is useful to note some of the purposes of comparative education identified by scholars at earlier points in history. A good place to start is with one of the great-grandfathers of the field of comparative education, Sir Michael Sadler. Writing in 1900 (reprinted 1964, p.310), Sadler suggested that:

> The practical value of studying, in a right spirit and with scholarly accuracy, the working of foreign systems of education is that it will result in our being better fitted to study and understand our own.

The emphasis in this quotation is of an individual looking outwards, identifying another society and then comparing patterns with those in that individual's own society. In the case of the present book, it would describe a resident of Hong Kong seeking to learn more about Hong Kong through comparison with Macau; and it would describe a resident of Macau seeking to learn more about Macau through comparison with Hong Kong. Sadler suggested (p.312) that the comparison might encourage appreciation of domestic education systems as well as heightening awareness of shortcomings:

> If we study foreign systems of education thoroughly and sympathetically – and sympathy and thoroughness are both necessary for the task – I believe that the result on our minds will be to make us prize, as we have never prized before, the good things which we have at home, and also to make us realise how many things there are in our [own education systems] which need prompt and searching change.

However, while the editors and authors of this book certainly hope that the work will help residents of Hong Kong and Macau to value and critique their own education systems, the editors and authors also hope that it will prove instructive to readers elsewhere. These readers might include people who have never visited, and indeed do not expect to visit, either Hong Kong or Macau. Such an aspiration emphasises a higher goal of conceptual understanding and theoretical construction.

In aiming for such a goal, again the book has many antecedents within the field. Isaac Kandel, for example, was a key figure in the generation which followed Sadler's. Kandel's 1933 book (p.xix) listed a set of problems which, he suggested, raised universal questions. Kandel then pointed out that:

> The chief value of a comparative approach to such problems lies in an analysis of the causes which have produced them, in a comparison of the differences between the various systems and the reasons underlying them, and, finally, in a study of the solutions attempted.

The tone of such a statement is more closely allied to theoretical goals; and Kandel's book to some extent established a tradition into which the present book fits.

Nearly half a century later, however, Farrell (1979, p.4) justifiably pointed out weaknesses in the quality of theorising in the field. He observed that:

There is a lack of cumulation in our findings; we have many interesting bits and pieces of information, but they seldom seem to relate to one another. We have little in the way of useful and concise theory.

This situation partly arose from the fact that comparative education is a field in which scholars of many ideological persuasions converge. Since Farrell wrote those words, moreover, the field's principal academic journals have hosted further controversy and discord. Positivists have clashed with post-modernists, structural-functionalists have disputed with conflict theorists, and so on (Epstein 1986; Psacharopoulos 1990; Paulston 1997, 1999; Watson 1998; Crossley 1999).

Nevertheless, the goal of contributing to higher-level conceptual understanding remains not only legitimate in the scholarly arena but arguably the principal overall justification for undertaking academic studies. Such theorising, moreover, should not be seen as merely a form of self-gratification for small groups of thinkers whose work is distant from realities. As Farrell also pointed out (1979, p.4), it is through development of good theory that academics can be of greatest use to policy makers and practitioners:

> [We] will not find something useful to say simply by directing our efforts to studies of popular policy issues of the day – by being trendy. We will have something useful to say only when our observations regarding any particular policy problem are rooted in a more general understanding of how educational systems work, which is in turn based upon cumulated discoveries organized into and by theory.

Such remarks are pertinent to the present book as much as to others in the field.

Focus in Comparative Studies of Education

Locational Comparisons

Paralleling the diversity of ideological perspectives in the field of comparative education is a diversity in the foci of comparison. The field of comparative education is principally conceived in terms of locational comparisons, i.e. of phenomena in different places. Temporal comparisons may also be important, and are considered below, but historical and futuristic studies focusing on single locations are less likely to appear in the pages of comparative education journals.

Even within the category of locational comparisons, survey of the articles in the field's major journals would display a vast array of studies. The array would include diversity in the themes and in the countries, regions, levels of education, and types of education chosen for analysis. Within this array, however, two emphases have been dominant. First has been a stress on comparisons in which the main units of analysis are nations or countries (commonly treating these two words as synonyms, and ignoring the differences in meaning which are important to political scientists [e.g. Robertson 1993, p.331]). Second, a major focus has been on systems of education, many of which are described, rightly or wrongly, as national systems. Conceptually, of course, it is possible, and in many circumstances very desirable, to compare classrooms, schools and other units both between and within countries; but a considerable number of major works which have helped to define the field of comparative education have explicitly focused cross-nationally on systems of education. Sadler's 1900 presentation was in this category, as was Kandel's 1933 book. Subsequent works, spread over the decades, include Cramer & Browne (1956), Bielas (1973), Ignas & Corsini (1981), and Postlethwaite (1988).

To some extent, the present book fits in this tradition. The chapter by Adamson & Li on primary and secondary education sets part of the scene by describing what is widely called *the* Hong Kong education system, though Adamson & Li also observe the existence of schools and even of systems in Hong Kong which lie outside the mainstream. Macau, by contrast, has not had a dominant entity which can be described as *the* Macau education system. Instead it has had a plurality of systems – a fact which has been the focus of considerable and important comment in the present book.

In a strict sense, however, the main focus in this book is not on cross-national comparisons. Hong Kong and Macau cannot be described as nations, and not even as countries. Prior to the 1997 and 1999 changes of sovereignty they were administered as colonies, albeit with substantial autonomy from the United Kingdom and Portugal; and since the change of sovereignty they have been Special Administrative Regions (SARs) of the People's Republic of China (PRC). As such, the book may be seen as helping to redress an imbalance in the field of comparative education by focusing on a pair of units which, particularly after 1997 (in the case of Hong Kong) and 1999 (in the case of Macau) may be called *intra*national instead of *inter*national.

Figure 12.1: A Framework for Comparative Education Analyses

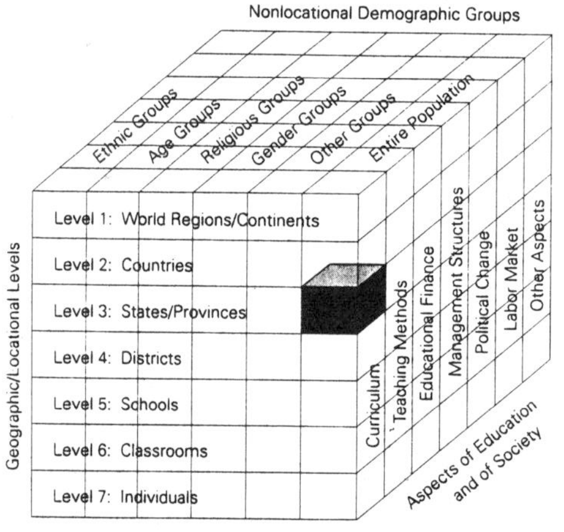

Source: Bray & Thomas (1995), p.475.

This observation may usefully be considered in conjunction with a comment about the value of multilevel analyses. Figure 12.1 reproduces a model for comparative analyses presented by Bray & Thomas (1995). The article from which it is taken pointed out that too many studies neglect discussion of the ways in which patterns at lower levels in education systems are shaped by patterns at higher levels, and vice versa. The article noted that the goals and resources available for some comparative studies necessarily limit their scope, but suggested that such studies should at least recognise both the mutual influences of other levels and the boundaries in their foci.

Along these lines, Figure 12.1 is helpful for showing what the present book has and has not covered. Within the figure, the smaller black cube represents a comparative study of curriculum in two or more states/provinces of a single country. That smaller cube would also be shaded if the contents of the present book were mapped against the large cube. In this case the vocabulary would refer to colonies/SARs rather than to states/provinces, but the basic idea is equivalent. This particular book has included a chapter on curriculum as a whole (by Lo), and separate chapters on civic and political education (by Tse), secondary school history (by Tan) and secondary school mathematics (by Tang). This list on the one hand shows how the book has gone into detail, but on the other hand indicates the extent to which further study is both possible and desirable. Many more subjects and cross-curricular domains remain to be analysed in the same way; and history and mathematics can instructively be compared at other levels in addition to the secondary level.

Other parts of the cube which would be shaded if the contents of the present book were mapped against Figure 12.1 would include levels of education as a whole. This would be done under age groups (or, if that is considered too rigid on the grounds e.g. that some 12-year olds may be in primary school while others are in secondary, under 'other groups') in the nonlocational demographic dimension of the cube. Concerning levels of education, the present book has compared pre-primary education in Hong Kong and Macau, and has given similar treatment to primary, secondary and higher education. Teacher education is not so much a level as a type of education. However, the book has omitted specific coverage of some other types of education, such as adult nonformal education and schooling for the blind, deaf and mentally handicapped. This again emphasises that although the present book is the product of a substantial amount of work, much further exploration remains to be done.

Concerning other levels of the cube, several chapters in the present book make explicit comparisons of institutions – particularly the chapters by Tan on secondary school history curricula, and by Yung and by Hui & Poon on higher education. Comparisons of classrooms and of individuals are mostly implicit rather than explicit. A similar observation applies to higher levels in the cube: several chapters refer to other countries and to world regions, but it has not been the goal of the authors to make systematic multilevel comparisons throughout each chapter. This certainly does not devalue the nature of the research; but the discussion does help to show the boundaries of the present book as well as its focus.

Temporal Comparisons
Turning to temporal comparisons, all chapters in this book place comments on contemporary events within the context of historical antecedents. Leung's chapter on church and state, for example, goes back to the 16th century with reference to Macau. Tang's chapter on mathematics curricula also has a strong historical element, albeit mainly confined to the 20th century. These and other chapters therefore contain comparisons over time as well as over place; and while temporal comparisons do not so readily find an accepted niche within the field of comparative education, they are considered legitimate and important by at least some major figures in the field (e.g. Cowen 1998, p.61; Thomas 1998, p.9).

Concerning the value of historical research in comparative education, Sweeting (1998c, p.2) pointed out that "efforts to stretch comparisons across places, with little or no attention paid to time, are likely to create a thin, flat, quite possibly superficial outcome". In contrast, he added, efforts to enable comparisons to encompass time in addition to place are likely to enhance the profundity of analysis. The editors and authors certainly hope that this observation applies to the present study. All projects must of course seek balances within the framework of their objectives. By restricting its primary spatial focus to two locations, the present book sacrifices the insights that would come from systematic comparison of more locations. However, because the primary spatial focus was restricted, greater depth has become possible through temporal comparison.

A further benefit from incorporating historical analysis is the possibility of clearer understanding of the actors and processes in education systems. As pointed out by Sweeting (1998c, p.5):

> There is an understandable tendency of writers on comparative education to concentrate on product-documents such as White Papers, Commission Reports, and Digests of Statistics rather than the type of process-documents that illuminate past decision-making (and fascinate historians). This leads, at times, to a failure to distinguish between the officially designated agents of policy-making and the actual ones.

Sweeting added that the superficiality necessitated when comparative education studies involve many locations may lead analysts to make false assumptions about sequence in policy making and implementation. Using the example of language policy for Hong Kong schools, Sweeting shows (p.6) that policy formulation does not necessarily precede implementation. Hong Kong has a long and tortuous history in the debate about appropriate policies for the medium of instruction, particularly at the secondary level. Only through historical comparisons is it possible to ensure that simplistic analyses are avoided. As observed elsewhere by Sweeting (1997, p.36):

> It could have helped the policy makers and advisers in 1973 and 1974, for example, as they debated whether to make Chinese the normal language of instruction in the early years of secondary education, if they had remembered to check what had happened in 1946 when language circulars proposing precisely this were withdrawn by the Education Department.... More recently, enthusiastic proponents of 'bridging programmes' to help students switch from one medium of instruction to the other would have benefited if they had examined both the strengths and weaknesses of the Special Classes Centre at Clementi Middle School in the years 1956-1963.

Readers will judge for themselves how well the chapters in this book have drawn insights from their historical frameworks and have avoided the superficiality which would have posed a stronger threat had the book taken more locations as its primary focus; but the methodological point remains that the restriction in the number of locations has permitted greater depth in historical analysis. This has permitted comparisons over time, which has been a key element enshrined even in the subtitle of the book about continuity and change. Temporal comparisons have also permitted authors to analyse processes of change, not relying on simplistic statements about products.

Changing Fashions and Opportunities

Discussion about focus in comparative education should include commentary about changing fashions in the types of topics which dominate the literature during particular decades. Kelly (1992, p.18) observed that the field "has always been influenced by contemporary events". At the same time, comparative education, like other fields, has some topics which remain strong foci for research and debate throughout the decades.

The contents of the present book were influenced by contemporary events in several ways. Most striking was the heightened sense of identity in both Hong Kong and Macau because of their changes of sovereignty. Hong Kong's transition attracted huge international media attention, and created considerable self-consciousness within the territory. Macau's transition attracted less international attention, but was obviously of major significance to the residents of Macau and to some extent also more widely. In this sense, the book fits Kelly's description as a product stimulated by a pair of contemporary events.

The book also results in several important ways from opportunity. The fact that no previous book of this type has been produced is not only because of the absence of a sharp stimulus such as the change of sovereignty. It also results from maturing expertise for work of this kind within the two locations. Partly as a result of the expansion of higher education described in the chapters by Yung, Ma and Hui & Poon, by the mid-1990s both Macau and Hong Kong had local research capacity of a scale and quality unprecedented in their histories.

This expansion of research capacity was especially obvious in Macau. Between the closure of St. Paul's University College in 1762 and the opening of the University of East Asia (UEA) in 1981, Macau had no local institution of tertiary education. The operation of the UEA, which in 1991 was renamed the University of Macau (UM), created a body of scholars who had a mandate to undertake research as well as to teach, and who had a strong reason to focus their research on the territory in which they lived. Prior to 1981, very little research was conducted in or on Macau. Its subsequent blossoming was due in no small measure to the establishment and growth of the UEA/UM. It is no coincidence that seven of the 15 contributors to this book have been or still are employees of the University of Macau.

However, the pattern has another instructive dimension: all seven of those people were residents of Hong Kong before moving to Macau. In part because Macau had not had a university for centuries, in the early years of the existence of the UEA/UM, Macau was unable from internal sources to provide even the majority of people needed to staff the institution. Hong Kong was an obvious ground for recruitment, since it had a much larger pool of suitable personnel, was close at hand, and had cultural and political affinities. The result for the present book was the formation of a group of people who already knew a great deal about education in Hong Kong and who subsequently learned a great deal about education in Macau. These people were therefore excellently placed to contribute to a comparative study of this sort.

A question which readers might next have in mind concerns the other authors in this book who have never taught at the University of Macau. One of them was born in Macau but then came to Hong Kong for much of his education and subsequent employment. A determining factor in his personal history was that Hong Kong had a stronger economy which attracted many migrants and their families; but the fact that he still had many relatives in Macau helped him to retain a strong interest in the territory. Others were born in Hong Kong but were drawn to undertake comparison by academic fascination with a neighbouring society which was both so similar and so different.

An additional factor in Hong Kong, which to some extent paralleled patterns in Macau but had a different emphasis, arose from the scale and nature of tertiary education. Hong Kong's first university, the University of Hong Kong, was founded in 1911 and has a much longer history than the UEA/UM. As recounted by Yung and by Ma, however, the 1990s brought considerable tertiary expansion. The higher education sector at this time was well resourced, but from the middle of the decade academics were placed under considerable pressure to produce evidence of productivity in research. For all disciplines, this combination of circumstances provided both the capacity and a strong incentive to undertake research.

Within this climate, comparative research has been a particular beneficiary. To the fact that some contributors were born in Hong Kong but worked in Macau, or vice versa, should be added that the majority of contributors gained at least part of their postgraduate training in neither place. Travel to other countries and other cultures for research training greatly promoted inclinations to undertake comparative studies. The growing prosperity of both Hong Kong and Macau were important factors in this, for economic strength provided both finance for people to go abroad for training and employment opportunities on their return. The governments of both Hong Kong and Macau endeavoured to take every opportunity to enhance international links since they perceived such links to be part of the safeguard of autonomy in the post-colonial era.

Yet another dimension of this environment helps explain the circumstances of the two contributors to this book who were not born in Hong Kong or Macau, nor indeed in the region. These two individuals were born in Europe, and had personal reasons for taking up employment in Hong Kong. The fact that they could do so was made easier by Hong Kong's economic strength and therefore employment opportunities. The significance for the field of comparative education was that they brought perspectives not only from their countries of origin but also from other places in which they had worked.

To summarise, this list of biographies has been presented not so much because of its intrinsic interest but to echo and elaborate on the observation by Kelly (1992, p.18) that the field of comparative education "has always been influenced by contemporary events". The contemporary events which led to this particular book included a confluence of stimulus and opportunity. Much of the stimulus lay in the change of sovereignty in the two places, while much of the opportunity lay in the existence of persons who had the skills and interest to undertake a study of this kind. In turn, the existence of these persons was partly the result of economic prosperity and a political desire for international connections. The Comparative Education Research Centre at the University of Hong Kong, which is the publisher of this book, was established in 1994 and to some extent is itself a product of this pattern of circumstances.

Allied to this, the influence of contemporary events is evident in one analytical theme which runs through the majority of chapters, namely the focus on colonialism and colonial transition. Because Hong Kong and Macau were scheduled for change of sovereignty in 1997 and 1999, it was natural for a book prepared at this point in history to make the transition a major focus. In turn, focus on colonial transition naturally led to focus on colonialism itself, including the main era and even, for some authors, the beginning of colonial rule.

However, survey of literature on comparative education shows that colonialism is a topic of sustained interest in the field as a whole. A sampling of books over the decades could include Murray (1929), Mayhew (1938), Furnivall (1943), Lewis (1954), Ashby (1966), Altbach & Kelly (1978), Watson (1982a), and Mangan (1993). Articles on the theme appearing shortly before the publication of the present book included Arnove & Arnove (1997) and Errante (1998). In this respect, the contents of this book are contributing to an existing body of knowledge on a topic which remains of widespread concern in the academic world. It does so, moreover, in at least two distinctive ways. The first is that comparison of Hong Kong and Macau requires comparison of British and Portuguese colonial styles. While a considerable body of literature compares education in British and French colonies (e.g. Clignet & Foster 1964; Gifford & Weiskel 1971; Asiwaju 1975), little direct comparison has been made of education in British and Portuguese colonies. Watson's (1982b) 23-page bibliography contained no direct reference to any such work, and the only direct reference to comparison of British and Portuguese (plus Belgian and French) colonial styles in Kay & Nystrom's (1971) 19-page bibliography was a 1949 article by Lewis. Likewise, Altbach & Kelly's (1991) book omitted all mention of Portuguese colonialism. Comparison of colonial styles on Hong Kong and Macau therefore helps to reduce a longstanding neglect.

A second distinctive way in which this book contributes to the conceptual literature on this topic arises from distinctive features of the colonial transition in the two territories. Among these features were that:

- the transitions in Hong Kong and Macau were at the end of the 20th century rather than earlier, and thus took place in a very different global climate;
- the transitions took place over an extended time period;
- the transitions were not to independent sovereign statehood, but to reintegration with the country from which the colonies had previously been detached; and
- the colonies being handed over had far higher per capita incomes than had been the case in previous decolonisation exercises.

Because these features are distinctive to Hong Kong and Macau, as a pair they provide instructive contrasts to colonial transitions in other parts of the world and at earlier times in history (Bray 1994, 1997c).

However, colonial transition is of course not the only theme that runs through the majority of chapters. Another pair of themes deserves to be highlighted because it can again be related to both sustained interests and fashions in the comparative study of education. One partner in the pair, which has been the focus of sustained interest (see e.g. Reller & Morphet 1964; Lauglo & McLean 1985; Cummings & Riddell 1994), concerns the control of education, including questions of centralisation or decentralisation and the role of churches and other non-government bodies at different levels of education systems. The more fashionable topic is privatisation in education – a topic which attracted particular attention during the 1980s and 1990s (see e.g. Walford 1989; Jimenez & Lockheed 1995; Bray 1998c).

Again, the book contributes perspectives which are important additions to the broader literature. Lo's chapter points out that in the domain of curriculum control, Hong Kong's mainstream education system is widely described as centralised. In Macau, by contrast, control of curriculum has been largely uncentralised (a word which is preferred to the term *de*centralised since the latter usually describes a situation which was previously centralised, whereas in Macau curriculum control was never centralised). During the 1990s, aspects of administration of Hong Kong schools were decentralised, with institutions being given stronger autonomy through the School Management Initiative and other schemes (K.C. Wong 1998). In other respects, however, control became more centralised. Perhaps the best example of this, explained in Lo's chapter, is the medium of instruction in secondary schools. Control also became more centralised in Macau, and in this respect the two societies not only began to resemble each other more, but also provided a useful counterpoint to the considerable literature which advocates decentralisation of educational administration (e.g. Winkler 1989; Fiske 1996; USAID 1997), often in a rather generalised way.

Likewise, analysis of both Hong Kong and Macau provides useful insights for debates about privatisation. Macau is one of the few places in the world in which the majority of schools have been left to operate on their own with almost no government support, interference or control. However, the resulting patterns have been far from the idealistic pictures of efficiency and quality painted by advocates of privatisation such as Chubb & Moe (1990) and Cowan (1990). Because of this, in Macau the 1990s brought processes of publicisation rather than privatisation, very much against the world trend. Patterns in Hong Kong were more complex, but they also included a measure of publicisation through the Direct Subsidy Scheme (Ip 1994; Bray 1995b).

Moreover, careful analysis of Hong Kong schools shows the danger of superficial judgements by authors who do not take the trouble to look beyond the surface. For example, James (1988, p.96) looked at Hong Kong statistics, found that only 8 per cent of primary and 28 per cent of secondary pupils were in schools operated by the government, and mistakenly assumed that all the rest were in private schools. Had she looked more closely, she would have found that although the aided schools are legally non-government bodies, almost all their funding comes from the government and they are subject to considerable government control. As such, the aided schools would be much more appropriately classified in the public than the private sector. Such remarks illustrate the danger of superficiality in large-scale comparative research, particularly when it requires data from diverse settings to fit simple categories, and emphasise the value of studies which can examine matters in depth.

Approaches and Tools in Comparative Study of Education

Watson (1996, p.381) has highlighted the plurality of methods in the field of comparative education:

> Because comparative education is the product of many disciplines it cannot lay claim to any single conceptual or methodological tool that sets it apart from other areas of education or from the applied social sciences. It must be stressed, therefore, that there is *no* single scientific comparative research method in spite of the efforts of some scholars to argue that there is.

Just as the aims and foci of comparative studies of education may vary widely, so too may the methods. Comparative studies, like most others, may be primarily quantitative or primarily qualitative; and they may rely on questionnaires, on interviews, on documentary analysis, and on many other bases (Rust et al. 1999).

The present book nevertheless has features which place it in a sub-group within the field. The various chapters are mainly analytical accounts based on description of both policy and practice. As such, they are very different from exploratory research which seeks to generate hypotheses, or evaluative research which seeks to test hypotheses. They are also very different from the carefully-constructed comparative studies of the International Association for the Evaluation of Educational Achievement (IEA), in which specific school subjects have been investigated on a cross-national basis through carefully designed questionnaires administered to equally carefully selected samples of schools and students (Postlethwaite 1999).

One strength of the present book, as mentioned in the Introduction, is that each chapter focuses on patterns in both Hong Kong and Macau, and undertakes explicit comparison. In this respect the book differs from many others in the field of comparative education. Some books (e.g. Mukherjee 1964; Sullivan 1997) place country chapters in sequence, and primarily present comparisons at the beginning and/or end rather than in each chapter. Other books which purport to be comparative (e.g. Fafunwa & Aisiku 1982; Mazurek & Winzer 1994) barely even do that; instead they are little more than collections of single-country studies bound together, and leave it to readers to make the comparisons. The present work, it may be suggested, is in this respect more actively comparative.

In the process, whether consciously or unconsciously, almost all contributors to the present book have followed an approach allied to that advocated by Bereday (1964). Figure 12.2 reproduces Bereday's recommended four steps for undertaking comparative studies of education in two countries. The first step in the model is description of pedagogical data for two countries separately. This is followed by evaluation within historical, political, economic and social contexts. The third step requires juxtaposition according to criteria for comparability and hypotheses for comparative analysis; and the final step requires simultaneous comparison according to the hypothesis to reach a conclusion.

Of course, not all authors in this book followed these steps in precisely that sequence. Indeed, as noted by Jones (1971, pp.89-92), Trethewey (1979, pp.75-77) and Watson (1996, p.371), that would be very difficult to do. Even at the first stage, in the words of Jones (1971, p.89), "the complete isolation of pedagogical facts is extra-ordinarily difficult, as rarely do they have meaning without the help of explanation, using other disciplines". Further, it is doubtful whether any researcher should be recommended to follow Bereday's sequence rigidly, moving from one step to another without going back over earlier ground to make several iterations. However, the model remains useful several decades after it was first presented because it stresses the value of systematic and balanced enquiry. The model further emphasises the importance of viewing education phenomena within their broader contexts.

The Bereday model also helps to underline why Hong Kong and Macau are a worthwhile pair for comparison, namely that they have sufficient in common to make analysis of their differences meaningful. The commonalities, as noted in the Introduction, include the fact that they are both situated on the south coast of China, are both mainly populated by Cantonese-speaking Chinese, are both urban societies with economies based mainly on services and light industry and with insignificant agricultural sectors, have both been colonies of European powers, and since the 1980s had both been scheduled to be returned to China and governed as Special Administrative Regions. Yet this book has shown that their education sectors have significant differences as well as similarities. This provides an excellent basis for meaningful comparison to identify the extent and the reasons for the differences and similarities, and to advance conceptual understanding through exploration of the forces at work and the relationships between those forces.

Figure 12.2: Bereday's Model for Undertaking Comparative Studies

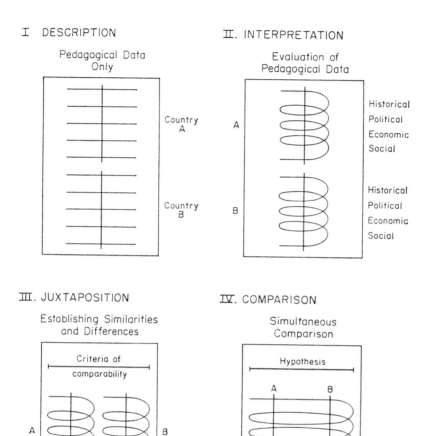

Source: Bereday (1964), p.28.

More detailed analysis of the approaches used by the various authors of this book again reveals both commonalities and variations. All the authors used documentary materials, which is a dominant characteristic of much comparative inquiry in education. These documentary materials included primary as well as secondary sources: many chapters refer to government reports and statistics, for example, and a few cite primary sources from archives or other sources. Several chapters also draw on interviews, and a few report data collected from questionnaires. In other words, the range of methods used to gather material for the comparison is broad. This matches the range that would be found in typical volumes of the major professional journals.

One further obstacle commonly encountered in comparative education is that of language. Translations are a poor substitute for direct communication, and, as observed by Halls (1990, p.63), "for comparative studies to thrive, the linguistic barrier remains the greatest to be overcome". Direct linguistic access to both secondary and primary sources permits researchers to identify important nuances, and to avoid some of the misconceptions which might arise from inadequate translation and linguistic cultural bias. The present book has benefitted from the fact that all authors have knowledge of both English and Chinese, and that several also have a working knowledge of Portuguese. The authors who did not have fluency in Portuguese may have been slightly handicapped in access to certain materials and people in Macau. However, in recent years much official documentation in Macau has been translated into Chinese; and the number of potential informants who did not speak Chinese or English was very small. As a result, lack of fluency in Portuguese has been much less of a handicap than it would have been if conducting research in Brazil or Cape Verde, for example. For the present research, English and Chinese were by far the most important languages, and competence in both languages has given the authors much greater access than would have been possible for monolingual researchers.

A final methodological point concerns the scale of the societies. With its population of below half a million, Macau is among the smallest of the small. Hong Kong has a much larger population, but is still very small compared with such neighbours as mainland China, Indonesia, Philippines and Vietnam. From a research perspective, smallness of scale may create some problems but can also have substantial benefits (Bray & Packer 1993). One benefit is that 100 per cent samples can be achieved with small numbers. Tang's chapter on mathematics curriculum is partly based on his PhD thesis (K.C. Tang 1999), which surveyed all the secondary schools in Macau. Because Hong Kong is larger, most researchers have to take samples when investigating education there; but their samples are usually still substantially greater proportions of the total number of schools than would be possible for research on mainland China, for example. In the domain of higher education, as shown by Yung's chapter, even in Hong Kong it is easy to make explicit reference to every institution.

Smallness of scale may also permit identification of the personal factors which shape education systems. Leung's chapter on the church and state exemplifies this in its reference to individuals who have shaped both policy and practice in Hong Kong and Macau. Tan's chapter on history curricula identifies individuals who have founded particular schools and shaped curricula. Since this chapter uses schools as units of analysis, a similar approach could have been used in larger societies. However, the schools sampled still represented a much greater proportion of the total in each territory; and the fact remains that all chapters would have been qualitatively very different had they focused on China and India, for example, rather than on Hong Kong and Macau. Focus on larger units would require greater anonymity and preclude the degree of attention to internal variations that is possible in smaller units.

Conclusions

As an academic study, this book aims to contribute to conceptual understanding more than to specific recommendations for policy and practice. Along the lines proposed by Farrell

(1979, p.4), however, the authors and editors hope that the book will still assist policy makers and practitioners by showing some of the ways that educational processes interact with and result from economic, social, political and other forces.

Returning to Sadler's remarks quoted above, one of the key roles of comparative education is to help individuals to understand more fully their own societies. Margaret Mead, the anthropologist, is reported once to have said (approximately): "If a fish were to become an anthropologist, the last thing it would discover would be water" (Spindler & Spindler 1982, p.24). Similar remarks might be made about research in comparative education. While the value of inside perspectives seems obvious, Mead's remark emphasises also the value of outside perspectives.

An alternative way to promote objective understanding of one's own society, however, is first to look outwards and then to look back. Comparative education, like other forms of comparative enquiry, should make "strange patterns familiar", i.e. should permit and encourage researchers and readers to become more familiar with the features of education systems and societies which are not well known to them. At the same time the reverse may also apply, i.e. that comparative education can make "familiar patterns strange", calling into question features of education systems and societies which had been taken for granted by insiders simply because they were so familiar with them (see Spindler & Spindler 1982, p.43; Choksi & Dyer 1997, p.271). The authors and editors of this book hope that on the one hand readers based in Hong Kong and Macau will learn about each other's society and patterns of education, but also that they will be encouraged to reflect on their own society and patterns of education. In the process, they may see features of their own society and education which had been overlooked and which perhaps deserve attention for encouragement or reform.

Within the book, historical features have been given considerable attention. As noted above, this is a strong tradition within the mainstream of comparative education. Writing in 1984, Noah (reprinted 1998, p.52) showed how temporal and locational comparisons can be combined in a fruitful way by observing that:

> Not only is the nation that forgets its history likely to repeat it, but the nation that forgets (or is blind to) the educational system of its contemporaries is risking either stagnation, or the perils of burdensomely expensive experimentation. Comparative understanding can help countries break with old ways of arranging the educational systems without the danger that they indulge in foolish daydreams that there are just one or two fairly simplistic things they need to do in order to set their schools aright.

Again, this shows the functional uses of comparative education to readers in particular societies, and in this case Hong Kong and Macau.

However, this chapter has also stressed that the book makes a contribution to broader literatures, and should interest readers who are not residents of either Hong Kong or Macau. The themes addressed in the book are certainly of interest to analysts in many other parts of the world; and even this methodological chapter may be of value to readers who seek to understand the processes by which comparative studies may be assembled in a range of contexts. Once again, this is the value of analytical works. Were the book to focus on recommendations to policy makers and practitioners in Hong Kong and Macau, it would have relevance to a limited audience and would rapidly become out of date. It seems likely that many of the themes on which the contributors to this book focus will have a relevance which is both enduring and which reaches considerably beyond the small part of the south coast of China with which the book is primarily concerned.

13

Continuity and Change in Education

Mark BRAY

The title of this final chapter follows the wording in the subtitle of the whole book. The chapter focuses on the lessons of the book for the understanding of continuity and change in education. Building on the methodological points made in the previous chapter, this one benefits from both temporal and locational comparisons. Although focus on continuity and change is most obviously a matter of temporal comparison, locational comparisons assist analysis because, even when they are 'snapshots' of particular places at particular points in time, they may still contribute to understanding. For example, much can be learned about the probable implications of colonial transition in Hong Kong and Macau at the end of the 20th century by comparing it with patterns in other colonies at their stages of colonial transition in earlier decades.

A considerable literature addresses the nature of change and continuity in education systems (e.g. Dalin 1978; Archer 1984; Fullan 1994; Morrison 1998). For present purposes, one of the most helpful frameworks for analysis was presented by Thomas & Postlethwaite (1983a) in a book entitled *Schooling in East Asia: Forces of Change*. As indicated by its title, the book focused directly on the East Asian region; and it included separate chapters on Hong Kong and Macau. Much has altered in both those territories and the region as a whole since the book was written, which itself underlines the importance of the topic. Nevertheless, the analytical framework remains both valid and useful, and is the starting point for this chapter. Discussion then proceeds to other models for change, and to interpretations of the various chapters in this book in the context of other theories and explanatory frameworks.

The Thomas & Postlethwaite Framework

Thomas & Postlethwaite began (1983b, p.7) by indicating that they used the terms 'force' and 'cause' synonymously. A force or a cause, they stated (p.7), is "a factor whose presence is necessary for an event to occur". Without each of the forces that press against each other in a kind of dialectical exchange, they added, events cannot happen in the way that they do. Use of the phrase "each of the forces" reflected the authors' commitment to the principal of multiple causation. According to this principle, an event is not simply the result of a single force but is always the result of many forces, some of which may be more powerful than others and therefore more worthy of note.

The principle of multiple causation, Thomas & Postlethwaite proceeded to observe (1983b, p.7), applies to both the horizontal and vertical dimensions of the timing of an event. By 'horizontal' they meant that several forces converge simultaneously to mould an event; and by 'vertical' they referred to the sequence or accumulation of causes over time. This, they pointed out, is the philosopher's principle of infinite regress: the idea that behind each cause is an earlier cause which brought the later one about. Thomas & Postlethwaite did not attempt the impossible task of identifying all forces that converge horizontally to cause an event. Nor did they endeavour to trace far back into the past to uncover all the links in a vertical web that recedes into ancient times. Instead they restricted their main focus to the 20th century, and to the major causes of the events they analysed.

Thomas & Postlethwaite distinguished between enabling and direct forces for change. An enabling force was identified (1983b, p.10) as:

> a causal condition that provides an opportunity for educational innovation but is not directly involved in the change. In other words, an enabling event can take place without affecting the schooling process.

A direct force, in contrast, was identified as one that applied specifically to the process of schooling. Such a force, Thomas & Postlethwaite added (1983b, p.10) was:

> a characteristic – such as an attitude – or an act of a person that motivates others to promote a given educational change, that furnishes an alternative to current educational practice, or that provides resources for implementing the change.

The converse of an enabling force was described as a disabling one, i.e. a condition that obstructed change; and the possibility was noted that direct forces could be either positive or negative. For the present chapter, inclusion of disabling forces and direct negative forces is important because analysis here focuses on continuity as well as change.

For Thomas & Postlethwaite, however, the main focus was on change. With this in mind, they constructed an analytical framework with seven dimensions of change, namely: the magnitude of intended change; availability of alternatives; motivation or philosophical commitment; social and organisational stability; resource accessibility; organisational and technical efficiency; and adequacy of funding. Figure 13.1 gives examples of each category in the seven dimensions. These are of course not the only ways in which change (and non-change) can be viewed and classified, as observed by Thomas & Postlethwaite themselves (1983b, p.6). However, the framework does promote understanding of patterns in Hong Kong and Macau, as well as in other parts of the world.

Application of the Thomas & Postlethwaite Framework

The most sensible place to start the task of seeing how the Thomas & Postlethwaite framework can be applied to Hong Kong and Macau is with the relevant chapters of the Thomas & Postlethwaite book. The present work can go further, however. This book benefits from the passage of time, having been published 16 years after the volume edited by Thomas & Postlethwaite. The book also benefits from considerably greater depth, because it focuses on only two territories and draws on the considerably expanded base of scholarship within those two territories.

Figure 13.1: The Thomas & Postlethwaite Classification of Determinants of Change and Non-Change

Positive Forces that Hasten Change   **Negative Forces that Retard Change**

Dimension 1: Magnitude of Intended Change

1.1 Population Size and Accessibility

Enabling forces: small population. Small territory, easily traversed terrain and waterways, mild climate. Advanced communication and transportation facilities – radio, telephone, television, electronic-computer systems, fast trains, ships, autos, aeroplanes.

Disabling forces: Large population. Large territory, rugged terrain and treacherous waterways, severe climate. Primitive communication and transportation facilities.

1.2 Complexity of Intended Change

Direct-positive forces: A few simple aspects of the education system to be changed.

Direct-negative forces: Many interrelated aspects of the education system to be changed.

Dimension 2: Availability of Alternatives

Enabling forces: A society with a high proportion of people holding modernisation views. A society that interacts freely with other societies and encourages new ideas.

Disabling forces: A society with a high proportion of people holding traditionalist views. A society isolated from interaction with other societies and that discourages innovation

Direct-positive forces: Educational leaders who seek new ideas and encourage varied opinions and proposals.

Direct-negative forces: Educational leaders who defend traditional practices, discourage differences of opinion and new proposals.

Dimension 3: Motivation or Philosophical Commitment

Enabling forces: A society with a high proportion of people holding modernisation views.

Disabling forces: A society with a high proportion of people holding conservative, traditionalist views.

Direct-positive forces: A high proportion of powerful educational leaders strongly committed to effecting the proposed change. Leaders have sanctions or propaganda techniques available for influencing educational personnel to support the change.

Direct-negative forces: A high proportion of powerful educational leaders who lack a strong commitment to the change or, more seriously, who choose to resist the change. Leaders have sanctions or propaganda techniques available to influence educational personnel to resist the change.

Dimension 4: Social and Organisational Stability

Enabling forces: Peace and amity in the society, continuity of the ruling government, regular pro-duction of sufficient goods to meet people's needs.

Disabling forces: War, revolution, rioting, frequent changes of government, and such 'natural' disasters as floods, earthquakes, and crop failures.

Direct-positive forces: Amicable relations among the education-system's staff members, rewards to staff for efficient service, clear leadership direction, infrequent organisational change.

Direct-negative forces: Dissension among the education-system's staff members, jealousies, frequent organisational change, frequent displacement of existing projects with new projects, lack of rewards for efficient service.

Dimension 5: Resource Accessibility

Enabling forces: A society with advanced industries and training systems.

Disabling forces: A society whose services for producing supplies and training personnel are few and inefficient.

Direct-positive forces: The use of efficient, nearby sources for producing the equipment and personnel required in the intended educational change.

Direct-negative forces: The lack of efficient, nearby facilities for producing the equipment and personnel required for the educational change.

Dimension 6: Organisational and Technical Efficiency

Enabling forces: A society with efficient organisational structures and a high degree of specialisation, technical expertise and advanced equipment for producing objects, processing data, communicating, training people, and the like.

Disabling forces: A society with ineffective organisational structures, little technical expertise in per-forming specialised tasks, and little or no advanced equipment for producing objects, processing data, communicating, training people and the like.

Direct-positive forces: The application in the educational-change system of advanced organisational structure, efficient specialisation, a high level of skill in the specialised tasks, and advanced equipment to per-form tasks that are more effectively done by machines than by people. An effective method for adapting these systems to the local culture.

Direct-negative forces: An educational change system that is inefficiently organised or poorly suited to the local culture, that involves little or no specialisation or expertise in performing specialised tasks, and that uses no equipment for performing tasks – that is, the system uses only people.

Dimension 7: Adequacy of Funding

Enabling forces: A society with enough wealth to expend large sums for improving services, including educational services.

Disabling forces: A society marked by widespread poverty.

Direct-positive forces: Educational change advocates who present a convincing case for their project's receiving a high priority in obtaining available education funds.

Direct-negative forces: Other agencies or projects that make a more convincing case for deserving funds to support their projects than is made by advocates of the change-project under review.

The individual country/territory chapters in the Thomas & Postlethwaite book began with Japan and then moved to Taiwan, mainland China, South Korea, North Korea, Hong Kong, and Macau. The Hong Kong chapter was written by Anthony Sweeting, whose subsequent work on the history of education in Hong Kong has been cited by several contributors to the present volume. The Macau chapter was written by R. Murray Thomas, the senior editor of the book. Thomas himself recognised that this was a second-best arrangement. In the Preface (p.vii), he wrote that:

> When the leading education officials in the Portuguese colony … were asked to suggest a suitable author, they explained that the limited size of their professional staff would not permit them to spare a member of it for such an assignment.

The University of East Asia was in its infancy, and could not furnish a suitable scholar. In the absence of an alternative, Thomas decided to write the chapter himself. However, he readily admitted (Thomas 1994) that he found the task challenging because he lacked the detailed knowledge necessary to conduct it thoroughly. As noted in Chapter 12, the subsequent growth of the number of scholars able to write in depth on education in Macau may be viewed with some satisfaction. Thomas would have much less difficulty today were he to prepare a revised edition and seek a knowledgeable author on the topic.

Magnitude of Intended Change

Under the heading of magnitude of intended change, Thomas & Postlethwaite highlighted the importance of such enabling/disabling factors as population, area, physical features, and availability of facilities for communication. Direct forces, they suggested, included the complexity of intended change, being positive if a few simple aspects of the education system were to be changed but negative if many interrelated aspects were to be changed.

In the prologue to the section of their book which focused on Hong Kong and Macau, Thomas (1983b, pp.266-267) wrote:

> Hong Kong and Macau are similar in the magnitude of their educational tasks and of the territory and populations they cover. Compared to the nations of East Asia around them, the two colonies are quite small. All schools in each colony can be reached by car within less than 1 hour, so that communication and the transport of supplies between the central headquarters and every unit of the school system is a simple matter.

This statement of similarity is important, because the people of Hong Kong and Macau sometimes perceive differences more than similarities when looking at each other. Hong Kong is of course much larger than Macau in both area and population; but both are very small when viewed in a regional context.

The point that educational reform may be easier to achieve in entities with smaller populations has also been made by other authors (e.g. Hassan 1990, p.4; Bray 1996, p.16). The Commonwealth Secretariat (1985, p.2) has observed that:

> success has a greater effect on a small system. Any successful achievement in any part of the system can shed its light over other parts so that all can share in the afterglow. This obviously helps morale, and strengthens the sense of corporate identity for all those working in the service. Success when it comes tends to come quickly in the smaller system and to be more clearly seen, and that in time acts as an encouragement and spur to further reform.

Brock & Parker (1985, pp.44-45) have added the observation that when allied with compactness, smallness in populations size:

> provides a degree of proximity and accessibility in respect of involvement and management that is simply not available to larger systems of education. The ability to communicate rapidly with (say), the Director of Education, the Minister of Education, Principal of the Teachers College, a Head Teacher and an individual class teacher on the same day, perhaps even in the same street, obviously provides these compact systems with advantages in terms of responsiveness to the community's point of view. By the same token, it makes the community very much more aware of the realities of what is going on....

In Macau, however, until the late 1980s the authorities made little use of this enabling factor; and if communities were strongly aware of what was going on, they appeared to have little power to ensure that the various actors in the education sector operated in a coordinated way. Several contributors to this book have observed that Macau's schools evolved in a largely laissez-faire environment, and that the university was founded as a result of private rather than government initiative. During the 1990s, the Macau government adopted a more interventionist stance and was no doubt facilitated by the small population and area of the territory. However, the authorities were confronted during the 1990s by long traditions of school-level autonomy which continued to obstruct coordination. Thus although small size was enabling, the nature of educational change and non-change was shaped by many other factors.

The importance of other factors is illustrated by the fact that change in mainland China's schools during the decade and a half after the publication of the Thomas & Postlethwaite book was perhaps even greater than in Macau. This was despite the fact that, in the opening words of Hawkins' chapter in the book (1983, p.136):

> From the Tian Shan range in the extreme West to the port of Shanghai in the East, from the cold steppes of Mongolia in the North to the tropical rain forests of Yunan in the South, China's 9½ million square kilometers of land contains almost one-fourth of the world's population.

Even in such a vast country, the administration of education, at least in the 1970s and 1980s and arguably even in the 1990s, was more centralised than in Macau. Rather more important were the macro-economic and macro-political contexts in China, which changed radically in the 1980s and 1990s and in turn altered the functioning of schools and universities (K.M. Cheng 1992a; Y.M. Leung 1995). The chief change in the environment which shaped schools was China's shift to a market economy and much greater freedom of personal expression. Specifically in the education sector, a set of reforms was launched in 1985 to universalise basic education, decentralise administration, restructure secondary education, promote technical and vocational education, and reshape the links between higher education and the labour market (Lewin et al. 1994). The pace and scale of change during the 1980s and 1990s were very dramatic despite the size of the population, the vastness of the country, its many geographic barriers arising from mountains, deserts and jungles, and the fact that the education and broader reforms had many interrelated components.

Hong Kong seems to provide a third model which was different from both Macau and mainland China. Over 50 sovereign states in the world have total populations which are smaller than that of Hong Kong, and on this scale Hong Kong might be considered relatively large. However, Hong Kong has a compact territory and excellent physical infrastructure. Moreover, during the 1980s and 1990s the government exercised centralised control over many aspects of Hong Kong's education system, which permitted both coordination and some reform. Hong Kong's schools did not change during these two decades as much as the schools in mainland China, but this was chiefly because the political and economic superstructures in Hong Kong were relatively stable, and because the authorities and the general population were content with incremental change rather than fundamental overhaul.

It is also instructive here to note a difference between the situations at the time that Thomas & Postlethwaite wrote and at the time of preparing this chapter. Page 309 of the Thomas & Postlethwaite book contained a table of population sizes in 1979. Hong Kong was listed as having a population of 4,622,000, and Macau as having a population of 320,000. Twenty years later, one is struck by the growth. At the end of 1997, Hong Kong had an estimated population of 6,617,000 (Hong Kong, Information Services Department 1998, p.380), and the population had continued to rise during 1998 and 1999. Likewise, Macau in 1997 had an estimated population of 422,000 (Macau, Department of Statistics & Census 1998a, p.29) and experienced similar continued growth. Postlethwaite & Thomas (1983, p.310) remarked that Hong Kong had succeeded in lowering its birth rate, and that "it is estimated that the colony's population will grow by only about 20 percent or one million people over the next 20 years if the low birth rate can be maintained and immigration reduced". The low birth rate was indeed maintained, but immigration was not reduced. As a result, within 18 years the population had increased by nearly two million and over 40 per cent. The proportionate increase in Macau was not much lower.

While initial size of population may have been an enabling/disabling factor, growth of population was a major direct force of change. It required expansion of education in the two territories, and in some respects permitted diversification. Yung's chapter in this book points out that in both Hong Kong and Macau, higher education was one area in which diversification was particularly marked. Some diversity is also evident at the school level, e.g. in the numbers and types of international schools in both Hong Kong and Macau. However, as noted by Adamson & Li, in both Hong Kong and Macau academic approaches are very dominant, and neither territory has particularly strong technical or prevocational education at the school level. Indeed in Hong Kong, growth of population has been accompanied by reduction of diversity in this respect because the 1980s and 1990s brought a trend in which technical and prevocational schools became increasingly like grammar schools.

On a related tack, Thomas & Postlethwaite suggested that change of a few simple aspects of an education system may be considered a direct-positive force, while change of many interrelated aspects of education would be a direct-negative force. While this statement seems intuitively true, the experience in mainland China shows that the combined weight of multiple changes can in fact become a direct-positive force. In contrast, reforms which are small may in fact be obstructed because they are piecemeal and do not take full account of other components in education and society. Dalin (1978, pp.9-10) observed that in many cases single innovations make little difference when pitted against the inertia of traditional ways of operation. Such remarks seem applicable to Hong Kong and Macau as well as to other parts of the world.

Availability of Alternatives

Under the heading of availability of alternatives, Thomas & Postlethwaite suggested that enabling forces included the existence in society of a high proportion of people holding modernisation views, and encouragement of new ideas through free interaction with other societies. Disabling forces included a high proportion of people holding traditionalist views, and isolation from other societies.

Both Hong Kong and Macau are widely considered open societies. In the Thomas & Postlethwaite book, they were sharply contrasted with North Korea, for example, which continued through the 1980s and 1990s as a 'hermit' society dominated by a rigid political structure and with minimal interaction with other countries. For Hong Kong and Macau, external interaction was assisted by the bilingual skills of large proportions of the population. The fact that the bulk of the people in each place could speak, read and write in Chinese facilitated interaction with Taiwan and mainland China, in particular; and the fact that many people could also speak, read and write English facilitated interaction with many other parts of the world. Also, in Macau a significant proportion of the leadership rank was fluent in Portuguese.

In practice, however, rather few innovations in the education sector were adopted from Chinese-speaking societies. The influences of mainland China and Taiwan were perhaps stronger in Macau than Hong Kong, because many of Macau's private schools recruited teachers and had other links with mainland China and Taiwan. Hong Kong educators and policy-makers had access to mainland China and Taiwan, but tended to feel that they had little to learn from those places. Instead, innovations tended to be imported from such countries as the Australia, Canada, the UK and the USA. Examples include the School Management Initiative, which was heavily influenced by models in Australia and to some extent the UK and USA (O'Donoghue & Dimmock 1998, p.52), and the Target Oriented Curriculum, which was heavily influenced by models in the UK and Australia (Carless 1998, p.228). Lest this be oversimplified, however, it must be stressed that most imported models were adapted and even substantially changed in the local context. With reference to the social studies curriculum, for example, Morris et al. (1998, p.123) point out that:

> There can be no dispute that the development of social studies in other countries, particularly the United Kingdom and the United States, influenced the curriculum in Hong Kong, especially at the policy and initiation stages. Nevertheless, the emergence of social studies in Hong Kong cannot be adequately explained simply by the influence of external models.

The authors added that although the external models provided exemplary materials, a rhetoric for change that enthused pioneers and policy-makers, and a means for justifying policies, the external models were modified beyond recognition in the design and adaptation to the local environment.

A related issue concerns the internationalisation of the leadership in Hong Kong and Macau. Colonial transition reduced the proportions of British and Portuguese admini-strators in the respective governments. However, in some respects, both Hong Kong and Macau became more internationalised because of the shortage of local higher education places during the 1980s. Shive (1992, p.216) reported that at the end of that decade, 35,000 Hong Kong students were enrolled in tertiary institutions outside the territory – a number far exceeding the 15,000 tertiary students within Hong Kong.

Academic staff in local institutions were also international in their outlook and experience. Data reported by Postiglione (1996a, p.196) indicated that in 1993, 33.0 per cent of academic staff in seven institutions funded by the University Grants Committee of Hong Kong were employed on non-local terms. Such academics brought with them perspectives from their home countries and elsewhere. Many local academics also had broad international experience. In 1993, 84.1 per cent of academic staff had obtained their highest qualifications outside Hong Kong (Postiglione 1996a, p.197). As observed by the chapters in this book by Yung and by Ma, Macau's tertiary education had been even more restricted in the 1980s; and Macau's institutions of higher education recruited external staff and local staff with non-local qualifications along the same lines as their counterparts in Hong Kong. Macau's institutions have had considerable proportions of Hong Kong staff (compared with an almost insignificant number of Macau staff in Hong Kong's institutions), and have also been more open to recruitment from mainland China as well as other parts of the world. In 1993/94, 91.4 per cent of academic staff at the University of Macau had gained their highest qualifications outside Macau (Koo 1999, p.12). The principal places in which the highest qualifications had been obtained were Portugal (25.1%), North America (24.3%), other Europe (13.6%), mainland China (11.9%), and Hong Kong (7.4%).

A related factor, which has been the focus of comment throughout this book, is the extent to which Hong Kong and Macau have been role models for each other. Wong's chapter does point out that at some points in history, Hong Kong pre-schools gained staff and ideas from their counterparts in Macau; and Adamson & Li highlight the shift of some

Macau schools to Hong Kong shortly after the commencement of the British colonial period. In general, however, the balance has been very much on the other side, i.e. Macau learning from Hong Kong. A major underlying factor has been the relative expertise of the two territories. Because Hong Kong is larger and has paid more attention to tertiary education, it has had greater pools of expertise. Educators in Hong Kong have not generally felt that they had much to learn from Macau; but educators in Macau have commonly scrutinised innovations in Hong Kong with care. Tang's chapter shows that in the domain of mathematics education, some Macau educators have paid heed not only to Hong Kong's innovations but have also retained some of the old Hong Kong models no longer in use in Hong Kong.

Stressing a point made in Chapter 12, it is also worth quoting a statement by Thomas (1983b, p.268) concerning research. He indicated that:

> In contrast to Hong Kong, educators in Macau have conducted very little research, so that few if any local studies are available as sources of educational innovation.

This aspect changed markedly during the period following publication of the Thomas & Postlethwaite book. Research output greatly increased in Macau, as evidenced by the chapters in this book and the references to other research that the various contributors make. The fact that the volume of research also greatly increased in Hong Kong to some extent maintained the gap between the two societies. However, the increased volume of research in the two territories meant that in both Macau and Hong Kong, data on alternative models for educational administration and implementation had become increasingly plentiful. Some actors in the two territories felt that this contributed to excessive change – that teachers, in particular, were subjected to a constant barrage of innovations as a result of the increased access to information on models in other parts of the world.

Motivation or Philosophical Commitment
As indicated in Figure 13.1, Thomas & Postlethwaite considered the enabling and disabling forces for motivation or philosophical commitment to be very similar to those for availability of alternatives. Overlap also exists in the nature of direct-positive and direct-negative forces. However, motivation and commitment move beyond mere availability of information about the nature of alternatives.

Specifically referring to Hong Kong and Macau, Thomas (1983b, p.269) observed that, especially in comparison with mainland China, Taiwan, South Korea and North Korea, education policy-makers had had strong laissez faire stances. This book has shown that in general, the approach of the Macau government was much more laissez faire than that of the Hong Kong government; but it is instructive to place the two territories next to other parts of the region and see that both of them occupied one end of the spectrum. Thomas added (p.269) that in neither Hong Kong nor Macau did the schools foster the type of cohesive cultural commitment evident in Japan:

> Instead, each of the colonies has permitted diverse socio-political and cultural purposes to be pursued in different schools – Christian and Buddhist versus communist, European language versus Chinese language, European culture versus Chinese culture. Apparently the dominant educational aim shared by the peoples of the two colonies is the pursuit of self-interest. Education is viewed not as a device for implementing a consciously designed socio-political program or a given set of

cultural goals, but rather as an instrument for achieving personal success, for rising in the economic system and for gaining … social prestige.

A similar observation has been made about Hong Kong by Luk (1992, p.117). In remarks which would also be applicable to Macau, Luk observed that:

Unlike most national governments with its own cultural agenda to follow and the interests of its domestic power-base to promote through its educational policies, the colonial government of Hong Kong has not tried to impose its own or any one group's core values on the populace; rather, it has allowed the various groups to 'do their own things', and to thrive, wither, or change in the evolving socio-economic environment.

However, the Hong Kong government was much more interventionist than the Macau government when faced by the threat of communism, especially in the 1950s and 1960s. Leung's chapter in this book notes the ways in which the colonial authorities allied with the Christian churches, using education as a tool to maintain existing political structures in the territory. In Macau, by contrast, the government collapsed in the face of leftist demonstrations, and for some years after 1966 social order and security were chiefly maintained by the pro-China neighbourhood associations and other influential social, religious and economic organisations rather than by the government. The 1966 riots in Macau also marked a turning point in education, with the rise of pro-China schools and the decline in Catholic ones.

By the 1980s, the era of colonial transition had begun and the governments of both Hong Kong and Macau became more interventionist. Most obvious were the changes in Macau, where the authorities embarked on reform initiatives which sought to coordinate institutions in a more coherent way. The Macau government purchased the University of East Asia, and launched a scheme for fee-free basic education. It also embarked on curriculum reform, and sought ways to upgrade the quality of teachers. Parallel moves of this type were less urgent in Hong Kong because the territory already had a strong public sector in tertiary education, fee-free basic education, and a strong teaching force. However, many curriculum changes were considered desirable. Among them, the thrust for civic education, documented in Tse's chapter, was particularly notable.

Social and Organisational Stability
Under this heading, Thomas & Postlethwaite suggested that enabling forces included peace and amity in the society, continuity of the ruling government, and regular production of sufficient goods to meet people's needs. Disabling forces included war, revolution, rioting, frequent changes of government, and disasters such as floods, earthquakes and crop failures. Direct-positive forces included amicable relations among the education system's staff members, rewards to staff for efficient service, clear leadership direction, and infrequent organisational change; and direct-negative forces included dissension among staff members, jealousies, frequent organisational change, frequent displacement of existing projects with new projects, and lack of rewards for efficient service.

As already noted, Macau and also to some extent Hong Kong experienced social dislocation in the mid-1960s as a result of overspill of the Cultural Revolution in mainland China. Also, during subsequent decades, at the level of top leadership Macau was much more directly affected by political changes in Portugal than Hong Kong was by political changes in the United Kingdom (Lo 1995, pp.41-44). However, during the 1970s, 1980s and 1990s both territories were characterised much more by stability than by change. Indeed this was a major policy goal not only of the Hong Kong and Macau governments but also of the British, Portuguese and mainland Chinese governments. This stability provided an environment for government-orchestrated and, particularly in Hong Kong, fairly cautious change. Even after Hong Kong's change of sovereignty, at least in the initial years the continuities were more striking than the discontinuities. Also, on one specific criterion identified by Thomas & Postlethwaite, neither Hong Kong nor Macau has suffered significantly from serious natural disasters in recent years.

However, the lack of abrupt changes in broad social and organisational structures should not cause observers to overlook more 'silent' social changes. Luk (1992, pp.117-118) has highlighted the significance of the processes of industralisation which changed Hong Kong society from the 1950s onwards. These processes, he suggested have "profoundly changed the occupational profile, appropriate knowledge, necessary skills, and general attitudes". Similar remarks would apply to Macau. In part, moreover, the broader changes have resulted from changes in the scale and nature of educational provision. Education and society have operated in relationships in which each has shaped the other. Supply of school places increased in both territories, and at the school level supply to a large extent kept up with demand. At the post-school level, supply of tertiary places was inadequate to meet demand in either Hong Kong or Macau during the period up to the late 1980s. However, during the 1990s this situation changed too. Yung's chapter in this book points out that Hong Kong entered an era of mass higher education during the 1990s, and that Macau was not far behind.

The fact that the social and organisational framework remained stable despite political changes deserves further comment. Thomas (1983b, p.270), writing before the Sino-British and Sino-Portuguese Joint Declarations, suggested that:

> there is within both colonies the constant realization that the direction of life and schooling could be sharply diverted at any moment, should the People's Republic of China choose to take over the colonies. This realization casts over the colonies a sense of impermanence. If Hong Kong and Macau should become part of the People's Republic, the colonies' *laissez faire* approach to education and their great array of private schools would disappear.

Reviewing this paragraph two decades later, it certainly seems that the laissez faire approach to education has diminished (though perhaps not altogether disappeared), especially in Macau. However, little threat is posed to private schools, not least because they are now tolerated and even encouraged in the PRC itself (Mok 1997). Most of Macau's private schools have sacrificed some of their autonomy in return for financial and other support from the government, and to some extent a parallel development was evident when the Hong Kong government developed its Direct Subsidy Scheme in the early 1990s (Bray 1995b). However, in no sense have either Macau or Hong Kong been subjected to a wave of nationalisation of schools because of reunification with the socialist motherland. Even if mainland China were not itself moving in the direction of privatisation, private schools in Macau and Hong Kong would be protected by the concept of 'One Country, Two Systems'.

This, moreover, is a domain in which colonial transition in Macau and Hong Kong, rather in contrast to dominant patterns in other parts of the world (Bray 1997a), has been characterised by continuity rather than change. Several chapters in this book point out that the long lead-times between the signature of the Joint Declarations and the actual change deserves particular mention, and one feature which comparative analysis helps to expose concerns official languages in the two territories. In Hong Kong, the Basic Law (China 1990, Article 9) indicates that for at least 50 years in addition to the Chinese Language, English may also be used as an official language. By itself, that clause might not cause much remark, since many former British colonies have chosen to retain English as an official language because of its uses in the international arena. However, when a comparison is made with Macau, and when further comparisons are made with other former Portuguese colonies, the clause might appear deserving of further scrutiny. The Macau Basic Law was closely modelled on the Hong Kong one, and contained a clause which was exactly the same except that it gave place to Portuguese rather than English (China 1993, Article 9). Given that Portuguese has a much weaker international role, this might seem remarkable. One cannot imagine the post-colonial rulers in Angola or Mozambique, for example, agreeing to use Portuguese as an official language for 50 years after the change of sovereignty; and yet the colony which had a negotiated return of sovereignty to its powerful motherland has such a clause. These are among the dimensions of continuity rather than change which make the cases of Macau and Hong Kong so interesting within a broader comparative framework.

Resources
Thomas & Postlethwaite (1983b) had three headings concerned with resources. The first was labelled resource accessibility, the second was labelled organisational and technical efficiency, and the third was labelled adequacy of funding.

In these categories, enabling forces included advanced industries, training services, technical expertise, and general prosperity; while disabling forces included widespread poverty, inadequate services for producing supplies and training personnel, and generally ineffective organisational structures. Direct-positive forces included educational change advocates who presented a convincing case for their projects to receive available funds, and efficient specialisation in the necessary tasks. Direct-negative forces included inability of innovations to attract the resources that were available, and inefficient organisation.

Specifically referring to Hong Kong and Macau, Thomas (1983b, p.270) stated that:

> Hong Kong is stronger than Macau in resources and efficiency. Hong Kong has more highly trained personnel and is far ahead in the completeness and regularity of administrative reports on the condition of the educational enterprise.

While Macau had achieved considerable advances, most observers would consider that this statement remained valid two decades later. Thomas proceeded (pp.270-271) to remark that both Hong Kong and Macau depended on similar sources of educational finance:

> Each colony maintains a small number of government-operated schools supported by public funds, and subsidies are provided by the governments to aid certain private institutions, with Hong Kong furnishing more financial subsidies than Macau.... From the viewpoint of furnishing instructional facilities, Hong Kong's schools appear more adequately funded than Macau's.

One indicator that this remained the case during subsequent decades was provided by Yung's chapter. Even in 1996, he observed, public expenditure on education as a proportion of Gross Domestic Product formed 3.0 per cent in Hong Kong but only 0.8 per cent in Macau.

On another dimension identified by Thomas (1983b), however, considerable change had been achieved. Thomas had written (p.271) that:

> In each of the colonies, the ability of the schools to attract apt, dedicated, and well-prepared teachers and administrators would apparently be enhanced if the schools paid salaries that competed more successfully with the income provided by other occupations in the colonies.

Macau's schools retained great diversity because the majority of them were private institutions. However, the reforms of the 1990s increased the government subsidies for private schools and generally raised teachers' salaries. By the mid-1990s, teachers were also considered well paid in Hong Kong – in comparison not only with other professions but also with teachers elsewhere. Brown (1997, pp.103-104) observed that a typical trained graduate with 10 years of experience earned HK$348,000:

> a figure that is well above the median for teachers in the United Kingdom and in all but a few of the United States. It is also far higher than the average income in business and industry.

Brown added (p.104) that the top point of the teachers' scale was equivalent to US$75,900 a year in 1995: "an unheard of salary for classroom teachers nearly anywhere else in the world". Teachers salaries had increased more rapidly than general inflation.

However, while Thomas (1983b, p.271) seemed to consider low salaries an inhibiting factor on educational change, Brown (1997, p.104) pointed out that high salaries may also inhibit change:

> One unexpected consequence of this relatively high level of income is that it substantially increases the recurrent costs of any educational reform that requires increasing the number of teachers.

Specifically, Brown referred to an estimate in Hong Kong's Education Commission Report No.5 (1992, p.7), which had observed that the cost of adding one non-graduate teacher to each primary and secondary school would be HK$330 million a year; and the additional cost of a graduate teacher would of course have been higher still.

Other Models of Stability and Change in Education

The Thomas & Postlethwaite framework for analysis of stability and change in education has been employed here because it is convenient, helpful, and relatively easy to comprehend. Also, it was originally designed specifically for analysis of East Asia, including Hong Kong and Macau. As noted at the beginning of this chapter, however, it is certainly not the only model that could be used. Indeed some readers may not even consider it the most appropriate, perhaps feeling that parts of the model are simplistic and that important components of stability and change are not captured by the model.

It would be impossible to review all the alternative models; and indeed it is impossible here even to review all of the major ones. However, specific mention should be made of the work of Margaret Archer (e.g. 1984, 1995), first because it has considerable significance in evolving theoretical understanding of the subject, and second because it was an explicit basis for part of Tang's chapter in the present book.

Tang's chapter presented only a short commentary on the potential contribution of Archer's theory, which he linked to the work of such other scholars as Bernstein and Bourdieu in a section entitled "Proposing a Conceptual Framework for Further Analysis". However, Tang has developed this theme elsewhere with specific reference to Macau (Tang 1999). Tang's elaboration contributes also to an understanding of Hong Kong, as well as of other societies.

For some readers, Archer's framework, rather in contrast to the framework presented by Thomas & Postlethwaite, suffers from complexity and opaqueness. It was developed within the sociological domain, and uses both concepts and vocabulary which are not easy for non-sociologists to understand. Even Tang (1999), in a scholarly thesis of which the main text (i.e. excluding annexes) had 258 pages, felt (p.50) that he could not summarise the theory unmistakably within a few pages. The fact that even fewer pages are devoted to it here underlines the need for readers who wish to explore the topic thoroughly to go to Tang's more extended treatment and, more directly, to Archer's own books.

Nevertheless, for present purposes at least a few dimensions should be highlighted. First, for the present book which was conceived explicitly within the framework of comparative education, it is useful to note that Archer's own work arose from cross-national investigation. Her 1979 book drew particularly on analysis of Denmark, England, France and Russia. Second, referring back to the methodological observations of the previous chapter, Archer made explicit use of comparisons over time as well as over location. However, Archer also stressed (1984, p.14) that her analysis applied only to countries in which macroscopic change emerged autonomously; and not to settings where it can be attributed to external intervention via conquest, colonisation or territorial redistribution. Examination of the ways in which Archer's models do or do not apply to other settings is one way to develop her theories and to test the validity of some pro-positions.

The basic questions addressed by Archer (1984, p.1) were similar to those addressed by Thomas & Postlethwaite. First, she asked, why does education have the particular structure, relations to society and internal properties which characterise it at any given time? The basic answer was held to be very simple: education has the characteristics it does have because of the goals pursued by those who control it. The second question Archer asked was why these characteristics change. The basic answer was equally simple: change occurs because new goals are pursued by those who have the power to modify education's previous structural form, definition of instruction, and relationship to society. However, Archer then proceeded to show that these answers have deceptive simplicity. Yet although the real answers are more complex, she added, they supplement rather than contradict the simple answers. Archer emphasised (1984, p.2) that "to understand the nature of education at any one time, we need to know not only who won the struggle for control, but also how: not merely who lost, but also how badly they lost out".

Archer's overall concern, as highlighted in the title of her 1984 book, was not so much with educational processes as with educational systems. While many analysts now take the existence of systems for granted, Archer pointed out (1984, p.3) that educational systems were rare before the 18th century. They emerged within complex social structures and cultures, which Archer set out to study. She identified two cycles of evolution in education systems in which the starting point of the first cycle was a collection of privately-owned schools which were gradually brought together into a relatively unified system. The second cycle commenced with the existence of state systems, and showed a range of patterns in which some moved towards centralisation while others moved towards decentralisation.

The focus on systems brings out, once more, the idiosyncratic nature of Macau, in particular. Despite the fact that few countries had educational systems before the 18th century, by the early and mid- 20th century few countries and even colonial territories did not have them. As noted by Adamson & Li's chapter, a key date in the construction of Hong Kong's dominant education system was the passage of the 1913 Education Ordinance, which gave the government's Education Department power over, and some responsibility for, a large group of private schools which had previously operated independently (Sweeting 1990, pp.220-221, 284-288). Macau only reached what may be considered an equivalent stage in 1991 with the passage of a comparable law (Government of Macau 1991). As a result, even up to the late 1990s Macau's situation corresponded to a pattern which most other parts of the world had passed decades or even centuries previously. Changes in Hong Kong, by contrast, were more easily comparable to patterns in other relatively mature education systems, with significant (though not entirely linear or consistent) moves to reduce the role of the state.

In this connection, it is also useful to note the work of Green (1990), who explored relationships between education and state formation. Green considered Archer's descriptive typology of different educational structures to be "the most powerful comparative framework that has yet been produced" (Green 1990, p.73). However, he added, for all its sophistication and comparative insight, Archer's study was missing a crucial dimension. He observed (p.75) that in England and France, and also in countries which were not included in Archer's study, "it was not only the nature of group conflict which determined educational change, but also the nature of the state and the relation of classes in civil society to the state". While this statement emphasises change, it also has relevance to continuity and non-change.

While the present book has not made relationships with the state a central theme, the matter has been addressed directly and indirectly by several authors. Green's 1990 book was mainly concerned with England, France and the USA; and while a subsequent work (Green 1997) broadened his scope to consider other parts of the world including Asia, Green was necessarily constrained in the extent to which he could examine all dimensions that could be relevant to Macau and Hong Kong. One of the threads running through the present work has been the relationship between education and the colonial state in Macau and Hong Kong. The fact that both were colonies of European powers led to considerable commonalities, e.g. in the role of Christian churches and the introduction of European languages. On the other hand, differences in the orientations of the Portuguese and British colonial regimes were among the major reasons for differences in the nature of educational provision in Macau and Hong Kong.

At the same time, the prospect of reunification with China brought a third state actor to the fore. This affected both territories in comparable ways, creating pressures on the one hand to consolidate local identity during the years prior to the change of sovereignty, and on the other hand to find ways to promote values in the local populations which would be harmonious with dominant values espoused by leaders in the PRC. This must necessarily be seen as a long-term process, requiring decades rather than years; and much will depend on how mainland China evolves as well as how Hong Kong and Macau evolve. In the meantime, some observers argued that mainland China was a recolonising force (Law 1997); and although the operation of 'One Country, Two Systems' seemed to be working well, the shadow of Beijing was felt to be never far from policy-makers' minds.

Running alongside these developments have been forces of economic globalisation which have impacted on curricula and labour-market attributes (Spring 1998). Globalisation has become what Ilon (1997, p.609) calls the "silent partner" in the process of educational planning:

> While a global system of production may seem at first blush only vaguely linked to the classroom or educational policy, the distance between them is an illusion. The parameters established by this emerging system pervade every aspect of formal institutional, financial, and social systems. In fact, the global economic system directly influences the opportunities for employment, wage rates, the ability of governments to fund public services, and the returns individuals face when investing in schooling. As these very basic parameters change, so too do the systems by which education is organized.

Schools in Hong Kong and Macau have come to resemble each other not only in part because they also resemble schools in almost all other parts of the world. Williams (1997, p.119) points out that almost all over the world, schools are now basically similar in their functions and organisation. They house groups of students who sit in rows, holding books and facing a single teacher who stands in front of a black or green chalkboard and teaches or tests the ideas found in the books. As noted by Adamson & Li, the schools of Hong Kong and Macau do exhibit traditions derived from their Chinese cultural ancestry as well as from imported models; but in basic organisation and function, the schools fit closely to a model which has become globalised and which is affected by transnational economic forces as well as by local ones.

However, as shown by such authors as Gopinathan (1997) and Green (1997), the power of globalisation does not always overwhelm that of the state. This is especially evident in mainland China, where the state remains strong and central policy-makers still feel able to manipulate variables within the borders of the nation. It is also evident in Hong Kong and Macau, where the policies of central government certainly do have an effect on the nature of educational provision. For reasons such as this, fascinating domains for continuing research will include the relationships between the local state as evidenced by the governments of the Macau and Hong Kong Special Administrative Regions, the nation state in the shape of the People's Republic of China, and the international forces of globalisation. It seems likely that multiple forces will continue to operate, and that they will have the effect of promoting elements of continuity as well as change. Such a research agenda would fit well into the vision set out by Arnove (1999), who stressed the need to "reframe" comparative education with reference to the dialectic of the global and the local.

Conclusions

Throughout this book, analysis of change and non-change in education has been linked to patterns in the wider environments. This approach is among the strong traditions in the field of comparative education, and is among the contributions which the field can make to areas of educational studies which tend to be focused more narrowly. The importance of wider environments has been stressed by key figures in comparative education since the early history of the field. In the much-quoted words of Sadler (original 1900, reprinted 1964, p.310):

> In studying foreign systems of Education we should not forget that the things outside the schools matter even more than the things inside the schools, and govern and interpret the things inside.

And in the words of another pioneer in the field, Kandel (1933, p.xxi):

> Educational systems are in fact colored far more by prevailing social and political concepts than by psychological theories or educational philosophies which attempt to deal with the individual as an isolated personality.

Taking two particular societies as its main focus, and juxtaposing developments in those societies over a period of time, this particular book has been able to analyse many of the determinants and outcomes of continuity and change. As indicated in the Introduction to the book, Hong Kong and Macau make a particularly good pair for such comparative analysis because they have so much in common as well as some significant differences. Parts of this book have taken Hong Kong and Macau as a pair for comparison and contrast with other parts of the world as well as for comparison and contrast with each other. The editors and authors hope that the book will stimulate more work of this kind, deepening the analysis and exploring further dimensions that could not be covered here.

Notes on the Authors

Bob ADAMSON is an Associate Professor in the Department of Curriculum Studies and an Executive Committee member of the Comparative Education Research Centre at the University of Hong Kong. He teaches and publishes in the fields of English language teaching, curriculum studies and comparative education, with particular reference to the Chinese mainland and to Hong Kong. A consultant to the Ministry of Education of the PRC, he is working on textbook and teacher education projects related to the national English curriculum in Chinese secondary schools. *Correspondence*: Comparative Education Research Centre, The University of Hong Kong, Pokfulam Road, Hong Kong, China. E-mail: badamson@hkusua.hku.hk.

Mark BRAY is Director of the Comparative Education Research Centre and a Professor in the Department of Education at the University of Hong Kong. He previously taught in secondary schools in Kenya and Nigeria, and at the Universities of Edinburgh, Papua New Guinea and London. He has published extensively on aspects of the administration and financing of education, and on methodology in comparative education. In 1998 he was elected President of the Comparative Education Society of Hong Kong for a two-year period. He is the Asia-Pacific Editor of the *International Journal of Educational Development*. He is also Assistant Secretary General of the World Council of Comparative Education Societies. *Correspondence*: Comparative Education Research Centre, The University of Hong Kong, Pokfulam Road, Hong Kong, China. E-mail: mbray@ hku.hk.

HUI Kwok Fai, Philip is a Lecturer in the Department of Educational Studies at the Hong Kong Institute of Education. He previously taught at the University of Macau. He holds a doctorate in comparative education from the State University of New York at Buffalo. He is now the Team Leader of the project on the Preparation of a Code of Practice on Education under the Disability Discrimination Ordinance for the Equal Opportunity Commission. He has co-edited a book entitled *Reform of Educational Systems and Teacher Education: Asian Experience*. His current research focuses on policy studies in education, global studies in education, equal educational opportunity and IT in constructive learning. *Correspondence*: Department of Educational Studies, 10 Lo Ping Road, Tai Po, New Territories, Hong Kong, China. E-mail: phui@ied.edu.hk.

KOO Ding Yee, Ramsey is a Senior Lecturer in the Department of Educational Studies at the Hong Kong Institute of Education. He is also President of the Association for Childhood Education International (ACEI) Hong Kong & Macau Branch. He received his doctorate from the University of San Francisco, and was an Assistant Professor at Lincoln University in California during 1980-86.

From 1993 to 1995 he was Director of the Educational Research Centre at the University of Macau. In 1999 he was awarded by the Macau Government the Macau Curriculum Evaluation Project on civic education, social studies, mathematics, and visual arts and crafts. His research interests include education and society in Hong Kong and Macau, anthropological foundations in education, astronomy education, and academic achievement of Chinese-Americans in the United States. *Correspondence*: Department of Educational Studies, The Hong Kong Institute of Education, 10 Lo Ping Road, Tai Po, New Territories, Hong Kong, China. E-mail: rkoo@ied.edu.hk.

Kwo Wai Yu, Ora is an Associate Professor in the Department of Curriculum Studies at the University of Hong Kong. She has a particular interest in the theory and practice of teacher education, and is a member of the Executive Committee of the International Study Association on Teacher Thinking. In 1999 she was awarded a Universitas 21 fellowship for the study of links between teaching and research at the University of British Columbia, Canada. *Correspondence*: Department of Curriculum Studies, The University of Hong Kong, Pokfulam Road, Hong Kong, China. E-mail: wykwo@hku.hk.

Leung Kit Fun, Beatrice is an Associate Professor in the Department of Politics & Sociology of Lingnan University. She is the author of over 30 scholarly articles on various aspects of church-state relations, religious policy and religious education in China, Hong Kong SAR and Macau. She is also the author/editor of five books. *Correspondence*: Department of Politics & Sociology, Lingnan University, Tuen Mun, Hong Kong, China. E-mail: leungbea@ln.edu.hk.

Li Siu Pang, Titus is a Lecturer in the Faculty of Education at the University of Macau. He is also the co-ordinator of the primary teacher education course. He previously taught in primary and secondary schools in Hong Kong. His research interests include juvenile delinquency, comparative education, home-school links, special education and teacher education. *Correspondence*: Faculty of Education, University of Macau, P.O. Box 3001, Macau, China. E-mail: fedspl@umac.mo.

Lo Yiu Chun, Jennifer is a Senior Lecturer in the Department of Curriculum & Instruction at the Hong Kong Institute of Education. Prior to joining the Institute, she taught in the Faculty of Education at the University of Macau. Her research interests include curriculum reform, curriculum implementation, and interdisciplinary/cross-curricular studies. *Correspondence*: Department of Curriculum & Instruction, The Hong Kong Institute of Education, 10 Lo Ping Road, Tai Po, New Territories, Hong Kong, China. E-mail: yclo@ied.edu.hk.

Ma Hing Tong, William is a School Development Officer in the Hong Kong Accelerated Schools Project at the Faculty of Education of the Chinese University of Hong Kong. From the mid-1970s to the mid-1990s, he was a primary and secondary school teacher in Hong Kong. He then taught at the Hong Kong Polytechnic and the University of Macau, and served as a research fellow in Monash University (Australia) and the Chinese University of Hong Kong. His research interests include the costs and benefits of higher education, higher education and the labour force, environmental education, mathematics and science education, and special education. *Correspondence*: Accelerated Schools Project, Faculty of Education, The Chinese University of Hong Kong, Shatin, Hong Kong, China. E-mail: htma@cuhk.edu.hk.

Poon Lai Man, Helen is a Lecturer in the Department of the Educational Studies at the

Hong Kong Institute of Education. She obtained her Masters degree in International & Comparative Education from Indiana University, and is now a doctoral student at the University of Toronto. She has co-authored a report titled *A Study of the Adjustment Problems of Primary-one Students in Shatin*. Her research interests are in comparative education, gender, and teacher thinking. *Correspondence:* Department of Educational Studies, 10 Lo Ping Road, New Territories, Hong Kong, China. E-mail: hpoon@ied.edu.hk.

TAN Kang, John is Principal of Valtorta College. For his doctoral work at the University of Hong Kong, he studied Church-State relations during the period of Hong Kong's colonial transition. He also holds an MEd degree from the University of Hong Kong. Among his other posts of responsibility is the vice-chairmanship of the Liberal Studies Subject Committee of the Hong Kong Examinations Authority. *Correspondence*: Valtorta College, D.D.6, Lot 1822, Tai Po, Hong Kong, China. E-mail: johnktan@hotmail.com.

TANG Kwok Chun is an Assistant Professor in the Department of Education Studies at the Hong Kong Baptist University. He was born in Macau, and moved to Hong Kong when he was aged eight. He was a secondary mathematics teacher from 1983 to 1993 in Hong Kong. Subsequently he taught at the University of Hong Kong and the Open University of Hong Kong. His PhD study for the University of Hong Kong focuses on the stability and change of secondary school mathematics knowledge in Macau. His research interests include curriculum studies, sociology of knowledge, and mathematics teaching and learning. *Correspondence*: Department of Education Studies, Hong Kong Baptist University, Waterloo Road, Kowloon, Hong Kong, China. E-mail: kctang@hkbu.edu.hk.

TSE Kwan Choi, Thomas is an Assistant Professor in the Department of Educational Administration and Policy at the Chinese University of Hong Kong. He teaches and publishes in the fields of civic education, youth studies and sociology of education. He is currently working on a comparative study of civic education in mainland China, Taiwan, Hong Kong and Macau. *Correspondence*: Department of Educational Administration & Policy, The Chinese University of Hong Kong, Shatin, Hong Kong, China. E-mail: kctse@cuhk.edu.hk.

WONG Ngai Chun, Margaret is a Senior Lecturer in the School of Early Childhood Education at the Hong Kong Institute of Education. She previously worked for the Faculty of Education at the University of Macau, where she was co-ordinator of pre-school teacher education programmes. Her current research focuses on the assessment of pre-school programme quality, the project approach in pre-schools, and comparative studies of early childhood education. *Correspondence*: School of Early Childhood Education, The Hong Kong Institute of Education, 10 Lo Ping Road, Tai Po, New Territories, Hong Kong, China. E-mail: mwong@ied.edu.hk.

YUNG Man Sing, Andrew is a Guest Lecturer at the Hong Kong Institute of Education. He previously taught in secondary and evening schools, and served as an educational administrator in two school sponsoring bodies, namely Sik Sik Yuen and Tung Wah Group of Hospitals. His research interests include higher education, comparative education, economics of education, and educational administration. *Correspondence*: Department of Educational Studies, The Hong Kong Institute of Education, 10 Lo Ping Road, Tai Po, New Territories, Hong Kong, China. E-mail: andyyung@hk.super.net.

References

Adamson, Bob & Auyeung Lai, Winnie (1997): 'Language and the Curriculum in Hong Kong: Dilemmas of Triglossia', in Bray, Mark & Lee, Wing On (eds.), *Education and Political Transition: Implications of Hong Kong's Change of Sovereignty*. Hong Kong: Comparative Education Research Centre, The University of Hong Kong, pp.87-100.

Adamson, Bob & Morris, Paul (1998): 'Primary Schooling in Hong Kong', in Moyles, Janet & Hargreaves, Linda (eds.), *The Primary Curriculum: Learning from International Perspectives*. London: Routledge, pp.181-204.

Agelasto, Michael & Adamson, Bob (1998): 'Editors' Introduction', in Agelasto, Michael & Adamson, Bob (eds.), *Higher Education in Post-Mao China*. Hong Kong: Hong Kong University Press, pp.1-10.

Ahamad, Bashir & Blaug, Mark (1973): *The Practice of Manpower Forecasting*. Amsterdam: Elsevier Scientific Publishing Company.

Almond, G.A. & Verba, S. (1963): *The Civic Culture*. Princeton, NJ: Princeton University Press.

Altbach, Philip G. (1987): 'The Oldest Technology: Textbooks in Comparative Context'. *Compare*, Vol.17, No.2, pp.93-106.

Altbach, Philip G. & Kelly, Gail P. (eds.) (1978): *Education and Colonialism*. New York: Longman.

Altbach, Philip G. & Kelly, Gail P. (eds.) (1984): *Education and the Colonial Experience*. New Brunswick: Transaction Books.

Altbach, Philip G. & Kelly, Gail P. (eds.) (1988): *Textbooks in the Third World: Policy, Content and Context*. New York: Garland.

Altbach, Philip G. & Kelly, Gail P. (eds.) (1991): *Education and the Colonial Experience*. Revised 2nd edition. New York: Advent Books.

Anon. (1991): *World History*, Vol.2. Beijing: Renmin Jiaoyu Publishing Press. [in Chinese]

Anon. (1992): *World History*, Vol.3. Beijing: Renmin Jiaoyu Publishing Press. [in Chinese]

Apple, Michael (1990): *Ideology and the Curriculum*. 2nd Edition. London: Routledge.

Archer, Margaret Scotford (1979): *Social Origins of Educational Systems*. London: Sage Publications.

Archer, Margaret Scotford (1981): 'Educational Systems'. *International Social Science Journal*, Vol.33, No.2, pp.261-284.

Archer, Margaret Scotford (1983): 'Process without System'. *Archives Européennes de Sociologie*, Vol.24, No.1083, pp.196-221.

Archer, Margaret Scotford (1984): *Social Origins of Educational Systems*. University

Edition, London: Sage.

Archer, Margaret Scotford (1993): 'Bourdieu's Theory of Cultural Reproduction: French or Universal?' *French Cultural Studies*, Vol.3, No.12, pp.225-240.

Archer, Margaret Scotford (1995): *Realist Social Theory: The Morphogenetic Approach*. Cambridge: Cambridge University Press.

Arnove, Anthony K. & Arnove, Robert F. (1997): 'A Reassessment of Education, Language, and Cultural Imperialism: British Colonialism in India and Africa', in Cummings, William K. & McGinn, Noel F. (eds.), *International Handbook of Education and Development: Preparing Schools, Students and Nations for the Twenty-First Century*. Oxford: Pergamon Press, pp.87-101.

Arnove, Robert F. (1999): 'Introduction – Reframing Comparative Education: The Dialectic of the Global and the Local', in Arnove, Robert F. & Torres, Carlos Alberto (eds.), *Comparative Education: The Dialectic of the Global and the Local*. Lanham, MD: Rowman & Littlefield, pp.1-23.

Ashby, Eric (1966): *Universities: British, Indian, African – A Study in the Ecology of Higher Education*. London: Weidenfeld & Nicholson.

Ashworth, John (1997): 'A Waste of Time? Private Rates of Return to Higher Education in the 1990s'. *Higher Education Quarterly*, Vol.51, No.2, pp.164-188.

Asiwaju, A.I. (1975): 'Formal Education in Western Yorubaland, 1889-1960: A Comparison of the French and British Colonial Systems'. *Comparative Education Review*, Vol.19, No.3, pp.434-450.

Australia, Bureau of Statistics (1994): *Labour Force Status & Educational Attainment, Australia, Feb. 1994*. Canberra: Australian Government Publishing Service.

Australia, Department of Employment, Education, Training & Youth Affairs (1997): *Overseas Student Statistics 1996*. Canberra: Australian Government Publishing Service.

Auyeung, W.Y. (1991): *Civic Education in Geography Teaching in Lower Forms of Secondary Schools in Hong Kong*. M.Ed. dissertation, University of Stirling.

Ball, Christopher (1994): *Start Right: The Importance of Early Learning*. London: Royal Society for the Encouragement of Arts, Manufactures & Commerce.

Ball, Stephen J. (1983): 'Imperialism, Social Control and the Colonial Curriculum in Africa'. *Journal of Curriculum Studies*, Vol.15, No.3, pp.237-263.

Barnett, Ronald (1994): *The Limits of Competence: Knowledge, Higher Education and Society*. Buckingham: The Society for Research into Higher Education & Open University Press.

Barnett, W.S., Frede, E.C. & Mobasher, H. (1987): 'The Efficacy of Public Pre-school Programs and the Relationship of Program Quality to Efficacy'. *Education Evaluation and Policy Analysis*, Vol.10, No.1, pp.37-49.

Becker, Gary S. (1964): *Human Capital: A Theoretical and Empirical Analysis, with Special Reference to Education*. Chicago: University of Chicago Press.

Becker, Gary S. (1975): *Human Capital: A Theoretical and Empirical Analysis, with Special Reference to Education*. 2nd edition. Princeton: Princeton University Press.

Bennell, Paul (1996): 'Using and Abusing Rates of Return: A Critique of the World Bank's 1995 Education Sector Review'. *International Journal of Educational Development*, Vol.16, No.3, pp.235-248.

Bennell, Paul (1998): 'Rates of Return to Education in Asia: A Review of the Evidence'. *Education Economics,* Vol.6, No.2, pp.107-120.

Bereday, George Z.F. (1964): *Comparative Method in Education*. New York: Holt,

Rinehart & Winston.

Bickley, Gillian (1997): *The Golden Needle: The Biography of Frederick Stewart (1836-1889).* Hong Kong: David C. Lam Institute for East-West Studies, Hong Kong Baptist University.

Bielas, Léon (1973): 'Comparison of Systems of Education in Two Countries with Common Historical Traditions and Different Social Orders: The German Democratic Republic and the Federal Republic of Germany', in Edwards, R., Holmes, B. & van de Graaf, J. (eds.), *Relevant Methods in Comparative Education.* Hamburg: Unesco Institute for Education, pp.143-149.

Biggs, John (1996): 'The Assessment Scene in Hong Kong', in Biggs, John (ed.), *Testing: To Educate or To Select?* Hong Kong: Hong Kong Educational Publishing Company.

Blakemore, Kenneth & Cooksey, Brian (1980): *A Sociology of Education for Africa.* London: George Allen & Unwin.

Blaug, Mark (1970): *An Introduction to the Economics of Education.* London: Penguin.

Bond, Michael Harris (1991): *Beyond the Chinese Face: Insights from Psychology.* Hong Kong: Oxford University Press.

Bourke, S. (1994): 'Some Responses to Changes in Australian Education', *Australian Educational Researcher,* Vol.21, No.1, pp.1-18.

Boutilier, J.A. (1978): 'Missions, Administration and Education in the Solomon Islands 1893-1942', in Boutilier, J.A., Hughes, D.T. & Tiffany, S.W. (eds.), *Mission, Church and Sect in Oceania.* Lanham, MD: University Press of America, pp.139-161.

Bowman, Frank (1936): *Elementary Calculus.* London: Longman.

Bray, Mark (1992a): 'Colonialism, Scale and Politics: Divergence and Convergence of Educational Development in Hong Kong and Macau'. *Comparative Education Review,* Vol.36, No.3, pp.322-342.

Bray, Mark (1992b): 'Centralisation versus Decentralisation in Curriculum Development: Contrasting Patterns in Hong Kong and Macau'. *New Horizons,* No.33, pp.15-23.

Bray, Mark (1992c): *Educational Planning in Small Countries.* Paris: UNESCO.

Bray, Mark (1993): 'Financing Higher Education: A Comparison of Government Strategies in Hong Kong and Macau', in Bray, Mark (ed.), *The Economics and Financing of Education: Hong Kong and Comparative Perspectives.* Education Paper No.20, Hong Kong: Faculty of Education, The University of Hong Kong, pp.32-50.

Bray, Mark (1994): 'Decolonisation and Education: New Paradigms for the Remnants of Empire'. *Compare,* Vol.24, No.1, pp.37-51.

Bray, Mark (1995a): 'Macau', in Morris, Paul & Sweeting, Anthony (eds.), *Education and Development in East Asia.* New York: Garland, pp.185-201.

Bray, Mark (1995b): 'The Quality of Education in Private Schools: Historical Patterns and the Impact of Recent Policies', in Siu, Ping Kee & Tam, Tim Kui, Peter (eds.), *Quality in Education: Insights from Different Perspectives.* Hong Kong: Hong Kong Educational Research Association, pp.183-198.

Bray, Mark (1996): 'Educational Reform in a Small State: Bhutan's New Approach to Primary Education'. *International Journal of Educational Reform,* Vol.5, No.1, pp.15-25.

Bray, Mark (1997a): 'Education and Decolonization: Comparative Perspectives on Change and Continuity', in Cummings, William K. & McGinn, Noel F. (eds.), *International Handbook of Education and Development: Preparing Schools, Students and Nations for the Twenty-First Century*. Oxford: Pergamon Press, pp.103-118.

Bray, Mark (1997b): 'Education and the Labour Market', in Postiglione, Gerard A. & Lee, Wing On (eds.), *Schooling in Hong Kong: Organization, Teaching and Social Context*. Hong Kong: Hong Kong University Press, pp.43-63.

Bray, Mark (1997c): 'Education and Colonial Transition: The Hong Kong Experience in Comparative Perspective', in Bray, Mark & Lee, Wing On (eds.), *Education and Political Transition: Implications of Hong Kong's Change of Sovereignty*. Hong Kong: Comparative Education Research Centre, The University of Hong Kong, pp.11-23.

Bray, Mark (1998a): 'Education and Political Transition in Hong Kong and Macau: A Comparative Analysis', in Ramos, R., Dinis, J.R., Wilson, R. & Yuan, D.Y. (eds.), *Macau and its Neighbors toward the 21st Century*. Macau: University of Macau and Macau Foundation, pp.199-209.

Bray, Mark (1998b): 'Regional Examinations Councils and Geopolitical Change: Commonality, Diversity, and Lessons from Experience'. *International Journal of Educational Development*, Vol.18, No.6, pp.473-486.

Bray, Mark (1998c): 'Privatisation of Schooling: Strategies and Policy Implications in Less Developed Countries', in Aggarwal, Yash & Premi, Kusum K. (eds.), *Reforming School Education: Issues in Policy Planning and Implementation*. New Delhi: Vikas Publishing House, pp.275-299.

Bray, Mark, Clarke, Peter B. & Stephens, David (1986): *Education and Society in Africa*. London: Edward Arnold.

Bray, Mark & Hui, Philip Kwok Fai (1991a): 'Curriculum Development in Macau', in Marsh, Colin J. & Morris, Paul (eds.), *Curriculum Development in East Asia*. London: Falmer Press, pp.181-201.

Bray, Mark & Hui, Philip Kwok Fai (1991b): 'Structure and Content of Education', in Cremer, R.D. (ed.), *Macau: City of Commerce and Culture – Continuity and Change*. 2nd edition. Hong Kong: API Press, pp.299-313.

Bray, Mark & Ieong, Pedro (1996): 'Education and Social Change: The Growth and Diversification of the International Schools Sector in Hong Kong'. *International Education*, Vol.25, No.2, pp.49-73.

Bray, Mark & Lee, Wing On (1993): 'Education, Democracy and Colonial Transition: The Case of Hong Kong'. *International Review of Education*, Vol.39, No.6, pp.541-560.

Bray, Mark & Lee, Wing On (eds.) (1997): *Education and Political Transition: Implications of Hong Kong's Change of Sovereignty*. Hong Kong: Comparative Education Research Centre, The University of Hong Kong.

Bray, Mark & Packer, Steve (1993): *Education in Small States: Concepts, Challenges and Strategies*. Oxford: Pergamon Press.

Bray, Mark & Tang, Kwok Chun (1994a): 'Imported Textbooks, Non-interventionist Policies and School Curricula in Macau'. *Curriculum and Teaching*, Vol.9, No.2, pp.29-43.

Bray, Mark & Tang, Kwok Chun (1994b): 'Comparative Education in a Microcosm: Diversity and Evolution of Secondary School Curricula in Macau'. *Educational*

Research Journal [Hong Kong], Vol.9, No.1, pp.5-14.

Bray, Mark & Thomas, R. Murray (1995): 'Levels of Comparison in Educational Studies: Different Insights from Different Literatures and the Value of Multilevel Analyses'. *Harvard Educational Review*, Vol.65, No.3, pp.472-490.

Brimer, Alan & Griffin, Patrick (1985): *Mathematics Achievement in Hong Kong Secondary Schools*. Hong Kong: Centre of Asian Studies, The University of Hong Kong.

Brock, Colin & Parker, Roy (1985): 'School and Community in Situations of Close Proximity: The Question of Small States', in Lillis, Kevin (ed.), *School and Community in Less Developed Areas*. London: Croom Helm, pp.42-56.

Brock, Colin & Tulasiewicz, Witold (1988): 'Western Christianity, Educational Provision and National Identity: An Editorial Introduction', in Brock, Colin & Tulasiewicz, Witold (eds.), *Christianity and Educational Provision in International Perspective*. London: Routledge, pp.1-16.

Bronfenbrenner, U. (1992): 'Ecological Systems Theory', in Vasta, Ross (ed.), *Six Theories of Child Development: Revised Formulations and Current Issues.* London: Jessica Kingsley, pp.187-250.

Brown, Hubert O. (1997): 'Teachers and Teaching', in Postiglione, Gerard A. & Lee, Wing On (eds.), *Schooling in Hong Kong: Organization, Teaching and Social Context*. Hong Kong: Hong Kong University Press, pp.95-116.

Bruning, Harald (1999): 'Macau Jobless Rate Doubles as GDP Forecast to Decline', *South China Morning Post*, 2 February, p.6.

Budiardjo, C. & Liem, S.L. (1984): *The War Against East Timor*. London: Zed Books.

Burke, G. & Rumberger, R.W. (1987): *The Future Impact of Technology on Work and Education.* London: Falmer Press.

Burney Report (1935): *Report on Education in Hong Kong.* London: Crown Agents for the Colonies.

Carless, David R. (1998): 'Managing Systemic Curriculum Change: A Critical Analysis of Hong Kong's Target-Oriented Curriculum Initiative', in Stimpson, Philip & Morris, Paul (eds.), *Curriculum and Assessment for Hong Kong: Two Components, One System*. Hong Kong: Open University of Hong Kong Press, pp.223-244.

Carmody, B.P. (1992): *Conversion and Jesuit Schooling in Zambia*. New York: E.J. Brill.

Carnoy, Martin (1974): *Education as Cultural Imperialism.* New York: David McKay.

Carnoy, Martin (1995): 'Introduction to Section IV: Education, Economic Growth, and Technological Change', in Carnoy, Martin (ed.), *International Encyclopedia of Economics of Education*. 2nd edition. Oxford: Pergamon Press, pp.191-192.

Carnoy, Martin (1996): 'Universities, Technological Change, and Training in the Information Age', in Salmi, Jamil & Verspoor, Adriaan (eds.), *Revitalizing Higher Education*. Oxford: Pergamon Press, pp.41-91.

Castelnuovo, Emma (1989): 'The Teaching of Geometry in Italian High Schools during the Last Two Centuries: Some Aspects Related to Society', in Keitel, Christine (ed.), *Mathematics, Education, and Society.* Paris: UNESCO, pp.51-52.

Chan, Che Po & Leung, Beatrice (1996): 'The Voting Behaviour of Hong Kong Catholics in the 1995 Legislative Council Election', in Kuan, H.C., Lau, S.K., Louie, K.S. & Wong, K.Y. (eds.), *The 1995 Legislative Council Elections in Hong Kong.* Hong Kong: Institute of Asia-Pacific Studies, The Chinese University of

Hong Kong, pp.275-314.

Chan, K.I. (1991): *Special Publication for the 65th Anniversary of St. Joseph's College.* Macau: St. Joseph's College. [in Chinese]

Chan, K.W. (1992): *Footprints of the Trailblazers: 300 Years of Chinese Education Overseas.* Toronto: Royal Kingsway Inc. [in Chinese]

Chan, Y.Y. (ed.) (1993): *The Present State of Development in Macau.* Hong Kong: Wide Angle. [in Chinese]

Chan, Y.Y. (ed.) (1995): *Social Problems in Macau.* Hong Kong: Wide Angle. [in Chinese]

Chang, Jaw-ling Joanne (1988): *Settlement of the Macao Issue: Distinctive Features of Beijing's Negotiating Behavior (with text of 1887 protocol and 1987 declaration).* Baltimore: University of Maryland.

Chapple, Christopher (1993): 'Introduction', in Chapple, Christopher (ed.), *The Jesuit Tradition in Education and Missions: A 450-Year Perspective.* Scranton: University of Scranton Press, pp.1-18.

Chen, E. (1994): 'The Present Situation and Problems in Macau's Education'. Paper presented in International Conference on Chinese Education in Southeast Asia, 6-8 June.

Cheng, Christina Miu Bing (1999): *Macau: A Cultural Janus.* Hong Kong: Hong Kong University Press.

Cheng, Joseph Y.S. (1995): 'Higher Education in Hong Kong: The Approach to 1997 and the China Factor'. *Higher Education*, Vol.30, No.4, pp.257-271.

Cheng, Kai Ming (1992a): *Educational Reform in China.* Hong Kong: Commercial Press. [in Chinese]

Cheng, Kai Ming (1992b): 'Educational Policymaking in Hong Kong: The Changing Legitimacy', in Postiglione, Gerard A. with Leung, Julian Y.M. (eds.), *Education and Society in Hong Kong: Toward One Country and Two Systems.* Hong Kong: Hong Kong University Press, pp.97-116.

Cheng, Kai Ming (1997a): 'Realise the Weakness of the Present Education System and Make Necessary Innovation to Catch up with Asian Countries'. *Shun Pao,* 6 November. [in Chinese]

Cheng, Kai Ming (1997b): 'Hong Kong Education in Retrospect', in Wang, Gungwu (ed.), *Hong Kong History: New Perspectives,* Vol.II. Hong Kong: Joint Publishing Company, pp.465-491. [in Chinese]

Cheng, Kai Ming (1998): 'The University in School and Community – New Challenges and New Roles'. Keynote Paper at the ASAIHL Conference, Brunei Darussalam 12-14 November.

Cheng, T.C. (1949): *The Education of Overseas Chinese: A Comparative Study of Hong Kong, Singapore and the East Indies.* M.A. thesis, University of London.

Cheong, C.M., Lai, I.M. & Vong, S.K. (1992): 'A Comparison of Education between Hong Kong and Macau, and Preview of their Prospects.' Paper presented at the 9th Annual Conference of the Hong Kong Educational Research Association. [in Chinese]

Cheong, Pak Lin (1991): 'Relationships between School Autonomy and Government Administration', in Wong, Hon Keong (ed.), *Education Reform in Macau.* Macau: Centre of Macau Studies, University of East Asia, pp.115-119. [in Chinese]

Cheung, Anthony B.L. (1991): 'The Civil Service', in Sung, Yun Wing & Lee, Ming Kwan (eds.), *The Other Hong Kong Report 1991.* Hong Kong: The Chinese University Press, pp.27-54.

Cheung, C.F. (1955): *Overseas Chinese Education New Issue*. Taipei: Central Cultural Material Supplier. [in Chinese]

Cheung, C.F. (1956): *Simplified Developmental History of Culture and Education of Overseas Chinese*. Taipei: Ng Tai Publisher. [in Chinese]

Cheung, Chau Kiu & Leung, Kwan Kwok (1994): *Political Attitudes of Senior Secondary Students during the Transition Period in Hong Kong*. Hong Kong: Department of Applied Social Studies, City Polytechnic of Hong Kong.

Cheung, H.K. (1987): 'The Secondary School Chinese History Curriculum in Hong Kong over the Post War Forty Years'. *Education Journal*, Vol.15, No.2, pp.76-82. [in Chinese]

Cheung, H.K. (1990): *The Turbulent Years*. Hong Kong: Youth Book House. [in Chinese]

Cheung, Kwok Cheung (1996): 'Teacher Education in Macau: Achievements and Challenges during the Transition Period', in Ramos, R., Dinis, J.R., Wilson, R. & Yuan, D.Y. (eds.), *Macau and its Neighbours in Transition*. Macau: University of Macau & Macau Foundation, pp.339-349.

China, National Affairs Office (1996): 'The National Affairs Office's Circular to the State Education Commission and Other Departments. On Reinforcing the Work of Early Childhood Education', in Jiangsu Education Commission (ed.), *A Selection of Early Childhood Education Documents*. Jiangsu: Jiangsu Education Commission, pp.27-33.

China, People's Republic of (1982): *The Constitution of the People's Republic of China*. Beijing: Government of the People's Republic of China.

China, People's Republic of (1990): *The Basic Law of the Hong Kong Special Administrative Region of the People's Republic of China*. Hong Kong: Consultative Committee for the Basic Law of the Hong Kong Special Administrative Region of the People's Republic of China.

China, People's Republic of (1993): *Lei Básica da Região Administrativa Especial de Macau de República Popular da China*. Macau: Conselho Consultivo da Lei Básica da Região Administrativa Especial de Macau de República Popular da China.

China, State Education Commission (1996a): 'Kindergarten Management Regulations in the People's Republic of China', in Jiangsu Education Commission (ed.), *A Selection of Early Childhood Education Documents*. Jiangsu: Jiangsu Education Commission, pp.7-23.

China, State Education Commission (1996b): 'Statute of Kindergartens in the People's Republic of China', in Jiangsu Education Commission (ed.), *A Selection of Early Childhood Education Documents*. Jiangsu: Jiangsu Education Commission, pp.1-6.

Chiu, Iok San & Ng, Cheong San (1991): 'Cooperation between Guangdong and Macau in Teacher Education', in Wong, Hon Keong (ed.), *Education Reform in Macau*. Macau: Centre of Macau Studies, pp.167-169. [in Chinese]

Choi, C.C. (1991): 'Settlement of Chinese Families in Macau', in Cremer, R.D. (ed.), *Macau: City of Commerce and Culture – Continuity and Change*. 2nd edition. Hong Kong: API Press, pp.61-80.

Choi, P.K. (1995): '1997 and Decolonization', in Romaniuk, Susan & Tong, Denise K.W. (eds.), *Uncertain Times: Hong Kong Women Facing 1997*. Hong Kong:

Hong Kong Women's Christian Council, pp.27-33.

Choksi, Archana & Dyer, Caroline (1997): 'North-South Collaboration in Educational Research: Reflections on Indian Experience', in Crossley, Michael & Vulliamy, Graham (eds.), *Qualitative Educational Research in Developing Countries: Current Perspectives.* New York: Garland, pp.265-299.

Chubb, John E. & Moe, Terry M. (1990): *Politics, Markets and America's Schools.* Washington DC: The Brookings Institution.

Chung, Yue Ping (1990): 'The Expansion of Hong Kong University Education'. *Ming Pao Monthly,* Vol.25, No.3, pp.52-55. [in Chinese]

Chung, Yue Ping & Ma, Hing Tong (1997): 'The Supply of Overseas University Manpower: From Dependence to Independence'. Paper presented at the Annual Conference of the Comparative & International Education Society, Mexico City.

Clayton, Thomas (1999): *Education and the Politics of Language: Hegemony and Pragmatism in Cambodia, 1979-1989.* Hong Kong: Comparative Education Research Centre, The University of Hong Kong.

Cleverley, John (1991): *The Schooling of China: Tradition and Modernity in Chinese Education.* 2nd edition. Sydney: Allen & Unwin.

Clignet, Remi & Foster, Philip (1964): 'French and British Colonial Education in Africa'. *Comparative Education Review,* Vol.8, No.3, pp.191-198.

Collins, K.T., Downes, L.W., Griffiths, S.R. & Shaw, K.E. (1973): *Key Words in Education.* London: Longman.

Commonwealth Secretariat, The (1985): 'Educational Development for the Small States of the Commonwealth: A Review of Issues'. Paper for the Pan-Commonwealth Meeting on Educational Development for the Small States of the Commonwealth, Mauritius.

Cooper, Barry (1985): *Renegotiating Secondary School Mathematics: A Study of Curriculum Change and Stability.* London: Falmer Press.

Correia, Celina Veiga de Oliveira Eisabel (1994): *São Paulo: Historia de um Colégio.* Macau: Committee of Celebration of the Portuguese Discovery.

Cowan, L. Gray (1990): *Privatization in the Developing World.* New York: Greenwood Press.

Cowen, Robert (1998): 'Thinking Comparatively about Space, Education and Time: An Approach to the Mediterranean Rim', in Kazamias, Andreas M. & Spillane, Martin G. (eds.), *Education and the Structuring of European Space: North-South, Centre-Periphery, Identity-Otherness.* Athens: Seirios Editions, pp.61-72.

Crahay, M. (1990): *Which Research Paradigm for the IEA Longitudinal Quality of Life Study?.* Paper prepared for the preprimary study, International Association for the Evaluation of Educational Achievement. Michigan: High/Scope Education Research Foundation.

Cramer, John Francis & Browne, George Stephenson (1956): *Contemporary Education: A Comparative Study of National Systems.* New York: Harcourt, Brace & Company.

Cremer, R.D. (1991): 'From Portugal to Japan: Macau's Place in the History of World Trade', in Cremer, R.D. (ed.), *Macau: City of Commerce and Culture – Continuity and Change.* 2nd edition. Hong Kong: API Press, pp.23-38.

Crisswell, C.N. (1974): *Modern Europe 1870-1960.* Hong Kong: Longman.

Cross, Michael (1987): 'The Political Economy of Colonial Education: Mozambique, 1930-1975'. *Comparative Education Review,* Vol.31, No.4, pp.550-569.

Crossley, Michael (1999): 'Reconceptualising Comparative and International Education'. *Compare*, Vol.29, No.3, pp.225-241.

Cummings, William K. & Riddell, Abby (1994): 'Alternative Policies for the Finance, Control and Delivery of Basic Education'. *International Journal of Educational Research*, Vol.21, No.8, pp.751-776.

Curriculum Development Committee (1985): *Guidelines on Civic Education in Schools*. Hong Kong: Government Printer.

Curriculum Development Committee (1995): *The Development of Civic Awareness of Hong Kong Primary and Secondary School Students*. Hong Kong: Government Printer.

Curriculum Development Council (1984): *Guide to the Kindergarten Curriculum*. Hong Kong: Government Printer.

Curriculum Development Council (1993): *Guide to the Primary School Curriculum*. Hong Kong: Government Printer.

Curriculum Development Council (1996): *Guidelines on Civic Education in Schools*. Hong Kong: Curriculum Development Council.

Curriculum Development Institute (1993): *Guide to the Kindergarten Curriculum*. Hong Kong: Government Printer.

Curriculum Development Institute (1996): *Guide to the Pre-Primary Curriculum*. Hong Kong: Government Printer.

Curriculum Development Institute (1999): *Enhancing Learning, Knowing China – Teaching Resources*. Hong Kong: Government Printer. [in Chinese]

Curriculum Reform Group, Department of Education & Youth (1995a): *Moral and Civic Education Syllabus (Primary Education)*. Macau. [in Chinese]

Curriculum Reform Group, Department of Education & Youth (1995b): *Moral and Civic Education Syllabus (Junior Secondary Education)*. Macau. [in Chinese]

Dalin, Per (1978): *Limits to Educational Change*. Basingstoke: Macmillan.

Dearing, Ron (Chairman) (1997): *The National Committee of Inquiry into Higher Education in the United Kingdom*. London: Her Majesty's Stationery Office.

Deng, K.Z. & Lu, X.M. (1997): *Relations between Hong Kong and Guangdong 1840-1984*. Hong Kong: Qilin Press. [in Chinese]

Dove, Linda (1986): *Teachers and Teacher Education in Developing Countries: Issues in Planning, Management and Training*. London: Croom Helm.

Doyle, W. (1978): 'Student Mediating Responses in Teaching Effectiveness: An Interim Report'. Paper presented at the meeting of the American Education Research Association, Toronto.

Duffy, James (1959): *Portuguese Africa*. Cambridge: Harvard University Press.

Durell, Clement V. (1920): *Modern Geometry: The Straight Line and Circle*. London: Macmillan.

Eckstein, Max A. & Noah, Harold J. (eds.) (1992): *Examinations: Comparative and International Studies*. London: Pergamon Press.

Edmonds, R.L. (1989): 'Introduction', in Edmonds, R.L. (ed.), *Macau*. World Bibliographical Series, Vol.105. Oxford: Clio Press, pp.xxiii-xxv.

Education Commission, The (1984): *Education Commission Report No.1*. Hong Kong: Government Printer.

Education Commission, The (1986): *Education Commission Report No.2*. Hong Kong: Government Printer.

Education Commission, The (1988): *Education Commission Report No.3: The Structure of Tertiary Education and the Future of Private Schools.* Hong Kong: Government Printer.

Education Commission, The (1990): *Education Commission Report No.4: The Curriculum and Behavioural Problems in Schools.* Hong Kong: Government Printer.

Education Commission, The (1992): *Education Commission Report No.5: The Teaching Profession.* Hong Kong: Government Printer.

Education Commission, The (1995): *Education Commission Report No.6: Enhancing Language Proficiency – A Comprehensive Strategy.* Hong Kong: Government Printer.

Education Commission, The (1997): *Education Commission Report No.7: Quality School Education.* Hong Kong: Government Printer.

Educational Group of Christians for Hong Kong Society, The (1994): *Youngsters Brave the Road to Democracy.* Hong Kong: The Educational Group of Christians for Hong Kong Society. [in Chinese]

Endacott, George B. (1962): 'The Beginnings', in Harrison, Brian (ed.), *University of Hong Kong: The First 50 Years, 1911-1961.* Hong Kong: Hong Kong University Press.

Endacott, George B. (1964): *A History of Hong Kong.* Hong Kong: Oxford University Press.

Epstein, Erwin P. (1986): 'Currents Left and Right: Ideology in Comparative Education', in Altbach, Philip G. & Kelly, Gail P. (eds.), *New Approaches to Comparative Education.* Chicago: University of Chicago Press, pp.233-259.

Ernst & Young Ltd. (1996): *Hong Kong Government Student Financial Assistance Agency Report: Consultancy Study on the Local Student Finance Scheme.* Hong Kong: Ernst & Young Management Consultancy Ltd.

Errante, Antoinette (1998): 'Education and National Personae in Portugal's Colonial and Postcolonial Transition'. *Comparative Education Review*, Vol.43, No.3, pp.267-308.

Fafunwa, A. Babs & Aisiku, J.U. (eds.) (1982): *Education in Africa: A Comparative Survey.* London: George Allen & Unwin.

Fägerlind, Ingemar & Saha, Lawrence J. (1986): *Education and National Development.* Oxford: Pergamon Press.

Fan, K. (1995): 'An Examination of the Effects of Hong Kong Education Policy on Chinese Language Teaching Materials in Secondary Schools from the 1950s to 1970s', in Siu, Ping Kee & Tam, Tim Kui Peter (eds.), *Quality in Education: Insights from Different Perspectives.* Hong Kong: The Hong Kong Educational Research Association, pp.233-245. [in Chinese]

Farrell, Joseph P. (1979): 'The Necessity of Comparisons in the Study of Education: The Salience of Science and the Problem of Comparability'. *Comparative Education Review*, Vol.23, No.1, pp.3-16.

Fehr, H.F. (1970): 'Education for Change: What Change?'. *New Trends in Mathematics Teaching*, Vol.II, Paris: UNESCO, pp.199-213.

Feitor, R. & Cremer, R.D. (1991): 'Macau's Modern Economy', in Cremer, R.D. (ed.), *Macau: City of Commerce and Culture – Continuity and Change.* 2nd edition. Hong Kong: API Press, pp.202-206.

Ferreira, Hugo Gil & Marshall, Michael W. (1986): *Portugal's Revolution: Ten Years on.* Cambridge: Cambridge University Press.

Fey, J.T. (1978): 'Change in Mathematics Education since the late 1950's – Ideas and Realisation: U.S.A.'. *Educational Studies in Mathematics*, Vol.9, No.3, pp.339-353.

Fine, H.B. (1905): *College Algebra*. New York: Dover Publications.

Firth, Stewart & Darlington, Robert (1993): 'Racial Stereotypes in the Australian Curriculum: The Case-study of New South Wales', in Mangan, J.A. (ed.), *The Imperial Curriculum: Racial Images and Education in the British Colonial Experience*. London: Routledge, pp.79-92.

Fiske, Edward B. (1996): *Decentralization of Education: Politics and Consensus*. Washington DC: The World Bank.

Foley, Douglas (1984): 'Colonialism and Schooling in the Philippines, 1898-1970', in: Altbach, P. & Kelly, G. (eds.), *Education and the Colonial Experience*. New Brunswick: Transaction Books, pp.33-53.

French, Nigel (1997): *Higher Education in Hong Kong: Recent Developments and Future Challenges*. Hong Kong: University Grants Committee Internet Virtual Library, www.ugc.edu.hk.

Fry, Gerald W. (1984): 'The Economic and Political Impact of Study Abroad', in Barber, Elinor G., Altbach, Philip G. & Myers, Robert G. (eds.), *Bridges to Knowledge*. Chicago: University of Chicago Press, pp.55-72.

Fu, K.Y., Chan, Y.F. & Kuong, L.K. (1994): 'Teacher Education: Responding to the New Realities in a Changing Society', in Koo, Ramsey Ding Yee & Ma, Hing Tong (eds.), *Macau Education: Continuity and Change*. Macau: Macau Foundations, pp.100-109. [in Chinese]

Fullan, Michael (1991): 'The Nature of Curriculum Innovations', in Lewy, Arieh (ed.), *The International Encyclopedia of Curriculum*. Oxford: Pergamon Press, pp.279-280.

Fullan, Michael (1994): *Change Forces: Probing the Depths of Educational Reform*. London: Falmer Press.

Fung, H.S. (1960): *Overseas Chinese Education in Macau*. Taipei: Overseas Publication Service. [in Chinese]

Fung, P.W. (1980): *World History*. Hong Kong: Everymans Book Co. Ltd.

Fung, Y.W. & Lee, C.K. (1987): 'Development of Geographical Education in Hong Kong in Postwar Years'. *Education Journal*, Vol.15, No.2, pp.60-67. [in Chinese]

Furnivall, J.S. (1943): *Educational Progress in South East Asia*. New York: Institute of Pacific Relations.

Gifford, Prosser & Weiskel, Timothy C. (1971): 'African Education in a Colonial Context: French and British Styles', in Gifford, Prosser & Louis, William Roger (eds.), *France and Britain in Africa*. New Haven: Yale University Press, pp.663-711.

Gillespie, J. (1992): 'Trends in Secondary-School Mathematics in the United Kingdom', in Morris, R. & Arora, M.S. (eds.), *Studies in Mathematics Education*. Vol.8, Paris: UNESCO, pp.90-101.

Gimmestad, M.J. & Hall, G.E. (1995): 'Structure of Teacher Education Programs', in Anderson, Lorin W. (ed.), *International Encyclopedia of Teaching and Teacher Education*, 2nd edition, Oxford: Pergamon Press, pp.548-552.

Ginsburg, M., Cooper, S., Raghu, R. & Zegarra, H. (1990): 'National and World-system Explanations of Educational Reform'. *Comparative Education Review,* Vol.34, No.4, pp.474-499.

Giroux, Henry A. (1983): *Theory and Resistance in Education: A Pedagogy for the Politics of the Opposition.* New York: Bergin & Garvey.

Gomes dos Santos, Domingos Maurício (1968): *Macau: Primeira Universidade Occidental do Extremo-Oriente.* Lisboa: Academia Portuguesa da Historia.

Gopinathan, Saravanan (1997): 'Globalisation, the State and Education Policy in Singapore', in Lee, Wing On & Bray, Mark (eds.), *Education and Political Transition: Perspectives and Dimensions in East Asia.* Hong Kong: Comparative Education Research Centre, The University of Hong Kong, pp.68-80.

Governo de Macau (1990): *Analise Curricular no Ensino Secundario.* Macau: Direcção dos Serviços de Educação.

Granville, William Anthony (1909): *Plane and Spherical Trigonometry.* New York: Ginn.

Green, Andy (1990): *Education and State Formation: The Rise of Education Systems in England, France and the USA.* London: Macmillan.

Green, Andy (1997): *Education, Globalization and the Nation State.* London: Macmillan.

Guillen-Nuñez, Cesar (1984): *Macau.* Hong Kong: Oxford University Press.

Gunn, Geoffrey C. (1996): *Encountering Macau: a Portuguese City-State on the Periphery of China, 1557-1999.* Boulder: Westview Press.

Halls, W.D. (1990): 'Trends and Issues in Comparative Education', in Halls, W.D. (ed.), *Comparative Education: Contemporary Issues and Trends.* London: Jessica Kingsley, pp.21-65.

Hanson, E. (1978): *Catholic Politics in China and Korea.* Maryknoll, New York: Orbis Books.

Harber, Clive (1985): 'Weapon of War: Political Education in Zimbabwe'. *Journal of Curriculum Studies,* Vol.17, No.2, pp.163-174.

Harber, Clive (1989): *Political Education in Africa.* London: Macmillan.

Hargreaves, Andy (1995): *Changing Teachers, Changing Times.* London: Cassell.

Harms, T. & Clifford, R.M. (1980): *Early Childhood Environment Rating Scale.* New York: Teachers College, Columbia University.

Harris, D. (1995): 'Endogenous Learning and Economic Growth', in Carnoy, Martin (ed.), *International Encyclopedia of Economics of Education.* 2nd edition. Oxford: Pergamon Press, pp.199-204.

Harrison, Brian (1962): 'The Years of Growth', in Harrison, Brian (ed.), *University of Hong Kong: The First 50 Years, 1911-1961.* Hong Kong: Hong Kong University Press, pp.45-57.

Hassan, Mohammed Waheed (1990): 'Educational Planning in Small Countries: The Case of Maldives'. Paper presented at the UNESCO International Congress on Educational Planning & Management, Mexico City.

Havelock, R.G. (1973): *The Change Agent's Guide to Innovation in Education.* New York: Educational Technology Publications Inc.

Hawkins, John N. (1983): 'The People's Republic of China (Mainland China)', in Thomas, R. Murray & Postlethwaite, T. Neville (eds.), *Schooling in East Asia: Forces of Change.* Oxford: Pergamon Press, pp.136-187.

Hayhoe, Ruth (1984): 'The Evolution of Modern Chinese Educational Institutions', in Hayhoe, Ruth (ed.), *Contemporary Chinese Education.* London: Croom Helm, pp.26-46.

Heads of Universities Committee (HUCOM) (1998): *Working Group on Duration of Undergraduate Programmes: Consultation Document.* Hong Kong: Lingnan

College Internet Home Page, www.ln.edu.hk.

Heater, Derek Benjamin (1990): *Citizenship: The Civic Ideal in World History, Politics and Education.* London: Longman.

Heater, Derek Benjamin (1991): 'What is Citizenship?'. *Citizenship*, Vol.1, No.2, pp.3-5.

Hinchliffe, Keith (1995): 'Manpower Analysis', in Carnoy, Martin (ed.), *International Encyclopedia of Economics of Education.* 2nd edition. Oxford: Pergamon Press, pp.370-375.

Ho, S.C. (1990): *A Study of the Relationship between School Climate and the Effectiveness of Civic Education.* M.A. dissertation, The Chinese University of Hong Kong. [in Chinese]

Ho, V.O. (1997): 'Localization of Macau Civil Servants', in Wu, Z., Fung, S.W. & Ieong, W.C. (eds.), *Macau 1997.* Macau: Macau Foundation, pp.28-40.

Hok Yau Shek [Learning-mate Group] (1987): *Report on the Opinion Survey of Hong Kong Secondary Teachers on Civic Education.* Hong Kong: Hok Yau Shek. [in Chinese]

Holmes, Brian (ed.) (1967): *Educational Policy and the Mission Schools: Case Studies from the British Empire.* London: Routledge & Kegan Paul.

Hong Kong, Board of Education (1994): *Report of the Ad Hoc Sub-committee on Pre-primary Education.* Hong Kong: Board of Education.

Hong Kong, Census & Statistics Department (1996): *Quarterly Report on General Household Survey October to December 1996.* Hong Kong: Census & Statistics Department.

Hong Kong, Census & Statistics Department (1997): *Facts on Hong Kong.* Hong Kong: Government Printer.

Hong Kong, Census Household Survey (1998): *Unemployment Rate by Levels of Education.* Press Release of Hong Kong SAR Government.

Hong Kong, Education & Manpower Branch (1994): *Manpower 2001 Revisited.* Hong Kong: Education & Manpower Branch, Government Secretariat.

Hong Kong, Education & Manpower Bureau (1997): *Degree and Sub-degree Tuition Fees Rate, 1997-2001.* Press Release, 15 July.

Hong Kong, Education & Manpower Bureau (1998): *Review of the Education Department (Consultation Document):* Hong Kong: Printing Department.

Hong Kong, Education Department (1971): *Education Regulations.* Hong Kong: Government Printer.

Hong Kong, Education Department (1986): *Report on the Evaluation of the Implementation of the Guidelines on Civic Education in Schools.* Hong Kong: Government Printer.

Hong Kong, Education Department (1987): *Second Report on the Evaluation of the Implementation of the Guidelines on Civic Education in Schools.* Hong Kong: Government Printer.

Hong Kong, Education Department (1993): *School Education in Hong Kong: A Statement of Aims.* Hong Kong: Government Printer.

Hong Kong, Education Department (1994): *Manual of Kindergarten Practice.* Hong Kong: Government Printer.

Hong Kong, Education Department (1997a): *Education Indicators for the Hong Kong School Education System.* Hong Kong: Government Printer.

Hong Kong, Education Department (1997b): *Medium of Instruction: Guidance for Secondary Schools.* Hong Kong: Education Department.

Hong Kong, Education Department (1998): *Enrolment Survey 1998.* Hong Kong: Statistics Section, Education Department.

Hong Kong, Financial Secretary (1999): *The 1999/2000 Budget: Onward with New Strengths.* Hong Kong: Government of the Hong Kong Special Administrative Region.

Hong Kong, Government of (1955a): *General School Circular No.22: List of Chinese Textbooks Approved for Schools.* Hong Kong: Department of Education. [in Chinese]

Hong Kong, Government of (1955b): *General School Circular No.25: List of English Textbooks Approved for Schools.* Hong Kong: Department of Education.

Hong Kong, Government of (1958): *Education Report.* Hong Kong: Government Printer.

Hong Kong, Government of (1959): *Education Report.* Hong Kong: Government Printer.

Hong Kong, Government of (1962): *Suggested Syllabus for Mathematics in Chinese-Middle Schools.* Hong Kong: Department of Education. [in Chinese]

Hong Kong, Government of (1972): *Education Report.* Hong Kong: Government Printer.

Hong Kong, Government of (1981): *Primary Education and Pre-primary Services* [White Paper]. Hong Kong: Government Printer.

Hong Kong, Government of (1982a): *Child Care Centres Ordinance* (revised edition) Hong Kong: Government Printer.

Hong Kong, Government of (1982b): *Child Care Centres Regulations* (revised edition) Hong Kong: Government Printer.

Hong Kong, Government of (1986): *Activity Guidelines for Day Nurseries.* Hong Kong: Government Printer.

Hong Kong, Government of (1997): *Policy Address: Building Hong Kong for a New Era.* Hong Kong: Government Printer.

Hong Kong, Government of (1998): *Hong Kong: A New Era.* Hong Kong: Information Services Department.

Hong Kong, Government of (1999): *Hong Kong 1998.* Hong Kong: Information Services Department.

Hong Kong, Quality Education Fund (1998): *Quality Education Fund: Project Statistics.* Hong Kong: Quality Education Fund.

Hong Kong, Social Welfare Department (1963): *Social Welfare Department Report.* Hong Kong: Government Printer.

Hong Kong, Social Welfare Department (1977): *Social Welfare Department Report.* Hong Kong: Government Printer.

Hong Kong, Social Welfare Department (1995): *Department Report, 1993-1995.* Hong Kong: Government Printer.

Hong Kong, Social Welfare Department (1997): *Department Report, 1996-1997.* Hong Kong: Government Printer.

Hong Kong, Social Welfare Department (1999): *Department Report, 1998-1999.* Hong Kong: Government Printer.

Hong Kong Baptist College (1957): *Hong Kong Baptist College Annual Bulletin.* Hong Kong: Hong Kong Baptist College.

Hong Kong Baptist College (1988): *Manual of Academic Regulations, Policies and Procedures*. Hong Kong: Hong Kong Baptist College.

Hong Kong Catholic Education & Studies Centre, Group of Educational Studies (1989): *A Preliminary Study on Democracy Education in Hong Kong Catholic Secondary Schools*. Hong Kong: Hong Kong Catholic Education & Studies Centre. [in Chinese]

Hong Kong Christian Institute & Action Group for Education (1994): *Party Politics and Voting: Sources of Materials*. Hong Kong: Hong Kong Christian Institute & Action Group for Education. [in Chinese]

Hong Kong Council of Early Childhood Education & Services (1993): *Training Needs Analysis of Early Childhood Workforce in Hong Kong*. Hong Kong: Hong Kong Council of Early Childhood Education & Services.

Hong Kong Educationists' Association & Hong Kong Resource Centre (1996): *Basics in Civic Education: Knowing Your Own Country*. Hong Kong: Fai Ho Publisher. [in Chinese]

Hong Kong Examinations Authority (1994a): *HKALE Annual Report 1994*. Hong Kong: Hong Kong Examinations Authority.

Hong Kong Examinations Authority (1994b): *HKCEE Annual Report 1994*. Hong Kong: Hong Kong Examinations Authority.

Hong Kong Federation of Youth Groups, The (1996): *The Youth Today: An Analysis of the Development of Youth in Five Places*. Hong Kong: The Hong Kong Federation of Youth Groups. [in Chinese]

Hong Kong Insititute of Education, The (1998): http://www.ied.edu.hk/acdprgs/programs.htm.

Howes, C. (1986): 'Quality Indicators for Infant-Toddler Child Care'. Paper presented at the Annual Meeting at the American Educational Research Association, San Francisco.

Howes, C. & Marx, E. (1992): 'Raising Questions about Improving the Quality of Child Care: Child Care in the United States and France'. *Early Childhood Research Quarterly*, Vol.7, No.3, pp.347-366.

Howson, A.G. (1978): 'Change in Mathematics Education since the late 1950's – Ideas and Realisation: Great Britain'. *Educational Studies in Mathematics*, Vol.9, No.2, pp.183-223.

Huang, H.P. & Chiu, L.H. (1991): 'Moral and Civic Education', in Smith, Douglas C. (ed.), *The Confucian Continuum: Educational Modernization in Taiwan*. New York: Praeger.

Huang, W.C. (1988): 'An Empirical Analysis of Foreign Student Brain Drain to the United States'. *Economics of Education Review*, Vol.7, No.2, pp.231-243.

Hughes, A.S. (1991): 'Curriculum Policies', in Lewy, Arieh (ed.), *The International Encyclopedia of Curriculum*. Oxford: Pergamon Press, pp.137-138.

Hui, Philip Kwok Fai (1990): *Development of Higher Education in the Context of Political and Economic Changes: The Case of Macau*. M.Ed. dissertation, The University of Hong Kong.

Hui, Philip Kwok Fai (1994): 'Higher Education in Macau: From Private to Public', in Koo, Ramsey Ding Yee & Ma, Hing Tong (eds.), *Macau Education: Continuity and Change*. Macau: Macau Foundation, pp.46-59. [in Chinese]

Hui, Philip Kwok Fai (1999): *A Comparative Historical Analysis of Higher Education*

Development in Macau and Hong Kong: State Intervention, Portuguese and British Imperialism and Colonialism, Ph.D. thesis, State University of New York at Buffalo.

Ichilov, O. (1994): 'Political Education', in Husen, T. & Postlethwaite, T.N. (eds.), *International Encyclopedia of Education*. 2nd edition. Oxford: Pergamon Press, pp.4568-4571.

Ieong, Pedro (1993): 'The Financing of Hong Kong Kindergartens', in Bray, Mark (ed.), *The Economics and Financing of Education: Hong Kong and Comparative Perspectives*. Education Paper No.20, Hong Kong: Faculty of Education, The University of Hong Kong, pp.96-121.

Ieong, S.L. (1994): 'Reflections on the Language Issues in Macau: Policies, Realities, and Prospects', in Koo, Ramsey Ding Yee & Ma, Hing Tong (eds.), *Macau Education: Continuity and Change*. Macau: Macau Foundation, pp.60-69. [in Chinese]

Ignas, Edward & Corsini, Raymond (eds.) (1981): *Comparative Education Systems*. Itasca, Illinois: F.E. Peacock Publishers.

Igwe, S.O. (1987): *Education in Eastern Nigeria 1847-1975, Development and Management: Church, State and Community*. London: Evans Brothers.

Ilon, Lynn (1997): 'Educational Repercussions of a Global System of Production', in Cummings, William K. & McGinn, Noel F. (eds.), *International Handbook of Education and Development: Preparing Schools, Students and Nations for the Twenty-First Century*. Oxford: Pergamon Press, pp.609-629.

Imrie, Bradford (1998): 'Professional Development as Quality Assurance: Now and Zen'. Hong Kong: University Grants Committee Internet Virtual Library, www.ugc.edu.hk.

Ip, Kin Yuen (1994): *Organisational Change: The Case of a 'Leftist School' in Joining the Direct Subsidy Scheme*. M.Ed. dissertation, The University of Hong Kong.

James, Estelle (1988): 'The Public/Private Division of Responsibility for Education: An International Comparison', in James, Thomas & Levin, Henry M. (eds.), *Comparing Public and Private Schools*. Vol.I, New York: Falmer Press, pp.95-127.

Jansen, Jonathan (1989): 'Curriculum Reconstruction in Post-Colonial Africa: A Review of the Literature'. *International Journal of Educational Development*, Vol.9, No.3, pp.219-231.

Jimenez, Emmanuel & Lockheed, Marlaine E. (1995): *Public and Private Secondary Education in Developing Countries: A Comparative Study*. Discussion Paper No.309, Washington DC: The World Bank.

Jones, Catherine (1990): *Promoting Prosperity: The Hong Kong Way of Social Policy*. Hong Kong: The Chinese University Press.

Jones, Philip E. (1971): *Comparative Education: Purpose and Method*. St. Lucia: Queensland University Press.

Jones, V. (1965): 'The Content of History Syllabuses in Northern Nigeria in the Early Colonial Period'. *West African Journal of Education*, Vol.9, pp.145-148.

Kamens, D.H. & Benavot, A. (1992): 'A Comparative and Historical Analysis of Mathematics and Science Curricula, 1800-1986', in Meyer, J.W., Kamens, D.H. & Benavot, A. with Cha, Y.K. & Wong, S.Y., *School Knowledge for the Masses: World Models and National Primary Curricular Categories in the Twentieth Century*. London: Falmer Press, pp.101-123.

Kandel, I.L. (1933): *Studies in Comparative Education*. London: George G. Harrap &

Company.

Kay, Stafford & Nystrom, Bradley (1971): 'Education and Colonialism in Africa'. *Comparative Education Review*, Vol.15, No.3, pp.240-259.

Kellaghan, Thomas & Greaney, Vincent (1992): *Using Examinations to Improve Education: A Study in Fourteen African Countries.* Technical Paper No.165, Washington DC: The World Bank.

Kelly, Albert Victor (1987): *Education.* London: Heinemann.

Kelly, Gail P. (1984): 'Colonialism, Indigenous Society, and School Practices: French West Africa and Indochina, 1918-1938', in Altbach, Philip G. & Kelly, Gail P. (eds.), *Education and the Colonial Experience.* New Brunswick: Transaction Books, pp.9-32.

Kelly, Gail P. (1992): 'Debates and Trends in Comparative Education', in Arnove, Robert F., Altbach, Philip G. & Kelly, Gail P. (eds.), *Emergent Issues in Education: Comparative Perspectives.* Albany: State University of New York Press, pp.13-22.

Kelly, Gail P. & Altbach, Philip G. (1984): 'Introduction: The Four Faces of Colonialism', in Altbach, Philip G. & Kelly, Gail P. (eds.), *Education and the Colonial Experience.* New Brunswick, N.J.: Transaction Books, pp.1-8.

Kerr, Clark (1982): 'The Idea of a Multiversity', in Kerr, Clark, *The Uses of the University.* Cambridge, Mass: Harvard University Press, pp.1-34.

King, Ambrose Y.C. (1981a): 'Administration Absorption of Politics in Hong Kong: Emphasis on the Grass Roots Level', in King, Ambrose Y.C. & Lee, Rance P.L. (eds.), *Social Life and Development in Hong Kong.* Hong Kong: The Chinese University Press, pp.127-146.

King, Ambrose Y.C. (1981b): 'The Political Culture in Kwun Tong: A Chinese Community in Hong Kong', in King, Ambrose Y.C. & Lee, Rance P.L. (eds.), *Social Life and Development in Hong Kong.* Hong Kong, The Chinese University Press, pp.147-168.

Kong, S.M. (1992): 'An Experience in Organising Programmes of Civic Education', in Wong, H.K. (ed.), *Civic Education in Macau.* Macau: Macau Research Centre, University of Macau, pp.157-160. [in Chinese]

Kontos, S. & Fiene, R. (1987): 'Child Care Quality, Compliance with Regulations and Children's Development: The Pennsylvania Study', in Phillips, D. (ed.), *Quality in Child Care: What does Research Tell Us?* Washington, D.C.: National Association for the Education of Young Children, pp.57-79.

Koo, Ramsey Ding Yee (1994a): 'Degree Expectations of Senior High School Students in Macau by Country of Origin', in Ramos, Rufino & Yuan, D.Y. (eds.), *Population and Development in Macau.* Macau: University of Macau & Macau Foundation, pp.433-445.

Koo, Ramsey Ding Yee (1994b): 'Reconstructing the Future of our Postsecondary Education: The Choice of Community College', in Koo, Ramsey Ding Yee & Ma, Hing Tong (eds.), *Macau Education: Continuity and Change.* Macau: Macau Foundation, pp.24-45. [in Chinese]

Koo, Ramsey Ding Yee (1997): 'Macau Education: Critical Changes and Challenges in the Post-transitional Period'. *Asian Studies,* Vol.22, No.1, pp.217-234. [in Chinese]

Koo, Ramsey Ding Yee (1998a): 'A Comparative Perspective on Education Development in the Transition Period for Hong Kong and Macau', in Yee, Albert (ed.), *A*

Tale of Two Cities: Political, Economic, and Social Development in Hong Kong and Macau. Macau: Macau Association for Social Sciences, pp.327-345. [in Chinese]

Koo, Ramsey Ding Yee (1998b): 'A Study of the Relationships between Father's Educational Level, Self-Expectation, and Academic Performance of Junior High School Students in Hong Kong'. Paper presented at the UNESCO-ACEID International Conference on Secondary Education and Youth at the Crossroads, Bangkok, 10-13 November.

Koo, Ramsey Ding Yee (1999): 'Academic Status of Women at a Public University in Macau'. Paper presented at the annual conference of the Comparative & International Education Society, Toronto, 14-18 April.

Koo, Ramsey Ding Yee & Ma, Hing Tong (eds.) (1994): *Macau Education: Continuity and Change.* Macau: Macau Foundation. [in Chinese]

Kopf, D. (1984): 'Orientalism and the Indian Educated Elite', in Altbach, Philip G. & Kelly, Gail P. (eds.), *Education and the Colonial Experience.* New Brunswick, N.J.: Transaction Books, pp.117-136.

Lai, I.F. (1995): 'Teacher Education in Macau: The Present and the Direction of the Future', in South China Normal University, *The Collection of Year 91.* China, Guangdong Education Press, pp.180-195. [in Chinese]

Lai, I Meng (1996): 'The Other Side of "The Contribution of Catholic Education in Macau"'. Macau: manuscript. [in Chinese]

Lam, A.W.C. (1994): *Evaluation of Civic Education in Hong Kong Secondary Schools.* M.Phil. thesis, University of Birmingham.

Lam, K., Fan, Y. & Skeldon, R. (1995): 'The Tendency to Emigrate from Hong Kong', in Skeldon R. (ed.), *Emigration from Hong Kong.* Hong Kong: The Chinese University Press, pp.79-110.

Lam, K.K. (1994): *Interaction Between Politics and Education: A Case Study of a Patriotic School in Hong Kong.* M.Phil. thesis, The Chinese University of Hong Kong. [in Chinese]

Lan, M.L. (1993): *A Study of the Chinese-Cultural Essential Elements in the Text Content of the Chinese Language Subject in Hong Kong Secondary School.* M.A. dissertation, The Chinese University of Hong Kong. [in Chinese]

Lau, Siu Kai (1982): *Society and Politics in Hong Kong.* Hong Kong: The Chinese University Press.

Lau, Siu Kai & Kuan, Hsin Chi (1988): *The Ethos of the Hong Kong Chinese.* Hong Kong: The Chinese University Press.

Lau, Sin Peng (1994): *A Preliminary Study of Historical Value of St. Paul's University College in Macau.* Macau: Department of Culture. [in Chinese]

Lau, Sin Peng (1996): 'Macau Education in the World War II', in Macau Chinese Education Association, *Selection of Educational Papers.* Macau: Macau Education Publisher, pp.3-17. [in Chinese]

Lau, Sin Peng (1997): 'The Main Duty and Timely Task of Educational Organisation is Providing the Status of Teaching Professionalism for Teachers'. Paper presented at the 4th Two Coasts Plus Hong Kong & Macau Regions Educational Studies Conference, 25-26 October, Macau. [in Chinese]

Lauglo, Jon & McLean, Martin (eds.) (1985): *The Control of Education: Issues in the Centralisation-Decentralisation Debate.* London: Heinemann.

Law, Wing Wah (1997): 'The Accommodation and Resistance to the Decolonisation,

Neocolonisation and Recolonisation of Higher Education in Hong Kong', in Bray, Mark & Lee, Wing On (eds.), *Education and Political Transition: Implications of Hong Kong's Change of Sovereignty*. Hong Kong: Comparative Education Research Centre, The University of Hong Kong, pp.41-63.

Lazzarotto, A. (1982): *The Catholic Church in Post-Mao China*. Hong Kong: Holy Spirit Study Centre.

Lee, S.M. (1987): 'Political Education and Civic Education: The British Perspective and Hong Kong Perspective'. *International Journal of Educational Development*, Vol.7, No.4, pp.251-263.

Lee, Wing On & Bray, Mark (1995): 'Education: Evolving Patterns and Challenges', in Cheng, Joseph & Lo, S.H. (eds.), *From Colony to SAR: Hong Kong's Challenges Ahead*. Hong Kong: The Chinese University Press, pp.357-378.

Leung, Beatrice (1992): *Sino-Vatican Relations: Problems of Conflicting Authority*. Cambridge: Cambridge University Press.

Leung, C.K. (1995): 'Foreword by the Director', in HKIEd, *Course Handbook 1995-96*. Hong Kong: Hong Kong Institute of Education.

Leung, Julian Y.M. (1992): 'Education in Hong Kong and China: Toward Convergence?', in Postiglione, Gerard A. with Leung, Julian Y.M. (eds.), *Education and Society in Hong Kong: Toward One Country and Two Systems*. Hong Kong: Hong Kong University Press. pp.265-272.

Leung, K.K. (1995): 'The Basic Law and the Problem of Political Transition', in Cheng, Y.L. & Sze, M.H. (eds.), *The Other Hong Kong Report 1995*. Hong Kong: The Chinese University Press, pp.33-50.

Leung, K.T. (1980): 'Development of Mathematics Curriculum in Recent Two Decades in Hong Kong'. *Dou Sou*, Vol. 38, pp.44-56. [in Chinese]

Leung, Sai Wing (1995): 'Depoliticization and Trivialization of Civic Education in Secondary Schools: Institutional Constraints on Promoting Civic Education in Transitional Hong Kong', in Siu, Ping Kee & Tam, Tim Kui Peter (eds.), *Quality in Education: Insights from Different Perspectives*. Hong Kong: The Hong Kong Educational Research Association, pp.283-312.

Leung, Sai Wing (1997): *The Making of an Alienated Generation: The Political Socialization of Secondary School Students in Transitional Hong Kong*. Aldershot: Ashgate.

Leung, Yat Ming (1995): 'The People's Republic of China', in Morris, Paul & Sweeting, Anthony (eds.), *Education and Development in East Asia*. New York: Garland, pp.203-242.

Leung, Yan Wing & Lau, Kit Fai (1997): *Political Education in a Hong Kong Setting: Theory and Practice*. Hong Kong: Hong Kong Christian Institute. [in Chinese]

Lewin, Keith M., Xu, H., Little, A.W. & Zheng, J. (1994): *Educational Innovation in China: Tracing the Impact of the 1985 Reforms*. Harlow, Essex: Longman.

Lewis, Leonard John (1949): 'Education in Africa', in *The Year Book of Education 1949*. London: Evans Brothers, pp.312-337.

Lewis, Leonard John (1954): *Educational Policy and Practice in British Tropical Areas*. London: Nelson.

Lewy, Arieh (1991): *National and School-based Curriculum Development*. Paris: International Institute for Educational Planning.

Li, Sui Pang Titus (1997): 'A Comparative Study on the Innovation of Primary and

Pre-school Teacher Education between Macau, Hong Kong and Canton'. Paper presented at the Oxford International Conference on Education and Development, 11-15 September.

Liu, Keung and Lee, Sheung (1997): 'What's Bothering the Economy of Macau'. *Asian Research*, No.22, pp.8-17. [in Chinese]

Liu, Z. (1973): *Overseas Chinese Education.* Taipei: Chung Hwa Book Company Ltd. [in Chinese]

Llewellyn, John (Chairman) (1982): *A Perspective on Education in Hong Kong: Report by a Visiting Panel.* Hong Kong: Government Printer.

Lo, Shiu Hing Sonny (1993): 'Decolonisation of Hong Kong and Macau: A Comparison'. *Hong Kong Journal of Social Sciences*, No.1, pp.79-99.

Lo, Shiu Hing Sonny (1995): *Political Development in Macau.* Hong Kong: The Chinese University Press.

Lo, Yiu Chun (1995): *The Implementation of the School-based Curriculum Project Scheme in Hong Kong.* Ph.D. thesis, The University of Hong Kong.

Louisy, Pearlette (1997): 'Dilemmas of Insider Research in Small-Country Settings: Tertiary Education in St. Lucia', in Crossley, Michael & Vulliamy, Graham (eds.), *Qualitative Educational Research in Developing Countries: Current Issues.* New York: Garland, pp.199-220.

Lugard, Frederick J.D. (1909): *The Conception and Foundation of the University of Hongkong: 1908-1913 Miscellaneous Documents.* Hong Kong: Hong Kong University.

Lugard, Frederick J.D. (1910): *Speech at the Laying of the Foundation Stone of the Hongkong University Building.* Hong Kong: Hong Kong University.

Lugard, Frederick J.D. (1912): *Present Position, Constitution, Objects and Prospects.* Hong Kong: Hong Kong University.

Luk, Hung Kay Bernard (1991): 'Chinese Culture in the Hong Kong Curriculum: Heritage and Colonialism'. *Comparative Education Review*, Vol.35, No.4, pp.650-668.

Luk, Hung Kay Bernard (1992): 'Hong Kong', in Wielemans, Willy & Chan, Choi Ping Pauline (eds.), *Education and Culture in Industrializing Asia.* Leuven: Leuven University Press, pp.111-150.

Ma, Hing Tong (1994): 'A Profile of Overseas University Education and Employment in Macau'. Paper presented at the Annual Conference of the Hong Kong Educational Research Association, 26-27 November.

Macau, Department of Administrative Services & Public Works (1994): 'Localization of Civil Servants'. *Hou Keng: Journal of the Macau Society of Social Sciences,* No.13, pp.53-67.

Macau, Department of Education & Youth (1994a): *Organização Curricular: Ensinos Pre-escolar, Preparatorio, Primario e Secundario Geral,* Decreto-Lei No.38/94/m de 18 de Julho. Macau: Imprensa Oficial.

Macau, Department of Education & Youth (1994b): *Caracteristicas dos Sistema de Ensino de Macau, 1992/93: Curriculo.* Macau: Department of Education & Youth.

Macau, Department of Education & Youth (1994c): *Estabelecimentos de Ensino de Macau.* Macau, Department of Education & Youth.

Macau, Department of Education & Youth (1997a): *Estabelecimentos de Ensino de Macau 1996-97.* Macau, Department of Education & Youth.

Macau, Department of Education & Youth (1997b): *Educação e Formação em Números*. Macau: Department of Education & Youth.

Macau, Department of Education & Youth (1998): *Estabelecimentos de Ensino de Macau 1997-98*. Macau, Department of Education & Youth.

Macau, Department of Statistics & Census (1989): *Inquérito ao Ensino 1987/88*. Macau : Department of Statistics & Census.

Macau, Department of Statistics & Census (1990): *Inquérito ao Ensino 1988/1989*. Macau: Department of Statistics & Census.

Macau, Department of Statistics & Census (1994): *Inquérito ao Ensino 1992/1993*. Macau: Department of Statistics & Census.

Macau, Department of Statistics & Census (1995): *Macau in Numbers*. Macau: Department of Statistics & Census.

Macau, Department of Statistics & Census (1997a): *Yearbook of Statistics 1996*. Macau: Department of Statistics & Census.

Macau, Department of Statistics & Census (1997b): *Inquérito ao Ensino 1995/1996*. Department of Statistics & Census.

Macau, Department of Statistics & Census (1998a): *Yearbook of Statistics 1997*. Macau: Department of Statistics & Census.

Macau, Department of Statistics & Census (1998b): *Inquérito ao Ensino 1996/1997*. Department of Statistics & Census.

Macau, Department of Statistics & Census (1999): *Macau in Figures*. Macau: Department of Statistics & Census.

Macau, Government of (1984): *Linhas de Acção Governativa: Plano de Investimentos*. Macau: Imprensa Oficial.

Macau, Government of (1991): *Sistema Educativo de Macau: Lei No.11/91/M*. Macau: Imprensa Oficial.

Macau, Government of (1992): *Decreto-Lei No.81/92/M*. Macau: Imprensa Oficial.

Macau, Government of (1993): *Decreto-Lei No.38/93/M*. Macau: Imprensa Oficial.

Macau, Government of (1994): *Decreto-Lei No.38/94/M*. Macau: Imprensa Oficial.

Macau, Government of (1995): *Decreto-Lei No.29/95/M*. Macau: Imprensa Oficial.

Macau, Government of (1996): *Decreto-Lei No.15/96/M*. Macau: Imprensa Oficial.

Macau, Government of (1997): *Decreto-Lei No.41/97/M*. Macau: Imprensa Oficial.

Macau Chinese Education Association (1951): *Macau Education (Vol.1-5):* Macau: Macau Chinese Education Association. [in Chinese]

Macau Chinese Education Association (1957): *Macau Education (Vol.11):* Macau: Macau Chinese Education Association. [in Chinese]

Macau Chinese Education Association (1966): *Macau Education (Vol.25):* Macau: Macau Chinese Education Association. [in Chinese]

Macau Chinese Education Association (1967): *Macau Education (Vol.26-29):* Macau: Macau Chinese Education Association. [in Chinese]

Macau Chinese Education Association (1968): *Macau Education (Vol.30-31):* Macau: Macau Chinese Education Association. [in Chinese]

Macau Chinese Education Association (1974): *Macau Education (Vol.67):* Macau: Macau Chinese Education Association. [in Chinese]

Macau Chinese Education Association (1975a): *Macau Education (Vol.74):* Macau: Macau Chinese Education Association. [in Chinese]

Macau Chinese Education Association (1975b): *Macau Education (Vol.76):* Macau:

Macau Chinese Education Association. [in Chinese]

Macau Chinese Education Association (1979): *Macau Education (Vol.102):* Macau: Macau Chinese Education Association. [in Chinese]

Macau Daily (1997): 'Increasing Enrolment of Macau's Students in Higher Education Institutions in China'. 23 July. [in Chinese]

Macau Ling Nam Middle School (n.d.): *Chinese History*, Vol.2. Macau: Macau Ling Nam Middle School.

Macau Research Centre (1994): *An Overview of Macau.* Macau: Macau Foundation.

MacKenzie, C.G. (1993): 'Demythologising the Missionaries: A Reassessment of the Functions and Relationships of Christian Missionary Education under Colonialism'. *Comparative Education*, Vol.29, No.1, pp.45-66.

Maglen, Leo (1991): 'The Impact of Education Expansion on the Distribution of Earnings in Australia'. *Australian Bulletin of Labour,* Vol.17, No.2, pp.132-159.

Maglen, Leo (1993): *Assessing the Economic Value of Education Expansion: A Preliminary Review of the Issues and Evidence.* Canberra: Economic Planning Advisory Council Background Paper, No.27.

Mak, Grace C.L. & Postiglione, Gerard A. (1996): 'Hong Kong', in Postiglione, Gerard A. & Mak, Grace C.L. (eds.), *Asian Higher Education: An International Handbook and Reference Guide.* Armonk, NY: M. E. Sharpe, pp.57-73.

Makagiansar, M., Beynon, J., de la Cruz, L., Selim, M., Sakya, T.M., Qureshi, M., Khan, A., Tun Lwin, M., Kasaju, P.K. & Djaka, E. (1989): 'Educational Policies Leading to Reform in Asia and the Pacific: An Overview', in *Educational Reforms in Asia.* Bangkok: UNESCO Principal Regional Office for Asia & the Pacific.

Mangan, J.A. (ed.) (1993): *The Imperial Curriculum: Racial Images and Education in the British Colonial Experience.* London: Routledge.

Manuel, P.C. (1996): *The Challenges of Democratic Consolidation in Portugal.* Westport, Conn.: Praeger.

Marques de Oliveira, A.H. (1972): *History of Portugal, Vol.II: From Empire to Corporate State.* New York: Columbia University Press.

Marsh, Colin & Morris, Paul (eds.) (1991): *Curriculum Development in East Asia.* London: Falmer Press.

Marshall, T.H. (1950): *Citizenship and Social Class and Other Essays.* Cambridge: Cambridge University Press.

Massy, William (1997): 'Teaching and Learning Quality Process Review: The Hong Kong Programme'. *Quality in Higher Education*, Vol.3, No.3, pp.249-262.

Mathews, John C. (1985): *Examinations: A Commentary.* London: George Allen & Unwin.

Mayhew, A. (1938): *Education in the Colonial Empire.* London: Longmans.

Mayne, A.B. (1938a): *The Essentials of School Arithmetic.* London: Macmillan.

Mayne, A.B. (1938b): *The Essentials of School Algebra.* London: Macmillan.

Mazurek, Kas & Winzer, Margret (eds.) (1994): *Comparative Special Education.* Washington DC: Gallaudet University Press.

McClelland, J.A.G. (1991): 'Curriculum Development in Hong Kong', in Marsh, Colin & Morris, Paul (eds.), *Curriculum Development in East Asia.* London: Falmer Press, pp.106-128.

McMahon, Walter (1991): 'Relative Returns to Human Capital and Physical Capital in the U.S. and Efficient Strategies'. *Economics of Education Review*, Vol.10, No.3, pp.283-296.

McMahon, Walter (1998): 'Recent Advances in Measuring the Social and Individual Benefits of Education'. *International Journal of Educational Research*, Vol.27, No.6, pp.447-532.

Mellor, Bernard (1988): *The University of East Asia: Origin and Outlook.* Hong Kong: UEA Press.

Memmi, A. (1965): *The Colonizer and the Colonized*. Boston: Beacon Press.

Miners, Norman John (1996): *The Government and Politics of Hong Kong*. 5th edition. Hong Kong: Oxford University Press.

Ming Pao (1997): 'Curriculum Development and Design'. 4 November. Hong Kong.

Modern Educational Research Society, Ltd. (1994): *Macau Modern Society.* Hong Kong: Modern Educational Research Society. [in Chinese]

Mok, Ka Ho (1997): 'Privatization or Marketization: Educational Development in Post-Mao China'. *International Review of Education*, Vol.45, Nos.5-6, pp.547-567.

Moon, Bob (1986): *The 'New Maths' Curriculum Controversy: An International Story*. London: Falmer Press.

Morgan, G. (1985): 'The Government Perspective', in Morgan, G., Curry, N., Endsley, R., Braradbard, M., Rashid H. & Epstein A. (eds.), *Quality in Early Childhood Programs: Four Perspectives*. High/Scope Early Childhood Policy Papers No.3, Ypsilanti, MI: High/Scope.

Morris, Paul (1988): 'The Effect on the School Curriculum of Hong Kong's Return to Chinese Sovereignty in 1997'. *Journal of Curriculum Studies*, Vol.20, No.6, pp.509-520.

Morris, Paul (1990): *Curriculum Development in Hong Kong*. Education Paper No.7, Hong Kong: Faculty of Education, The University of Hong Kong.

Morris, Paul (1992a): 'The Context of Curriculum Development in Hong Kong: Problems and Possibilities', in Morris, Paul, *Curriculum Development in Hong Kong*. 2nd edition. Education Paper No.7, Hong Kong: Faculty of Education, The University of Hong Kong, pp.4-22.

Morris, Paul (1992b): 'Teachers' Attitudes towards a Curriculum Innovation', in Morris, Paul, *Curriculum Development in Hong Kong*. 2nd edition. Education Paper No.7, Hong Kong: Faculty of Education, The University of Hong Kong, pp.33-46.

Morris, Paul (1992c): 'Preparing Pupils as Citizens of the Special Administrative Region: Curriculum Change and Control during the Transitional Period', in Morris, Paul, *Curriculum Development in Hong Kong*. 2nd edition. Education Paper No.7, Hong Kong: Faculty of Education, The University of Hong Kong, pp.120-143.

Morris, Paul (1996): *The Hong Kong School Curriculum: Development, Issues and Policies.* Hong Kong: Hong Kong University Press.

Morris, Paul (1997): 'Civics and Citizenship Education in Hong Kong', in Kennedy, Kerry (ed.), *Citizenship Education and the Modern State*. London: Falmer Press, pp.107-125.

Morris, Paul (1998): *The Hong Kong School Curriculum: Development, Issues and Policies.* 2nd edition. Hong Kong: Hong Kong University Press.

Morris, Paul, Adamson, B., Au, M.L., Chan, K.K., Chan, W.Y., Ko, P.Y., Lai Auyeung, W., Lo, M.L., Morris, E., Ng, F.P., Ng, Y.Y., Wong, W.M. & Wong, P.H. (1996): *Target Oriented Curriculum Evaluation Project: Interim Report.* Hong Kong: In-service Teacher Education Programme, Faculty of Education, The University of Hong Kong.

Morris, Paul, Adamson, B., Chan, K.K., Che, M.W., Chik, P.M., Fung Lo M.L., Ko, P.Y., Kwan, Y.L., Mok, A.C., Ng, F.P. & Tong, S.Y. (1999): *Final Report: The Project on Feedback and Assessment.* Hong Kong: Curriculum Development Institute.

Morris, Paul & Chan, Ka Ki (1997): 'The Hong Kong School Curriculum and the Political Transition: Politicisation, Contextualisation and Symbolic Action', in Bray, Mark & Lee, Wing On (eds.), *Education and Political Transition: Implications of Hong Kong's Change of Sovereignty.* Hong Kong: Comparative Education Research Centre, The University of Hong Kong, pp.101-118.

Morris, Paul, McClelland, J.A.G. & Leung, Y.M. (1994): 'Higher Education in Hong Kong: The Context of and Rationale for Rapid Expansion'. *Higher Education,* Vol.27, No.1, pp.125-140.

Morris, Paul, McClelland, Gerry & Wong, Ping Man (1998): 'Explaining Curriculum Change: Social Studies in Hong Kong', in Stimpson, Philip & Morris, Paul (eds.), *Curriculum and Assessment for Hong Kong: Two Components, One System.* Hong Kong: The Open University of Hong Kong Press, pp.103-124.

Morris, Paul & Sweeting, Anthony (1991): 'Education and Politics: The Case of Hong Kong from an Historical Perspective'. *Oxford Review of Education,* Vol.17, No.3, pp.249-267.

Morris, Paul & Tang, C.K. (1992): 'The Abuse of Educational Evaluation: A Study of the Evaluation of the Implementation of the Civic Education Guidelines', in Morris, Paul, *Curriculum Development in Hong Kong.* 2nd edition. Education Paper No.7, Hong Kong: Faculty of Education, The University of Hong Kong, pp.102-119.

Morris, Robert (ed.) (1981): *Studies in Mathematics Education,* Vol.2, Paris: UNESCO.

Morris, Robert & Arora, M.S. (eds.) (1992): *Studies in Mathematics Education,* Vol.8, Paris: UNESCO.

Morrison, Keith (1998): *Management Theories for Educational Change.* London: Paul Chapman.

Mouat Jones, B. & Adams, Sir Walter (1950): 'Visit to University of Hong Kong, April, 1950: Report by Mouat Jones, B. & Adams, Sir Walter'. London: The Inter-University Council for Higher Education in the Colonies.

Mukherjee, L. (1964): *Comparative Education for Students and Educationists.* 2nd edition. Allahabad, India: Kitab Mahal.

Murray, A. Victor (1929): *The School in the Bush: A Critical Study of the Theory and Practice of Native Education in Africa.* London: Longmans, Green & Co..

Musgrove, F. (1955): History Teaching within a Conflict of Cultures. *History,* Vol.15, No.140, pp.300-318.

Nadel, George H. & Curtis, Perry (1964): *Imperialism and Colonialism.* New York: The Macmillan Company.

National Association for the Education of Young Children (1991): *Accreditation Criteria and Procedures.* Washington, DC: National Association for the Education of Young Children.

Neves, P.A. & Almeida, V.C. (1990): *Descoberta da Historia 9.* Lisboa: Porto Editora.

Ng, Cherry S.C. (1997): *Civic Education in Hong Kong and Macau: A Comparative Analysis.* M.Ed. dissertation, The University of Hong Kong.

Ng, F.K. (1992): *Comparing Education in Hong Kong and Macau.* Guangzhou: Zhongshan University Press. [in Chinese]

Ng Lun, Ngai-ha (1984): *Interactions of East and West: Development of Public Education in Early Hong Kong*. Hong Kong: The Chinese University Press.

Ngai, Gary (1994): *Free Talks on Macau*. Macau: Macau Foundation.

Ngai, K.Y., Lee, C.S. & Ko, H.Y. (1987*): History of Secondary Mathematics Education in China*. Beijing: The People's Education Press. [in Chinese]

Nicholson, Annie (1988): *A Study of the Implementation of a Curriculum Innovation in a Secondary School in Hong Kong: The Case of Form I-III Social Studies*. M.Ed. dissertation, The University of Hong Kong.

Nkabinde, Zandile P. (1997): *An Analysis of Educational Challenges in the New South Africa*. Lanham, MD: University Press of America.

Noah, Harold J. (1998 reprint [original 1984]): 'Use and Abuse of Comparative Education', in Noah, Harold J. & Eckstein, Max A., *Doing Comparative Education: Three Decades of Collaboration*. Hong Kong: Comparative Education Research Centre, The University of Hong Kong, pp.57-67.

O'Donoghue, Tom & Dimmock, Clive (1998): *School Restructuring: International Perspectives*. London: Kogan Page.

Okoth, P.G. (1993): 'The Creation of a Dependent Culture: The Imperial School Curriculum in Uganda', in Mangan, J.A. (ed.), *The Imperial Curriculum: Racial Images and Education in the British Colonial Experience*. London: Routledge, pp.135-146.

Oldham, E. (1989): 'Is there an International Mathematics Curriculum?', in Greer, B. & Mulhern, G. (eds.), *New Directions in Mathematics Education*. London: Routledge, pp.185-224.

Oliver, Paul (1996): 'The Concept of Change Management', in Oliver, Paul (ed.), *The Management of Educational Change: A Case-Study Approach*. Aldershot: Arena, pp.1-9.

Opper, Sylvia (1989): 'Child Care and Early Education in Hong Kong', in Olmsted, Patricia P. & Weikart, David P. (eds.), *How Nations Serve Young Children: Profiles of Child Care and Education in 14 Countries*. Ypsilanti, MI: High/Scope, pp.119-142.

Opper, Sylvia (1993): 'Kindergarten Education: Cinderella of the Hong Kong Education System', in Tsui, Amy B.M. & Ivor Johnson (eds.), *Teacher Education and Development*. Education Paper No.8, Hong Kong: Faculty of Education, The University of Hong Kong, pp.80-89.

Opper, Sylvia (1996): *Hong Kong's Young Children: Their Early Development and Learning*. Hong Kong: Hong Kong University Press.

Organisation for Economic Co-operation & Development [OECD] (1997): *Education at a Glance: OECD Indicators*. Paris: Organisation for Economic Co-operation & Development.

Paulston, Rolland G. (1997): 'Mapping Visual Culture in Comparative Education Discourse'. *Compare*, Vol.27, No.2, pp.117-152.

Paulston, Rolland G. (1999): 'Comparative Education after Postmodernity'. Occasional Papers Series, Pittsburgh: Department of Administrative & Policy Studies, University of Pittsburgh.

Pennycook, Alistair (1994): *The Cultural Politics of English as an International Language*. London: Longman.

Phillips, D.A. (1988): 'Quality in Child Care: Definitions and Dilemmas'. Paper presented at the Mailman Family Foundation Symposium, White Plains, NY.

Phillips, D. & Howes, C. (1987): 'Indicators of Quality in Child Care: Review of Research', in Phillips, D. (ed.), *Quality in Child Care: What Does the Research Tell Us?* Washington DC: National Association for the Education of Young Children, pp.43-56.

Pires, B.V. (1991): 'Origins and Early History of Macau', in Cremer, R.D. (ed.), *Macau: City of Commerce and Culture – Continuity and Change.* 2nd edition. Hong Kong: API Press, pp.7-21.

Pong, L.W. (1987): 'The Secondary School Chinese History Curriculum in Hong Kong over the Past Forty Years'. *Education Journal*, Vol.15, No.2, pp.68-75. [in Chinese]

Pong, Y.W. (1997): 'Some Questions on Primary Teacher Education in Hong Kong'. *Sing Tao Yat Pao*, 5 November. [in Chinese]

Ponte, Joao P., Matos, Joao F., Guimaraes, Henrique M., Leal, Leonor C. & Canavarro, Ana P. (1994): 'Teachers' and Students' Views and Attitudes towards a New Mathematics Curriculum: A Case Study'. *Educational Studies in Mathematics*, Vol.26, pp.347-365.

POSTE Team (1996): *Preparation of Students for Tertiary Education (Final Report).* Hong Kong: Faculty of Education, The University of Hong Kong.

Postiglione, Gerard A. (1992): 'The Decolonization of Hong Kong Education', in Postiglione, Gerard A. with Leung, Julian Y.M. (eds.), *Education and Society in Hong Kong: Toward One Country and Two Systems.* Hong Kong: Hong Kong University Press, pp.3-38.

Postiglione, Gerard A. (1996a): 'The Future of the Hong Kong Academic Profession in a Period of Profound Change', in Altbach, Philip G. & Boyer, Ernest L. (eds.), *The International Academic Profession: Portraits of Fourteen Countries.* Princeton, New Jersey: The Carnegie Foundation for the Advancement of Teaching, pp.191-227.

Postiglione, Gerard A. (1996b): 'Attitudes and Attributes of Hong Kong Academics'. *Higher Education Management*, Vol.8, No.3, pp.122-140.

Postiglione, Gerard (1998): 'Maintaining Global Engagement in the Face of National Integration in Hong Kong'. *Comparative Education Review*, Vol.42, No.1, pp.30-45.

Postiglione, Gerard A. & Lee, Wing On (eds.) (1997): *Schooling in Hong Kong: Organization, Teaching and Social Context.* Hong Kong: Hong Kong University Press.

Postlethwaite, T. Neville (ed.) (1988): *The Encyclopedia of Comparative Education and National Systems of Education.* Oxford: Pergamon Press.

Postlethwaite, T. Neville (1999): *International Studies of Educational Achievement: Methodological Issues.* Hong Kong: Comparative Education Research Centre, The University of Hong Kong.

Postlethwaite, T. Neville & Thomas, R. Murray (1983): 'Country Comparisons and Future Prospects', in Thomas, R. Murray & Postlethwaite, T. Neville (eds.), *Schooling in East Asia: Forces of Change.* Oxford: Pergamon Press, pp.308-342.

Priestley, Kenneth (1962): 'Changing Aims', in Harrison, Brian (ed.), *University of Hong Kong: The First 50 Years, 1911-1961.* Hong Kong: Hong Kong University Press, pp.93-102.

Psacharopoulos, George (1985): 'Returns to Education: A Further International Update and Implications'. *Journal of Human Resources*, Vol.20, No.4, pp.584-604.

Psacharopoulos, George (1990): 'Comparative Education: From Theory to Practice, or Are You A:\neo.* or B:*.ist?'. *Comparative Education Review*, Vol.34, No.3, pp.369-380.

Psacharopoulos, George (1994): 'Returns to Investment in Education: A Global Update'. *World Development*, Vol.22, No.9, pp.1325-1343.

Psacharopoulos, George (1995): *Building Human Capital for Better Lives.* Washington D.C.: The World Bank.

Psacharopoulos, George & Woodhall, Maureen (1985): *Education for Development: An Analysis of Investment Choices.* New York: Oxford University Press.

Ramirez, Francisco O. (1997): 'The Nation-State, Citizenship, and Educational Change: Institutionalization and Globalization', in Cummings, William K. & McGinn, Noel F. (eds.), *International Handbook of Education and Development: Preparing Schools, Students, and Nations for the Twenty-First Century.* Oxford: Pergamon Press, pp.47-62.

Rangel, Jorge A.H. (1989): 'The Role of Macau in the Exchange of Oriental Culture', translated by Ng, C.L. *Administration.* No.3/4: 201-210. [in Chinese]

Rangel, Jorge A.H. (1991): 'Prospects and Directions for Education', in Cremer, R.D. *Macau: City of Commerce and Culture – Continuity and Change.* 2nd edition. Hong Kong: API Press, pp.315-322.

Reller, Theodore L. & Morphet, Edgar L. (1964): *Comparative Education Administration.* Englewood Cliffs, N.Y.: Prentice Hall.

Reynolds, Charles (1981): *Modes of Imperialism.* Oxford: Martin Robertson.

Ride, Lindsay (1962): 'The Antecedents', in Harrison, Brian (ed.), *University of Hong Kong: The First 50 Years, 1911-1961.* Hong Kong: Hong Kong University Press, pp.5-22.

Robertson, David (1993): *The Penguin Dictionary of Politics.* London: Penguin.

Rosa, Alexandre (1990): 'Macau Education in the Period of Transition: An Overview and Prospects'. Paper presented at the UNESCO International Congress of Planning and Management of Educational Development, Mexico City.

Rosa, Alexandre (1991): 'A Situação da Educação em Macau e a Necessidade da Reforma', in Wong, Hon Keong (ed.), *Education Reform in Macau.* Macau: Centre of Macau Studies, University of East Asia, pp.31-36.

Rulcker, T. (1991): 'Curriculum Reform', in Lewy, Arieh (ed.), *The International Encyclopedia of Curriculum.* Oxford: Pergamon Press, pp.281-289.

Ruopp, R., Travers, J., Glantz, L. & Goelen, C. (1979): *Children at the Centre: Final Results of the National Day Care Study.* Cambridge, MA: Abt Associates.

Rust, Val D., Soumaré, A., Pescador, O. & Shibuya, M. (1999): 'Research Strategies in Comparative Education'. *Comparative Education Review*, Vol.43, No.1, pp.86-109.

Sadler, Sir Michael (1964 reprint [original 1900]): 'How Can we Learn Anything of Practical Value from the Study of Foreign Systems of Education?'. *Comparative Education Review*, Vol.7, No.3, pp.307-314.

Sautman, B. (1991): 'Politicization, Hyperpoliticalization, and Depoliticization of Chinese Education'. *Comparative Education Review*, Vol.35, No.4, pp.669-689.

Schleicher, K. (1993): *Nationalism in Education.* Frankfurt am Main: Peter Lang.

Schultz, T.W. (1961): 'Education and Economic Growth', in Henry, N.B. (ed.), *Social*

Forces Influencing American Education. Chicago: University of Chicago Press, pp.46-88.

Schultze, Arthur, Sevenoak, Frank Louis & Stone, L.C. (1901): *Plane and Solid Geometry.* New York: Macmillan.

Scott, Ian (1989): *Political Change and the Crisis of Legitimacy in Hong Kong.* London: Hurst.

Scott, Peter (1995): *The Meanings of Mass Higher Education.* Buckingham: The Society for Research into Higher Education & Open University Press.

Shipp, Steve (1997): *Macau, China: A Political History of the Portuguese Colony's Transition to Chinese Rule.* Jefferson, North Carolina: McFarland & Company.

Shive, Glen (1992): 'Educational Expansion and the Labor Force', in Postiglione, Gerard A. with Leung, Julian Y.M. (eds.), *Education and Society in Hong Kong: Toward One Country and Two Systems.* Hong Kong: Hong Kong University Press, pp.215-231.

Sigel, I.E. (1991): 'Pre-school Education: For Whom and Why?'. *New Directions in Child Development,* Vol.53, No.1, pp.83-91.

Sing Tao Daily (1998): 'More than Half of the Anglo-Chinese Schools would use Mother-tongue for Teaching Cultural Subjects'. 20 March. Hong Kong. [in Chinese]

Sit, Victor F.S., Cremer, R.D. & Wong, S.L. (1991): *Entrepreneurs and Enterprises in Macau: A Study of Industrial Development.* Hong Kong: Hong Kong University Press.

Siu Chan, F.K., Chow, W.M. & Suen, S.N. (1997): *ES361 - Teaching Mathematics in Secondary Schools.* Hong Kong: Open Learning Institute.

Smith, Percy Franklyn & Gale, Arthur Sullivan (1912): *New Analytical Geometry.* London: Ginn.

Soares, Mario (1989): 'Address', delivered to the assembly of the University of East Asia on the occasion of the visit of His Excellency. [in Portuguese]

Spindler, George & Spindler, Louise (1982): 'Roger Harker and Schönhausen: From Familiar to Strange and Back Again', in Spindler, George (ed.), *Doing the Ethnography of Schooling: Educational Anthropology in Action.* New York: Holt, Rinehart & Winston, pp.20-46.

Spring, Joel (1998): *Education and the Rise of the Global Economy.* Mahwah: Lawrence Erlbaum Associates.

Stanic, G.M.A. (1987a): 'A Historical Perspective on Justifying the Teaching of Mathematics', in Goodson, I.F. (ed.), *International Perspectives in Curriculum History.* London: Croom Helm, pp.209-227.

Stanic, G.M.A. (1987b): 'Mathematics Education in the United States at the Beginning of the Twentieth Century', in Popkewitz, T.S. (ed.), *The Formation of School Subjects: The Struggle for Creating an American Institution.* New York: Falmer Press, pp.145-175.

Stokes, G. & Stokes, J. (1975): *Europe 1870-1960.* Hong Kong: Longman.

Sullivan, Keith (ed.) (1997): *Education and Change in the Pacific Rim: Meeting the Challenges.* Wallingford, Oxfordshire: Triangle Books.

Sweeting, Anthony (1983): 'Hong Kong', in Thomas, R. Murray & Postlethwaite, T. Neville (eds.), *Schooling in East Asia: Forces of Change.* Oxford: Pergamon Press, pp.272-297.

Sweeting, Anthony (1990): *Education in Hong Kong, Pre-1841 to 1941: Fact and*

Opinion. Hong Kong: Hong Kong University Press.

Sweeting, Anthony (1991a): 'Politics and the Art of Teaching History in Hong Kong'. *Teaching History* [U.K.], Vol.64, pp.30-37.

Sweeting, Anthony (1991b): 'The Medium of Instruction in Hong Kong Schools', in Crawford, Nick & Hui, Eadaoin K.P. (eds.), *The Curriculum and Behaviour Problems in Schools: A Response to Education Commission Report No.4.* Education Paper No.11, Hong Kong: Faculty of Education, The University of Hong Kong, pp.67-78.

Sweeting, Anthony (1992): 'Hong Kong Education within Historical Processes', in Postiglione, Gerard A. with Leung, Julian Y.M. (eds.), *Education and Society in Hong Kong: Toward One Country and Two Systems.* Hong Kong: Hong Kong University Press, pp.39-81.

Sweeting, Anthony (1993): *A Phoenix Transformed: The Reconstruction of Education in Post-war Hong Kong.* Hong Kong: Oxford University Press.

Sweeting, Anthony (1995): 'Hong Kong', in Morris, Paul & Sweeting, Anthony (eds.), *Education and Development in East Asia,* New York: Garland, pp.41-77.

Sweeting, Anthony (1997): 'Education Policy and the 1997 Factor: The Art of the Possible Interacting with the Dismal Science', in Bray, Mark & Lee, Wing On (eds.), *Education and Political Transition: Implications of Hong Kong's Change of Sovereignty.* Hong Kong: Comparative Education Research Centre, The University of Hong Kong, pp.25-39.

Sweeting, Anthony (1998a): 'Teacher Education at Hongkong University: A Brief History (Part 1: 1917-1951)'. *Curriculum Forum,* Vol.7, No.2, pp.1-44.

Sweeting, Anthony (1998b): 'Teacher Education at the University of Hong Kong: A Brief History (Part 2: 1951-circa 1976)' *Curriculum Forum,* Vol.8, No.1, pp.1-32.

Sweeting, Anthony (1998c): 'Doing Comparative Historical Research: Problems and Issues from and about Hong Kong'. Paper presented at the inaugural conference of the British Association of International & Comparative Education, University of Reading.

Sylva, K. & Wiltshire, J. (1993): 'The Impact of Early Learning on Children's Later Development'. A Review Prepared for the RSA Inquiry 'Start Right'. *European Early Childhood Education Research Journal,* Vol. l, No.1, pp.17-40.

Tai, Hung Chao (1989): *Confucianism and Economic Development: An Oriental Alternative?* Washington, D.C.: Washington Institute Press.

Taiwan, Director General of Budget, Accounting & Statistics (1996): *Statistical Yearbook of the Republic of China 1996.* Taipei: Director General of Budget, Accounting & Statistics. [in Chinese]

Taiwan, Education Department (1995): *The Republic of China Education Report: Vision in Education Towards the Twenty-first Century.* Taipei: Ministry of Education. [in Chinese]

Tam, C.C.K. (1994): *Disputes Concerning Macau's Sovereignty between China and Portugal (1553-1993).* Taipei: Yong Ye Publication. [in Chinese]

Tam, Tsz Wai Edith (1995): *A Comparative Study on the Contributions of Missionaries to the Formative Years of Colonial Education in Hong Kong and Macau.* MA dissertation, The University of Hong Kong.

Tan, Jason (1997): 'Education and Colonial Transition in Singapore and Hong Kong:

Comparisons and Contrasts', in Bray, Mark & Lee, Wing On (eds.), *Education and Political Transition: Implications of Hong Kong's Change of Sovereignty*. Hong Kong: Comparative Education Research Centre, The University of Hong Kong, pp.157-166.

Tan, John Kang (1997): 'Church, State and Education: Catholic Education in Hong Kong during the Political Transition', in Bray, Mark & Lee, Wing On (eds.), *Education and Political Transition: Implications of Hong Kong's Change of Sovereignty*. Hong Kong: Comparative Education Research Centre, The University of Hong Kong, pp.65-86.

Tang, Hou Chung (1995): *History of Macau (1840-1949)*. Macau: Macau History Society.

Tang, James Tuck Hong (1992): *Britain's Encounter with Revolutionary China, 1949-54*. New York: St. Martin's Press.

Tang, Joan Fun Hei & Morrison, Keith (1998): 'When Marketisation does not Improve Schooling: The Case of Macau'. *Compare*, Vol.28, No.3, pp.245-262.

Tang, Kwok Chun (1998): 'The Development of Education in Macau', in Ramos, R., Dinis, J.R., Wilson, R. & Yuan, D.Y., *Macau and its Neighbors toward the 21st Century*. Macau: University of Macau and Macau Foundation, pp.221-238.

Tang, Kwok Chun (1999): *Stability and Change in School Mathematics: A Socio-Cultural Case Study of Secondary Mathematics in Macau*. Ph.D. thesis, The University of Hong Kong.

Tang, K.K. (1997): 'The Cultural Manner Demonstrated by the 400 Years of Education in Macau', in To, Y.O. (ed.), *Proceedings of Education, History and Culture of Macau*. Guangzhou: Academic Studies Publisher, pp.55-59. [in Chinese]

Teichler, Ulrich (1996): 'Comparative Higher Education: Potentials and Limits'. *Higher Education*, Vol.32, No.4, pp.431-465.

Teixeira, Manuel (1969): *D. Melchior Carneiro: Fundador da Santa Casa da Misericórdia de Macau*. Macau: Comissão Executiva das Comemorações do IV Centenário da Santa Casa da Misericórdia.

Teixeira, Manuel (1982): *A Educação em Macau*. Macau: Direcção dos Serviços de Educação e Cultura.

Teixeira, Manuel (1991): 'The Church in Macau', in Cremer, R.D. (ed.), *Macau: City of Commerce and Culture – Continuity and Change*. 2nd edition. Hong Kong: API Press, pp.39-49.

Thion, Serge (1993): *Watching Cambodia: Ten Paths to Enter the Cambodian Triangle*. Bangkok: White Lotus.

Thomas, R. Murray (1983a): 'Macau', in Thomas, R. Murray & Postlethwaite, T. Neville (eds.), *Schooling in East Asia: Forces of Change*. Oxford: Pergamon Press, pp.301-307.

Thomas, R. Murray (1983b): 'The Two Colonies – A Prologue', in Thomas, R. Murray & Postlethwaite, T. Neville (eds.), *Schooling in East Asia: Forces of Change*. Oxford: Pergamon Press, pp.265-271.

Thomas, R. Murray (1994): personal communication to Mark Bray.

Thomas, R. Murray (1998): *Conducting Educational Research: A Comparative View*. Westport, Connecticut: Bergin & Garvey.

Thomas, R. Murray & Postlethwaite, T. Neville (eds.) (1983a): *Schooling in East Asia: Forces of Change*. Oxford: Pergamon Press.

Thomas, R. Murray & Postlethwaite, T. Neville (1983b): 'Describing Change and

Estimating its Causes', in Thomas, R. Murray & Postlethwaite, T. Neville (eds.), *Schooling in East Asia: Forces of Change.* Oxford: Pergamon Press, pp.1-36.

Ticozzi, S. (1983): *The Anecdotes of Catholic Church in Hong Kong.* Hong Kong: Holy Spirit Study Centre, pp.1-4. [in Chinese]

Tong Sin Tong (1992): *Centenary Anniversary of Tong Sin Tong.* Macau, Management Board of Tong Sin Tong.

Trethewey, A.R. (1979): *Introducing Comparative Education.* Rushcutter's Bay, Australia: Pergamon Press.

Trow, Martin (1974): 'Problems in the Transition from Elite to Mass Higher Education', in *Policies for Higher Education.* Paris: Organisation for Economic Co-operation & Development.

Tsang, W.K. (1984): 'Review and Prospect of the Political Education in Hong Kong'. *Hong Kong Economic Journal,* Vol.8, No.5, pp.34-40. [in Chinese]

Tsang, W.K. (1994): 'Decolonized Citizenship Education: A Framework of Post 1997 Hong Kong School's Civic Education'. *Journal of Education,* Vol.22, No.2, pp.237-248. [in Chinese]

Tsang, W.K. (1998): 'Patronage, Domestification, or Empowerment? Citizenship Development and Citizenship Education in Hong Kong', in Ichilov, O. (ed.), *Citizenship and Education in a Changing World.* London: Woburn Press, pp.221-252.

Tse, Kwan Choi Thomas (1997a): *The Poverty of Political Education in Hong Kong Secondary Schools.* Occasional Paper, Hong Kong: Hong Kong Institute of Asian-Pacific Studies, The Chinese University of Hong Kong.

Tse, Kwan Choi Thomas (1997b): 'Social Subjects and Civic Education in Secondary Schools'. *New Horizons in Education,* Vol.38, pp.10-14. [in Chinese]

Tse, Kwan Choi Thomas (1997c): *Preparing Students for Citizenship? Civic Education in Hong Kong Secondary Schools.* Ph.D. thesis, The University of Warwick.

Tse, Kwan Choi Thomas (1997d): 'This is Hong Kong? The Composite Images of Citizenship and Hong Kong Society Reflected in the Lower Form EPA and Social Studies Textbooks in Hong Kong'. Hong Kong: manuscript.

Tse, Kwan Choi Thomas (1998): 'A Comparative Study of Political Education in Four Chinese Societies: Mainland China, Taiwan, Hong Kong & Macau'. Paper presented at the International Conference on 'Restructuring the Knowledge Base of Education in Asia', Hong Kong, February 12-14. [in Chinese]

Tsurumi, Patricia E. (1977): *Japanese Colonial Education in Taiwan (1895-1945).* Cambridge: Harvard University Press.

Tsurumi, Patricia E. (1984): 'The Non-Western Colonizer in Asia: Japanese Educational Engineering in Taiwan', in Altbach, Philip G. & Kelly, Gail P. (eds.), *Education and the Colonial Experience.* New Brunswick: Transaction Books, pp.55-74.

Tulviste, P. (1994): 'History Taught at School versus History Discovered at Home: The Case of Estonia'. *European Journal of Psychology of Education,* Vol.9, No.2, pp.121-126.

Tung, Chee Hwa (1997a): *Inaugural Speech by the Chief Executive the Honourable Tung Chee Hwa, 1 July 1997.* Hong Kong: Government Printer.

Tung, Chee Hwa (1997b): *Policy Programme: The 1997 Policy Address.* Hong Kong: Government Printer.

UNESCO (1990): *Innovations and Initiatives in Teacher Education in Asia and the Pacific Region. Vol.1: Comparative Overview of Fifteen Countries.* Bangkok: UNESCO Asia and the Pacific Programme of Educational Innovation for Development.

UNESCO (1998): *World Education Report 1998: Teachers and Teaching in a Changing World.* Paris: UNESCO.

United States, Bureau of the Census (1996): *Statistical Abstract of the U.S. 1996.* Washington: Department of Commerce, Bureau of the Census.

University Grants Committee (1996): *Higher Education in Hong Kong: A Report by the University Grants Committee of Hong Kong.* Hong Kong: Government Printer.

University Grants Committee (1998): *Student Statistics.* University Grants Committee internet homepage www.ugc.edu.hk.

University of Macau, Faculty of Education (1996): *Course Description of Professional Continuing Education Programme 1996-1997.* Macau, University of Macau. [in Chinese]

University of Macau, Faculty of Education (1997a): *Course Description of Faculty of Education 1997/98.* Macau: Faculty of Education, University of Macau. [in Chinese]

University of Macau, Faculty of Education (1997b): *Number of Graduates (1989-1997) of the Faculty of Education.* Macau: Faculty of Education, University of Macau.

University of Macau (1997): *Admission Information.* Macau: University of Macau internet homepage www.umac.mo.

USAID (1997): *Education Decentralization in Africa: As Viewed through the Literature and USAID Projects.* Washington DC: United States Agency for International Development.

van der Berg, O. & Buckland, P. (1982): 'History as a Subject in South African Schools'. *Teaching History* [U.K.] Vol.34, pp.22-25.

van der Blij, F., Hilding, S. & Weinzwig, A.I. (1981): 'New Goals for Old: An Analysis of Reactions to Recent Reforms in Several Countries', in Morris, Robert (ed.), *Studies in Mathematics Education*, Vol.2, Paris: UNESCO, pp.105-188.

Walford, Geoffrey (ed.) (1989): *Private Schools in Ten Countries: Policy and Practice.* London: Routledge.

Wan, W.K. (1990): *Political Attitudes of Hong Kong Adolescents Towards the PRC: A Study of Political Socialization.* M.Phil. thesis, The Chinese University of Hong Kong.

Wang, Ying Jie (1996): 'Faculdade de Ciêcias da Educação', in *Os Estudos Superiores em Macau: Seminário Internacional.* Macau: University of Macau, Macau Polytechnic and Macau Foundation, pp.45-47.

Watson, Keith (1982a): 'Colonialism and Educational Development', in Watson, Keith (ed.), *Education in the Third World.* London: Croom Helm, pp.1-46.

Watson, Keith (1982b): 'Selected Bibliography on Colonialism and Educational Development', in Watson, Keith (ed.), *Education in the Third World.* London: Croom Helm, pp.201-224.

Watson, Keith (ed.) (1982c): *Education in the Third World.* London: Croom Helm.

Watson, Keith (1996): 'Comparative Education', in Gordon, P. (ed.), *A Guide to Educational Research.* London: Woburn Press, pp.360-397.

Watson, Keith (1998): 'Memories, Models and Mapping: The Impact of Geopolitical Changes on Comparative Studies in Education'. *Compare*, Vol.28, No.1, pp.3-31.

Weale, Martin (1992): 'Externalities from Education', in Hahn, Frank (ed.), *The Market: Practice and Policy*. London: Macmillan, pp.112-135.

Weigel, George (1987): *Tranquillitas Ordinis: The Present Failure and Future Promise of American Catholic Thought on War and Peace*. New York: Oxford University Press.

Weigel, George (1992): *The Final Revolution: The Resistance Church and the Collapse of Communism*. New York: Oxford University Press.

Wen Wei Po (1998): 'Mother-tongue Teaching must be Accomplished Consistently'. 20 March, Hong Kong. [in Chinese]

Whitebook, M., Howes, C. & Phillips, D.A. (1990): *Who Cares? Childcare Teachers and the Quality of Care in America*. The National Child Care Staffing Study. Oakland: Child Care Employee Project.

Whitehead, Clive (1988): 'British Colonial Educational Policy: A Synonym for Cultural Imperialism?', in Mangan, J.A. (ed.), *Benefits Bestowed? Education and British Imperialism*. Manchester: Manchester University Press, pp.211-230.

Whitty, Geoff (1985): *Sociology and School Knowledge: Curriculum Theory, Research and Politics*. London: Methuen.

Whitty, Geoff & Young, Michael (eds.) (1976): *Explorations in the Politics of School Knowledge*. Driffield: Nafferton Books.

Williams, Gareth (1996): *Paying for Education Beyond Eighteen: An Examination of Issues and Options*. London: The Council for Industry & Higher Education.

Williams, James H. (1997): 'The Diffusion of the Modern School', in Cummings, William K. & McGinn, Noel F. (eds.), *International Handbook of Education and Development: Preparing Schools, Students and Nations for the Twenty-First Century*, Oxford: Pergamon Press, pp.119-136.

Winkler, Donald R. (1989): *Decentralization in Education: An Economic Perspective*. Working Paper No.143, Washington DC: The World Bank.

Wong, C.L. (1995): 'How to Raise the Quality of Macau Teachers', in South China Normal University, *The Collection of Year 1991*. China: Guangdong Education Press, pp.161-179. [in Chinese]

Wong, Hon Keong (ed.) (1991): *Education Reform in Macau*. Macau: Centre of Macau Studies, University of East Asia.

Wong, Hon Keong (ed.) (1992): *Civic Education in Macau*. Macau: Centre of Macau Studies, University of Macau.

Wong, Hon Keong (1996): 'Problems of Policies of Population', in Wong, Hon Keong (ed.), *As Condições e a Politíca de População Para o Desenvolvimento de Macau: Comunicações do Simpósio Realizado na Universidade de Macau 3 de Septembro de 1994*. Macau: University of Macau, pp.109-116.

Wong, Hung Chiu (1987): *History of Macau*. Hong Kong: The Commercial Press. [in Chinese]

Wong, H.T. (ed.) (1993): *Hong Kong Education Handbook*. Hong Kong: The Commercial Press. [in Chinese]

Wong, Hin Wah (1988): *A Study of Hong Kong Secondary School Civic Education Curriculum Development (1984-1986)*. Ph.D. thesis, University of California, Los Angeles.

Wong, Ka Fu (1992): 'Private and Social Rates of Return to Investment in Education', in Chung, Yue Ping & Wong, Yue Chim Richard (eds.), *The Economics and Fi-*

nancing of Hong Kong Education. Hong Kong: The Chinese University Press, pp.17-37.

Wong, Kam Cheung (1998): 'Organizing and Managing Schools', in Postiglione, Gerard A. & Lee, Wing On (eds.), *Schooling in Hong Kong: Organization, Teaching and Social Context*. Hong Kong: Hong Kong University Press, pp.81-94.

Wong Leung, So Nga C. (1969): *A Comparative Study of Some of the Salient Features of the Curricula of Ordinary Middle Schools in Mainland China, Taiwan and Hong Kong between 1949-1966*. M.A. dissertation, The University of Hong Kong.

Wong, Ngai Chun Margaret (1997): *Pre-school Quality and Child Development in Macau*. Ph.D. thesis, The University of Hong Kong.

Wong, Ping Man (1981): *The Civic Education and the Curriculum of the Subject 'Economic and Public Affairs' in Hong Kong after World War II: A Comparative Perspective*. M.A. dissertation, The Chinese University of Hong Kong. [in Chinese]

Wong, Ping Man (1983): 'What Kind of 'Hong Kong Citizen' Does the EPA Curriculum Produce?'. *Ming Po Monthly*, Vol.18, No.12, pp.56-59. [in Chinese]

Wong, Ping Man (1992): *The Evolution of the Secondary School Subject in Hong Kong: The Case of Social Studies*. Ph.D. thesis, The University of Hong Kong.

Wong, Suk Ying (1991): 'The Evolution of Social Science Instruction,1900-86: A Cross-national Study'. *Sociology of Education*, Vol.64, No.1, pp.33-47.

Wong, Wing Ping (1997): 'The Role of Higher Education and its Future Development'. Speech at the Lingnan College Public Seminar on Quality Higher Education in Hong Kong: Issues, Models and Future Directions. Hong Kong University Grants Committee Internet Virtual Library, www.ugc.edu.hk.

Wong, Yin Li (1996): *A History of the Hong Kong Baptist University*. Hong Kong: Hong Kong Baptist University. [in Chinese]

Wong, Y.N. (1990): *New Solid Geometry*. Macau: Sacred Heart Cannossian College. [in Chinese]

Wong, Yui Tim (1995): 'Labour and Employment', in Cheung, Stephen Y.L. & Sze, Stephen M.H. (eds.), *The Other Hong Kong Report 1995*. Hong Kong: The Chinese University Press, pp.287-302.

Woodhall, Maureen (1995a): 'Student Fees', in Carnoy, Martin (ed.), *International Encyclopedia of Economics of Education*. 2nd edition. Oxford: Pergamon Press, pp.426-429.

Woodhall, Maureen (1995b): 'Student Loans', in Carnoy, Martin (ed.), *International Encyclopedia of Economics of Education*. 2nd edition. Oxford: Pergamon Press, pp.420-425.

World Bank, The (1994): *Higher Education: The Lessons of Experience*. Washington DC: The World Bank.

Wu, John B. (1989): *March Towards a Bright Decade: Pastoral Exhortation of Cardinal John B. Wu on the Pastoral Commitment of the Catholic Diocese of Hong Kong*. Hong Kong: Catholic Diocese Office.

Wu, Kok Lin (1994): 'An Exploratory Study on Issues of Macau Educational Policy and Resources', in Koo, Ramsey and Ma, Hing Tong (eds.), *Macau Education: Continuity and Change*. Macau: Macau Foundation, pp.13-23. [in Chinese]

Wu, Z.L. (1998): *The Way of Survival: On Macau's Political Institution and Political Development*. Macau: Macau Association of Adult Education. [in Chinese]

Xu, Jiatun (1995): *Xu Jiatun's Hong Kong Memoir*. Taipei: Luenjin. [in Chinese]

Yau, S.K.R., Leung, K.L. & Chau, S.L.T. (1993): *Education in Hong Kong: Past and Present*. Hong Kong: The Urban Council.

Yee, A.H. (1990): 'A Comparative Study of Macau's Education System: Changing Colonial Patronage and Native Self-reliance'. *Comparative Education*, Vol.26, No.1, pp.61-71.

Yee, H., Liu, B.L. & Ngo, T.W. (1993a): *The Political Culture of the Macau Chinese*. Macau: Macau Foundation. [in Chinese]

Yee, H., Liu, B.L. & Ngo, T.W. (1993b): 'Macau's Mass Political Culture'. *Asian Journal of Public Administration*, Vol.15, No.2, pp.177-200.

Young, Michael F.D. (ed.) (1971): *Knowledge and Control: New Directions for the Sociology of Education*. London: Collier-Macmillan.

Yu, S.T. (1990): *A Study of the Effects of Formal Curriculum on Students' Civic Consciousness in Hong Kong Secondary Schools*. M.A. dissertation, The Chinese University of Hong Kong. [in Chinese]

Yue, K.L. (1994): 'The Controversy on Language of Instruction in Macau'. *Yazhou Zhoukan,* 28 August, 64-65. [in Chinese]

Yuen, B.K. & Yuen, K.S. (1988): *A Brief History of Macau*. Hong Kong: Chung Liu. [in Chinese]

Zhou, Li Go (1997): 'Fostering Higher Level Manpower in Macau from the View of the University of Macau'. *Macau Daily*, 27 July. [in Chinese]

Index